ANGLO-NORMAN STUDIES VI

PROCEEDINGS OF THE BATTLE CONFERENCE
1983

The Director and Mr Ian Peirce on the battlefield, Pyke House, 1983 (Photo, Nigel Holland, Evening Argus, Brighton)

ANGLO-NORMAN STUDIES

VI

PROCEEDINGS OF THE BATTLE CONFERENCE

1983

Edited by R. Allen Brown

BOYDELL PRESS

© by contributors 1983, 1984

First published 1984 by The Boydell Press, an imprint of Boydell &
Brewer Ltd, PO Box 9, Woodbridge, Suffolk IP12 3DF and
Dover, New Hampshire, U.S.A.

British Library Cataloguing in Publication Data

Battle Conference on Anglo-Norman Studies
    (6th: 1983)
    Proceedings of the Battle Conference on
    Anglo-Norman Studies 1983.
    1. Great Britain — History — Norman period,
    1066-1154 2. Great Britain — History —
    Angevin period, 1154-1216
    I. Title   II. Brown, R. Allen
    942.02   DA195

ISBN 0-85115-197-3

The cover illustration is from BL MS Cotton Domitian AII f.21, and is reproduced
by kind permission of the Trustees of the British Library

Printed by St Edmundsbury Press
Bury St Edmunds, Suffolk

CONTENTS

LIST OF ILLUSTRATIONS

PREFACE

An acknowledgement of the success of the sixth Battle Conference requires a formal expression of thanks to those who made it possible, not least to those who contributed the papers here printed. In addition we give thanks to the British Academy for a further generous grant towards the expenses of overseas contributors, to the East Sussex County Council for continuing to sponsor the Conference in these hard times, and to the warden and staff of Pyke House — together with the management of our annexe, the 'Chequers', next door — for the comfort and comforts provided. We are very much obliged, also, to the Headmaster of Battle Abbey School for allowing us to continue the tradition of holding our reception in the admirably appropriate surroundings of the abbey and the Abbot's Hall.

The Outing this year was principally directed to the 'Lewes Group' of church wall-paintings, in particular those of Clayton, Hardham and Coombes. It is especially well-integrated with the text that follows because it was led by Dr David Park who also read a paper on the subject, while Dr Gem has contributed his customary note arising from the Outing, this time upon the Templar church of Shipley, Sussex.

An unusual feature of the sixth Battle Conference was that the customary display of arms and armour by Mr Ian Peirce was developed into a mounted exhibition. It is not given to everyone to ride fully armed and accoutred up the hill of Hastings as Mr Peirce and the Director did. They both hope that the fact that they made a mess of it will be taken by the erudite company present, if not by the media also present, as further proof that Norman knights were professional in their expertise.

R. Allen Brown

Thelnetham, Suffolk
30 December 1983

ABBREVIATIONS

Antiqs. Journ.	*The Antiquaries Journal* (Society of Antiquaries of London).
Arch. Journ.	*Archaeological Journal* (Royal Archaeological Institute).
ASC	*Anglo-Saxon Chronicle*, ed. D. Whitelock et al., London 1969.
Battle Chronicle	*The Chronicle of Battle Abbey*, ed. Eleanor Searle, Oxford Medieval Texts, 1980.
BIHR	*Bulletin of the Institute of Historical Research*
BL	British Library
BN	Bibliothèque Nationale
BT	*The Bayeux Tapestry*, ed. F. M. Stenton, 2nd ed. London 1965.
Cal. Docs. France	*Calendar of Documents preserved in France* . . . i, 918-1216, ed. J. H. Round, H.M.S.O., 1899.
Carmen	*The Carmen de Hastingae Proelio of Guy bishop of Amiens*, ed. Catherine Morton and Hope Munz, Oxford Medieval Texts, 1972.
De gestis pontificum	William of Malmesbury, *De gestis pontificum Anglorum*, ed. N. E. S. A. Hamilton, RS 1870.
De gestis regum	William of Malmesbury, *De gestis regum Anglorum*, ed. W. Stubbs, RS 1887.
Domesday Book	*Domesday Book, seu liber censualis* . . ., ed. A. Farley, 2 vols., 'Record Commission', 1783.
Dudo	*De moribus et actis primorum Normanniae Ducum auctore Dudone Sancti Quintini Decano*, ed. J. Lair, Société de Antiquaires de Normandie, 1865.
Eadmer	*Historia novorum in Anglia*, ed. M. Rule, RS 1884.
EHD	*English Historical Documents*, i, ed. D. Whitelock, London 1955; ii, ed. D. C. Douglas, London 1953.
EHR	*English Historical Review*
Fauroux	*Recueil des actes des ducs de Normandie (911-1066)*, ed. M. Fauroux, Mémoires de la Société des Antiquaires de Normandie, xxxvi, 1961.
GEC	*Complete Peerage of England, Scotland, Ireland, Great Britain and the United Kingdom*, 13 vols. in 14, London 1910-59.
Gesta Guillelmi	William of Poitiers, *Gesta Guillelmi* . . ., ed. R. Foreville, Paris 1952.
Historia Novella	William of Malmesbury, *Historia Novella*, ed. K. R. Potter, Nelson's Medieval Texts, London 1955.
HMSO	Her Majesty's Stationery Office, London.
Huntingdon	Henry of Huntingdon, *Historia Anglorum*, ed. T. Arnold, RS 1879.

Journ. BAA	*Journal of the British Archaeological Association*
Jumièges	William of Jumièges, *Gesta Normannorum Ducum*, ed. J. Marx, Société de l'histoire de Normandie, 1914.
Lanfranc's Letters	*The Letters of Lanfranc Archbishop of Canterbury*, ed. H. Clover and M. Gibson, Oxford Medieval Texts, 1979.
Med. Arch.	*Medieval Archaeology*
MGH	*Monumenta Germaniae Historica*, Scriptores.
Monasticon	William Dugdale, *Monasticon Anglicanum*, ed. J. Caley, H. Ellis and B. Bandinel, 6 vols. in 8, London 1817-30.
ns	New Series
Orderic	Ordericus Vitalis, *Historia Ecclesiastica*, ed. M. Chibnall, Oxford Medieval Texts, 1969-
PRO	Public Record Office
Procs. BA	*Proceedings of the British Academy*
Regesta	*Regesta Regum Anglo-Normannorum*, i, ed. H. W. C. Davis, Oxford 1913; ii, ed. C. Johnson, H. A. Cronne, Oxford 1956; iii, ed. H. A. Cronne, R. H. C. Davis, Oxford 1968.
RS	Rolls Series, London.
ser.	series
Trans.	Transactions
TRHS	*Transactions of the Royal Historical Society*
VCH	Victoria County History
Vita Eadwardi	The Life of Edward the Confessor, ed. F. Barlow, Nelson's Medieval Texts, London 1962.
Vita Herluini	ed. J. Armitage Robinson in his *Gilbert Crispin abbot of Westminster*, Cambridge 1911.
Wace	Wace, *Le Roman de Rou*, ed. A. J. Holden, 3 vols. Société des anciens textes français, Paris 1970-3.
Worcester	Florence of Worcester, *Chronicon ex Chronicis*, ed. B. Thorpe, English Historical Society, London 1848-9.

BATTLES IN ENGLAND AND NORMANDY, 1066-1154

Jim Bradbury

There has been a tendency in recent years to neglect the study of battles, as a somewhat outmoded approach to history. An example would be the excellent volume on the Hundred Years War, edited by Fowler, in which virtually every possible aspect of the war is considered, with the exception of the battles.[1] It is true that such an approach has in the past been used at the expense of studies of campaigns, or political and social sides of warfare. Views on battle have certainly been modified by a study within the broader context, but this should encourage cross-fertilisation between the various fields, and not neglect of any one. A study of battles can indeed stimulate ideas in other areas of history. For example, if dismounted knights are significant in twelfth-century battles, can one find a social explanation of that significance? Perhaps Anglo-Norman historians are less narrow than some of their colleagues, and the example given is of course one provided by Dr Chibnall.[2]

The intention of this paper is to ask some questions of the battles in the century following the Norman Conquest, without necessarily anticipating clear answers. A question raised by those with even a passing interest in the period is, why there were so few battles. Professor Hollister, in his important work on 'The Military Organization of Norman England', discusses five battles which he suggests were 'the only ones of any significance in the Anglo-Norman age'.[3] Some would see this as a sign that battles were not especially important in the warfare of this period: sieges were common, and therefore more significant. But significance surely does not rest only in quantity. In any case, one of the most obvious features of Norman warfare is the close, almost inseparable, relationship between sieges and battles. Two responses to the question come to mind. Professor Hollister was concerned with those battles which had been described in sufficient detail to allow some discussion of tactics. There were certainly more battles, many of which were at least as large in scale as Bourgthéroulde, but are given little space by the chroniclers. There were at least fifteen lesser battles in the period.[4] A second consideration is the frequency with which battles were avoided. Sometimes this was achieved by a form of truce or treaty, sometimes simply by backing down from a challenge.

[1] K. Fowler, *The Hundred Years War*, London 1971.
[2] Dr Chibnall presented a paper on this subject to the conference at St Mary's, Strawberry Hill, on 'Knighthood and Chivalry'. The paper will not be published, but the material will appear in Dr Chibnall's forthcoming book on *Orderic Vitalis and His World*. Professor Hollister's work, including his paper in these proceedings, is another honourable exception.
[3] C. W. Hollister, *The Military Organization of Norman England*, Oxford 1965, 128.
[4] Other battles include: Fagaduna 1075, Gerberoi 1079, Chaumont 1098 where seven hundred horses were killed, Exmes 1102, Alençon 1118, Vaudreuil 1136 where five hundred knights fought on one side, Caen 1138, Clitheroe 1138, Barnstaple 1139, Winchester 1141, Wilton 1143, Montfort 1154, and in Wales in 1088, 1095, 1097 with two battles in 1136.

Negotiation before battle was a common occurrence, and should not be treated as an empty formality, since there were occasions when it succeeded in preventing a fight. Presumably this occurred when neither side was confident of ultimate victory. An obvious reason for avoiding battle was the knowledge that one's opponents had greater numerical strength. The more cautious commander often took note, and abandoned the field, as for example, Robert of Gloucester at Faringdon, or Louis of France at Cosne, when he was 'brought to his senses by sound counsel', and moved off. Matilda intended to leave Winchester when the arrival of the Londoners gave the edge to her opponents, but in that instance the decision could not be executed in time.[5] The older and wiser were generally those to advise that discretion was the better part of valour. Louis VI at Brémule, Waleran at Bourgthéroulde, David of Scots at the Standard, and Stephen at Lincoln, were all advised to avoid battle because of their opponents' strength.[6] In all these cases the advice was ignored, and the commanders lived to rue their decisions. Age seems commonly to have engendered caution, and is expressed nicely in the words of the mother of Sulpice of Amboise, when her son decided on war without consulting her: I am not an imbecile yet. My advanced age still leaves me some sense. Look at the forces against you. 'It is uncertain who will be favoured by the chance of arms, but I fear it will not be you.'[7] She was right.

Numerical inferiority was not the only consideration; lack of morale, unreliable troops, poorly trained, armed or disciplined men had also to be taken into account before risking battle. Stephen in Normandy was clearly worried about the loyalty of his forces, and in the end their quarrels caused him to abandon the campaign. In the year of the Standard, Stephen led an expedition north, but called it off when it was feared his own men were in league with the Scots. Other reasons given were the onset of Lent, and the failure of supplies, both perfectly valid reasons for backing out of a campaign, but perhaps in this instance excuses. In the case of the Scots at the Standard, it was the quality of the troops that led to Robert Bruce advising David against fighting. He asked the king if he wanted his future to depend upon the hotheaded but poorly armed and disciplined Galwegians.[8]

Nor should we exaggerate the Norman eagerness for blood. No doubt religious scruples were useful as excuses, and could be ignored on occasion, but they must also have played a real part in the decision-making of commanders. The avoidance of bloodshed, the observance of truces, the necessity to have a just cause, were important for propaganda purposes, but perhaps in practice too. There was a twelfth-century code of war, as well as that so brilliantly examined by Keen in the later medieval period.[9] Orderic speaks of a 'brotherhood of arms'. This may have been a kind of class solidarity, and certainly common soldiers were not treated in the same manner as knights, but it contains at least the germs of a more humane attitude to war. No doubt Orderic was being idealistic when he wrote that at Brémule: 'as Christian soldiers they did not thirst for the blood of their brothers'. But Geoffrey

---

5 Faringdon: ed. R. Howlett, *Chronicles of the Reigns of Stephen, Henry II and Richard I*, RS 1889, iv, 150; Cosne: L. Halphen and R. Poupardin, *Chroniques des Comtes d'Anjou et des Seigneurs d'Amboise*, Paris 1913, 200; Winchester: Huntingdon, 275.

6 Brémule: Orderic, vi, 234; Bourgthéroulde: Orderic, vi, 350; Standard: Ailred in Howlett, iii, 192; Lincoln: K. R. Potter, *Gesta Stephani*, Oxford 1976, 112.

7 Halphen and Poupardin, 126-7.

8 Normandy: Orderic, vi, 482-6; Scotland: T. Arnold, *Symeon of Durham*, RS 1882-5, ii, 284; Standard: Howlett, iii, 192.

9 M. H. Keen, *The Laws of War in the Late Middle Ages*, London 1965.

of Anjou expresses a similar sentiment in the 'Historia Gaufredi Ducis': 'If we are knights, we should have compassion on fellow knights, especially those at our mercy'.[10] There was a growing concern in the Church about the circumstances in which war could be approved, and especially about the fighting of Christian against Christian. It is unlikely that men were eager for battle on every possible occasion. One tag quoted in the Angevin chronicle is: 'Nothing is more shameful than to wage war on one with whom you have lived in friendship'; and Robert son of Lisiard expresses the desire to avoid battle with his own previous household comrades.[11] Clearly also there were anxieties in confronting one's feudal lord, except in approved circumstances.

Common sense, religious scruples, practical difficulties, the realistic weighing of consequences, could all be important pressures against battle, but undoubtedly the most potent deterrent was fear of defeat. Consider the consequences of defeat for some of those involved in our Norman battles. Harold Godwinson lost his throne, his kingdom, his estates, his family, as well as his life. For Robert Curthose, defeat meant the loss of his duchy and life imprisonment. For Louis, Brémule meant a loss of face, sighs and sniggers in every corner of Europe north of the Alps. For Waleran, Bourgthéroulde meant the blighting of his ambitions and imprisonment. For three of his leading tenants is meant blinding: two for breaking liege homage to the king, one at least in part for composing satirical verses against Henry.[12] Through Lincoln, Stephen lost his throne temporarily and the duchy of Normandy for good. He was imprisoned at Bristol, in chains after he had shown a tendency to wander.[13] He was indeed fortunate not to suffer the same fate as Robert Curthose, saved only by the victory his supporters won in the Rout of Winchester. Such could be the consequences of defeat, and they were not to be contemplated lightly.

Wise commanders therefore avoided battle whenever possible. The outstanding success in this respect must be Geoffrey le Bel. In his invasion of Normandy between 1135 and 1145, he undertook a series of sieges, and used diplomatic pressure. He was prepared to retreat when discretion dictated and in the event won the duchy without having to fight a single pitched battle. Other commanders were not so fortunate as Geoffrey, but some at least shared the same attitude. Battle was a last resort, to be avoided unless victory seemed assured, in the knowledge that chance would always be a factor in what Orderic called 'the uncertain verdict of battle'.[14]

One begins to wonder why battles occurred at all. The answer must be, when either both commanders were confident of victory, in which case one of them had probably miscalculated, or when one expected victory and the other was physically or mentally trapped in a situation from which he could not or would not back down. The point in fighting a battle was to make sure of victory, and equally therefore to make certain one would not be defeated. Let us see how far this attitude is reflected in the battle tactics of Norman warfare in the west.

In order to examine tactics fruitfully we need to clear the ground in two respects. Firstly it is important to value the evidence we use, chiefly chronicle evidence, to

---

[10] Orderic, vi, 240; Halphen and Poupardin, 196.

[11] Halphen and Poupardin, 206.

[12] Orderic, vi, 242, 352. I am grateful to David Crouch for allowing me to read the draft of his thesis (Cardiff 1983) on the Beaumonts, particularly with regard to their tenants and Bourg-théroulde.

[13] *Historia Novella*, 50.

[14] Orderic, ii, 309: 'ambiguum certamen'; compare Ailred in Howlett, iii, 185: 'incertos de victoria, fluctuare animo'.

employ the best and earliest accounts. This may seem an unnecessary point, until one uses some modern accounts and realises that the normal process is to take every piece of evidence from all quality of sources and construct a jigsaw account of battles. What is needed is chiefly an exercise in pruning. As a part of this process it is also necessary to review the practice of evaluating medieval tactics by consideration of the ground over which the battles were fought. In ninety-nine cases out of a hundred, precise location of a battle is guesswork, often very broad guesswork indeed. It may be fun to try and identify a site, but to give a proper account we should rely on historical evidence, and not historical fiction.

Our starting point is the Battle of Hastings, the details of which need not detain us long, since Professor Brown has so recently reviewed the battle for this conference. 'If he could blunder here he could blunder anywhere', refers of course to Freeman and Hastings, and is not a comment that we require.[15] Harold seems to have miscalculated in choosing to fight at this time, apparently in order to achieve surprise. Hastings is the exception in our battles, as being the only one where a positive location can be asserted with some assurance. Traditionally the high altar of the Abbey was sited on the spot where Harold set his standard and was killed. But even Hastings may require some caution in this respect. The earliest detailed account, in William of Poitiers, gives only an approximate location, telling us little more than that the battle was fought on a hill near the edge of the woodlands. The Anglo-Saxon Chronicle, though giving few details of the conflict, mentions that the English assembled by the hoary apple tree.[16] This has normally been identified as on Caldbec Hill, and most accounts then take the Saxon army forward, but the Chronicle gives the impression that this is where the battle was fought. The Malfosse provides another difficulty. Professor Searle has made the interesting suggestion that the local place-name might relate not to an incident in the battle, but to a burial ditch.[17] If this were so, its siting to the north is also odd, since one would expect a burial ditch to be near the centre of action. On the evidence quoted so far, one might be inclined to locate the battle on Caldbec Hill. The identification with the present site depends of course on the Battle Abbey Chronicle, which is not an absolutely reliable witness. Its account of William's vow has been questioned by Professor Searle.[18] It is true that the words put into William's mouth, forecasting that the supply of wine in the Abbey would be more abundant than water, seem to have been confirmed by the recent sherry reception, but it remains true that the tale of the hill has no greater antiquity than that of the vow. Nevertheless, common sense would agree that the tradition of placing the Abbey named after the battle on the actual site seems likely and remains acceptable. The point here is not to move the battlefield, but to demonstrate the problems of locating battles even when one has apparently sound evidence. Our other battles are far more difficult to locate with precision than Hastings.

There are a few points in the tactics of Hastings that we need to linger over. It must be asserted that the English fought on foot. Glover's view that Snorre is 'an important and dependable' witness for this eleventh-century battle is not acceptable,

[15] R. A. Brown, 'The Battle of Hastings', *ante*, iii, 1980. J. H. Round, *Feudal England*, London 1895, 332.
[16] *Gesta Guillelmi*, 186; *ASC*, 143: C. Plummer, *Two of the Saxon Chronicles Parallel*, 2v, Oxford 1892, i, 199.
[17] *Battle Chronicle*, 16.
[18] *Battle Chronicle*, 16, 20, 23, 38, 40, 44, 46; 36-44.

and on it depends the argument for Anglo-Saxon cavalry.[19] The comment in Florence of Worcester on the Welsh border incident of 1055 is decisive: that Earl Ralph 'ordered the English to fight on horseback against their custom'.[20] Equally convincing is the fact that, although Hastings is well covered for a medieval battle, there is no mention of English cavalry. If the Anglo-Saxons had normally used cavalry, they would surely have employed it at Hastings.

On the Norman side we need to consider the two main elements in their attack. There is no question that the Normans used cavalry, but there is a problem over how they used it. Ross has suggested that the couched lance was only now in the process of development, and the evidence of the Tapestry on this is certainly ambiguous: some lances are used couched, and some over-arm.[21] One thing is clear, the English line was not broken by one massive cavalry charge, though there seems no reason against believing that feigned flights were used and with effect. The other main factor in the Norman victory was archery. Its significance at Hastings has sometimes been overlooked. The dispute over the arrow in the eye seems now to have been settled.[22] Archery was used at two points in the battle: to open hostilities, apparently without great effect; and in the final assault, during which Harold was killed. In the Tapestry the archers are using ordinary wooden bows, not short-bows which are composite and have a distinctive shape.[23] Ordinary wooden bows are technically the same as longbows, but of a lesser length, to judge by the Tapestry. The bows at Hastings were effective, however, and could not have been much shorter than five feet or they would have lacked sufficient range and impact. Despite the suggestion by Morton and Muntz, the editors of the 'Carmen', that one archer on the Tapestry is a crossbowman, it must be asserted that all the archers shown are using ordinary bows, there are no crossbowmen. The 'Carmen' mentions the use of crossbows in the battle, but its value as an early source is now open to doubt.[24] There is, however, no need to discard this idea, since William of Poitiers also refers to 'balistae' in a context where crossbowmen must be meant.[25] References to crossbows in the eleventh and twelfth centuries are common enough, and clearly were used in the Norman armies of the period. One of the more interesting mentions of the weapon is in Orderic's account of the quarrel between Henry I and his natural daughter, Juliana. Henry besieged his daughter, and was not prepared for her reaction when invited to see her. 'She had a crossbow ready drawn for the purpose and shot a bolt at her father, but failed to injure him since God protected him.' She had to surrender, and her father, more lenient than was his wont, allowed her to escape by leaping down from the walls 'to fall shamefully with bare buttocks into the depths of the moat' and the freezing February waters.[26] We may then summarise that the

[19] R. Glover, 'English Warfare in 1066', *EHR* xvii, 1952, 1-18.

[20] Worcester, i, 213: 'Anglos contra morem in equis pugnare jussit'.

[21] D. J. A. Ross, 'L'originalité de "Turoldus": le maniement de la lance', *Cahiers de Civilisation Médiévale* vi, 1963, 127-38.

[22] D. Bernstein, 'The Blinding of Harold and the Meaning of the Bayeux Tapestry', *ante*, v, 1982. Although I do not accept all the author's conclusions, the discovery of evidence for an arrow in the falling figure removes any doubt that the Tapestry's version showed Harold to have been hit by an arrow.

[23] Twenty-nine archers are depicted on the Tapestry, all have ordinary wooden bows. These are analysed in more detail in J. Bradbury, *The Medieval Archer*, to be published shortly.

[24] *Carmen*, 115. *BT*, pl. 61, pl. X. R. H. C. Davis, 'The *Carmen de Hastingae Proelio*', *EHR* xciii, 1978, 241-61; and the discussion on the Carmen in *ante*, ii, 1979.

[25] *Gesta Guillelmi*, 185: 'Pedites in fronte locavit, sagittis armatos et balistis'.

[26] Orderic, vi, 212-14.

Norman tactics that won Hastings involved a combination of cavalry and archers, using both ordinary bows and crossbows.

The first major battle in either England or Normandy after Hastings was at Tinchebrai in 1106, exactly forty years after the great victory, as William of Malmesbury noted.[27] It brought to a climax the struggle between the sons of the Conqueror for control of kingdom and duchy. Like so many other battles in the period, Tinchebrai arose from a siege, both sieges and battles being essentially tests of lordship. Henry I had besieged the castle of Tinchebrai during the course of his invasion of Normandy. The castle belonged to William, Count of Mortain, who appealed to Robert Curthose for aid. In such a situation, the overlord either admitted the loss, or had to contest the siege in the field. In this case Curthose chose to accept the challenge, and brought an army to the relief of Tinchebrai. Often, especially if outnumbered, the challenger would then, his bluff called, abandon the siege, but Henry chose to make a stand.

Henry I himself, in a letter, tells us that the battle was fought 'before Tinchebrai'.[28] During the siege Henry had constructed a siege castle, but we do not know its position. The ruins of the castle now sit on the hill of Tinchebrai, and clearly the battle was fought on the level ground below the castle, closer than that we cannot get. Similarly, we know that Henry placed a force of cavalry under Helias of Maine at a distance, out of sight of Curthose, but we do not even know in which direction.

For many years historians disputed the extent of Henry I's use of dismounted knights in the battle, according to whether they favoured the account by Orderic or that by Henry of Huntingdon. The matter was settled through the use of the letter from a priest of Fécamp. This document has had an extraordinary history. It was first printed in 1872 by Delisle in his edition of Robert of Torigny, but ignored until its 're-discovery' by H. W. C. Davis in 1909. It afterwards emerged that Davis had not himself seen the original, only a copy made for him. This copy made exactly the same error as the version by Delisle, omitting an important line. Only in 1910 was this corrected. Even then, oddly enough, the missing line was printed with a minor mistake, the addition of a word that does not appear in the manuscript. The line refers to the dismounting of Henry's second division. This letter was written immediately after Tinchebrai, and gives a detailed account of Henry's army.[29] According to the priest Henry's first line consisted of men from Bayeux, Avranches and Coutances, all on foot. In the second line were the king and his barons, all similarly on foot. Seven hundred cavalry were ranged with each line. In addition there was the flanking cavalry force under Helias of Maine. According to Henry of Huntingdon and the sources that followed him, Curthose also dismounted men, but with no indication of the numbers. Curthose charged against his brother's army, and with some effect 'since the duke and his troops had been well trained in the wars of Jerusalem'. The meaning of this can only be conjectured, but following Smail's analysis of crusading methods, it probably should be taken as indicating a

---

27 *De gestis regum*, ii, 475.

28 Eadmer, 184: 'ante Tenerchebraicum'.

29 L. Delisle, *Chronique de Robert de Torigni*, Rouen 1872, i, 129; H. W. C. Davis, 'A Contemporary Account of the Battle of Tinchebrai', *EHR* xxiv, 1909, 728-32; 'The Battle of Tinchebrai: A Correction', *EHR* xxv, 1910, 295-6. The letter is in Bodleian, Jesus College MS li, f.104, where the actual line reads: 'omnes pedites. In secunda rex cum innumeris baronibus suis omnes similiter/pedites'.

concerted cavalry charge using couched lances.[30] The charge made an impact, but it was held. To the sound of shouts, presumably as a signal, the hidden cavalry force now attacked from the side. The ducal army was shattered and Curthose himself captured.

The second of our main battles was fought at Alençon in 1118. It does not appear in most military discussions of the period. One reason for this may be that it does not figure in the Anglo-Norman chronicles, except briefly in Orderic, no doubt because Henry I suffered a defeat which most chroniclers in England and Normandy thought it best to pass over in silence. There is, however, an account of the battle in the Angevin chronicles.[31] There is not time here to discuss in detail the difficulties of the Angevin sources, but some brief explanation must be made, since we are now dealing with a source that cannot compare in authority with the letter of the priest of Fécamp.

The earliest manuscripts of the 'Gesta Consulum Andegavorum' are mid twelfth-century, and already show signs of numerous alterations to lost originals. The best known of these chroniclers is John of Marmoutier, who revised the 'Gesta', and added a life of Geoffrey le Bel. John names a series of earlier writers on whom he depended. The historians of the chronicles have played subtle games attempting to ascribe particular versions and additions to the authors named by John.[32] It is a somewhat unprofitable game, since there are too many unknown factors, and it seems better to refer to manuscripts than to conjectural authors. In the form we possess them, the 'Gesta' are mid twelfth-century revisions and additions to earlier versions, in the form of deeds ascribed in chronological order to the Counts of Anjou. From internal evidence it is clear that sources from Loches and Tours played an important part in this compilation.

It has been generally agreed that BN. 6218 is the earliest version, and this was used for Halphen and Poupardin's edition. BN. 6006, however, comes from about the same period, and was preferred for the earlier Marchegay and Salmon edition. The latter manuscript includes the account of Alençon, which would therefore seem to be an addition of the mid twelfth-century. The account demonstrates an interest in Maine, particularly in emphasising the role of Lisiard of Sablé in the battle. As a battle account it is detailed and interesting, but also has inaccuracies and seems already to contain elements of legend.[33] At the same time, the basic outline of the account is confirmed by Orderic. Clearly it is not an account on which to rely too heavily, but it is a narrative of an important battle, and at the very least reflects the ideas of battle in the mind of its writer.

[30] On Curthose dismounting, see Huntingdon, 235, and the 'Draco' in Howlett, ii, 649. On 'wars of Jerusalem' see Huntingdon, 235: 'assuetusque bellis Jerosolimitanis'. R. C. Smail, *Crusading Warfare, 1097-1193*, Cambridge 1956, 199, 203; and compare F. Gabrieli, *Arab Historians of the Crusades*, London 1969, 58.
[31] The Angevin account appears in P. Marchegay and A. Salmon, *Chroniques des Comtes d'Anjou*, 2nd edn, 1871, 144-51; and in Halphen and Poupardin, 155-61. Briefer references are in Orderic, vi, 206-8; and H. Waquet, *Suger: Vie de Louis VI le Gros*, Paris 1929, 192.
[32] For commentary on the authorship of the Angevin chronicles, see the introduction by E. Mabille to Marchegay and Salmon, 1871; L. Halphen, *Étude sur les Chroniques des Comtes d'Anjou et des Seigneurs d'Amboise*, Paris 1906; and the introduction to Halphen and Poupardin.
[33] P. J. Odolant-Desnos, *Mémoires Historiques sur la Ville d'Alençon et sur ses Seigneurs*, 2nd edn, Paris 1858, i, 371, discussed the problem of people mentioned in the Angevin Chronicle in connection with Alençon who could not have been present, though possible solutions can be offered. For a comment on the legendary aspect, see K. Norgate, *England under the Angevin Kings*, 2 v, London 1887, i, 236.

Alençon had long been a bone of contention, just on the Norman side of the
Maine boundary. Its citizens had no great reason to recall the past with any fondness
for the Normans. Robert I had made its lord sue for mercy with a saddle on his
shoulders, and, according to William of Jumièges, poison in his heart.[34] On another
famous occasion the Conqueror had taken bitter revenge on the citizens for taunting
him with skins over the walls. In 1118 Alençon was held for Henry I by his nephew
Stephen. The latter had created resentment by his treatment of the citizens and
their wives, and they, probably needing little encouragement, had invited in Fulk
of Anjou. The latter came to besiege the castle, setting himself up in a defended
'park'.[35] Yet again, the challenge of a siege was accepted. Henry, coming to the
relief of Alençon, faced battle if he wished to succeed. Fulk's forces remained
within the park, and in the early stages there was a series of sorties rather than a
pitched battle. Fulk sent out three groups, each consisting of knights and archers,
and each in turn forced to return to the park. In the meantime a second Angevin
force, under Lisiard of Sablé, was approaching the scene. At a distance of four miles
they could hear the clamour and wails from the conflict. They speeded up in order
to join the fight. They dismounted in a wooded valley, mustered and, when dressed
for war in leg armour, mail coats and helmets, drew up their lines. The first consisted
of Lisiard of Sablé with knights, archers and foot. As they approached, they shouted
and at a signal rushed upon the enemy. The horses, knights and foot of Henry I
suffered severely at the hands of the Angevin archers, and Theobald of Blois was
wounded by a light blow on the forehead. Fulk then issued from the park with his
main army, calling, 'Look knights, knights, here comes your count. I am your brother,
lord and master, and whatever you see me doing, you do the same.' The final assault
was a cavalry charge, reinforced by archers and crossbowmen. After the victory,
Alençon surrendered to Fulk. The Latin does not make it clear if Lisiard's force
remained dismounted and fought on foot, or whether they were also cavalry, but
the Angevin tactics involved a combination of archers and cavalry, and perhaps
dismounted men as well.[36]

The Battle of Brémule in 1119 is a deservedly famous occasion, though the size
of the armies involved does not seem to have been great. It was the 'battle of the
two kings', the supreme test of lordship after Louis' invasion of Normandy.[37] Again
the sources require some discussion. It is useful to have accounts from both sides,
and the assistance of such chroniclers as Suger, Orderic and Henry of Huntingdon.
One important source, although not unknown, has been rather neglected by military
historians, and that is the Hyde Chronicle.[38] The reason for the neglect is not clear,
since it has long been in print, is a full account, and possibly the earliest, being in a
manuscript that breaks off in 1121 and was probably written soon after that. Like
many works it displays partisanship, in this case for the Warenne family. There are
some difficulties in that the Hyde Chronicle differs in some details from other

---

34 Jumièges, 139, 193; 171. *Gesta Guillelmi*, 43.
35 Halphen and Poupardin, 156. There is a modern park in Alençon in an ideal position for
besieging the castle.
36 Halphen and Poupardin, 158: 'descenderuntque in quadam valle amena et nemorosa,
disellatis equis et recenciatis, induti etiam toracibus, loricis et galeis, ordinaverunt acies suas'.
37 Orderic, vi, 240: 'In duorum certamine regum'; Suger, 196; Huntingdon, 241-2; Orderic, vi,
234-42.
38 E. Edwards, *Liber Monasterii de Hyda*, RS, 1866, 316-18. The Manuscript is BL, Cotton
MS, Domitian xiv.

accounts, but not to any greater extent than the other sources differ from each other. In the overall picture there is general agreement.

The precise site cannot be identified, beyond noting that Henry's scouts were posted on the hill of Verclives, and according to Orderic 'near the hill is an open field and a wide plain called Brémule', and here the battle was fought.[39] Verclives is only a small height, and again the battle was fought on level ground suitable for cavalry. This is significant when one recalls that Henry I chose the point of contact and, although using dismounted men, seems also to have taken into consideration his intended use of cavalry. Louis did not have a large force, but ignored advice not to fight, being himself impatient and angry. It is not clear if Henry's sons were mounted or not, but Henry stationed himself with the dismounted men. Louis ordered a charge, which all the chroniclers agree lacked discipline, and we might suggest was not properly concerted. Although archers are not specifically mentioned, it is likely, as Dr Chibnall suggests, that Orderic's mention of William Crispin's horses being 'quickly killed' means by archery.[40] Despite lack of order, the French charge had some impact, but was held by the line of dismounted men. In the fighting Henry I was wounded by blows on the head, but was saved by the mail hood of his hauberk. The French were broken, and Louis, after further adventures, returned to Andely.

Bourgthéroulde in 1124 was a relatively minor affair with no kings, one side even lacking a magnate to command. It remains an interesting conflict for us, because of Orderic's detailed narrative.[41] It is quite impossible to provide a location for this battle. Most of the brief notices of the battle refer to it as being at or near Bourg-théroulde, Robert of Torigny referring to it as 'near to the town which they call Bourgthéroulde', and a chronicle of Rouen places it between Bourgthéroulde and Boissy-le-Chatel. Orderic seems to support this in his main account, but on a second occasion mentions apparently the same battle as being at Rougemoutiers, several miles away to the north.[42] The whole area in any case is pretty level, and we can only note that the battle occurred when Waleran of Meulan, in revolt against Henry I, was returning from a relief expedition to his besieged and isolated castle at Vatteville in the direction of Beaumont. He found his return blocked by a force of Henry's household troops collected from nearby castle garrisons. The young Waleran insisted on fighting against advice. After discussion, the royal household troops, being set an example by Odo Borleng, decided to dismount. Odo outlined the plan 'for one section of our men to dismount for battle and fight on foot, while the rest remain mounted ready for the fray. Let us also place a force of archers in the first line and compel the enemy troop to slow down by wounding their horses.'[43] It would be difficult to give a clearer analysis of the general tactics of the period. Robert of Torigny says that mounted archers were sent forward against the enemy right.[44] Probably they fought on foot, but certainly these household archers decided the issue. The charging horses were brought down, including that of Waleran himself who was captured.

The battlefield of the Standard fought in 1138 is marked by a monument beside the A167 road north out of Northallerton, but like most such markers seems to have

[39] Orderic, vi, 236: 'latissima planicies quae ab incolis Brenmula vocitatur'.
[40] Orderic, vi, 238; Orderic, vi, xxi.
[41] Orderic, vi, 346-56.
[42] Jumièges, 295: 'haud procul a villa, quam vocant Burgum Turoldi'. *RHF*, xii, 784: 'prope Burgum-Turoldi et Buxeium'. Orderic, vi, 348: 'prope Burgum Turoldi', but Orderic, vi, 356: 'in territorio Rubri Monasterii'.
[43] Orderic, vi, 348.
[44] Jumièges, 294-5.

been positioned rather arbitrarily. Some historians have placed the battle eastwards of the town, but this northern spot is the most likely. The English battle speech was made from a hill, but this has been given more significance than it deserves. There are several low rises in the vicinity, any one of which would answer, but the main feature of the area is its general flatness. Ailred, who should have been familiar with the geography, says it was fought 'in a broad plain' near Northallerton.[45] There is a tradition of burials at Scotpits Lane.[46] This is the most promising indication of the site, and would place it some way south of that traditionally accepted. The move would fit better with Richard of Hexham's two miles from Northallerton. There are several full accounts of the battle, including that by Richard of Hexham, but most of the others seem to stem from Henry of Huntingdon.[47]

The composition of the armies was less unusual than is often suggested. There were undisciplined Galwegians in the Scottish armies, whose presence proved disastrous to King David, and parish levies on the English side, but both sides were controlled by Norman knights. The importance of Stephen's household knights under Bernard of Balliol has certainly been underestimated. It was only after their arrival that the English felt numerically strong enough to engage in battle.[48] The pattern of the English army fits closely to that found in the battles we have already covered: archers, dismounted knights, and a reserve force of cavalry. David of Scots also dismounted part of his force. David, like Harold Godwinson at Hastings, pinned his hopes on a surprise attack, in this case through the fog, and like Harold he failed to achieve it. The battle hinged on his decision to allow the Galwegians to disrupt his plan so they could take what they saw as their rightful place in the van. They made an aggressive but ill-disciplined advance and were shot down by the English archers. One of the Lothian chiefs was felled by an arrow, and the Galwegians fled. According to Ailred, 'as a hedgehog is covered with spines, so were the Galwegians with arrows'.[49] The king's son, Henry, led a gallant charge, which had initial success, but was held off, apparently by the English cavalry.

Finally, we come to Lincoln in 1141, the last major battle of the Norman period. Some historians have located this battle to the north of the city, but a position to the west is more likely, though the chronicles are not specific. They do tell us of the rebel forces crossing marshy ground, after changing their line of approach, and this probably indicates the Foss Dyke. But again, the main point is that, apart from the rise of Lincoln itself, the whole area is flat and the battle was fought over level ground.

Once more the battle arose from a siege. Ranulf of Chester had seized Lincoln castle by a trick and Stephen had responded to an appeal from the bishop and the citizens to attempt recovery by a siege. An army was collected in the west by Ranulf and Robert of Gloucester, and came to the relief. Their army seems to have been larger, and Stephen again was faced with problems over the loyalty of his own force. Against advice, he chose to fight, primarily it would seem for psychological reasons, not wishing to emulate the cowardice of his father. He refused 'to stain his reputation by the disgrace of flight'.[50] Baldwin FitzGilbert made Stephen's battle speech for

---

45 Howlett, iii, 182: 'in campo latissimo'. See also VCH, *Yorkshire*, i, 160.
46 A. H. Burne, *More Battlefields of England*, London 1952, 96-9.
47 Huntingdon, 262-5; Howlett, iii, 162; Orderic, vi, 522.
48 Howlett, iii, 160-1.
49 Howlett, iii, 196.
50 *Gesta Stephani*, 112; Huntingdon, 271-3.

him. Henry of Huntingdon indulges himself with the battle speeches, in which most of the commanders are insulted for reasons ranging from cowardice to unutterable filthiness in behaviour. Again both sides dismounted some knights but retained some cavalry. The first clash destroyed the poorly armed Welsh on the rebel side, but the earls retaliated and dealt the decisive blow by breaking the royal cavalry. Stephen was left with infantry forces, and surrounded. He fought with his sword till it broke, and then with an axe given him by a citizen of Lincoln. He resisted 'like a lion, grinding his teeth and foaming at the mouth like a boar' until hit on the head by a rock.[51]

Let us then summarise the battle tactics employed in this century after Hastings. There are three common elements: knights who are dismounted to fight with the foot; archers usually placed in a forward position; and cavalry normally reserved for a decisive charge. Our final problem is to try and explain why these tactics were used.

Were they novel or unique tactics, something confined to England and Normandy? It seems not. Leo the Wise had said of the Franks: 'when their soldiers are hard pressed in a cavalry fight, they will turn their horses loose, dismount, and stand back to back against superior numbers, rather than flee'. At the Battle of the Dyle in 891, knights were dismounted by Arnulf against the Vikings. According to Morice, the Bretons dismounted against the Angevins in the second Battle of Conquereux in 992, and it is possible that knights dismounted at Pontlevoy in 1016. In a later period, during the Second Crusade, Conrad III dismounted knights at Damascus in 1148, and William of Tyre makes the interesting comment that this was the 'custom of the Teutons when they were faced with a crisis in battle'. The famous Byzantine remark that the Franks were ungainly when they fought on foot, nevertheless suggests that this did occur.[52]

It seems likely then that this was not a new practice in 1106, nor one confined to England and Normandy. The view of Professor Hollister, and of Lachauvelaye before him, that this was a result of Anglo-Saxon influence, does not therefore seem to be supported.[53] No doubt the experience of Hastings reinforced the view that good infantry could be effective against cavalry, but twelfth-century tactics were far from being a reproduction of English tactics, and there is little evidence that the knights who dismounted were of Old English extraction. Only one Englishman is mentioned in any situation where dismounting occurred, and that is the somewhat unusual case of Edgar the Atheling with Curthose. When 'English' knights are mentioned, it is never certain that they were Anglo-Saxons, and generally more likely that they were Normans who had settled in England. Of the many named examples of men who dismounted, all were of Norman or French extraction. The interesting incident in 1101, when Henry I 'went among the ranks (of the English assembled to face the anticipated invasion of Curthose) instructing them how to elude the ferocity of the cavalry by opposing their shields, and how to return their strokes', does not

---

51 Howlett, iv, 140-1.

52 C. Oman, *A History of the Art of Warfare in the Middle Ages*, 2v, 2nd edn, 1924, i, 204, 357; F. C. Liskenne and J. B. B. Sauvan, 'L'Empereur Leon: Institutions Militaires', *Bibliothèque Historique et Militaire*, iii, Paris 1850, 524-5. On the Dyle, *MGH*, 1, 1826. On Conquereux and Pontlevoy, P-H. Morice, *Histoire Ecclésiastique et Civile de Brétagne*, 2v, Paris 1750, i, 65. On Damascus, E. A. Babcock and A. C. Krey, *William Archbishop of Tyre, A History of Deeds done Beyond the Sea*, New York 1943, i, 189. On the Franks, E. R. A. Sewter, *The Alexiad of Anna Comnena*, Harmondsworth 1969, 416.

53 J. Lachauvelaye, *Guerres des Français et des Anglais du XIe au XVe siècle*, Paris 1875, i, 13, 34. Hollister, 127-9. Compare Norgate, i, 13.

suggest that the expertise and influence in developing the tactics against cavalry was of English origin.[54] It is nonetheless interesting in showing Henry I's familiarity with such tactics several years before Tinchebrai. The fact that both sides dismounted in that battle also argues against it as the result of English influence, and in favour of a development in continental warfare by that time.

It remains interesting that dismounting knights in the Norman period became almost invariable in battle. There was no hint of the practice at Hastings, where the Conqueror's knights were 'astonished to see him on foot', when he was unhorsed.[55] The chronicles give some explanation of dismounting, which may be analysed as 'lest they take to flight', 'to remove the hope of flight', and in order that 'they might fight with more determination', usually in conjunction with an oath 'to conquer or to die'.[56] Can we interpret this in tactical terms? The greatest fear of any commander was defeat. Cavalry offered the best hope of a sudden blow and victory, but how could one insure against an opponent's cavalry charge? On the defensive, cavalry was likely to break, horses were vulnerable. Good infantry had a better chance of withstanding a charge. Both the Normans and the English at Hastings possessed heavy infantry, but in this period there was a limit to how many well armed infantry could be provided. A simple solution to the problem of strengthening infantry, particularly in a crisis, was to take some of your best armed and trained men, even if trained as cavalry, and use them to reinforce the infantry. Stephen at Lincoln, in the view of Henry of Huntingdon, dismounted knights and disposed his lines for 'maximum safety'.[57] As Geoffrey of Monmouth put it: the side that stands firm in the first assault, achieves victory in the end.[58]

A related explanation is to be found in the use of archers. Western armies were not the only ones that had to find an answer to the growing power of the concerted charge. On crusade, several responses were attempted to what the Byzantines called the 'irresistible' charge of the Franks: wagons pushed forward at the moment of the charge, iron caltrops, or especially missile weapons that could hit the vulnerable horses before the charge was delivered.[59] This last answer was also employed in the West. Archers were effective, but they were also vulnerable. In the East the archers were mounted, and could shoot and move away from danger. In the West they were normally on foot, and on their own would be vulnerable against cavalry, hence the use of dismounted men and spearmen to protect them, hence at the Standard the dismounted men were 'mixed in' with the archers in the front line.[60] It was a tactic that would re-emerge in the Hundred Years War.

In short, the tactics of this period were probably not of English origin, though they might have received some influence from that quarter. They were tactics that developed out of ordinary Frankish methods of war, and were distinguished by the combination of archers, heavy infantry and cavalry, in a period when the greatest threat was the concerted cavalry charge, and the greatest concern of military commanders was to find an answer to that charge.

54 *De gestis regum*, ii, 472.
55 *Gesta Guillelmi*, 198: 'Mirantes eum peditem sui milites'.
56 Huntingdon, 235, 269, 271. Suger, 196. Howlett, iii, 189.
57 Huntingdon, 271: 'cum summo securitate'.
58 A. Griscom, *The Historia Regum Britanniae of Geoffrey of Monmouth*, London 1929, 486. Geoffrey is of considerable interest for the warfare of his own age.
59 Alexiad, 163, 416, 165, 416.
60 Huntingdon, 263: 'sagittarii equitibus inmixti'.

FORTRESS-POLICY IN CAPETIAN TRADITION
AND ANGEVIN PRACTICE
ASPECTS OF THE CONQUEST OF NORMANDY BY PHILIP II

Charles Coulson

The Director of these conferences in 1959 first established that the treatment of non-royal fortresses in Britain in the period 1154 to 1216 was sufficiently systematic and purposeful to constitute a 'castle-policy', in Professor Allen Brown's words, 'consciously directed to the augmentation of royal power, chiefly at the expense of the baronage'.[1] Taken together with the programme of royal castle-building under Henry II, Richard and John (already in 1955 analysed and financially quantified) this 'Angevin castle-policy', by a calculated campaign of seizure, confiscation, escheat and demolition, changed the ratio of royal to recorded baronial castles markedly in favour of the Crown. By the close of 1214, before the Civil War broke out, ninety-three were physically or lawfully in royal possession compared with forty-nine in 1154; in effect, 'nothing less than a drastic alteration in the balance of power'.[2] Although various documentary estimates of the number of seignorial castles in the later twelfth century have been shown by D. J. Cathcart King's recently published ground-survey to have been too low by a factor of about three, the siege-worthiness of the great majority of unrecorded sites was arguably so slight that Professor Brown's conclusion, on its own terms of reference, is not greatly affected. Whether the ratio in 1214 was two to one, or in fact ten to one, all numerical assessments are vitiated by problems of reconciling modern structural and military criteria with the original usage of *castrum* and *fortericia* and by such extraneous factors as manpower, stocking and political will; and it may be that an official presence might be better established by a dense network of administrative bases (even sub-fortified manors) than by a handful of major strongholds, strategically significant perhaps but sparsely scattered, their phases of active service brief and occasional, military value somewhat equivocal, and their construction, guard and repair decidedly bur-

[1] For his tolerant supervision of the thesis upon which this paper is largely based (C. L. H. Coulson, 'Seignorial Fortresses in France in Relation to Public Policy c.864 to c.1483', University of London Ph.D., February 1972 — hereafter Coulson 1972) and for many subsequent kindnesses my thanks are due to R. Allen Brown; and for discussion of 'rendability' over many years to H. R. Loyn, R. H. C. Davis, J. C. Holt and to the members of the Medieval and Renaissance Seminar at Eliot College, University of Kent at Canterbury.
[2] R. Allen Brown, 'A List of Castles 1154-1216', *EHR* lxxiv, 1959, 249, 256 and 249-80 *passim*; 'Royal Castle-Building in England 1154-1216', *EHR* lxx, 1955, 353-98. R. Allen Brown, H. M. Colvin, A. J. Taylor, *The History of the King's Works*, London 1963, I, 64-81, II, 553-894 *passim*, 1023. Dr Brown's supplementary notes to F. M. Powicke, *The Loss of Normandy* 2nd edn (Manchester 1961 — hereafter Powicke 1961) and D.Phil. thesis ('The Place of English Castles in the Administrative and Military Organization 1154-1216 with Special Reference to the Reign of John', Oxford University 1953) and his *English Castles* (London 1976 — with revised estimates of the total of operative castles c.1200) have also been of great value and deserve special acknowledgement.

densome. Territorial power obviously correlated with castle-building; but exactly how, be it psychologically or in contemplation of war, or as the celebration and guarantee of a *fait accompli* of local dominance, clearly varied in time and place. In addition, there is value in thinking of a *fortress*-policy, comprehending all kinds of fortifications and especially the walled-towns.[3]

Acknowledging this dimension of Angevin statecraft at once directs attention to seeing how public policy originally in France, and that of the Capetians subsequently, may have intervened in the world of seignorial fortresses. Comparisons with Anglo-Norman practice particularly during that part of the struggle for Normandy between John's accession and the battle of Bouvines, offer some illumination. Philip Augustus had a fortress-policy of his own, which evolved out of traditions differing hardly at all in doctrine but markedly in their implementation from the Angevin. These antecedents may repay examination.[4] Down to the treaty of Le Goulet (January 1200) Capetian practice was conditioned by the underdog situation of the Kings of France. Philip II succeeded in 1180 at the age of fifteen to an insecure throne with wide pretensions but power confined narrowly to the Île de France, the Orléannais and to Berri. The Crown had survived partly because it had appeared too weak to evoke any lethal combination of feudatories. Philip may have been a Carolid, as Sir Maurice Powicke has it, intent from the outset on destroying the Angevin Empire and going on to develop ambitions to revive the power of the house of Charlemagne, but he had twenty years of uphill endeavour before he could make much progress and what distinguishes his fortress-policy is that he was the first of the Capetians to break with tradition; to discard the imperial and sub-Carolingian pretence of royal control as such over all the fortresses of his kingdom, irrespective of their

---

3 Mr D. J. Cathcart King has most generously allowed me over many years use of the draft of his virtually exhaustive site-catalogue and bibliography listing about 1500 'fortified' places datable between 1052 and c.1500 (*Castellarium Anglicanum*, 2 vols, New York 1982). Ella Armitage (*Norman Castles*, London 1912) appended 'a schedule of English castles known (from documents) to date from the eleventh century' (total 84). Sidney Painter ('English Castles in the Early Middle Ages . . .', *Feudalism and Liberty*, Baltimore 1961, 126-8, reprinting *Speculum*, x, 1935, 321-32) stressed the problem of ephemeral works and twelfth-century abandonment but was 'inclined to believe' in a peak of 500-600 in use c.1100 and 'reasonably certain' of a decline to about 200-250 'castles' by c.1200. His confidence as to criteria and terminology, and assumption that early thirteenth-century records omitted relatively few, are not supported by King, especially with subinfeudated places. Structural definitions apart, *castellum* is often used for the lordship as a whole (e.g. 1154 Saint-Clair-sur-Epte, *Monuments Historiques*, J. Tardif, Paris 1866, no. 529). On the statistical and terminological problems even of detailed fief rolls, listing at least 341 'fortresses' in a single county, see Charles Coulson 'Castellation in the County of Champagne in the Thirteenth Century' (*Château-Gaillard*, ix-x, Caen 1982 – hereafter Coulson 1982 – 349-56, 362-3). Documentary mention usually indicates a place in use ('militarily'?) but the totals given by John Beeler (*Warfare in England 1066-1189*, New York 1966, 427-38) of 'castles built before 1189' (England 298, Wales 80) and by Brown (1959) for 1154-1216 (with Wales 327 'castles') are dwarfed by unrecorded sites (cf. Brown, 1959, 259; Beeler, 397-426) especially if those disregarded as merely manorial are included (e.g. *Bibliography of Moated Sites*, ed. H. Mytum, Moated Sites Research Group, Newcastle on Tyne 1982; on the general issues see Charles Coulson 'Hierarchism in Conventual Crenellation . . .', *Med. Arch.*, xxvi, 1982, 69-100).

4 The few *addenda* to Powicke (1961), 180-6 are required by his entire omission of rendability. The traditional French caricature of patriotic monarchs warring with usurping castle-building 'barons' (for the *genre* see the 'nobles brigands' of A. Luchaire in *Louis VI, le Gros . . .*, Paris 1890, ch. iv; Ch. Petit-Dutaillis, *Etude sur la Vie et le Règne de Louis VIII*, Paris 1894, 403) still persists (J.-F. Finó, *Forteresses de la France Médiévale*, Paris 1970, 72-3) despite R. Aubenas' important 'Les Châteaux Forts des Xe et XIe Siècles' (*Revue Historique de Droit français et étranger*, 4e série, 1938, 548-86).

tenure. He chose instead to rebuild monarchy by consent upon the rights which feudal evolution had placed in the hands of direct lords over the fortresses of their immediate vassals. While Philip was patiently laying new foundations of power to supplement the old, Henry II continued to implement prerogatives of monopolistic and imperial type over the fortresses in his vast empire using force, fear and not a little fraud, just as John was to do with such ultimately disastrous results. The contrast with Capetian castle-policy pointedly bears out the francophile Gerald of Wales' opinion that the despotic governmental methods employed by the Norman dukes in England alienated their continental subjects and crushed their desire to resist the French: nevertheless, the castle-liberties so dear to the baronage on both sides, and likewise the public accountability for those franchises, derived from common parentage; for all that the fortress-policy of Philip II until after Bouvines was moderate and only mildly interventionist, whereas John's was ruthlessly *dirigiste* and opportunistic from first to last.[5]

How much of either was innovation can be judged only by considering the inheritance which the Angevin, Norman and other comital dynasties, along with the Capetian dukes of *Francia*, received from late Carolingian government. Powicke's proposed late-eleventh-century origin for what he called the Norman dukes' 'right of entry' to castles must be questioned; the final part of clause 4 of the 1091 *Consuetudines et Justicie* not only refers back to the mid-century but has been modelled upon contemporary rendability, namely the formerly royal and now widespread lordly right to take over temporarily at pleasure the possession or use of a vassal's fortress.[6] Sufficient direct and corroborative evidence survives to establish the monarchical provenance of fortress-control, comprising licensing and rendability, notably the very suggestive terms of many Carolingian ecclesiastical privileges of mid-ninth-century date onwards, which explicitly or tacitly acknowledge monastic and episcopal fortifying. With conventual establishments claustral jurisdictional immunities were redefined so as to accord with the alignment of the newly fortified

---

[5] W. L. Warren, *King John*, London 1961, 22 (map), 37, 259; Powicke (1961), 17, 105, 297-302; Ch. Petit-Dutaillis, *The Feudal Monarchy in France and England*, London 1964, 181. Brown (1959), on the 100 cases of confiscations and appropriations of baronial castles and 30 cases of demolition by the Crown, comments (pp. 257-8) 'the Angevin kings . . . seem often to have ridden rough-shod over right and precedent . . . Not infrequently no cause is known, and we seem faced with the brute facts that the king desired certain castles and felt himself strong enough to take them.' The suggestion is then made that this 'castle-policy' was a factor in the baronial revolt of 1215, drawing attention to *Magna Carta* clause 52 and to a clinching passage in the *Brut Y Tywysogion*. Capetian comparisons amply confirm this view.

[6] Text below; Powicke (1961), 180, citing C. H. Haskins, *Norman Institutions*, New York 1918, 282 cl. 4 – *nulli licuit in Normannia fortitudinem castelli sui vetare domino Normannie si ipse eam in manu sua voluit habere*. R. Allen Brown, *The Normans and the Norman Conquest*, London 1969, 239; J. H. le Patourel (*The Norman Empire*, Oxford 1976, 304-6) refers to ducal 'control' of castles but does not elaborate upon Haskins, Powicke (1961) or Jean Yver (note 8 below). Rendability awaits systematic publication but see Ch. L. H. Coulson, 'Rendability and Castellation in Medieval France', *Château-Gaillard*, vi, Caen 1972, 59-67 and Coulson 1972 for the *vetare* formula etc. Index 'Rendability'. This phrase was already conventional c.1034 (C. Brunel, *Les Plus Anciennes Chartes en Langue Provençale*, Paris 1926, 3-5, cf.11-12, 13-14 etc.) and may be discerned in Aquitaine-Poitou c.1022-8 e.g. 546, 548) but R. Richard, 'Le Château dans la structure féodale de la France de l'est au XIIe siècle' (*Probleme des 12 Jahrhunderts*, Reichenau Vorträge 1965-7, 169-76) found no evidence of (feudal) rendability (in Burgundy) before that time. Robert Boutruche (*Seigneurie et Féodalité* . . ., Paris 1970, 38) more correctly regarded it as going back 'à la fin du XIe siècle' but cited only charters of 1182 and 1245.

circuits (*castra* and *castella*) leaving very little doubt but that this was done to avert being taken over as fortifications, under colour of royal warrant, by the local count or those claiming his authority. Fortress-rights, rendability chief among them, were already eluding central control and similarly Charles the Bald's famous second capitulary of Pîtres in 864, ordering the destruction of all *castella, firmitates et haias*, built *sine nostro verbo*, shows that local initiative was already participating in the defence of the lower Seine and elsewhere against the Norsemen. The doctrine of royal monopoly persisted nonetheless, insisting that all kinds of fortress, including the newly prominent and multiplying personal strongholds, popular refuges of all kinds, as well as episcopal, comital and sub-comital city-seats and other walled towns and citadels, possessed by virtue of being fortifications of a public character which vested in the local agent of imperial authority (arrogated or legitimate) whatever substance or remnant of monarchical control had survived.[7] Robert Aubenas has stressed the continuity of public authority in tenth and eleventh-century France with a wealth of examples, but he concentrated on the construction of fortresses not their use. Jean Yver developed the theme as it applies to Normandy down to the mid-twelfth century and their powerful testimony is emphatically endorsed if we trace rendability back from the feudal age to its source. Far from doing so, Yver and Aubenas entirely ignored rendability which deprived them of some of the strongest evidence against the perverse dogma that castles were contrary to public policy unless kept in the hands of the ruler. Yver quoted but did not appreciate the statement by Robert of Torigni, that Henry I had 'used the fortresses of many of his barons as though they were his own'. Like the joint declaration of 1091, this represents normal rendability not some peculiarly Norman ducal act of sovereign power. Whenever the sub-Carolingian comital rôle in the regions survived the upheaval and transformations of society, the construction and use of fortresses remained the peculiar sphere of public authority.[8]

7 Rendability survived best where Charlemagne's successors' rule had been strong and outside the regions disrupted by invasion, within an area probably once coextensive with Carolingian Gaul, including Catalonia, Lombardy, Provence, Lotharingia, Netherlands, Germany (Charles L. H. Coulson, 'Fortresses and Social Responsibility in Late-Carolingian France', *Zeitschrift für Archäologie des Mittelalters*, 4, 1976, 29-36). For the Edict of Pistes MGH Legum II, II 310-28 (328 cap I) cf. 302-10, 355-61; MGH I, 62-4 (739 AD); also *Recueil des Actes de Charles III* . . . , ed. Ph. Lauer, Paris 1949, nos. 2, 10, 34, 41, 67, 90, 98, 101; *Recueil des Actes de Louis IV* . . . , ed. Ph. Lauer, Paris 1914, nos. 2, 9, 14, 18; *Recueil des Actes de Lothaire et de Louis V* . . . , ed. L. Halphen, F. Lot, Paris 1908, nos. 4, 18, 21. Cf. the royal and papal immunity, dispensable only for defence and by abbatial consent, accorded to Sainte-Trinité, Péronne, in 1046 (*Catalogue des Actes d'Henri Ier* . . . , ed. F. Soehnée, Paris 1907, no. 72). For the *castellum* of Compiègne see note 12 below.

8 Powicke (1961) 181 and n.10 on *aedificare*; S. Painter (1961), 17-40, and *Speculum*, xxxi, 1956, 243-57 on 'Castellans of the Plain of Poitou . . .'; R. Aubenas (1938) *passim*; Jean Yver, 'Les Châteaux Forts en Normandie jusqu'au milieu du XIIe siècle . . .', *Bulletin de la Société des Antiquaires de Normandie*, liii, 1955-6, 111, 112 *et passim* 28-115. To R. Boutruche (1970, 36) it was still axiomatic that the seignorial castle was (*de seipso*) 'un signe de l'anarchie féodale' just as it had been to W. S. McKechnie (*Magna Carta*, Glasgow 1905, 176) who supposed that 'it was the aim of every efficient ruler to abolish all fortified castles'. With *id genus omne* (likewise Boutruche, 38) he insisted that any castle without royal licence was 'adulterine' in contradiction to his text (1217 version cap 47) which precisely defined the *castra adulterina* as illegal because the product of recent wartime force. Even Yver was nervous about the baronial fortress as such while Auguste Longnon's antipathy was muted only because 'nos comtes pouvaient en temps de guerre faire occuper par leurs chevaliers certains châteaux ou maisons-fortes . . . rendables' (*Histoire des Ducs et Comtes de Champagne*, H. d'Arbois de Jubainville, vii, Paris 1869, 93). The continuity of public authority is correctively stressed by Marcel Garaud

Their different circumstances caused the Anglo-Normans and the early Capetian kings to deal divergently with the Carolingian legacy of fortress-rights. Four years' disorderly rule in Normandy by Robert Curthose required the ban pronounced jointly with William Rufus upon any substantial earthwork and timber fortification, the making of any *fortitudo* on a naturally defensible site (*in rupe vel in insula*), and on the usurped creation of any castellany (*castellum*). Their forthright *nulli licuit in Normannia* applied the rule to the whole territory of the duchy, irrespective of immunity, liberty or mode of tenure. It was part of a general reassertion of the rule of law, intended to deal with the illicit and adulterine gains of violence and lawlessness and typical of such pacifications of which in England 1154 and 1217 are the most familiar.[9] The realities of Capetian power were very different. About the year 1005, the monks of Cormery by Tours, having seen their lands and rights diminished and threatened for the future by the Count of Anjou's new castles of Montbazon and Mirebeau, persuaded Fulk Nerra to guarantee them harmless and prevailed upon him to seek King Robert's corroboration. Cormery esteemed the honour and sanction, and perhaps valued the security and permanence, of a solemn charter so highly, and Fulk no doubt cynically or piously humoured them, because the royal authority over fortresses had retained its aura while losing its material reality. Abbot Gauzelin of Saint-Bénoît-sur-Loire rejoiced at the destruction in a storm of Yèvre-le-Châtel (Loiret), and having seized the opportunity to buy out the irksome *avouerie* owned by its thunderstruck lord, tried to make both changes stick by expensively purchasing the moral backing of his royal brother. Gauzelin's biographer, André de Fleuri explains: *utque eversio castri Evere omnium saeculorum permaneret tempore, centum nonaginta quinque libras Gauzelinus abbas probatissimi argenti Regis Roberto regali proli contulit, quod et scripto corroborat*. Gauzelin also hoped to procure the endorsement 'of the bishops of the whole of Gaul' to complete a familiar cocktail of sanctions; the more naturally since the Church also exercised, by default or by right, the monarchical power to ban. As late as 1148, when the right was already feudalised like rendability, the bishops at the Council of Reims fulminated against the usurpation of clerical property associated with the 'new plague' of castle-building, among other grievances inveighing against 'undue works of castles' being imposed on their men

in his 'La construction des châteaux et les destinées de la *vicaria* et du *vicarius* Carolingiens en Poitou' (*Revue Historique du Droit* . . ., 4e série, 1953, 54-78) and, in a more 'feudalised' context, by J. Richard in his important paper 'Châteaux, châtelains et vassaux en Bourgogne aux XIe et XIIe siècles' (*Cahiers de Civilisation Médiévale*, iii, 1960, 433-47). Rendability in Normandy was already seignorial (as well as ducal) by the twelfth century as elsewhere (note 15 below).

[9] *Castellum* and *castrum* are persistently juridical not architectural terms (unlike *munitio*, *firmitas*, *fortalicium*) meaning not just the fortified *caput* but the whole parcel of appurtenant lordly rights (note 3 above; *Rotuli Chartarum*, Record Commision 1837, 93a) whence the suggested translation of cl.4 which avoids the usual tautology and equally implausible juxtaposing of *fortitudo* in its literal and figurative senses. Attempts to apply the very precise wording to include masonry and major works (the diagnostic *turris* is absent) are conventional but questionable (A. H. Thompson, *Military Architecture in England during the Middle Ages*, Oxford 1912, 89-90; Armitage (1912), 337-8; Powicke (1961), 180; M. de Boüard, 'Les Petites Enceintes Circulaires . . .', *Château-Gaillard*, i, Caen 1964, 32; Brown (1976), 17, 49). The illegality lay in the usurpation as much as in the fortifying and imperial doctrines are no longer applied e.g. in 1088 against Robert de Mortagne, or in 1087-99 against Count Henry (*Cal. Docs France* nos. 39, 424). The maintenance and up-dating of established castles were not touched, unless by special compact as in 1144 with Humphrey de Bohun for Malmesbury and William de Albini in 1203 at Belvoir (*Regesta*, iii, no. 111; *Rotuli de Liberate ac de Misis et Praestitis* . . ., Rec. Comm. 1844, 34-5).

and seeking to submit to parochial discipline the clergy serving the new chapels *in munitionibus et turribus*.[10]

As new socio-political relationships coagulated, feudal custom brought a new pluralism to bear on inherited Carolingian principles. Monarchism becomes little more than a reminiscence in the pronouncements of ecclesiastics affecting fortresses, and in the atavistic grandiloquence of early Capetian charters. Old and new elements mingle in the 'sacred ban' established by the Council of Anse in 994 in favour of Cluny Abbey. The diploma preserves many of the elements of a later Carolingian protection, *inter alia* forbidding intrusion by any *judex publicus aut exactionarius, comes quoque*, but also including the up-to-date injunction that no such intruder should *castrum facere aut aliquam firmitatem* within or near the monastic lands or *burgus*. The Church habitually defended her own by such means but the King's special rôle was acknowledged by obtaining his confirmation. The young Robert le Pieux, in association with Duke Henry, his uncle, and their respective magnates, put their names to a new charter which defined the Cluny *banlieue* to comprise a tract of surrounding country, about 35 miles by 20 miles, in the most fulsome style of royal majesty. The consent of Robert's nobles is acknowleged but the ban was evidently a hallowed and pious act of kingship, combining the royal attributes of protector of the Church and overseer of fortifications in one documentary celebration of regality.[11] His grandson, Philip I, continued to prefer monarchical theory to feudal

---

10 *Thesaurus Novus Anecdotorum . . .*, E. Martène and U. Durand, iv, Paris 1717, cols 141-4. The analogy of castle licensing with chapels, mill-bans and market-bans etc. deserves attention. R. W. Southern, *The Making of the Middle Ages*, London 1953, 84-5 (map of Anjou 987-1040); *Catalogue des Actes de Robert II . . .*, ed. W. M. Newman, Paris 1937, nos. 25, 95. Late in the eleventh century the knowledgeable forgers of Saint-Denis fathered upon Robert II, as 'the successor of Dagobert, Charlemagne, Louis I and Charles III', in order to strengthen their hand against the Montmorency family, a charter confirming the monks' immunity in the conventual *castellum* (precinct; genuinely granted 898, *Recueil . . . Charles III*, no. 10) and banning (not synonymous with forbidding in the medieval era) fortifying on the Ile Saint-Denis. They relied on this forgery in 1219 successfully (*Catalogue . . . Robert II . . .*, nos. 80, 120, pp. 294-5; *Layettes du Trésor des Chartes*, i, Paris 1863, no. 1372). On the early thirteenth-century Yèvre-le-Châtel, see Finó (1970), 445-7; cf. the symbiotic not confrontational relations with a castle-based *avoué* at Corbie and Montier-en-Der in 1016-42 and 1027-35 (*Catalogue . . . Robert II . . .*, no. 45; *Catalogue . . . Henri Ier . . .*, no. 62, cf. note 24 below; *Catalogue des Actes des Comtes de Brienne, 950-1350*, ed. H. d'Arbois de Jubainville, Bibliothèque de l'Ecole des Chartes, xxxiii, 1872, no. 5). The clergy seem only to have anathematised (usually in much-used and unduly influentially lurid language) castle-building from which they did not benefit (e.g. near Châlons-sur-Marne in 1048-63, note 13 below). The Touraine Peace of God decretals issued at the Council of Clermont (1095) ordered that no *nova munitio* be built in churches or church-yards. Only very indirect general condemnation of fortresses can be inferred from making the community of the *receptacula* and *munitiones* of Touraine used as bases by malefactors collectively liable to make redress (*Thesaurus Novus . . .*, iv, cols 121-4).

11 To comment that 'Robert n'était pas un méchant homme mais c'est bien certainement un des plus nuls qui ait jamais porté la couronne' (d'Arbois de Jubainville, *Histoire . . . Champagne*, ii, Paris 1860, 278) fails to grasp that he was keeping alive an imperial tradition which he had no power to implement otherwise. *Recueil des Chartes de l'Abbaye de Cluny*, ed. P. Bernard and A. Bruel, i, Paris 1876, no. 2255, cf. iv (Paris 1888) no. 2800; *Catalogue . . . Robert II . . .*, 2-4, 18-19 (as 996-1002). The Council, by the 'pontifical authority' of the archbishops of Lyon and Vienne and nine other bishops from central eastern Gaul, accorded to Odilo (abbot 994-1049) the petition of Maieul of Cluny (died May 994) that the abbot be vested with episcopal rank (*praesulatus dignitas*) to repress the evils and *angustiae* about the *locus Cluniacensis sanctissimus* by power of anathema. Any infractor was also decreed excommunicated in advance. King Robert adduced royal precedents (giving only unspecific acknowledgement to *privilegia apostolica*) and expanded this spiritual protection of all Cluniac property into a geographical,

reality in his protection to the canons of Compiègne dated at the ancient palace in 1092. The atavism of this charter is substantial and illuminating, particularly the statement in the preamble that the house had been *sic nobilitata et premunita* by the Emperor Charles (?II) and Pope John (?VIII) that any attempt to violate it, to construct any *munitio* or to usurp lordship in the lands of the abbey would incur the full rigour of royal justice and the Church's anathema besides. Philippe le Gros admitted that the royal wrath and eternal damnation, manifest or merely presumed, had alike been impotent; *munitiones et turris* had even been built near the abbey church, although the outrage is said to have occurred *ante tempora nostra*. The phraseology here is all of a piece. When, we are told, Philip assumed the *imperium . . . totius Francie* (in 1059) he had the encroaching tower destroyed by mining and to avert any recurrence, now in 1092, transferred to the canons the reversion of his right, namely *jus regie potestatis et dominationis*, to prohibit fortifying upon or near their properties. Such powers devolved upon the greater franchises, and even lesser ones, most often not by grant but by mere user.[12] Between 1111 and 1118 the struggles of Louis VI to eradicate the castle of Hugh du Puiset in the Beauce, to stop Thibaud of Blois fortifying at Allaines, and to remove the castle of Quierzy, near Laon, make better sense as acts of partisan majesty than of peace-keeping. The royal example was copied as widely as the Carolingian mantle of fortress-control had fallen. Propaganda by local potentates against castles, when their construction was still technically an official act and possessory right did not yet apply, has combined with the interested complaints of dispossessed ecclesiastical first-comers to

non-feudal and non-proprietorial, castellation *banlieue* extending 35 miles from Châlon to Mâcon on the Saône, 30 miles west from Mâcon to Charolles, thence 20 miles to Mont-Saint-Vincent. This banal zone influenced castle-building in c.1147, c.1122-56, 1166, 1173, 1264, 1309-10 (*Recueil . . . Cluny*, v, Paris 1894, nos.4131, 4244; *Les Olim ou Registres des Arrêts rendus par la Cour du Roi . . .*, ed. Beugnot, Paris 1839, i, no. 6; iii nos.34, 69). It is unique among ecclesiastical, royal and ducal protections to Cluniac houses; the urban *banlieues* of Ponthieu afford a later parallel (note 15 below), cf. *Recueil . . . Cluny*, ii, Paris 1880, no. 980; iii, nos.1950, 2270, 2465, 2466; iv, nos.2949, 2976, 3389, 3632; v, nos.3689, 3720 all dating between 955 and 1097.

12 *Recueil des Actes de Philippe Ier . . .*, ed. M. Prou, Paris 1908, no. 125, from three thirteenth-century copies whose glosses (eg. *Philippus rex de firmitatibus non edificandis in Compendio vel in vicinio Compendii absque licentia nostra*) confirm that the canons were dispensing the ban (such bans were invitations to treat, not prohibitions *d'en haut*) in normal franchisal fashion. Other late sixteenth-century glosses show this was used to stop building on the bridge and riverside by the rival town authorities. King Charles II (840-77) founded the abbey; Charles III rebuilt it and (917) exempted from all (non-royal) takeover (rendability *de facto*) the fortified precinct and outworks (*de castello autem et propugnaculis ejus et de terra exteriori inter murum et fossatum, ut nullus externus ejusdem loci quasi ad praevidendum castellum principatum accipiat et nemo ibi mansionem accipiat concedimus eis; Recueil . . . Charles III . . .*, no. 90). Philip I's other affirmations of undisturbed tenure of fortified precincts were made to Senlis cathedral (1068; *firmitates omnium domorum canonicorum*), and to Reims Abbey *castrum* (1090; *Recueil . . . Philippe Ier . . .*, nos. 39, 102). Louis VI did likewise for the new *castellum* of Vézelai Abbey, adapting an immunity charter of Louis II (Luchaire (1890) no.253). At Compiègne the comital *fisc* was already vested in the abbey in 917, very likely with a (small) geographical castellation *banlieue* anticipating Cluny. Philip's ban *ne aliquis possit aut presumat construere turrim aut munitionem sive domum defensabilem in toto territorio et convicinio Compendii*, 'within or without the town on the islands or beyond the river' (Oise). The abbey of Ferrières-en-Gâtinais (Loiret) undoubtedly enjoyed a similar ban (valid even against the Crown), with other extensive monopolies, granted or confirmed by Philip I and defined by Louis VI on request as operative within the abbey lordship not territorial circumscription (Luchaire (1890) no.500, cf. feudal redefinition in 1208 of 1156 old-style castellation franchise of the see of Maguelone, notes 16, 27 below, and Corbie Abbey *banlieue*, note 24 below).

bias our own views, but it is profoundly significant that in the proto-feudal age fortress-control, along with protection of the Church, was inherent in regalian authority; and, conversely, that fortress-tenure was conditional and precarious *ab ovo*.[13]

Such allusions to the erstwhile royal monopoly of fortress-control as survive before Philip Augustus naturally occur predominantly in ecclesiastical contexts. In this facilitating environment Capetian practice most nearly approached its theory. Philip I's Compiègne declaration on the royal banning of fortification matches the Norman statement of 1091; and the latter assertion of universal ducal rendability compares closely with Louis VI's statement in 1119 that the 'Crown of France' could take over the fortresses dependent on Cluny Abbey (and by implication others), 'whenever the public defence should require'.[14] Similarly, the protection granted by Louis VII in 1156 to the abbot and monks of Villemagne in the diocese of Béziers (Hérault) continued the traditional policy of affirming ecclesiastical franchises on application, especially in Languedoc and beyond the royal demesne of the Île de France. By endorsing fortifying *carte blanche*, abbey, town and else-

---

13 But Philip I, according to Suger, advised his son to keep the *turris* (and castle) of Montlhéry, near Corbeil, in his own hands for 'it has caused me untold trouble. Frankly, that tower has made me old before my time' (quoted R. Fawtier, *The Capetian Kings of France*, trans. L. Butler and R. J. Adam, London 1962, 17). Luchaire (1890) nos.108, 117, 118, 128, 609; *Histoire ... Champagne*, ii, 194-202, suggesting Allonnes but A. Molinier and A. Luchaire prefer Allaines (also Eure et Loir) only 1¼ miles from le Puiset. Before the *donjon* there was destroyed by fire the first time Thibaud (*per* Suger) opportunistically alleged his right to build a tower at Allaines, within the lordship but held of Louis VI in chief, offering to prove his right by judicial duel between his seneschal and the king's. Hugh du Puiset and his castle jointly were blamed for local brigandage as was Quierzy castle (Aisne), formerly royal but given by Philip I (c.1068-98) for refuge from attacks to the bishop of Noyon (*Recueil ... Philippe Ier .... no.*136). Suger's almost obsessive clerical animosity towards seignorial fortresses was probably excited in this case by the territorial competition in the Beauce between lay magnates and the clergy of Saint-Père de Chartres and with the influential abbot of Saint-Denis. Compare the lurid denunciation of castle-oppression against Saint-Mard Abbey, Soissons, in 1048 (*Veterum Scriptorum ... Amplissima Collectio*, E. Martène and U. Durand, vii, Paris 1733, 58-9); Compiègne (above, probably drafted by the canons), and in Fulbert of Chartres' (died 1028) request to Robert II to obtain action by Count Eudes over the new castle of Illiers (16 miles south-west of Chartres) and to stop the rebuilding of Gallardon castle (6 miles north-west). Fulbert protested at the very possibly justified efforts by Geoffroi de Châteaudun to restore the separate integrity of the viscounty on the death (1023) of his uncle Hugh, both viscount and archbishop of Tours (*Histoire ... Champagne*, i, Paris 1859, 275-8; clericalist tone and argument taken directly from Nicolas Brussel, *Nouvel Examen de l'Usage Général des Fiefs en France ...*, Paris (1727) 1750, 378, ch.30 *passim*). Comital righteousness also imbues Geoffrey Plantagenet's solemn charter celebrating his siege and destruction of 'the entire tower and defences' of Montreuil-Bellay, near Saumur (1151; *Recueil des Actes de Henri II Roi d'Angleterre ... concernants ... les Affaires de France*, L. Delisle ed. E. Berger, i, Paris 1916, no.18; cf. Sempigny, razed in 1171 by the archbishop of Reims allegedly as a brigand lair, *Histoire ... Champagne*, iii, Paris 1861, 77-80). A good corrective is Pierre Héliot's 'Sur les Résidences Prinçières bâties en Frances du Xe au XIIe siècle', *Le Moyen Age*, série 4, 10, 1955, 27-61, 291-319 *passim*.

14 *Fortalicia autem, castra et munitiones, propter necessitates et deffensiones corone regni Francie publice faciendas, in manu corone Francie habebimus, abbate et conventu Cluniacensi prius requisitis. Predicta autem aliquo casu extra manum et coronam regni Francie non poterunt ad aliquam aliam personam aliquo modo transferri sive pervenire* (*Ordonnances des Rois ...*, iii, Paris 1732, 545-8); recognised as rendability by the editor Secousse from Du Cange's 1668 treatise, 'Des fiefs jurables et rendables', appended to his edition of Joinville (reprinted ed. Petitot, *Collection Complète des Mémoires ...*, Ire série, iii, Paris 1819, 490-527). Louis VI's charter was royally confirmed in 1270, 1294, 1314 etc. (*Chartes ... Cluny*, v, no.3943; vi, Paris 1903, no.5154; and *Layettes*, i, no.46).

where, *viz ut possitis munire fossa et vallo et muro et turribus et munitionibus*, Louis le Jeune really did no more (but it might be crucial) than facilitate the exercise of their lordship in competition with magnates less well disposed to the Crown. Conversely, any fortifying by intruders on abbey land would be met by the royal ban fulminated by proxy; and, if no more, the royal power would not die of disuse. Having little to lose, the authority of the distant monarch could only benefit by acts done in his name. By solemnly 'assigning' to the monks in advance the *fortias* which he had authorised them to build, Louis perpetuated the doctrine that all castles, however created or held, were public works at the king's disposal. In somewhat modernised language but still conventional manner the charter then confirms the monastic immunity to lay intrusion, omitting the old threats of Divine retribution but warning infractors simply that no prescriptive right will accrue to seizures however long enjoyed. Time will not run against the abbey; in particular, any previous rendering of their fortresses (forbidden henceforth) shall be reputed null and void, *quia hec redditio regii juris esse dignoscitur*. Because, with the multiplication of fortresses and of subinfeudation, rendability was in fact percolating down through the strata of tenure and was becoming a normal attribute of immediate lordship, any such precedent had to be quashed; but the new world of feudal relationships could not be set aside simply by declaring it *de facto* and of no legal effect.[15] Four similar ecclesiastical franchises with corresponding fortress-rights were endorsed by Louis VII down to 1186, all in the south; namely, the bishoprics of Maguelone (1156, 1161) and Lodève (1162, 1188), and the abbacies of Sarlat (1181) and of Figeac (1186), both in Périgord. These were in no way 'des privilèges assez extraordinaires', as Leopold Delisle would have it (1856). In each case the initiative lay with the grantee and the king readily lent his authority whenever he might acquire the credit of obedience and establish some vicarious presence. The early Capetians were responding to events but they kept their powder dry, realisti-

---

[15] Louis VII's text recited in 1210 confirmation *Recueil des Actes de Philippe Auguste, roi de France* (hereafter *Rec. Ph. Aug.*), iii, Paris 1966, no.1120. It applied to all possessions *ad jus monasterii pertinentia* as enumerated, comprising a region in the north-west of Béziers diocese (Hérault); a full baronial-level castellation franchise, monopolising the right to fortify and license others, linked by the Compiègne ban with the pre-feudal Cluny-type *banlieue*; another link is the control often exercised over the environs of major towns (cf. Carolingian *pagus*) e.g. Dijon, 1153; bishop of Langres and Duke Hugh of Burgundy (*Recueil Général des Anciennes Lois Françaises* ..., i, Paris 1822, 150-3); markets and fortifications within 6 miles of Carpentras (Vaucluse) banned 1155 by the bishop and Raymond of Toulouse (*Layettes*, i, no.139). That *de facto* territorial urban circumscriptions were far from obsolete is suggested by ducal licensing in Gascony (Coulson 1972, appendix B 3) and the formal castellation *banlieues* of such northwestern towns as Corbie, Abbeville, Crécy-en-Ponthieu, Noyelles-sur-Mer, Waben, Marquenterre, Ponthoile, Doullens, Rue, Ergnies all confirmed 1180-1210 (*Rec. Ph. Aug.*, i, Paris 1916, nos.10, 52; *Ordonnances des Rois* ..., iv, Paris 1734, 53-9; *Recueil des Actes des Comtes de Ponthieu (1026-1279)*, ed. C. Brunel, Paris 1930, nos.131, 134, 150, 152, 155, 206, 212, 298). The rendability to the Crown of the *munitiones* of the monks of Villemagne, alodial tenure notwithstanding, apparently pre-dates the feudalisation of rendability; cf. licence by Louis VII in 1174 to fortify Bourges Cathedral precinct under renewable oath to render it on demand, omitted in Louis VI's licence (1120) for Sens Cathedral close; renounced except in vacancies (1122) over the archbishop of Bourges' castle of Saint-Palais; and left uncertain in the reservation of 'regalian rights' (1134) over the lands and fortresses of the bishops of Le Puy (*Ordonnances des Rois* ..., xi, Paris 1769, 206-7; Luchaire (1890) nos. 295, 317, 532). Non-royal rendability was ubiquitous and is the essential complement to the present study (Coulson 1972, appendix A), however rarely found (recorded) in Angevin Normandy e.g. Robert de Neubourg's oath 'not to with-hold' his castle (Eure) from Count Waleran of Meulan's use at will (*Cal. Docs France*, no. 338) 'c.1155' but *rectius* 1141-2 (information supplied by Mr D. B. Crouch).

cally eschewing the pyrotechnics and the *machismo* displayed by the Angevin treatment of baronial fortresses. Philip II's predecessors made such use as they were able
of their meagre political and financial resources. This necessary moderation was
vindicated by the contribution made by their fortress policy to the worsting of
King John.[16]

It may be allowable to regard Angevin castle-policy as a programme of investment
in governmental plant, designed to maximise the Crown's portfolio of fortresses: or,
less plausibly, as a campaign of military preparedness on Vegetius' maxim that *qui
desiderat pacem praeparet bellum*; but legality of title and acceptability were essential
to political security. *Realpolitik*, nevertheless, has a seductive glamour. By such a
view it matters little whether a castle was demolished preventively, punitively or
purely vindictively if firm government was thereby manifested — but no vassal was
likely to acquiesce. It may well be that tenurial right in fortresses lagged behind
other forms of realty so that fortress-tenure had remained precarious: the hypothesis
would see Henry II and his sons acting within Carolingian doctrine, with unmitigated
monarchy strengthened by conquest. Such terms as 'appropriation', 'resumption' or
'seizure' of baronial castles need careful use; 'receive in pledge', or 'borrow' might
often be more correct. It may be significant beyond semantics that Henry II's legis-
lation made seisin the *prima facie* test of right whereas under rendability the castle-
tenant's occupation was interruptible but not his right of tenure and restitution. In
one case before the Parlement of Louis IX, proof of delivery of a fortress for war to
the count of Brittany as lord established that it was an act of rendability vindicating
the claimant's right to restitution, despite prolonged deprivation. That rendability
was indeed the principle of Henry II's resumption of 'all the castles in England and

---

16 Delisle's dogmatic prejudice is most significant regarding the 1186 Figeac grant (although
confirmed 1257, 1302, 1442, 1463. *Catalogue des Actes de Philippe Auguste . . .*, Paris 1856,
xcvii-iii). Delaborde (*Rec. Ph. Aug.*, i, no.167) was also worried by 'l'énormité de quelques-
un des privilèges concédés' (*sic*) that despite finding no diplomatic fault he labels it 'acte suspect'.
The misconception is fundamental but could hardly have survived the briefest consideration of
the whole group of franchises, to go no further (*Layettes*, i, nos.143, 167, cf. 141; *Ordonnances
des Rois . . .*, xvi, Paris 1814, 226-9; *Rec. Ph. Aug.*, i, nos. 22, 242). The Figeac ban (dép. Lot)
which Philip merely endorsed (*annuentes pariter . . .*) was defined by lordship and applied to
forts or *bastides* and religious foundations *viz. ne quis etiam infra metas possessionum ecclesie
oppida seu municipia seu habitaciones alia sive domos religiosas, sine voluntate abbatis et capituli,
edificare valeat*. The sporadically archaic phraseology is still more marked in the protection to
Sarlat Abbey (Dordogne, about 35 miles north-west of Figeac) *. . . juxta tenorem . . . privilegii
Ludovici Regis* (prob. Louis VI) *. . . nullus judex publicus . . .* etc., enjoining the abbey tenants
not to build any *turris* in Sarlat town or any *castellum* in the monks' lordships or around Sarlat
proprius quam sit hodie absque eorum licentia. This ban was upheld against Castelréal, a *bastide*
project of Henry III and Edward I of England in 1268 and 1281 (*Les Olim*, i, no. 21; ii, no. 25).
Louis VII's first protection (Feb. 1155) to Bishop John of Maguelone (Hérault) modelled on
Louis VI (*sanximus ut nullus comes, nullus princeps, nulla alia layca potestas . . .*) has no castellation provision, added next year for Bishop Raymond *viz. et si castrum vel aliquam munitionem
per te vel per alium ibi* (in the demesnes listed) *facere volueris, liceat tibi et successoribus tuis de
nostra concessione absque omni contradictione* (confirmed 1208, 1271, 1287). Power to ensure
security and due recognition of superior lordship is still clearer in Louis VII's (again very atavistic)
protection to Bishop Gauzelin of Lodève (Hérault) confirming (1162) royal *licenciam faciendi
. . . turres, municiones, muros, portarum tuiciones* (*munitiones* in 1188), *vallos* (*sic*) in all his
alodial properties and extensive *regalia* including (judicial cognisance of) *novas forcias*, especially
within church appurtenances *et jus prohibendi facere novas forcias in toto episcopatu*. Philip II
renewed this with insignificant modifications in 1188 (also confirmed 1210, 1283, 1464).
Lordship support was the aim not restriction of fortifying as such; indeed, the grantee's castellation was facilitated.

the March' (in Normandy also says Howden) by sending custodians to take them over, after the Young King's rebellion, at the Council of Windsor in 1176, can scarcely be doubted. Ceremonies of notional royal takeover, whether by exercising right of entry, by banner-placing *in signum dominii*, by receiving keys or by other acts reasserting Henry's lordship, could soon be performed at all the castles of bishops, earls and barons, as we are told was done, without recorded charge to the Exchequer. Rendability entailed such acts of recognition as well as delivering fortifications on demand for war or other purposes. English practice tallies equally with continental doctrine in the authorising of fortifying, except that the needs of the Conquest implied general franchises and until John's accession few licences survive or seem to have been given, at least in writing. In that it was centralised and decisive, albeit comparatively elementary, Angevin castle-policy seemingly radiates statecraft. In France, however, where pragmatic feudal management with Philip Augustus displaced imperial ideology, we look somewhat hard for that reawakening of national monarchy attributed to his reign. His was certainly not a fortress-policy of Angevin type: but if the methods are less recognisable Capetian aims become no less clear, for all that control of fortresses was necessarily more subtle and much more diversified than the Angevin.[17]

The *trésor des chartes*, apparently established in the castle of the Louvre after Richard's surprise attack at Fréteval in July 1194, still contains some eighty non-royal charters which directly relate to Philip II's fortress-policy and another forty-five which illuminate the intra-seignorial fortress-politics of the reign, often in great detail. Most of these eighty are rendability charters, that is, sworn undertakings, some with mainpernors and penalty clauses, obliging particular fortresses to be delivered to Philip whenever he should require, by summons under letter patent. A few are additionally summarised among the records of royal acts in Philip's three initial Registers for extra security and ease of reference, the originals being stored in the coffers or *layettes* later in the Sainte Chapelle treasury. The peripatetic records were largely reconstituted and successive rearrangements and up-dating of the Registers provided an accessible administrative memory for exercising the Crown's feudal and other powers, fortress-rights prominent among them. The new comprehensive Register of c.1211-20, for instance, was organised under ten sections with a separate folio for the communes and another for the services due from royal fiefs. Louis IX's

---

[17] A social interpretation of licences to crenellate and of castle-building is outlined in my 'Structural Symbolism in Medieval Castle Architecture' (*Journ. BAA*, 132, 1979, 73-90) whose specifically religious aspects are developed in my 'Hierarchism in Conventual Crenellation . . .' (note 3 above). W. L. Warren exults conventionally at royal ruthlessness with baronial castles but also stresses the heavy political cost of Angevin behaviour (*King John*, 50, 109, 170, 175-6, 181-3; Brown 1959, 252-3 for citations *et passim*). The reign of Henry I was a 'turning point' in the development of hereditary tenure, even landed security being precarious. Henry 'took for his own use the castle of Blyth' before Michaelmas 1102 (*Regesta*, i, no. 598; R. W. Southern, 'The Place of Henry I in English History', *Procs BA*, 48, 1962, 145; Marjorie Chibnall, 'Robert of Bellême and the Castle of Tickhill', in *Droit Privé et Institutions Régionales . . . (études historiques offertes à Jean Yver)*, Rouen 1976, 151-6). Carolingian doctrines of public utility applied as much to the pre-Conquest *burh* (C. Warren Hollister, *Anglo-Saxon Military Institutions on the Eve of the Norman Conquest*, Oxford 1962, 142-5; and, less happily on 'The Conqueror's castle-policy', 141-2; J. M. Hassall and D. Hill, 'Pont de l'Arche: Frankish Influence on the West Saxon Burh?', in *Arch. Journ.*, 127, 1970, 188-95) as to post 1052 'castles'. Under rendability length of disseisin was no bar to title provided delivery for war on demand was duly proved; the tenant of Roche Derrien (Brittany) rendered the castle in 1230-5, his heir winning restitution from Duke John in 1272 (*Les Olim*, i, 311-13, 395-6, 904; *Actes du Parlement de Paris*, ed. E. Boutaric, i, Paris 1863, nos.1456, 1788, 1845).

Registrum Guarini improved upon it further, having eighteen sections, the first three being entitled *Feoda, Civitates, Castella*. A copy was made for the king to take on the Seventh Crusade (1248-55), leaving the original for his mother's use as Regent. Clearly, there is much more to this administrative thrust than bureaucratic tidiness. From the *securitates* granted to Philip II (or incidentally involving him) and from the seventy or so relevant royal issues down to 1214, a threefold distinction emerges; namely, fortress-cases due to the royal appeal jurisdiction; cases brought to the king as alternative to the pope, a bishop or a great feudatory for mediation and record; and thirdly, that category of cases, initially very small, which concerned the royal demesne or the royal power directly and arose from the king's own intervention and initiative, in all probability.[18]

The medieval usage of *castrum* and *castellum* suggests that 'castle-policy' to contemporaries would have signified what 'fortress-policy' means to us, but no philological purism is needed to justify giving a major place here to the walled towns and especially those chartered by Philip Augustus. The reserves of manpower, arms and money controlled by the *villes fermées* made them as important strategically as they were financially. Significantly, nearly all of Philip II's relate directly to the struggle for Normandy in the north-west and fall within the scope of the present paper. Their juridical status gives them immense importance in any consideration of the roots and evolution of fortress-customs, reaching back to Roman times. That public character which generically belongs to fortifications is the quintessence of the Gallo-Roman and Merovingian *civitas*, no less than the Carolingian, and it clung nowhere more tenaciously than to the ancient walled cities of Gaul. The contrast is very great with the relative absence of continuity in Anglo-Saxon England where the word *castrum*, vernacularised to variants of *chester* (*Ceaster*; *Caer* in the Celtic fringe) and tagged on to corrupted remnants of Latin names, became a popular term for almost any kind of major Roman fortified site. Soldier merged with civilian in the later Roman Empire and large fortified complexes, whether military-gone-native or urban militarised, became Frankish and eventually royal, comital or episcopal administrative centres, or capitals of lesser dignity, their special status still denoted by the style *castrum* in tenth and eleventh-century France. Direct links with the Crown, or the

---

18 Royal judicial arbitrations were unsystematically recorded prior to 1254 but Boutaric appended to his preface an exceptionally notable case of June-September 1180, conducted at Pierrepertuis near Vézelai, which is very pertinent here (*Actes du Parlement . . .*, i, lxxx, ccxcvii; also *Rec. Ph. Aug.*, i, no. 8). The castellar (and seignorial) rivalry in Mâcon between the bishop and Count Gerard of Vienne was resolved by upholding a charter of Louis VII exempting the cathedral from comital lordship, the corollary being that Gerard *in villa Matisconensi nullam firmitatem habere debeat preter turrim suam quam tum temporis habebat*, whereas the clergy were entitled to fortify (*firmare*) both of their city precincts at will and likewise *firmitates aedificare vel augere* at all their extramural *ville* previously having defences. In Mâcon the count was neutralised symbolically and architecturally; his (other) dwelling there *quia supra consuetum statum firmitatem eidem domui adjecerat* (evidently part of his feudal aggrandisement) was adjudged rendable at will to the king to receive a large or small number of troops (significantly, *cum ad jura feodi nostri eadem pertineret*, not by regalian right, cf. Cluny 1119, Villemagne 1156, above) on pain of demolition of the newly fortified superstructure. For the archival details quoted see A. Teulet, *Layettes*, i, v-vi; H. F. Delaborde, *Layettes*, v, Paris 1909, ij-x; *Rec. Ph. Aug.*, i, v-xl; ii, Paris 1943, vj-xiii. The rubrics to licences to fortify on the English Rôles Gascons are comparatively haphazard, cf. Champagne record-keeping e.g. the c.1172 list of direct fiefs and dependent fortresses taken on the Third Crusade by Henri *le Libéral* (*Documents Relatifs au Comté de Champagne . . .*, A. Longnon, i, Paris 1901, xiij *et passim*; Coulson 1982 *passim*).

top comital échelons, ecclesiastical or lay, enhanced and perpetuated this rank especially as the *villes fermées* were both public fortresses and jurisdictional entities.[19] When evidence becomes more available in the charters of the twelfth century, the convention is ubiquitous that the defences of towns were public property, vested in the local ruler or in the Crown, or delegated to a plenary commune. Repair was commonly a first charge on general or specific revenues and cognisance of the crime of dilapidation, and the right to oversee upkeep and guard in emergencies, belonged to the public domain. References abound to deleterious encroachment by house-building which so often obstructed the circulation within the *enceinte*, encumbered or blocked the *chemin de ronde* at the summit, or even endangered the walls themselves owing to the thrust of floor joists and roof timbers. Latrines built to overhang the ditch and windows (worse still, posterns) illicitly pierced in the wall, particularly by religious establishments desiring both wall-side seclusion and private access to extra-mural gardens, continually jeopardised urban defensibility. Philip II's predecessors proclaimed their peculiar authority over all such works in walled towns in direct royal lordship as insistently as over rendability and licensing but they were too easily seduced by the revenue-potential of dispensing their ban. In 1112 Louis VI sold back to the canons of Sainte Croix the right to build onto the city wall of Orléans next to their precinct, on condition of not making any doorway through it; but in 1127 he ratified the bishop's charter permitting them to do just that. Louis VII in 1163 licensed one Vulgrin d'Étampes to support his house on the wall and gave him a charter to produce if the work was challenged by the citizens.[20]

---

[19] The analogy with immune religious precincts is both intimate, ancient and persistent. S. E. Rigold pointed out that in Carolingian *Francia* and across the Channel coins and seals provide complementary evidence of the styles of rulers and the formal status of towns. Of the over eighty mint-towns of Charles II nearly all fortified, 'about half are *civitates*, representing practically every see in *Francia* proper. The next most numerous category is *castra* or *castella*, other sites fortified since Roman days ... Then there are the privileged religious houses ... and the royal establishments, *palacia* and *fisci* ...' On the early *castrum* etc. see also J. Richard (1960, note 8 above, 433-7; S. E. Rigold, Presidential Address, *British Numismatic Journal*, 44, 1974, 101-3, 106). Jean Mesqui has recently shown that the Crécy agglomeration was collectively styled *castrum* until 1289 when town and 'castle' are first distinguished. He gives a valuable note on terminology and attributes the style *castrum* in Champagne to the *statut juridique* of the site ('Les Enceintes de Crécy-en-Brie ...', *Mémoires, Fédération des Sociétés Historiques et Archéologiques de Paris et de L'Ile de France*, 30, 1979, 15-16, 18-19, 44 note (2), 75 note (1) etc.). The defences of Langres (*munitio civitatis*) market and mint were 'delegated' to the bishop as early as 814 (*Recueil ... Lothaire ...*, no. 29; confirmed 887; again, adding the *comitatus* and tolls taken at the gates, in 967). Licensing of town fortification has (2nd-century) Roman precedent and Imperial symbolism became increasingly military. MacMullen comments 'everything to do with the emperor ... was already called *castrensis* before Septimius Severus ever entered the scene' (J. Wacher, 'A Survey of Romano-British Town Defences', *Arch. Journ.*, 119, 1962, 107 notes 16, 17, map 108 etc.; R. M. Butler, 'Late Roman Town Walls in Gaul', *Arch. Journ.*, 116, 1959, 25-50; R. MacMullen, *Soldier and Civilian in the Later Roman Empire*, Harvard 1963, 169). On the *chester* names a convenient summary is K. Cameron, *English Place Names*, London 1977, 35-6, 54-5, 90, 110-12, 116, 154-5, 214; varied examples in *Arch. Journ.*, 124, 1967, 65; 127, 1970, 243-4; 128, 1971, 31-2 etc.

[20] Luchaire (1890) nos. 137, 392. *Monuments Historiques*, no. 583. Orléans in 1057 was not a commune or privileged to have custody of its defences so royal officials had to be asked to keep the gates open during the *vendenge* (*Catalogue ... Henri Ier ...*, no. 109; instances collated in Coulson 1972, Index 'Towns, Fortified'). By the customs of Hénin-Liétard (Pas-de-Calais) confirmed c. 1071-1111 (Count Robert I or II of Flanders) and renewed in 1144 by Count Thierry as *avoué*, again by Philip II in 1196, *valli munitionem et firmitatem tocius ville ... burgenses ... absque perjurio nequeunt pejorare*. Fines for damage allocated to repairs were

The power latent in the walled towns had to be cultivated, which is doubtless why Philip II in confirming (1181-2) the privileges granted by his father to Bourges (c.1175) conceded permission, which Louis VII had expressly refused, for houses to be built against and upon the city wall. Philip also made over his judicial cognisance of *muri pejoratio*, thus allowing an offender to fine and make good the damage at the citizens' discretion. Civic trusteeship in law enhanced the urban franchise and also the renown of the place and of its lord, which compensated for any resultant loss of defensibility. Moreover, the traditional belief that, of all fortification, work on town defences was pre-eminently publicly beneficial, indeed pious, was no lip-service. Urban oligarchies were habitually entrusted by kings and other lords with the upkeep, guarding and improvement of their fortifications; and when this duty and privilege was withheld, not fear of wartime treachery explains it most often but resentment of encroachment upon the lord's *dominatio* or his revenues. Resident ecclesiastical lordships, under whose tutelage a borough had originated or grown up, were notably sensitive about pressure on their lien on the fortifications; but lordly status was the cause not military strategy: indeed, fortress-policy cannot be shorn of its social dimension. A complex of compelling reasons induced lords of towns to give up, not just defer for future increment, large sums of potentially taxable borough income by virtually irrevocable allocations at source of tolls and dues to be spent on the walls, along with streets, bridges and other common utilities; and to make on application continuous or *ad hoc* grants of timber, stone and other materials in addition to money, whether in cash or in tax remissions. This important part of Philip Augustus' fortress-policy merely applied the general and inherited principle more abundantly. It was regalian only insofar as it was also seignorial.[21]

His father's confirmation as early as 1150 to the river-port and arsenal at Mantes of a comprehensive set of privileges, including full control over the town barriers,

---

kept in the burgesses' hands not the lord's (*Rec. Ph. Aug.*, ii, no. 529) Louis VII seems to have accepted a fine from the townsmen of Tournon *videlicet de domibus eorum quas intra et extra et supra murum nostri castelli et in fossatis nostris edificaverant, et altius solito levaverant, et de chiminis nostris supra et intus occupatis* (i.e. both the wall-walks and circulation at ground level; *Layettes*, i, no.75). Henry I in 1101 alienated to Eudo *Dapifer* 'the city and tower and castle and all the fortifications of Colchester' with interesting emphasis (*Regesta*, ii, no.552).

21 Louis VII's charter was to Bourges, Dun and the people of the *castellania* and *septena* (*Rec. Ph. Aug.*, i, no.40; *Catalogue . . . Ph. Aug.*, 270, 395-6 for alienation in 1209/10 and 1218 of a postern and a gatehouse in his new enceinte of Paris. Defence was one factor only among many). On the licence to Bourges cathedral (1174) see note 15 above. Some walled towns were rendable in set form (e.g. Périgueux, 1204, below) particularly in the south. For examples 1095-1180 see *Layettes* i, nos.39, 49, 59, 81, 186, 207, 250; v, ed. H. F. Delaborde, Paris 1909, nos.34, 53, 70, 72, 78. Most of these are styled 'castle' (on vernacular 'castle' names cf. J. Gardelles, *Les Châteaux du Moyen Age dans la France du Sud-Ouest . . .*, Geneva 1972, 7-12 *et passim*). The *castrum* or *castellum* of Montchauvet (Seine et Oise) founded perhaps c.1120, was a refuge for the rural populace in war and had a civilian population (*Rec. Ph. Aug.*, ii, no.732). The lord's right of access to towns (fortress-customs distinguish entry rights to towns; lordly refuge in danger, lordly garrisoning and/or requisitioning) seldom had to be spelled out, but lordship-competition might require explicitness (e.g. 1153, Le Tremblay town, Seine et Oise, *Monuments Historiques*, no.523; 1155, city of Vienne, Isère, in Denis de Salvaing, *De L'Usage des Fiefs et Autres Droits Seigneuriaux*, Grenoble 1731, 81). Seignorial parallels are Anseau de Gallande's charter (1193, *Layettes*, i, no.410) to his burgesses of Tournan (Seine et Marne); the liberties included cooperative fortification and licence: abbatial licence c.1100 to Saint Sever town (Landes): licence by the count of Sancerre to the abbey to fortify la Charité-sur-Loire town, 1164 in perpetuity (*Thesaurus Novus . . .*, i, Paris 1717, 277-81, 464). For the lord-townsmen conflicts at Corbie and Noyon see note 24 below.

the repair, defence and funding of the fortifications, showed the way forward. To his new commune at Chaumont-en-Vexin (Oise), not far from Saint-Clair-sur-Epte, Philip gave in 1182 the same perpetual power to fortify and levy murage, terms closely followed for the new communes of Pontoise and Poissy (Seine and Oise), both probably in 1188, all three like Mantes outposts of Paris against Normandy. The customs of Mantes were much used, notably in 1204 after the fall of Château-Gaillard for the borough of Les Andelys (Eure), but the equally popular customs of Lorris (Loiret) provide only for common works, and the studied omission of the fortification clauses from some Mantes-type charters shows that this culminating privilege, apogee of bourgeois liberty and prestige, was conferred selectively and with deliberation. In the exposed north-western region of Picardy four towns received charters modelled upon that of 1195 for Saint-Quentin, or, it may be, upon Roye-en-Vermandois (both Somme) dated between 1185 and 1205. The others are Chauny-sur-Oise (Aisne, 1213) and Crépy-en-Valois (Oise, 1215). Each contains a slight variant of the clause *ubicumque major et jurati villam firmare voluerint, in cujus-cumque sit terra, sine forisfacto eam firmabunt*. Specified court-fines are allocated to the defences, except in the Roye charter; and since all four were authorised to purchase land compulsorily, as with the Mantes-group, their officials evidently had power to extend their fortifications not just to maintain them.[22]

In form all eight charters by Philip II confer the fullest licence to fortify without time limit, and royal authorisation is almost as explicit and fully as effectual in the privileges of Amiens (Somme, 1190), whereby two-thirds of the 9li. fine for wounding one of the jurats is payable *firmitati urbis et communie*. Permanent assignment of fines *ad firmitatem ville* by view of the *échevins* figures also in the charter of Péronne, adapted for Cappy (both Somme) and for the *castellum* and *villa* of Hesdin (Pas de Calais), all issued in 1207 and specifying penalties for assault (100s), wounding with edged weapons (10li.), and for slander and brawling (50s). The elimination of all allusion to fortifications (clauses 3, 4, 9) from the grant to Athies near Péronne, an otherwise almost *verbatim* version, confirms the careful discrimination between fortified and open towns in the same custumal group. In the case of Athies, rivalry with Péronne, or more likely with the non-royal town (*viz. castrum* or *castellum*) of Ham-en-Vermandois close by, may well explain it, but

---

[22] Issoudun in Berri (1213) is the only significant case noted of a (subinfeudated) town denied the right to fortify by Philip Augustus (*Layettes*, i, no.1040). Luchaire (1890) no. 254, confirming Louis VI (not recited), printed *Ordonnances des Rois* . . ., xi, 197 (8); *communes necessitates ut de excubiis, de cathenis et fossatis faciendis et de omnibus ad ville munitionem et firmitatem pertinentibus communiter ab omnibus procurentur*, according to individuals' means (Mantes). Between 1 Nov. 1201 and 13 April 1202, Philip II confirmed their fiscal advantages *pro servitio quod nobis faciunt et antecessoribus nostris (sic) fecerunt videlicet quod adjuvant ad honerandum et ad exhonerandum nostras machinas infra Meduntam* (i.e. shipping siege engines on the Seine to and from Normandy). The fortification clause (7 or 8) is almost *verbatim* 1150 in the other charters (*Rec. Ph. Aug.*, i, nos.59, 233, 234; ii, 782, Les Andelys April-October 1204. Château-Gaillard fell on 6 March). The confident extension of such a degree of military-juridical autonomy to Les Andelys reflects the firm Capetian *entente* with their own communes (Powicke 1961, 279 note 169; cf. Petit-Dutaillis, *Feudal Monarchy* . . ., 195-7 on borough-policy and the Lorris customs initiated by Louis VI). The Picardy formula lacks explicit delegation of custody of the defences. Artois with part of Vermandois, including Saint-Quentin, whose comital customs were ratified 1188-1197, became royal demesne in 1183 (*Rec. Ph. Aug.*, ii, nos.491, 540, 1295, 1389). There may well be a sub-Carolingian regalian echo in *sine* (or *absque*) *forisfacto* as also in compulsory purchase for fortification (Coulson 1972, Index).

this charter of Athies does make clear that under the Péronne customs the Crown was relinquishing a half-share in these judicial profits. Péronne was strategically crucial and Philip not only renewed the 1207 charter, itself consolidating existing privileges, but renewed it two years later (1209) and on a visit there in May 1214, shortly before Bouvines was fought to the north-east (27 July), he supplemented the fortification-fund by giving up his rights over a plot of land close to the walls which could conveniently be inundated to make cress-beds to yield it further revenue.[23] As usual, the king reserved no powers of supervision or audit, other than implied by the presence of a royal bailiff, and he evidently had such confidence in the loyalty, fiscal probity and technical expertise of his communes in general that he was able, as also at Noyon (1181-2) and at Saint-Omer (1197), to entrust them unreservedly with their own defence. Such emergency subsidies and interventions as were resorted to both by Philip Augustus (e.g. 1209-14) and by John (e.g. 1203-4, 1215-16) might be no more than ephemeral partnerships forged in the heat of crisis, but in Philip's case his borough charters are part of a long-term fortress-policy which had consistent aims and shows a shrewd grasp of the political and feudal realities.[24]

The essential context and understanding was, of course, that the royal host would be admitted at need to use the town defences as military base, refuge and arsenal like any other fortress, in cooperation with the citizenry. Rendability and the whole gamut of fortress-customs had long since articulated these obligations in terms of direct tenure in fief, lending a new feudal vigour to ancient monarchical right whenever no immediate (and prior) lordship intervened. There was no ambiguity about the military duties of royal walled towns, but it was otherwise when the burgesses of distant Périgueux (Dordogne) chose the climax of Philip's conquest of Normandy, in May 1204 at the siege of Rouen, as the appropriate moment to submit their city to his protection. Because direct royal lordship over Périgord had hitherto been in dispute with the Angevins, the envoys' act of recognition naturally took the form

---

23 Amiens: *Rec. Ph. Aug.*, i, no. 319; iii, no. 1072 at Lorris; renewed *verbatim* 1209. Amiens must have had these powers of fortification and ground-purchase long before 1471 when enumerated (*Ordonnances des Rois* . . ., xvii, Paris 1820, 401-3). Péronne: *Rec. Ph. Aug.*, iii, nos. 977, 1067, 1333 cf. 408; renewed 1209, there was an earlier charter than 1207. Cf. *Recueil* . . . *Ponthieu*, no. 197 for the peat-revenues shared between Count William and the fortifications of Montreuil in 1210; Cappy cf. Athies, 1212 (*Rec. Ph. Aug.*, iii, nos. 984, 1217, 1237); Hesdin (*Rec. Ph. Aug.*, i, 408; iii, no. 983, as to Péronne, text lost) conceded *pacem et communiam propter amorem quam erga burgenses Hesdini habere volumus, tam propter ejusdem castelli commodum*. Philip acquired the fief from the bishop of Thérouanne (Petit-Dutaillis, *Feudal Monarchy* . . ., 201). In the Hesdin charter (1192) half the redemption fines of houses penally to be razed (especially for anti-commune crimes; a Picard feature, see J. H. Round, *Feudal England*, London 1964, 416-19) were allocated half to the king and half *ad villam firmandam*. For Ham town see note 26 below.
24 The contribution to Philip's army at Bouvines of civic levies is familiar (C. W. Oman, *A History of the Art of War in the Middle Ages*, 1924, i, 474). All kinds of 'Grants for Fortification in France' are listed, including for Ponthieu after 1283 under Edward I and ducal Gascony, in Coulson 1972 appendix C I. They are of great significance, whether perpetual and vested or *ad hoc* for one to three years mostly, as in England where a number of murage grants were obtained by mesne lords (outlined in H. L. Turner, *Town Defences in England and Wales*, London 1970, appendix etc.). Embezzlement might occur, as shown by Edward I's great enquiry of 1274-6, but grants were still made on application (*Calendar of the Patent Rolls passim*; *Rotuli Hundredorum* . . ., Rec. Comm. 1834, i, 105, 108, 115, 131, 314-15, 322, 327-8, 353, 372, 398-9). At Noyon and at Corbie (Somme 1182) Philip II backed the townspeople against anciently entrenched ecclesiastical lords over the crucial seignorial test of control of the fortifi-

of a very explicit rendability charter. The cooperation between Philip and the men of Reims against the Anglo-Imperial coalition, prompted by his lending them 4000 li. to expedite their fortification in 1209, had to be expressed differently since the archbishop was lord of Reims and consequently had the defences under his authority, symbolised and to some extent implemented by custody of the keys of the gates.[25] Rendability had preserved but feudalised the uniquely public and regalian quality of fortifications in France, fragmenting and distributing the former royal monopoly, so that a subinfeudated fortress could be rendered only to the immediate lord who became answerable for it to his vassal and might not transfer his temporary right of use to his own superior. Walled towns present a few exceptions to this rule against 'sub-rendability', the pressures on mesne lordship being particularly strong from above and below. Odo lord of Ham-en-Vermandois agreed to the 'castle' being rendable by his burgesses to the king in 1223, and the public character of the major

.cations. At Noyon (near Compiègne) the bishop sought his support but *patrum nostrorum inherentes vestigiis* Philip confirmed the commune accorded by Louis VII and Louis VI and declared (clause 1): *Pro quacumque commonitione quam fecerint sive pro banno, sive pro fossato vel firmatione ville, neque episcopus neque castellanus habent ibi aliquid justicie vel implacitationis.* Notably this was probably not long after the count of Flanders had sacked Noyon (Nov. 1181). The later lordship-struggle is of great interest (*Rec. Ph. Aug.*, i, no. 43; etc.). At Saint-Omer control of the fortifications was probably completed by vesting the usufruct of the ditches, as at Doullens in 1202 (*Rec. Ph. Aug.*, ii, no. 557; *Recueil . . . Ponthieu*, no. 155). The sequence of events at Corbie is of exceptional interest: Charles III, in an assembly of counts and bishops (901) renewed Charles II's grant of immunity to the abbey, and by his mother's and local count's request reserved the newly fortified precinct to the monks' control *viz. . . . ut nullus judex publicus in castello propriis sumptibus ac juribus* (sic) *infra ipsa monasterii moenia constructo nullam ibi quasi potestative licentiam habeat discutiendi aut ordinandi aliquod aut disponendi.* By the abbot's plea and assent, we are told, Louis VI founded a joint commune comprising the clergy, knights and burgesses, which Louis VII *assecuravit et manutenuit* and Philip II confirmed (1180) adding (possibly initiating but probably modifying) the provision that *nulli firmitatem infra banlivam Corbie licebit edificare, nisi per nostram* (sic) *et communie licenciam* (renewed 1182 and 1225 despite unspecified objections by the abbot). In 1255 the burgesses' murage-fund was quashed; jurisdiction was regained by the abbey (1306) and violence, provoked by the abbot, ensued (1307). In 1310 the commune was dissolved for debt, all rights reverting to the abbey, except for royal use in emergencies of the town defences (i.e. rendability; *Recueil . . . Charles III*, no. 41; *Rec. Ph. Aug.*, i, nos. 10, 52; *Layettes*, ii, Paris 1866, no. 1735; *Actes du Parlement . . .*, i, i, 6; i, ii, 32, 40; *Registres du Trésor des Chartes*, i, Paris 1958, ed. R. Fawtier, 233).
[25] Coulson 1972, Index, 'Keys and their Symbolism'; both aspects are evident in the revolt of Najac town (Aveyron) on the death of Raymond VII (1249); at Tours in 1241 the symbolic dominates the practical (*Layettes*, ii, no. 2892; iii, no. 3947). The citizens of Reims promised repayment in two years and *quod personam vestram et omnes vestros, quotiens necesse fuerit, contra Imperium et alia regna, que vos vel regnum Francie vellent impugnare, bona fide Remis recipient et civitatem . . . defendent.* This may have aggravated the lordship rivalry alluded to in Philip's order to the burgesses to restore the keys (1211; i.e. custody of the gates and tolls) to the archbishop (cf. Duke Hugh of Burgundy's settlement of a similar conflict in Lyon in 1208: *Layettes*, i, nos. 855, 903; *Rec. Ph. Aug.*, iii, no. 1221). The Périgueux envoys bound to the king *tota communitas ville . . . in perpetuum facere fidelitatem contra omnes homines et feminas qui possunt vivere et mori; et tenemur ei et heredibus suis tradere totam villam de Petragolis integre, ad magnam vim et ad parvam, quocienscumque dominus rex noster Philippus et heredes sui inde nos requisierint.* Philip reciprocated with inalienability and protection; renewed in detail to Louis VIII on his accession (*Layettes*, i, no. 714; ii, no. 1602; *Rec. Ph. Aug.*, ii, no. 800). In 1197 Count Baldwin of Flanders and Hainault, by force and bribery, neutralised the royal lordship over Tournai by a treaty whereby the burgesses would *inter alia* neither *firmare* the town nor receive (*receptare*) any French or hostile troops. Reception in towns, under rendability, is wholly distinct from the (obsolescent) *droit de gîte* (*albergamentum*; *Thesaurus Novus . . .*, i, 664-6; cf. 1182, 1210 *Layettes*, i, nos. 309, 947).

towns facilitated Philip's intervention at Reims in 1209, and in 1193-4 to help Count Peter of Nevers obtain aid from the clergy of Auxerre (Yonne) for walling that town along the river-side. In the growing danger of May 1210, Philip combined military precaution with scrupulous feudal propriety in tactfully lending the townsmen of Châlons-sur-Marne 2000 li. to speed up their works of fortification, without prejudice to the rights of the bishop who had denied clerical liability to contribute.[26]

Fortresses under individual rather than collective lordship ('castles' according to modern convention) also required and rewarded a judicious fortress-policy but the seignorial niceties were here all-important: Philip, having put the theory of the past behind him, respected them impeccably. Castle-lords as of right and duty kept their defences up to date, fortified and licensed within their baronies, and had their vassals' castles rendered to them, looking to the king (if they held in-chief) to up-hold their right as a good lord should, in case of need. Philip Augustus therefore continued his predecessors' policy of endorsing ecclesiastical castellation franchises, as much in the period of initial consolidation (1181, Sarlat Abbey) as after the treaty of Le Goulet (1208, bishops of Maguelone; 1210, bishops of Lodève and monks of Villemagne). Royal *dirigisme* and initiative, nevertheless, during the decade from the fall of Rouen to the battle of Bouvines, clearly formed new patterns in the texture of seignorial castle-politics with Philip sensitively exploiting fortress-customs to strengthen his feudal and military resources and to deny advantages to his enemies. This interventionism intensified after 1214 in his dealings with King John's defeated allies in the north-west, most notably the restive Flemish communes, and is best considered not here but in the context of his fortress-policy as a whole. Feudal politics must never be under-rated. There is an obvious danger in interpolating modern strategic ways of thought.[27] In the three Anglo-French treaties which usher

---

[26] *Catalogue ... Ph. Aug.*, no. 396, non-prejudice by Peter; *Rec. Ph. Aug.*, iii, no. 1130; cf. voluntary castle-works by the clergy for Count Simon to Epernon town and Houdan castle in 1208-9 (*Catalogue des Actes de Simon et d'Amauri de Montfort*, ed. A. Molinier, Paris 1874, nos. 23, 28) and King John's exhortations to the clergy of Limoges to fortify the city (*Rotuli Litterarum Patentium*, Rec. Comm. 1835, 134a; 1215). On sub-rendability see Coulson 1972, Index. The vassal-lord nexus of rendability was unimpaired by the introduction of liege homage; nor was it much affected by the revival of monarchic universalism under Philip IV. Although corroborative undertakings directly by burgesses to the overlord do occur (Joigny *castrum*, 1220-2; Neufchâteau en Lorraine, 1252) it is towns only and rarely, e.g. the *castrum* or *castellum* of Ham, sworn rendable by Odo to the king and heirs *vel eorum certo mandato, sicut suum feodum, ad magnam vim et ad parvam, quotiens ... fuero requisitus*, underwritten by charter of the mayor and commune (*Registres du Trésor ...*, i, nos. 768, 794-8, 876, 1498; Coulson 1982, 349-50, 358, 361; *Layettes*, i, nos. 1583, 1584). The feudal reciprocity of rendability is fully expressed by the ex-*bailli* Philippe de Beaumanoir (c.1283, ed. A. Salmon, Paris 1970; *Coutumes de Beauvaisis*, 1662-5) very much from the vassal's standpoint, whose *forteresce* the lord might requisition at any time. Good lordship enabled Philip II in June 1214, just before Bouvines, confidently to abandon his *turris* of Montreuil-sur-Mer to the commune, despite the frontier location (*Rec. Ph. Aug.*, iii, no. 1336).

[27] The forthrightness of Lt Col. A. H. Burne (*The Crécy War*, London 1955, 12) about what he calls 'inherent military probability' is as rare as rigorous analysis, but see R. C. Smail (*Crusading Warfare 1097-1193*, Cambridge 1956, 1-17, 60-2, 204-44) and C. Warren Hollister (*The Military Organization of Norman England*, Oxford 1965, 161-6). Philip II's fortress-policy was no more 'anti-castle' than it was 'anti-feudal'. Diagnostic early cases, not cited elsewhere in this paper, are 1180/1, comital rights at Parai-le-Monial; 1181/2, section of town wall of Soissons removed to obviate harm to the royal castle; 1182/3, fortifying in the castellany (*firmitas ... cf. castellum ... castellania*) of Concressaut in coparceny; 1188, 1192 castellation-lordship arbitration, le Puy, Auvergne; 1204/5 ban continued in lands of lay abbacy of Seignelai (*Rec. Ph. Aug.*, i, nos. 17, 44, 71, 239, 425; ii, no. 852). Philip II extended or made more efficacious

in John's conflict with Philip Augustus, the fortresses are concerned primarily as tenurial entities: the body of law articulated safeguards and cease-fire lines. These are conventional elements in the treaties of 1194, 1195-6 and 1200, concluded respectively on Richard's return from his Austrian captivity; then after his partial retrieval of the situation in the duchy; and finally, after the accession of his brother. All the ramifications of fortress-tenure were within the law, but in such circumstances the liberties of castellans and of communes might suffer some usually temporary infringement, particularly to get assent to bans on fortifying. Such exceptions had to be carefully defined to preserve the quasi-demilitarised border zones from all but major and calculated breach; for example and most notably, Richard's building of Château-Gaillard after 1196.[28]

At this princely and pragmatic level the differences between Capetian and Angevin practice are submerged in common methods and concern to endow with legal durability the ephemeral effects of violence. Thus the 1194 armistice made 'between Verneuil and Tillières' debarred Richard from rebuilding any of the *munitiones* razed by the French during hostilities with four exceptions, but otherwise allowed both sides to fortify or to destroy all the *fortellescie* which were in their hands on 23 July. Richard gained more when the formal peace was duly concluded in early December 1195, as embodied in reciprocal charters dated 15 January 1196. The unstable balance of power had been forcibly tilted in his favour meanwhile. Philip's counterpart calls Richard his *amicus et fidelis* and royal right might be inferred from his apparently licensing Richard and Count Raymond of Toulouse to fortify within their lands henceforth as before *tanquam de sua*, but the reality was otherwise: it is a pact between equals, pragmatic not feudal, and Philip gained in return the right to fortify Châteauneuf-sur-Cher. All three treaties avoid the term *castrum* whenever the fortress proper not the castellany is meant, in accordance with this empirical spirit. Lesser magnates than these needed no licence from the Crown to fortify, and no vassalage was invoked here or elsewhere; the clause merely differentiated Richard's and Raymond's other territories from the sensitive war zone, where *ad hoc* and contractual restrictions were temporarily in force, on either side of the new frontier situated mid-way between the fortresses of Gaillon and Vaudreuil. The king of England similarly was permitted to rebuild Châteauneuf-de-Tours, but under

---

and up to date his father's four ecclesiastical castellation franchises giving Lodève (1188, 1210) power also to coin money; feudally re-defining Maguelone's castellation rights (1208); confirming Sarlat and Villemagne (1181, 1210) and originally recognising the castellation franchise exercised by Figeac Abbey, Lot (note 12 above; *Rec. Ph. Aug.*, i, nos. 22, 167, 242, iii, nos. 1037, 1119, 1120).

28 Rymer's *Foedera*, i, i, Rec. Comm. 1816, 64 (1194, *per* Howden); *Rec. Ph. Aug.*, ii, no. 517; *Layettes*, i, no. 431 (1196: Philip's and Richard's counterparts); *Rec. Ph. Aug.*, ii, no. 633 and *Layettes*, i, no. 578 (Philip's and John's counterparts); discussed e.g. Powicke (1961) 104, 107, 170-2, 192-6, 204-6. The ubiquitous *firmare* and *inforciare* made no distinction between such drastic feudal and strategic innovations caused by Château-Gaillard; extempore works such as the emergency 'enclosing' and 'fortifying' (*firmitas*, actually ditching) Evreux c.1193-4, partly on the bishop's land (the see and countship being vacant) *propter timorem regis Gallie* by an *ad hoc communia* of citizens and local villagers (challenged c.1205 as a civil trespass by the bishop and *ultra vires* though admitted to be within ducal powers: *Amplissima Collectio*, note 13 above, i, Paris 1724, 1061-2; also *Cal. Docs France* no. 414 n d); and thirdly, between mere stocking and 'garrisoning'. For comparisons of detail see e.g. the Franco-Castilian truce of 1280; 1176 Flanders-Hainault alliance; and 1173 Lyon-Forez partition, papally confirmed 1174 but not recorded in the royal court until 1183/4 (*Foedera*, i, ii, 581; *Thesaurus Novus . . .*, i, 585-6; *Rec. Ph. Aug.*, i, no. 103).

French supervision and he categorically agreed not to fortify within the archbishop of Rouen's manor of Les Andelys, which was explicitly neutralised in Angevin possession. This was a quite conventional way of resolving the strategic problem due in this case to the enclave or 'bulge' north and west of the river Epte. Although by May 1200 the Angevin position was much less strong, especially by John's advent, King Richard's 'Saucy Castle' was left defending the breach and the way to Rouen down the Seine, although the treaty made at Le Goulet awarded to Philip the Évrecin. All new fortifying by either party was renounced in respect of the tract of country lying between Évreux and Neubourg, safeguarded by razing the fortresses of Portes and Les Londes as was not uncommonly done to ensure the integrity of partitions and new frontiers.[29]

Although Philip II's fortress-rights served his needs as king they owed almost everything to lordship over immediate vassals, very little to overlordship and almost nothing to monarchy. Notwithstanding his few (but important) advantages after Le Goulet unavailable to the great feudatories, he relied as they did on making a feudal reality out of sub-Carolingian theory and dealt remarkably confidently with fortresses, especially after 1196, in his piecemeal conquest of Normandy. By the treaty set down in January he gained Nonancourt castle and the entire salient north-wards to Pacy and probably the castle of Grossœuvre also. Had the rôles been reversed, Angevin practice would surely have kept and garrisoned both with royal troops, alienation in custody at will, for term, life or in fief being less likely, and full hereditary enfeoffment hardly conceivable: and yet Philip, undeterred by briefly losing and promptly retaking Nonancourt, soon gave both away in full feudal right respectively to Peter Mauvoisin, and to his Pantler of the Household, William Poucin. The case is only one of many. Philip clearly judged that his vital interests were amply secured by the explicit but customary conditions of rendability attached to both enfeoffments, although his grip upon the fringes of Normandy remained precarious until Richard's death; likewise with the fortresses of Ivry, on the road to Évreux and near Grossœuvre, and of Avrilli, both taken from the duchy since the death of Henry II but in 1200 rendably enfeoffed to Robert of Ivry. The king was thus enabled to requisition them as often as he wished and Robert conventionally swore that he would deliver both fortifications *quotiens et quandocumque eas ipse . . . rex . . . vellet habere*, an oath underwritten by six mainpernors including Mauvoisin.[30]

---

29 Jurisdictional boundaries of all kinds and scale up to inter-state frontiers were habitually defined topographically, and castellanies by reference to the component manors or units (e.g. Powicke 1961, 197-201, map IV; R. Allen Brown on *castellarie, The Normans and the Norman Conquest*, 215; C. Warren Hollister (1965) 150, 153). Whereas the knightly castle-guard circumscription of Montereau c.1172 was the *castellania*, at Provins it was specially delimited (*Histoire . . . Champagne*, ii, nos.62, 70). Lordship-competition and war swept aside bounds of this kind, substituting a patrolling radius of effective surveillance (R. C. Smail, 1956, 61-2 *et passim*; Coulson 1972, Index, 'military functions of fortresses'; 'operational bases'). Precise topography and vaguely defined marches coexist in these treaties e.g. (1194) *citra Ligerim versus Normanniam*. Because the castle-proper of Châteauneuf-de-Tours was meant (1196) it is styled *domus Castelli Novi Turonis*. Fortifying at Quitteboeuf was forbidden in 1200 since it was on the English side of the new frontier but had been allocated to Philip (Powicke 1961, 170). Radepont castle (Seine Maritime, note 33 below) was razed in 1219 so as to favour neither co-heir, truly a judgement of Solomon. Cf. the 1201 partition between the four sons by her two husbands of the Poitevin lands of Lady Agnes (*Amplissima Collectio . . .*, i, 1138; *Catalogue . . . Ph. Aug.*, no.1886; *Layettes*, v, no.131.

30 *Layettes*, i, no. 594; cf. *Catalogue . . . Ph. Aug.*, no. 632; Peter, Gui and Manasses Mauvoisin and three others pledged all their lands. Robert's charter is not present. The *castellum* of Nonan-

Absence of trust and reciprocity of good-will, by contrast, pervade King John's very characteristic treatment of Ranulph of Chester over the earl's castle of Semilly (Manche) during the crisis of 1202. John first seized Semilly for suspicion then restored the castle on receiving guarantees from the archbishop of Canterbury and the bishop of Ely that Ranulph would acquiesce in a renewed arbitrary dispossession; which was, in fact, demanded and duly obeyed, discharging the guarantors from their obligations once for all but still giving the earl no promise of restitution. John was admittedly at a disadvantage: so much depended on moral and legal rectitude, sanctioned as it may be by success in arms. These assets he was losing or had already lost. Pledging of castles on an *ad hoc* basis, in which fear of treachery was balanced by fear of lasting disseisin, could not achieve that certainty of operation and security for both vassal and lord which rendability operated by the rule-book afforded. The Angevin record was bad and John's erratic seizures, hostage-taking and vindictive expedients inflicted on loyal and waverer alike, had implanted mistrust and hatred not duty and respect. Rendable fortresses could more easily be demanded as pledges of good conduct, or to abort revolt, since no suspicion on the lord's part or demonstration of good-faith on the vassal's but an unconditional duty was the motive. Although John occasionally did utilise his lordship to obtain rendability in Gascony and in his other continental dominions, and perhaps also in England, the combination of the mistrust and misfeasance peculiar to himself with the whole antifeudal and dispossessory thrust of Angevin fortress-policy was to deprive John in adversity of the support which the Capetian confidently obtained.[31] Philip lacked neither

court, close to the new (1196) border, in William the Breton's phrase *in fisci castellum jura reducit* was the entire castellany, as Powicke (1961, 199 and note) pointed out. The enfeoffment of Mauvoisin was apparently preceded by a grant to Robert of Dreux but is likely to be 1196, at the same juncture as the nearly identical charter for Grossœuvre (*Grandis Silva*, near Avrilli viz. *Aprilliacum*, Stapleton map). Delaborde, Petit-Dutaillis and Monicat follow Audoin in suggesting 1196 despite Delisle and their own '1196-1202' for both charters (*Rec. Ph. Aug.*, ii, nos. 548, 549 and notes; Léopold Delisle, *Cartulaire Normand ...*, Paris 1852, no.182 as c.1201). The standard French editorial gloss and calendarist's formula for rendability 'livrer ... à toute réquisition' is employed, vouched for by the phrase *ad magnam vim et ad parvam* but their comments betray some confusion with revocable grants, ignoring also that both are expressly hereditary despite their abbreviated Register men and apparent haste. Many instances show that such a phrase as *quotiens requisierimus nobis reddet Nonencurt et totam fortericiam* means 'Nonancourt, namely the fortress', and the habitual *quotiens* or *quocienscumque* cannot be translated as 'when'. Furthermore, both texts (but not the glosses supplied) make clear that the liege bond was personal to the vassal, just as the rendability was peculiar to the fortifications (not generally to the fief). In 1205 Nonancourt was granted under rendability with Conches castle to Robert de Courtenai and heirs who thereby *nobis ... tenentur tradere fortericias predictorum castrorum ad guerreandum et ad magnam vim et ad parvam.* Perhaps the male heir envisaged c.1196 had not materialised (*Rec. Ph. Aug.*, ii, no.875). Robert's counterpart states other restrictions but oddly omits the rendability again recognised in 1217 by his son (*Layettes*, i, nos. 747, 1262).

31 For Semilly (Similli) see *Rot. Litt. Pat.*, 7b, 28a; *Rotuli Normannie*, Rec. Comm. 1835, 96-7; Powicke (1961) 167. That John's conduct over baronial fortresses was true to his arbitrary style overall is unsurprising but still insufficiently pondered and related to fortress-custom (e.g. S. Painter, *The Reign of King John*, Baltimore 1949, 272, 352-3, 370; J. C. Holt, *The Northerners*, Oxford 1961, 94-5, 138; Warren, *King John*, 57-9, 109, 175-6, 181, 184-7, 190, 312). John's vindictive animosity in ordering castles and houses to be razed even without military expediency, reached a pitch of idiosyncrasy so that such an order seems to have been among the countersigns he used during the civil war to authenticate mandates to his henchmen. Even Henry II did not go so far nor, probably, did any ruler before Louis XI and the era of the Machievellian prince (*Rot. Litt. Pat.*, 33a, 46a, 58a, 98b, 99a, 112a, 124a, 135a, 137b, 138a, 148b, 184b, 186, 187a, 190a, 195b; *Rotuli Litterarum Clausarum*, Rec. Comm., i, 1833, 82a,

precedent nor legal precision, needing only, to cope with the exceptional strains of war and competing lordship, explicit charters of rendability, with collateral guarantees on occasion, to carry Capetian fortress-policy irresistibly forward to its vindication. As Philip's direct lordship was asserted within his conquests in Normandy, and as southwards towards Saintonge the wave of politic or coerced submission spread, so his feudal right of direct lordship attracted the prescribed formal recognition from fortress-tenants. Warfare afforded just the lawful occasion and military need to activate rendability where it was latent, or to extend it where lax lordship had let the practice fall into disuse despite the familiarity of the theory.[32]

The castle of Radepont (Seine Maritime) checked Philip's army for three weeks before being surrendered in late September 1203, as the blockade of Château-Gaillard began. Ruthlessly pursued through a severe winter and into the spring and as resol-

---

122a, 166b, 200a, 244b, 260a, 279a, 284, 291b; *Rot. Norm.*, 55, 59, 95, 97, 118). The case of Montrésor (Indre et Loire) is characteristic: Gerard d'Athies was to free Geoffrey de Palluau in August 1203 leaving his castle in Gerard's hands as security, but John ordered it to be razed when received, nominally as a military precaution. This seems not, in fact to have been obeyed, as was often the case in England also, but Geoffrey defected to Philip Augustus as soon as it was safe to do so (*Layettes*, i, nos.772-5; *Lettres de Louis XI . . .*, ed. J. Vaesen, E. Charavay, iv, Paris 1890, no. 566). Of the general doctrines of rendability signs in the English records from the later twelfth century are plentiful but lack legal precision. Continental phraseology used for Trim castle, co. Meath (1254) may be scribal confusion due to Gascon preoccupations, although repeated later (1267: *Calendar of the Patent Rolls, 1247-58*, 335; *1266-72*, 109). The position is still as stated by Brown in 1976 (*English Castles*, 18, 235 note 10) but the apparent borrowing of baronial castles requires case by case investigation; even instances in France of rendable requisitioning may not be obvious e.g. John's mandate, 30 Sept. 1206, to take over Fronzac castle, Gironde, *ad opus nostrum in custodia* removing any disloyal occupants, *quod plus nobis reportamus necessarium* (*Rot. Litt. Pat.*, 67b). John denounced Langton (1215) as a 'notorious and barefaced traitor to us since he did not deliver up our castle of Rochester to us in our so great need'. 'Necessity' is diagnostic. The bailey was in the archbishop's perpetual custody but William de Corbeil's dominant *turris* was their property since 1127 (*Regesta*, ii, 203, 356; R. Allen Brown, *Rochester Castle Guide*, HMSO 1969, 10-12; Warren, *King John*, 257). If rendability was, as we have suggested, more monarchical in England the efforts to preserve the Crown lien over castles given in longer-term custody (for life, life-fief, heritable fief) gain significance since the lien of rendability was a normal seignorial property, not a royal prerogative, within the European tenurial environment.

[32] The contrast is notable between Philip's and John's dealings with William de Guierche (1204-15, especially 1214) over his castle of Ségré (Normandy-Maine border). Seeking to regain his grip on Poitou, based at La Rochelle, John in March-June 1214 made various conciliatory castle-grants in terms more generous than the usual enigmatic e.g. Rochefort (*Rot. Chart.*, 196a) to be held *libere et quiete, bene et in pace* as for landed fiefs; cf. (*Rot. Litt. Pat.*, 68a, November 1206) grant of Châteauneuf and three other castles in full fief to R. de Talmont elliptically *salvo jure et servitio nostro*; similarly Coutures (Gironde) to the archbishops of Bordeaux but *quamdiu . . . fideliter versus nos continuebunt* (1214: *Rot. Chart.*, 201a; also *Rot. Litt. Pat.*, 112b, 118b, 119b). The lord of Ségré had apparently already promised Philip II *quod non denegabimus ei, vel mandato ejus, domum nostram de Segreio in magna vel parva necessitate* when John (23 June, just before his ignominious retreat from the siege of Roche-au-Moine, 2 July, forced by the Poitevin barons' disaffection) 'granted and confirmed' to William de Guierche in full fief the *castellum . . . cum omni castellaria*. John was reduced to persuasion of good faith by terms which impliedly renounced seizure though not rendability (the habitual *quiete et pacifice . . .* supplemented by *sine aliquo retenemento preter servicium . . .* with most explicit warranty and the bribe of Guiomarc'h's forfeited houses in Anjou (*Rot. Chart.*, 199a; *Catalogue . . . Ph. Aug.*, no.1496 as '1214, April?'; Du Cange, 'Dissertation', note 14 above, 506). Philip II in Anjou-Touraine-Poitou undoubtedly learned from John's *débâcle* (1202-4), negotiating pragmatically to obtain rendability and other fortress facilities with agreed penalties for breach, although by Capetian precedent or by current feudal law he could have demanded, and punished, non-compliance by outright forfeiture (Coulson 1972, 130-5, 221-31; note 33 below).

utely resisted, this siege is as well known as it was exceptional and untypical even of the military rôle of castles. The king's treatment of Radepont, about ten miles north and west on the river Andelle and essential to the blockading ring against English counter-attack, is therefore of the utmost interest. In 1202 an attempt to take it had failed but when he succeeded Philip promptly alienated Radepont to Peter de Moret in hereditary liege fief together with other lands late of Brice the Chamberlain, castellan for King John of Mortain and Tinchebrai, so that the fortress itself should be rendable on demand. Powicke found only the enfeoffment by Philip in 1206 of Montbazon castle in Touraine to compare with what he called the 'special conditions of service' attached to Radepont in the autumn of 1203. In fact, their peculiarity is confined to the stipulation that succession to the fief (*castrum*) should go only to Peter's children by his then wife and, secondly, to the extreme care with which the normal implications of rendability were applied to the local circumstances. In the traditional and elliptical phraseology habitual north of the Loire, worded as a perpetual grant, Peter de Moret undertook to hand over the *fortelicia ad magnam vim et ad parvam* to Philip in person and his heirs on demand, or to his well-known envoy bringing the king's mandate by letters patent. It was not unusual (and very natural at Radepont) to provide also that Peter's custodian for the time being should take the same oath, and likewise every member of the garrison, in case Peter or his heirs should be killed, captured or put under duress by the English.[33] The castle and town of the counts of Meulan at Beaumont-le-Roger, about thirty miles to the south-west on the river Risle, shared the strategic importance of Radepont at this juncture. This chief defence of central Normandy was betrayed in May 1203 by Count Robert's son Peter, although King John had observed feudal protocol and military prudence by sending in cash and supplies *ad emendam warnisionem ad castrum nostrum (sic) de Bello Monte*; perhaps it was in part a legacy of Richard's punitive and humiliating demolition of the *turris* of Beaumont in 1194. In October 1203 after Peter's death, by a charter dated 'at Gaillard', Philip II gave the *castellum* in liege fief to Guy de la Roche *tanquam aquestum nostrum*. As at Radepont, the fortified *caput* (*castellum cum fortelicia*) was to be rendered to the king as often as asked, by mere summons, under oath renewable by Guy's heirs. There is nothing to anticipate Philip's severe (but most interesting) punishment of Guy's offence of talking to 'the traitor and thief' Walter de Mondreville, for which complicity Beaumont town and all his rights there (evidently including the fortifications) were judicially forfeited, in January 1206. Guy was banned from central Normandy across

---

[33] Powicke (1961), 164-5 (including an excerpt of Philip's charter), 258 note, 275, map IV. John had fortified and garrisoned Radepont, crucial after the loss of the Norman Vexin, and financed the same at Stephen Longchamps' manor of Douville on the other bank of the Andelle (relevant fortification grants 1200-3 by John are *Rot. Norm.*, 26, 52, 74, 87, 88, 97; *Rot. Litt. Pat.*, 10b, 11a, 25a). Despite phraseology exclusive to rendability and peculiar the note to *Rec. Ph. Aug.*, ii, no. 761 infers that 'le roi a voulu tout de suite confier la place importante de Radepont à un homme sur, et les précautions qu'il prend montrent qu'on est en pleine guerre'. On this reckoning, royal garrisoning not alienation might be expected. The editors wrongly imply that Peter was custodian only and the tenure anomalous; it should be compared with Ségré (above) and Philip II's other fortress-pacts 1204-14 as well as with Montbazon (*Rec. Ph. Aug.*, ii, no. 839; *Catalogue . . . Ph. Aug.*, nos. 967, 1165; *Amplissima Collectio . . .*, i, 1099; *Layettes*, i, nos. 771, 772, 804, 805, 813, 892, 936, 954, 995, 1002, 1010, 1014). Even Radepont's military importance must not be exaggerated; under four years after Bouvines Philip readily agreed that the *forteritia* be razed and rebuilding forbidden in order to perfect an equal division of the fief between Peter de Moret's two sons (March 1219; *Amplissima Collectio . . .*, i, 1138; *Catalogue . . . Ph. Aug.*, no. 1886) cf. Portes and les Londes after Le Goulet (note 29 above).

the rivers Eure and Epte, and seven of his knights were made responsible for denouncing any future suspicious behaviour. In addition, 'all his other fortresses' were to be handed over to Philip on demand, ominously and abnormally *ad faciendum voluntatem suam* which is redolent of pledging not of rendability. The implied threat of disseisin may well have stiffened a pre-existing rendability since Guy's *quotiens . . . fuero requisitus* and Philip's absolute discretion are diagnostic. And rendability, in that it affirmed lordship, was not employed punitively and even the banning of fortifying by individuals was seldom precautionary in any military sense. The tenure of a fortress in fief implied and sometimes explicitly obliged repair and improvement. To remove this entitlement at the *caput*, or within the lordship at a new site, was an act of derogation of the vassal whereas by rendering his castle he signalised his feudal relationship and his lord's security.[34]

We have suggested that French fortress-customs, interwoven with the other ties of the castle-tenant to his immediate lord, very largely obviated the arbitrary expedients of Angevin practice. The continental context will supply the detailed proof. Rendability is no more than part (albeit the most expressive) of a complex of regional customs possessing a strong family resemblance throughout what was once Carolingian Gaul. Intimately and exclusively linked to direct lordship in the earliest feudal evidence (of the earlier eleventh century), fortress-customs comprise 'jurability', lordly refuge rights, protection and military support, 'razeability' or precarious existence, and also include rights of fortifying and of lordly authorisation. The recognitory procedures of banner-placing and delivery of control (*potestas* in the Languedoc); the mode and occasion of summons to render; the reciprocal duties of vassal and lord, and not least the formidable historiographical problem of the obscurity of fortress customs since the end of the Ancien Régime, all require systematic examination. What is true of thirteenth-century Champagne probably holds good for many of the provinces north of the Loire, and gives some indication of the prevalence of rendability; but its latent potentiality is no less important although much harder to quantify. In the provinces of the Provençal cultural area and throughout the south, rendability was evidently inherent in fortress-tenure to the point of being axiomatic by the thirteenth century. It is possible to speak of rendability as a con-

---

[34] Powicke (1961), 101-2, 161 note, 283, 344-5; *Rec. Ph. Aug.*, ii, no. 766; *Layettes*, i, no. 799; *Catalogue . . . Ph. Aug.*, no. 968. Guy was to hold *in ea saisina in qua Petrus de Mellento illud tenebat eo die quo decessit*. The distinction between his personal liege homage for the fief and the rendability attached to the fortifications clearly emerges, the latter (in the editor's conventional modern and inadequate phrase) Guy and heirs 'devront . . . remettre au roi à toute réquisition'. Guy's counterpart, not in the *Layettes*, will have been exchanged for the cancelled royal issue in 1206 when the town (and castle proper) was quitclaimed. No fortification ban (or prohibition) was imposed but Philip II interfered with such *seignoralia* extremely rarely. Castleworks were appurtenant rights of the Norman *mota* in a hauberk fief (*Jugements de l'Echiquier de Normandie . . .*, ed. L. Delisle, Paris 1865, nos.73, 341, 679). Security and symbolism dictated Philip's treatment of the defeated allies of Bouvines (Coulson 1972, 135-8) but the trusted partisan of Arthur of Brittany, Juhel de Mayenne, tenant in rendability of Guesclin castle (1210) was only stopped from fortifying (1211) at Bais (Mayenne) so as not to encroach upon the royal forest or lordship (*Layettes*, i, no. 936; *Rec. Ph. Aug.*, iii, no.1177; Powicke 1961, 74, 132, 146, 176). It must be stressed that Gui de la Roche's forfeiture by due process was for treason not connected with the contingent tenurial liability of Beaumont castle to be delivered on demand 'to great force and to small', (usually coupled in the Langue d'Oïl with a corresponding promise by the lord to restore the place *cessante negotio* or similar phrase) cf. Philip II's threat to Renaud de Dammartin (August-September 1211) demanding delivery of Mortain castle on his fealty in pledge to abate suspicion. The *fortericia* was not apparently rendable (*Rec. Ph. Aug.*, iii, nos.1202-3).

tingent liability at least throughout the north, judging from declarations of general and official record ranging from the Norman *Consuetudines* to the legist Beaumanoir, and from a sample of the charter material in print; but if the customs were demonstrably ubiquitous their application was clearly less than universal. The 1091 declaration might justify assuming that a fortress held *per consuetudines Normannie* would be rendable, at least if held in chief of the duke, but when individual specification is so precise silence in the record is very telling. One instance is the enfeoffment of Argentan (Orne) in June 1204 to Henry Clément, marshal to Philip Augustus, which does however state most exactly what use he might make of the forest there. Personal proximity, or otherwise, to the king gives no help, or scarcely any guidance, even less than do bans on fortifying. Exemption from rendability was so exceedingly rarely accorded, and then temporarily, that its presumptive effect is strong. Certainly, the nature of the sources and probably also the medieval legal mentality itself make any rigidly quantitative approach to fortress-customs somewhat misjudged.[35]

What mattered to William Marshal, earl of Pembroke, in his dilemma of double lordship in May 1204, and likewise in very many critical and run-of-the-mill contingencies of fortress-tenure, was that a legal code and chivalric *vade mecum* was always available which safeguarded vassal rights and lord's interests, clear in principles and precise in detail. Philip Augustus in the worsting of King John reaped the advantages of his record of good lordship and the Marshal was only the most noteworthy beneficiary, in the matter of his three Norman castles. He received far better treatment than at John's hands. His pact with Philip in late May 1204 at Lisieux hinges upon the central principle of rendability that the use, possession and control of a fortress may be temporarily but indefinitely transferred to the lord, without impugning the tenant's right or security of restitution; conversely, the lord's right to requisition or have assurance of the neutrality of the place made to him ('jurability') implied no derogation of and required no dispeace towards the tenant (*iratus seu pacatus*, as it was phrased in the Midi). William accordingly handed over *ad presens* (since the act unqualified of itself recognised Philip's lordship) his capital fortress of Orbec (*castrum Orbec et fortericia*), south-west of Lisieux, for the king to use for warfare or not. Longueville and Meulers, William's two lordships in the north near Dieppe, were beyond the war zone so the correct course was to place their capital fortresses (*castra . . . et fortericie*) in the hands of a non-suspect third party Osbert de Rouvrai under pledge of neutrality until midsummer. After that time Philip might requisition, garrison and use them also. For this respite of homage until mid-May 1205 William paid 500 marks by instalments but secured thereby recovery of his land and his

---

[35] *Rec. Ph. Aug.*, ii, no. 807; iii (1207/8), no. 986; cf. Powicke (1961), 257, 275; Coulson (1982), 362-3 *et passim*; general summary of Coulson 1972 in my 'Rendability and Castellation . . .' (note 6 above). A study is in preparation including the historiography of rendability since 1610 (Heinrich A. Rosentall, Cologne) *via* the *feudistes* (Salvaing, c.1667, Du Cange 1668, Brussel 1727) to Auguste Longnon (1869-1901) and Charles Bémont (1906). The contrast between Capetian rectitude and Angevin harshness can be ingenuously, or chauvinistically, exaggerated (R. Fawtier, 1962, note 13 above, vii-viii, 25-6, 38, 42, 45, 47 etc.) but in fortress-policy its significance can hardly be over-emphasised. Even when determinedly exploited feudal custom was the common *modus operandi* of noble social relations. After 1216 the Angevin monarchy was obliged to work more within the consensus afforded. Whereas their castle building slackened in pace that of the Capetians (notably in the construction of feudally eloquent *donjons*) accelerated after c.1214 (Raymond Ritter, *Châteaux, Donjons et Places Fortes*, Paris 1953, 55-8; R. Allen Brown, H. M. Colvin, A. J. Taylor, *The History of the King's Works*, London 1963, i, 113-19).

castra . . . in eo puncto in quo ei illa tradidi exactly according to the terms and phraseology of rendability. Until that time the Marshal would only suffer forfeiture if he failed to pay the instalments due in June and August 1204, or otherwise broke his side of the agreement. The sum was moderate and the terms quite generous. Indeed, Philip ignored his own promise to the count of Boulogne in 1203 to give to him the lordship of Meulers when it should be captured, but personal regard for the Marshal was one factor only in procuring this favourable treatment.[36]

The Marshal castles were duly restored in 1205 as was envisaged. Since rendability took no cognisance of the innovation (and rather brief efficacity) of liege homage the legal problems of serving two masters did not affect Longueville, Meulers and Orbec which, after the elimination of John's mesne lordship, were held directly from the French Crown. In July 1219, after the Marshal's death, these tenures were provisionally renewed without cavil in favour of his widow. The Countess Isabella undertook that her custodians would swear to render the castles, supplementing her personal oath (as non-resident and multi-castle tenants were occasionally asked to do) in war or peace *ad magnam vim et ad parvam* in the usual form. When her eldest son William passed on the family's Norman lands to Richard Marshal in 1220, the rendability of the three *fortericie* was reiterated as a matter of course.

Thinking of castles in a context of national politics no less than as part of such an armed and diplomatic struggle as was fought out between 1202 and 1204 over the duchy of Normandy predisposes one to concentrate on their military rôle, but feudal protocol was just as much attached to their symbolic aspect; perhaps more so. King Philip's counterpart contract for the surrender of Rouen dated 1 June 1204, if John failed to relieve the city, specified that it meant *civitas . . . integre cum omnibus forteliciis*. All knights holding fortresses were to provide hostages individually, in addition, surely so that due recognisance of Philip's lordship should be made in respect of them and rendability be written into their enfeoffments under the new dispensation.[37]

---

[36] The fortress-law aspects of this well known pact, made during the siege of Rouen, deserve attention (*Layettes*, i, no. 715; *Cartulaire Normand . . .*, no. 74; S. Painter, *Reign of King John*, 37-8, 213-14; Powicke (1961), 213-14, 251, 260, 262, 266, 294-7, 350; Warren, *King John*, 104-5, 184-7). W. L. Warren follows Sir Maurice Powicke in assuming that the lands primarily were made over but Philip's reversion in case of William's default governed *predicta castra*, the administrative centres and symbols of their respective lordships. Whereas William was to recover for his eventual homage *castra et terram meam* this looks like a catch-all phrase and although the form of words *castrum et fortericia*, habitually used to distinguish *caput* from fief, is not found here, clearly the castles were paramount. Philippe de Beaumanoir (c.1283) admirably expresses the chivalric mutuality which imbues the pact between Philip II and the Marshal. The aspect touching King John's personal proclivities most nearly is illustrated by *Coutumes du Beauvaisis* cap. 1662 denouncing abuse of rendability by a lord to oppress his vassal or to *pourchacier vilenie de sa fame ou de sa fille ou d'autre fame qui seroit en sa garde* (Salmon, 351).

[37] *Layettes*, i, nos.1354, 1397; *Rec. Ph. Aug.*, ii, no. 803. In 1219 at Pont de l'Arche William junior and Richard Marshal were given leave (severally) *veniendi in Franciam* but with five knights only in addition to their suites (*familia*). Rouen surrendered on midsummer's day 1204, six days before the very typical (but exceptionally detailed) truce ran out.

LA CRISE DE L'ORDRE DE SEMPRINGHAM AU XIIe SIECLE *
NOUVELLE APPROCHE DU DOSSIER DES FRERES LAIS

Raymonde Foreville

Le XIIe siècle, à la suite des fondations cisterciennes et à leur image, a vu l'essor d'une institution: celle des convers, frères laïques généralement issus de la paysannerie, véritables moteurs de la mise en valeur, dans un système autarcique, de terres le plus souvent incultes – bois, friches, landes, marécages – concédées aux nouvelles colonies religieuses. Il y eut un 'revers de médaille': ce fut, dans la seconde moitié du siècle, parfois avec récidives au début du XIIIe, l'esprit de rébellion entretenant l'agitation chez les frères lais, suscitant violences et crimes, engendrant ici ou là des scissions au sein des monastères. Cisterciens, Prémontrés, Grandmontains furent affrontés à de telles crises.[1] Toutefois, une des plus précoces et sans doute la plus grave fut celle que connut l'Ordre gilbertin un quart de siècle après l'établissement du chef d'Ordre, le prieuré Sainte-Marie de Sempringham en 1139. A l'époque – dans les années 60 du XIIe siècle – il comptait douze maisons, dont neuf nunneries. Il fut ébranlé dans ses oeuvres vives car la crise faillit compromettre irrémédiablement le statut même de celles-ci, c'est-à-dire la réunion en un même lieu, mais strictement séparées, de communautés masculines et féminines sous une même autorité et formant une unité économique et juridique, véritables monastères doubles (religieux et religieuses de choeur),[2] ceci après l'institution d'une quatrième branche celle des chanoines.

Si j'ai résolu de présenter ici l'affaire des frères lais de Sempringham, c'est à la faveur d'un nouvel examen de la question d'après les documents aujourd'hui disponibles, en vue d'une nouvelle édition du *Liber sancti Gileberti* pour les OMT. Lorsque je publiai, partiellement, le *Liber* en 1943, mon propos concernait le procès de canonisation, étude de droit canonique autant que d'histoire religieuse.[3] Je ne m'étais intéressée au dossier des frères lais qu'à titre subsidiaire, le croyant inédit, mon information n'ayant pu être complétée en raison des événements. L'édition que Dom Knowles en avait donnée et la mienne supportaient des conclusions assez proches. Toutefois, elles diffèrent sur un point essentiel, à savoir la transmission des documents et, en conséquence, le manuscrit de base. Dom Knowles avait établi son édition sur le Codex Bodl. Digby 36, du XVe siècle.[4] La mienne reposait sur le MS

---

* Je dois au Professeur C. R. Cheney l'inspiration de ce travail et je le remercie d'avoir bien voulu relire ce papier.

[1] Cf. Dom Jean Becquet, 'La première crise de l'Ordre de Grandmont', *Bull. de la Société archéologique et historique du Limousin*, lxxxvii, 1960, 283-324.

[2] Sur la définition des monastères doubles, cf. Dom Philibert Schmitz, *Hist. de l'Ordre bénédictin*, vii. *Les Moniales*, 46.

[3] R. Foreville, *Un procès de canonisation à l'aube du XIIIe siècle (1201-1202). Le Livre de saint Gilbert de Sempringham*, Paris 1943. – En attendant l'édition en préparation, nous citons les documents gilbertins d'après celle de 1943.

[4] M. D. Knowles, 'The revolt of the Lay Brothers of Sempringham', *EHR*, l, 1935, 465-87.

de la BL Cotton Cleopatra B I du début du XIIIe siècle. L'un et l'autre nous avions
négligé certaines des lettres pontificales émanant d'Alexandre III, conservées dans
le Cartulaire d'Old Malton et publiées dans les *Papsturkunden*: leur intérêt pour
l'Ordre tout entier et leur apport au dossier des frères lais apparaissent aujourd'hui
grâce aux documents découverts et publiés par le Professeur Christopher Cheney
dès 1946.

C'est donc à partir d'un dossier plus fourni et mieux assuré qu'il importe d'exa-
miner à nouveau l'affaire des frères lais de Sempringham, d'en déterminer la chronologie, mais aussi d'analyser la crise qu'elle engendra au sein de l'Ordre. Vous présentant
la primeur de cette recherche, je souhaite bénéficier de vos remarques et critiques en
vue de l'édition en cours de préparation. Je vous soumettrai d'abord le dossier tel
que j'ai pu l'établir, ensuite le déroulement de la crise telle que l'analyse des documents m'a permis de l'envisager.

I

Le dossier de l'affaire comporte deux sections. D'une part, les documents gilbertins
transmis par le *Liber sancti Gileberti*; d'autre part, des documents annexes transmis
par d'autres voies. Les documents gilbertins appellent une démarche primordiale, le
choix du manuscrit de base, critère de fiabilité.

Le *Liber* nous est parvenu à travers deux MSS de la British Library: Cotton Cleop.
B I (début XIIIe s.) et Harl. 468 (fin XIIIe s.). Un troisième MS, Bodl. Libr. Digby 36
(XVe s.), diffère notablement des précédents. Par son éclectisme, par la qualité des
lettrines enluminées, par la transcription intégrale de l'Office liturgique de saint
Gilbert, il s'apparente aux livres de dévotion. Au XVIIe siècle, il appartint au célèbre
bibliophile, Sir Kenelm Digby, dont les armoiries, imprimées au fer sur les plats de
la reliure en cuir marron portent la mention: INSIGNIA KENELMI DIGBY EQUITIS
AURATI, tandis qu'on peut lire en exergue au folio 4: *Vindica te tibi Kenelme Digby*.

Ce sont les manuscrits londoniens qui représentent véritablement le 'Livre de
saint Gilbert'. Le codex cottonien est un recueil composite de diverses oeuvres,
dont les documents gilbertins, d'une écriture très soignée, occupent les ff.33-168.
Ils dérivent, sinon directement du moins par un nombre minime d'intermédiaires,
de l'original présenté à l'archevêque Hubert Walter, ou du prototype autographe
d'auteur de ce volume. Le Codex harléien est une copie du manuscrit cottonien dont
il reproduit fidèlement toutes les caractéristiques, avec de rares altérations. Nous
connaissons la composition du Livre grâce au Prologue, Lettre dédicatoire à l'archevêque de Canterbury, Hubert Walter, ce qui permet également d'en fixer la date
dans la fourchette: 30 janvier 1202 (date de la bulle de canonisation) — 13 juillet
1205 (date de la mort du primat). D'autres indices laissent à penser que la compilation
fut réalisée au cours de l'année 1202.* Les lettres relatives à la révolte des frères lais
sont dans le MS cottonien au nombre de treize dont voici l'ordre et l'intitulé.

> 1. L'évêque de Norwich au pape
> 2. L'évêque de Norwich au pape
> 3. Le roi au pape
> 4. L'évêque de Winchester au pape
> 5. L'évêque de Norwich à saint Gilbert

---

* La lettre dédicatoire, énumérant les diverses composantes du *Liber*, précise que les leçons de
l'office de saint Gilbert y figurent, mais non les répons et antiennes propres que le compilateur
se propose, dans la suite, d'extraire des Ecritures canoniques. Ce qui laisse entendre que le *Liber*
était achevé avant la première fête solonnelle du nouveau saint (4 février 1203).

6. R. évêque d'York (*sic*) au même
7. Roger archevêque d'York au pape
8. Le prieur de Bridlington au pape
9. Le pape Alexandre à saint Gilbert
10. Le même aux évêques
11. Le même au roi
12. Le roi au pape
13. Saint Gilbert aux chanoines de Malton

Il faut ajouter à cette liste deux lettres transmises uniquement par le Codex bodleien — Henri II à Gilbert, Hugues cardinal et légat au pape — tandis que la lettre 6 n'y figure pas.

Le matériel de base est donc le même dans les deux traditions, à trois exceptions près, soit douze lettres communes. Dom Knowles, optant pour le MS d'Oxford qu'il jugeait plus correct, n'a pas pris garde que le dossier des frères lais fait partie intégrante du *Liber* tel qu'il est décrit dans le Prologue[5] et dont l'archevêque est, en quelque sorte, la caution. Or, le Codex bodleien s'en écarte, notamment dans la transcription des miracles, partielle et sans égard pour le recueil officiel tel qu'il fut présenté au pape Innocent III sous la garantie du serment. Ceci dit, il faut admettre que le matériel relatif aux frères lais est moins assuré que celui relatif au procès de canonisation, lequel constituait en 1201-1202 une documentation de première main, pratiquement contemporaine de la rédaction du *Liber*, d'autant mieux aisément accessible que l'auteur-compilateur, un chanoine de l'Ordre, gardien de la châsse de saint Gilbert, fut vraisemblablement l'un des membres de la délégation à la Curie.[6] Il n'en allait pas de même pour les lettres relatives à la révolte des frères lais, datant de plusieurs dizaines d'années; elles n'avaient sans doute pas fait l'objet d'une collection antérieure. Celles qui nous sont parvenues, dans l'un et l'autre codex, ne représentent qu'un échantillonnage: un nombre important de documents nécessairement impliqués manquent à l'appel.

Pour en venir à la critique textuelle, les variantes entre les deux traditions relèvent essentiellement de graphies différentes que l'écart de deux siècles entre les manuscrits suffit à justifier. Là où elles divergent vraiment, c'est dans la transcription des deux lettres de Henri II au pape. Le long passage final de la lettre 12: *Proinde obnixe rogamus* se trouve transposé à la suite de la lettre 3 dans le Codex bodleien (Knowles N° X). En revanche, ce même Codex ajoute à la lettre 12 ainsi tronquée deux phrases transcrites d'une main différente (Knowles N° XI), dont ni la syntaxe ni le sens ne s'avèrent satisfaisants eu égard au contenu, mais paraissent plutôt extraites d'un document vraisemblablement postérieur, plutôt accordé au style de la canonisation et consonant au roi Jean.[7] La lettre 3 telle que la présente le MS cottonien est une requête du roi concernant la coercition des rebelles par les censures ecclésiastiques, dont la phrase conclusive — 'Quod ne ullo modo contingat [totius ordinis excidium], sanctitas vestra malignantibus medullitus resistat' — ne saurait appeler des considérations autres liées par le terme *Proinde* (en conséquence). A cette lettre, Alexandre III répond positivement: d'une part, il enjoint aux évêques et archidiacres des diocèses concernés de dénoncer pour excommuniés ceux qui s'attaquent violemment aux membres de l'Ordre (lettre 10); d'autre part, il demande à Henri II d'exercer la justice royale envers les frères rebelles et contumaces que les censures ecclésiastiques n'auraient pas amenés à résipiscence (lettre 11). Enfin, le pape adresse à Gilbert une

---

[5] Foreville, 4. Introduction, xvii.
[6] Foreville, 4, 6-7. Introduction, xx-xxii.
[7] Knowles, xi, 486.

Lettres relatives à l'affaire des frères lais de Sempringham selon leur ordre dans les manuscrits

TABLE DE CONCORDANCE

		BL Cott. Cleopatra B I (et Harl. 468)			Bodl. Libr. Digby 36
A	1.	L'évêque de Norwich au pape	A	I	Guillaume évêque de Norwich au pape
B	2.	L'évêque de Norwich au pape	F	II	Roger archevêque d'York au pape
C	3.	Le roi au pape	E	III	Guillaume évêque de Norwich à Gilbert
D	4.	L'évêque de Winchester au pape	+	IV	Le roi Henri II à Gilbert
E	5.	L'évêque de Norwich à saint Gilbert	B	V	Guillaume évêque de Norwich au pape
+	6.	R. évêque d'York (*sic*) au même	D	VI	Henri évêque de Winchester au même
F	7.	Roger archevêque d'York au pape	++	[VII	Roger d'York au même]
G	8.	Le prieur de Bridlington au pape	G	VIII	Le prieur de Bridlington au même
H	9.	Le pape Alexandre à saint Gilbert	+	IX	Le cardinal Hugues légat au même
I	10.	Le même aux évêques	C	X	Le roi au même
J	11.	Le même au roi	H	–	Trois lettres du pape
K	12.	Le roi au pape	I	–	non transcrites par Knowles
L	13.	Saint Gilbert aux chanoines de Malton	J	–	mais figurant au Codex bodleien
			K	XI	Le roi au pape
			L	XII	Gilbert aux chanoines de Malton

+	6 omise sur Digby 36. Transcrite par Knowles d'après Cott. Cleop. B I sans correction d'attribution

+	IV et IX omises sur Cott. Cleop. B I
++	VII omise sur Digby 36

lettre de non préjudice concernant le droit de correction des abus dans l'Ordre (Lettre 9). C'est là un ensemble de mesures de caractère conservatoire ne touchant en rien au fond du débat, le statut de l'Ordre.

Examinons maintenant la teneur de la lettre 12. Le roi exprime d'abord sa gratitude envers le pape pour la protection qu'il a accordée à l'Ordre gilbertin, dont quelques-uns des frères lais de vie dissolue s'efforcent de renverser l'institution primitive. En conséquence, il supplie instamment le pape de délivrer un (ou plusieurs) privilège(s) (*Proinde obnixe rogamus quatinus ordinem prefatum faciatis inviolabiliter observari*) garantissant les institutions établies par Maître Gilbert (*secundum quod a prefato magistro prestitutus est*) et que lui-même avait confirmées (*et confirmatus a vobis*). S'il n'en allait pas ainsi, le roi et ses barons seraient prêts à révoquer les donations dont ils ont gratifié les maisons de l'Ordre. En revanche, ajoute le roi, — et c'est la réponse à la lettre d'Alexandre III — si vous confirmez l'Ordre dans son institution primitive, pour notre part, nous nous efforcerons de le maintenir, pour ce qui ressortit à notre justice. La supplique, ainsi assortie d'une sérieuse mise en garde, devait être présentée au pape et suivie à la Curie par deux émissaires, Me O. et J[ordan] archidiacre de Chichester.[8] On voit, ce qui est en jeu ici, ce n'est plus seulement, comme dans la lettre précédente, la répression des rebelles, mais bien

---

[8] Archidiacre de Lewes, mais toujours dénommé sous le titre du diocèse, Jordan de Melbourne détint l'office c.1164-1174 (*Acta of the Bishops of Chichester*, ed. Mayr-Harting, 1964, 211-13).

l'unité foncière − économique et juridique de l'Ordre gilbertin − c'est-à-dire le maintien des maisons doubles auxquelles ont été faites les donations (*sanctimonialibus de* [. . .] *et fratribus earum clericis et laicis*), ainsi que l'autorité des chanoines sur l'ensemble des communautés.[9] Syntaxe et argumentation paraissent dès lors en parfaite harmonie. Le manuscrit cottonien dans sa transmission des documents concernant l'affaire des frères lais, certes imparfaite, nous paraît cependant préférable à la tradition véhiculée par le Codex oxfordien.

Or la tradition originelle se trouve singulièrement confortée par le passage de la *Vita* qui termine le long chapitre relatif à la révolte des frères lais. Ce passage, reproduit aussi bien dans le codex bodleien, précise la teneur de la lettre 12 en cause ici. Ayant pris acte de l'unanimité des témoignages, épiscopaux et autres, en faveur de Gilbert et de la teneur des suppliques, à savoir que le Maître soit confirmé dans son propos initial, le texte poursuit: 'L'illustre roi Henri II dans son rescrit transmis par ses envoyés porte un témoignage identique et termine sa lettre par un sérieux avertissement. Si ces rustres et ces serfs [affranchis] obtenaient par leurs intrigues une altération [des statuts] de l'Ordre, lui-même et ses magnats révoqueraient les donations qu'ils lui ont concédées en raison de la fidélité de ses membres à l'observance religieuse. En revanche, si le pape confirme l'Ordre et en prescrit inviolablement l'institution primitive, pour sa part, il le maintiendra de tout son pouvoir, en ce qui ressortit, à la justice séculière, dans l'honneur et la révérence, comme il l'a toujours fait.[10]

Une dernière remarque s'impose quant aux documents gilbertins. Il s'agit de la lettre 6 transcrite littéralement par Dom Knowles (Nº VII) d'après le MS cottonien. L'intitulé: *Epistola R. Eboracensi episcopo* (sic) *ad eumdem pro eodem* recèle une double erreur. Elle n'est pas adressée au Maître de l'Ordre comme celle qui la précède et elle n'émane pas de l'archevêque d'York. Sans doute, y a-t-il eu, lors de sa transcription, soit inversion dans l'ordre des documents, soit omission d'une ou de plusieurs lettre(s). Or, si l'adresse rétablit le véritable destinataire, Alexandre III, elle n'en maintient pas moins la fausse attribution. Il suffit d'en comparer le texte avec celui de la lettre 7 qui émane bien de l'archevêque d'York (Knowles Nº II). Celui-ci, ayant procédé à l'enquête dans son propre diocèse, précise: 'Unica quippe domus est in Eboracensi diocesi in qua canonici et conversi cum monialibus infra eadem septa [. . .] honeste habitant'. Il s'agit là du prieuré de Watton. En revanche, le pseudo-évêque d'York désigne à trois reprises *les maisons* établies dans son diocèse. Il s'agit bien de prieurés doubles comme il le précise: '. . . de domibus illis que subjecte sunt regimini magistri Gileberti, videlicet quod [selon la suggestion de certains] canonici et fratres et moniales simul habitent . . .' Et plus loin: 'Si longe separarentur canonici et fratres a monialibus [. . .] non possent stare domus ille': Si les chanoines et les frères étaient éloignés des moniales, *ces maisons* ne pourraient se maintenir.

Seul, le diocèse de Lincoln possédait alors plusieurs maisons doubles. La lettre 6 émane donc de Robert de Chesney, ce qui signifie qu'elle est antérieure au 27 décembre 1166, date de la mort de l'évêque. L'inconséquence de l'adresse avait échappé à Dom Knowles. Or, l'implication de l'évêque de Lincoln dans l'affaire est attestée

---

[9] Cf. Major E. M. Poynton, 'Charters relating to the Priory of Sempringham', *The Genealogist*, New Ser. xv, xvi, xvii, *passim*, notamment xvi, 35. Cette formule est encore attestée à la fin du XIIe siècle: donation de deux portions de l'église de Stainton, 'concessione viri venerabilis Hugonis Lincolniensis episcopi' (1186-1200): *Transcripts of charters relating to the Gilbertine Houses* . . . , Alvingham ser., ed. F. M. Stenton (Lincoln Record Society), 107 (nº 10).

[10] 'Vita S. Gileberti', c.25, *Monasticon*, repr. 1970, *xix.

par Guillaume évêque de Norwich dans son rapport d'enquête (lettre 1): il s'agit d'un arbitrage entre Gilbert et quelques frères *coram domino Lincolniensi episcopo*. Les documents annexes ne prêtent pas à discussion critique, leur transmission et leur publication offrant les garanties requises. Ils se répartissent en trois séries:

1. Deux lettres de Thomas Becket à Gilbert. La première transmettant un mandement pontifical, citait Gilbert à comparaître en la fête de la Purification, 2 février [1166]. La seconde faisant état d'une autorité prééminente, est certainement postérieure à la mi-mai 1166. Le texte des deux lettres et la mention de *légat* dans l'adresse de cette dernière sont maintenant garantis par l'édition en cours d'Anne Duggan.*

2. La deuxième série comporte les lettres d'Alexandre III publiées par Walter Holtzman dans les *Papsturkunden in England* (1931). Ce sont les numéros 103, 112, 154, 184, 185, dont trois (103, 184, 185) figurent parmi les documents gilbertins. Dom Knowles n'avait pas jugé utile de les reproduire; datées de Bénévent, elles sont rapportées par l'éditeur à la période 1167-1169.

3. Enfin, deux privilèges pontificaux concernant les prieurés doubles d'Alvingham et de Chicksands publiés par Christopher Cheney. Le premier, daté du Latran 25 juin 1178, relève d'un train de privilèges de même date, englobant celui de Chicksands, en faveur de l'Ordre de Sempringham.[11]

Ainsi, de nouveaux repaires chronologiques permettent désormais d'appréhender la durée de la crise: son début c.1165 et son règlement final en 1178, après la légation d'Hugues de Pierleone (1175-76), mais encore de saisir les étapes de son déroulement. Envisagée dans une longue durée, la chronologie de la crise se démarque des positions prises antérieurement, aussi bien de la mienne (1165-70) que de celle de Dom Knowles (1167-69), *a fortiori* de celle avancée par Rose Graham (1170-75).[12] Elle est mieux accordée aux données de la *Vita*, mais aussi à la lenteur des procédures engagées auprès de la Curie romaine. Elle permet de prendre en compte une éventuelle suspension des négociations dans la conjoncture défavorable des années 1170-74. Au surplus, elle offre une meilleure approche de l'enjeu de la crise: non seulement le statut des frères lais — serfs affranchis par la profession religieuse — mais essentiellement la structure *sui generis* de l'Ordre gilbertin et sa raison d'être au milieu du foisonnement des fondations monastiques et canoniales au cours du XIIe siècle.

II

Voici comment, d'après l'ensemble des documents, on peut présumer du déroulement de la crise. La révolte des frères lais éclata au grand jour en 1165. Elle suivit une première vexation, Gilbert ayant été cité devant les juges royaux sur inculpation d'avoir fait parvenir à Thomas Becket des sommes d'argent, transgressant par là les ordres royaux.[13] Le pape et l'archevêque, l'un et l'autre alors en exil, en furent informés par la plainte d'une poignée de frères en rupture de ban auprès du pape qui résidait alors à Sens. Nous connaissons les noms de trois des principaux meneurs:

---

* L'auteur a bien voulu mettre à notre disposition le texte critique des lettres *Quantum te* et *Nos vobis*. L'apport principal est l'insertion du titre de légat dans le protocole de la seconde, d'après le MS BN Paris 5372 (Roger de Crowland, Quadrilogue II). La bulle d'Alexandre III accréditant Thomas est datée du Latran 24 avril 1166 (J.W. 11270).

11 C. R. Cheney, 'Papal Privileges for Gilbertine Houses', *Medieval Texts and Studies*, 1973, 39-65 (ed. révisée de l'article paru en 1946, *BIHR* xxi, 39-58). Nous nous référons uniquement au texte de 1973.

12 Knowles, 468; Graham, in VCH *Lincolnshire* ii, 181.

13 'Vita S. Gileberti', c. 24, *Monasticon* vi-2, *xvii-*xviii.

Le dossier de l'affaire des frères lais de Sempringham

ESSAI DE RECONSTITUTION CHRONOLOGIQUE

Circonstances	Documents préservés	Documents manquants
1165 – 1er recours des frères lais auprès d'Alexandre III	**1165** – 1ère lettre de Thomas B. à Gilbert	**1165** – Mandement du pape . à Thomas B. . à Gilbert
1166 – 2d recours des frères lais auprès du pape – Arbitrage de Robert évêque de Lincoln († *27 décembre*) – Comparution de Gilbert et des rebelles devant les juges pontificaux (diocèse de Lincoln)	**1166** – 2de lettre de Thomas, légat, à Gilbert (*après la mi-mai*) – Lettre de Robert év. de Lincoln au pape – Lettre de Guillaume év. de Norwich à Gilbert – Procès-verbal de l'audition par Guillaume de Norwich (*avant la fin décembre*)	**1166** – Mandat du pape . à Guillaume év. de Norwich . à Henri év. de Winchester . à Roger archev. d'York . à Hugues év. de Durham – Mandement du pape à Gilbert
1167 – Comparution de Gilbert et des rebelles devant les juges pontificaux (diocèse d'York) – Remise de l'amende royale *pro concelamento*.	**1166/67** – Procès-verbal de l'audition par Roger d'York et Hugues de Durham – Suppliques au pape . Henri év. de Winchester . Henri II	**1166/67** – Suppliques au pape . des évêques . des abbés et prieurs
1167/68 – Procédure en Cour de Rome		
	1169 – Alexandre III . à Gilbert 'prieur' de Malton et à ses successeurs *Bénévent 30 juillet* (Privilège) – . à Henri II (Lettre) – . aux archevêques, évêques et archidiacres (Lettre) – . à Gilbert Maître de l'Ordre de Sempringham *Bénévent 20 septembre* (Privilège)	**1169** – Alexandre III à chacun des prieurés de l'Ordre, sous couvert 'Gilbert prieur' (Privilèges)
1169-1176 – Nouvelle procédure en Cour de Rome. Entamée et éventuellement suspendue et prorogée (crises des années 1170-1174) – Nouvelle comparution de Gilbert devant les juges pontificaux – Mission de J[ordan] archidiacre de Chichester et O. auprès d'Alexandre III – Suite de la procédure en Cour de Rome	**1169-1176** – Lettre de remerciement et nouvelle supplique de Henri II à Alexandre III – Supplique de Guillaume év. de Norwich – Supplique du prieur de Bridlington à Alexandre III – Lettre de Henri II à Gilbert	**1169-1175** – Mandat d'Alexandre III aux nouveaux juges délégués – Mandement du pape à Gilbert – Nouvelles suppliques des évêques, abbés et prieurs au pape – Relation au pape des nouveaux juges délégués – Accréditif de la légation d'Hugues de Pierleone auprès de Henri II
1175-1176 – Légation en Angleterre du cardinal Hugues de Pierleone – Sa visite à Sempringham *janvier 1176* – Cession de Gilbert et promotion de Roger à la tête de l'Ordre	**1176** – Lettre d'Hugues de Pierleone à Alexandre III	**1176** – Suppliques de Gilbert, des chanoines et des moniales de l'Ordre
	1178 – Privilèges d'Alexandre III à Roger 'prieur' . de Malton – . d'Alvingham – . de Chicksands *25 juin*	**1178** – Privilèges d'Alexandre III à Roger 'prieur': pour chacun des autres prieurés de l'Ordre
1186 – Consécration d'Hugues évêque de Lincoln (*21 septembre*) **1186/89** – Arbitrage d'Hugues de Lincoln	**1176/78 ou 1186/89** – Gilbert aux chanoines d'Old Malton	**1176/78 ou 1186/89** – Gilbert aux autres prieurés de l'Ordre

Ogger, Gérard et Denis. Certains étaient des serfs, élevés depuis leur enfance sur le domaine, affranchis par l'entrée en religion. Ils n'avaient pas hésité à porter de graves accusations contre l'Ordre: relâchement de l'observance régulière parmi les membres des autres branches, scandales dans les maisons doubles, exigence d'une nouvelle profession contraire à celle qu'ils avaient émise à Sempringham. Alexandre III donna mandat à l'archevêque de Canterbury de procéder si nécessaire à la réforme de l'Ordre. Celui-ci, de son exil, écrivit à Gilbert, exprimant sa douleur d'apprendre que de tels scandales avaient pu naître au sein d'un Ordre qu'il chérissait entre tous et lui transmettait en même temps le mandement pontifical de correction des abus et de réforme auquel il devait se soumettre sous peine d'avoir à comparaître devant l'archevêque au terme de la Purification (2 février 1166), pour répondre des fautes imputées aux religieux et de non obéissance aux injonctions pontificales.[14]

Comme il devait l'attester dans la suite les lettres en question ne parvinrent pas à Gilbert, soit que le roi ait déjà dressé quelque obstacle aux relations entre l'archevêque exilé et sa province, soit que le porteur, Ogger lui-même, ait hésité à les présenter. Cependant, un premier arbitrage eut lieu: en présence de Robert de Chesney évêque de Lincoln, Gilbert délia les frères qui, spontanément, avaient prêté serment de maintenir l'Ordre (sans doute à l'encontre des rebelles).[15] Quant à Thomas Becket, il adressa une seconde lettre au Maître, lui enjoignant de rétablir la paix et l'unité au sein de son institut. Bien que prescrites en vertu d'une autorité prééminente – celle de légat dont Alexandre III l'avait investi au printemps de l'année 1166 – cette injonction n'était pas assortie d'une nouvelle citation, l'exilé étant privé de moyens d'action efficaces.[16] Les convers ayant réitéré leur plainte à la Curie, Alexandre III, de retour au Latran, résolut de procéder par voie judiciaire en nommant sur place des juges délégués. Gilbert fut donc cité à comparaître, d'une part devant les évêques de Norwich et de Winchester pour répondre des maisons du diocèse de Lincoln; d'autre part devant l'archevêque d'York et l'évêque de Durham, pour répondre de la maison double de Watton.

Procédure relevant du diocèse de Lincoln (1166)
Les relations des juges délégués nous informent pleinement sur les chefs d'accusation portés contre l'Ordre et le Maître de Sempringham. En l'absence de Henri de Winchester, malade, Guillaume de Norwich instruisit l'affaire de concert avec quelques abbés et prieurs. Furent évoquées la question d'une nouvelle profession contraire à celle émise à Sempringham et d'un serment insolite; celle de dissimulation de lettres apostoliques ou de refus de les recevoir sous allégation de faux;[17] celle enfin relative à la cohabitation des chanoines et des moniales. Gilbert dénia avoir exigé une nouvelle profession dérogeant à la première, sauf l'incident du serment réglé par devant l'évêque de Lincoln. Il se défendit également d'avoir eu connaissance des lettres pontificales adressées à lui-même et au chapitre de l'Ordre, et d'avoir excommunié le porteur, ce dont Ogger lui donna acte.[18] L'évêque de Norwich précise que les communautés masculines et féminines ont leurs cloîtres séparés: toutefois, pour obéir au mandement du pape, et bien que ce soit préjudiciable à l'Ordre, il fit

[14] *Materials for the history of Thomas Becket*, RS v, 261-2; Foreville, 90-1.
[15] Foreville, 93.
[16] *Materials*, v, 259-60; Foreville, 91-2.
[17] Foreville, 94.
[18] En 1167, Gilbert se vit remettre l'amende qui lui avait été infligée *pro concelamento*, i.e. dissimulation de lettres pontificales: *Liber rubeus de Scaccario*, éd. Hall, RS iii, 821.

promettre à Gilbert d'interdire l'accès des chanoines et des convers à la grande église — celle des moniales. Désormais, seuls deux ou trois chanoines devront assurer les messes solennelles, et les frères lais devront assister aux matines non plus dans la grande église, mais dans l'oratoire des chanoines. Quant aux rebelles, Gilbert dut s'engager à recevoir dans la communion de l'Ordre ceux qui se présenteraient en toute humilité. Quelques-uns, tel Denis et un certain W., refusèrent leur réintégration et déclarèrent émigrer dans un autre institut religieux. Ogger et les autres frères présents exigeaient un changement de statut assurant en chaque prieuré l'égalité des quatre branches — chanoines, moniales, convers et converses — dans l'obéissance à un préposé unique. Ces dispositions concernaient les maisons doubles établies dans le diocèse de Lincoln. Elles étaient alors, en toute probabilité, au nombre de sept: Sempringham, Haverholme, Alvingham, Bullington, Catley, Ormesby et Chicksands.

Procédure relevant du diocèse d'York (1166/67)

Ici l'instruction se déroula en deux temps. L'archevêque, Roger de Pont-l'Evêque, assisté de son suffragant, Hugues du Puiset, atteste l'existence en son diocèse d'une seule maison où chanoines et moniales vivent séparément et honnêtement dans une même enceinte d'ailleurs fort ample; il précise que Gilbert n'a procédé à aucune incarcération, excommunication, ou exigence de serment contraire à la profession émise par les frères; enfin, qu'il n'a pu arguer de faux des lettres pontificales qu'il n'avait ni reçues, ni même vues. Cependant, injonction lui a été faite d'éloigner, dans ce prieuré de Watton, les chanoines des moniales.

Insuffisamment instruits d'une cause qui sans doute ne les concernait pas, les convers de cette maison obtinrent un délai. L'affaire fut reprise en l'absence de l'évêque de Durham, mais en présence d'abbés et de prieurs. L'archevêque relate que les frères rebelles n'ont pu faire la preuve de leurs griefs; qu'en revanche, ceux relevant de son diocèse — où rien de contraire à la profession n'a été innové — ont été reçus au baiser de paix par le Maître. Ils demandaient cependant quelque tempérament afin d'affermir la paix; mais, en l'absence de mandat pontifical à cet égard, leur requête fut écartée. Quant à Ogger, il exigeait que fussent établies, à son propre arbitre, de nouvelles normes de vie dans l'Ordre.[19]

Crise au sein de l'Ordre et procédure en Cour de Rome

Au demeurant, il apparaît que les rebelles, rebutés après quelque trente à quarante ans de vie régulière, avaient constitué une sorte de bande organisée de malfaiteurs. Outre les calomnies dont ils accablaient les chanoines, ils tentaient de mettre la main sur les biens de l'Ordre, ne reculant ni devant le brigandage ni devant le meurtre; ils tentaient aussi d'en renverser l'organisation pour s'approprier l'administration temporelle des maisons gilbertines.[20] Leurs plaintes avaient cependant un fondement réel: l'assujettissement dans lequel ils étaient tenus par une règle plus dure que celles des chanoines ou des moniales. Et ces contraintes étaient devenues insupportables du jour où les chanoines avaient pris en main la direction effective des maisons de l'Ordre, reléguant les frères en des tâches subalternes. De telles révoltes, loin d'être l'apanage de Sempringham, affectèrent aussi bien des maisons cisterciennes ou cano-

---

19 Foreville, 97-8.
20 Foreville, 102-3.

niales vers la même époque. La rébellion des convers gilbertins ne laissa pas de susciter une crise grave au sein des prieurés du diocèse de Lincoln, ceux établis avant 1150 qui subirent de plein fouet le contre-coup de l'implantation des chanoines. Du moins, cette crise valut-elle au fondateur une quasi canonisation populaire de son vivant.

En effet, les juges ecclésiastiques dans leurs rapports au pape ne manquèrent pas de dresser un plaidoyer en faveur de Gilbert, attestant sa réputation de sainteté et le rayonnement de son oeuvre dans la société anglaise. Nombre d'évêques, d'abbés et de prieurs joignirent leurs suppliques au dossier qui serait transmis à la Curie. Nous sont parvenues, à titre exemplaire, celles des évêques de Lincoln et de Winchester.[21] Mais aussi celle de Henri II: le roi supplie le pape d'entendre les prières des évêques et celles des religieux; de donner aux pasteurs des diocèses concernés un mandat de coercition à l'encontre des rebelles; de maintenir les moniales sous la vigilance proche du Maître et des chanoines.[22] De la procédure en Cour de Rome, nous ne possédons aucune relation. On peut toutefois inférer, d'après les règles en usage à la Curie, que le dossier fut confié à un auditeur — cardinal ou notaire apostolique — que des témoins et des procureurs des deux parties, ayant été cités, déposèrent en audience contracdictoire devant le pape; qu'un procès-verbal fut établi et un renvoi requis pour complément d'information par devant les instances locales: ce qui implique une nouvelle procédure en Cour de Rome avant le dépôt de conclusions définitives. C'est là du moins ce que laissent entendre plusieurs lettres d'Alexandre III, réponses aux suppliques. Elles présentent, en l'année 1169, un caractère purement conservatoire, appelant par là-même une procédure ultérieure.

Premiers apaisements (1169)

Ces lettres — dont deux privilèges datés de Bénévent, 30 juillet 1169 et 20 septembre — sont en fait indissociables et il convient de les rapporter à l'été 1169. S'adressant aux archevêques, évêques et archidiacres des diocèses où sont sises les maisons gilbertines, le pape leur prescrit de défendre les membres de l'Ordre et de fulminer, d'autorité apostolique, l'excommunication sur les fauteurs de trouble.[23] Au roi, il écrit de contraindre et corriger — sans effusion de sang — les convers, contumaces et rebelles à l'Ordre, que les censures ecclésiastiques ne suffiraient pas à réprimer.[24] A Gilbert, il destine un privilège de non préjudice, lui confirmant, ainsi qu'à ses successeurs canoniques, avec le conseil des prieurs, le pouvoir de corriger et de réformer les abus, de sorte que ne puissent s'en prévaloir les personnes d'autres ordres religieux auxquelles il a confié, à diverses reprises, mandat de réprimer les dissensions et scandales survenus dans les maisons de l'Ordre (20 septembre).[25] Toutefois, un quatrième document doit être pris ici en considération.

Le privilège du 30 juillet 1169 a été tant par moi-même que par Dom Knowles, écarté du dossier, comme d'incidence purement locale.[26] La reconstitution et la publication par C. R. Cheney des privilèges du 25 juin 1178 adressés respectivement à Roger prieur d'Alvingham et à Roger prieur de Chicksands et rapprochés du privilège de même date adressé à Roger prieur de Malton[27] — prouvant qu'il s'agit du

21 Foreville, 95, 96.   22 Foreville, 102-3.
23 Foreville, 103-4.   24 Foreville, 104-5.
25 Foreville, 106-7.   26 *Papsturkunden* i, 377-9, Nº 112.
27 Cheney établit l'équivalence des titres décernés au supérieur majeur de l'Ordre gilbertin: *Magister*, *Prior*, *Summus prior* (p.46-50). Au XIIe siècle les chartes manifestent la diversité: Gilbert s'intitule *prior ordinis de Sempringham* (*Transcripts of charters*, Bullington ser., p.98);

même personnage, le successeur de Gilbert à la tête de l'Ordre – nous amène à reconsidérer la question du privilège de 1169 adressé à Gilbert prieur de Malton. Cette mention constitue le support unique d'un possible prieur local, homonyme du Maître, inséré entre le priorat de Robert et celui de Roger, lequel fut effectivement prieur d'Old Malton avant de succéder au fondateur.[28] Il semble raisonnable d'admettre qu'il s'agit bien du Maître lui-même. En effet, le prieuré canonial du Yorkshire a bénéficié d'une remarquable préservation de ses titres réunis dans le cartulaire, ce qui ne préjuge aucunement de l'inexistence de titres analogues en faveur des autres maisons gilbertines.[29] Or, dans la seconde lettre de Henri II au pape figurant au dossier – *epistola gratulatoria* – le roi remercie Alexandre III d'avoir pris sous sa protection 'les frères et *les* couvents de l'Ordre' et confirmé celui-ci par privilège (*autentico scripto*).[30] Dans le manuscrit d'Oxford, au lieu de *fratribus et conventibus* on lit: *canonicis et monialibus et universis conventibus ejus*.[31] Il ne faudrait cependant pas en conclure que l'affaire était terminée. Le privilège du 30 juillet, tel qu'il se présente pour Old Malton, outre la protection apostolique, la confirmation de *l'ordo canonicus*, selon la Règle de saint Augustin et l'institution de l'Ordre de Sempringham, confirme les possessions du prieuré, interdit violences et rapines et s'achève par des clauses formelles. La question subsiste de savoir si les autres prieurés de l'Ordre furent également gratifiés d'un privilège analogue en 1169, et dans quelle mesure cette concession concernait aussi bien les maisons doubles comme paraît l'attester la *Vita*.[32] Quoi qu'il en soit, la crise n'était pas éteinte ni le procès clos. Les institutions originelles – et originales – de l'Ordre demeuraient en suspens, notamment le statut des prieurés doubles.

Règlement final (1176-1178)

Il y a plus. La lettre de Henri II au pape revêt en même temps le caractère de supplique – une supplique assortie d'une mise en demeure: 'Nous vous supplions instamment de prescrire inviolablement que soit maintenu l'Ordre susdit selon ce que le Maître a institué et que vous aviez vous-même confirmé'. Suit la menace de révocation des possessions et domaines concédés par lui-même et ses barons aux maisons de l'Ordre 's'il advenait que fussent modifiées ses constitutions originelles, approuvées et confirmées par vous-même et par vos prédécesseurs. Mais, si vous prescrivez d'en observer l'institution première, alors nous en prendrons la défense en ce qui relève de notre justice séculière'.[33] C'est là une réponse directe à la précédente requête d'Alexandre III.[34] Sans doute y a-t-il lieu d'admettre que la supplique du roi, portée à la Curie par J[ordan] archidiacre de Chichester et O., était l'une des pièces d'un dossier comportant les suppliques d'évêques, d'abbés et de prieurs,

---

Roger Mustel confirme ses donations *in manu magistri Gileberti avunculi mei* (*Transcripts*, Sixhills ser., p.29).

[28] *Heads of rel. Houses, England and Wales*, ed. Knowles and Hadcock, 203.

[29] Le cartulaire de Sempringham, notamment, a été détruit dans un incendie: Poynton, *The Genealogist*, xv, 158. Comme l'a très justement noté, C. R. Cheney (p.42), les constitutions des maisons gilbertines variant de l'une à l'autre, il était difficile d'établir un privilège global, d'où la sollicitation de privilèges multiples auprès de la Curie romaine et un lot de privilèges de même date.

[30] Foreville, 105-6.

[31] Knowles, 485, lettre xi. Voir *supra*: critique textuelle, 41 et appendix ii, 55.

[32] 'Vita S. Gileberti', fin du c.25, *Monasticon* vi-2 *xix.

[33] Foreville, 106.

[34] Foreville, 104.

dont celle du prieur de Bridlington paraît bien donner le ton. Il reproche au pape de contrevenir aux privilèges de ses prédécesseurs: celui d'Eugène III qui approuva et garantit à perpétuité les constitutions, valables pour l'un et l'autre sexes, que Gilbert lui soumit, celui d'Adrien IV qui les confirma, et le sien propre. Il est impossible d'assigner une date précise à la nouvelle démarche du roi. Postérieure à l'été 1169, elle relève de la période 1169-1176.

Près de dix années allaient s'écouler avant le règlement final: une décennie ponctuée de crises au sein du royaume. A l'extrême fin de l'année 1169, Henri II avait resserré la surveillance du littoral dans la crainte d'éventuelles censures émanées du pape et du primat. En 1170, le couronnement du jeune roi, puis le meurtre de Thomas Becket, aggravèrent la tension entre Henri II et Alexandre III. Ce n'est guère avant la fin de l'année 1174 que furent jugulés obstacles et contretemps. Certes, le roi avait été relevé de l'interdit fulminé sur sa personne et réconcilié à Avranches (mai-septembre 1172), mais étaient survenus l'appel à Rome de Henri le Jeune, sa révolte, les hostilités en Normandie et l'invasion écossaise. C'est seulement en 1176 que resurgit dans nos documents l'affaire de Sempringham, lors de la légation en Angleterre du cardinal de Saint-Ange, Hugues de Pierleone, qui visita le chef d'Ordre au mois de janvier.[35] Dans sa relation au pape, le légat témoigne en faveur de Gilbert et des moniales, atteste la permanence du dessein pervers d'Ogger, et des autres frères irréductibles, de transgresser et bouleverser les institutions de l'Ordre, ainsi que la sentence d'excommunication dont le Maître les a frappés, conformément aux privilèges pontificaux. Il transmet enfin des suppliques de Gilbert, des chanoines et des moniales.

Les documents publiés par Christopher Cheney, qui à juste titre doivent être datés du 25 juin 1178, à l'instar de celui délivré à Old Malton, sont des privilèges solonnels de protection apostolique. Ils concernent les prieurés doubles d'Alvingham et de Chicksands, mais chaque maison gilbertine dut recevoir le sien. Ils ne confirment pas seulement les possessions de chaque établissement, menacées par les rebelles; ils spécifient et confirment spécialement les concessions octroyées par Henri II et Henri le Jeune. Enfin — ce qui répond aux requêtes des intéressés et règle le fond du litige — ces privilèges entérinent les institutions de l'Ordre établies par les archevêques Theobald de Canterbury, Henri d'York, et par Gilbert 'son premier père'. Il est remarquable que s'y trouvent nommément désignées les diverses branches: '. . . *ordo sanctimonialium et sororum, canonicorum et conversorum* . . .' Le statut des monastères doubles se trouvait avalisé, et l'unité foncière de l'Ordre confortée.[36]

Ainsi, bien qu'il manque des maillons à la chaîne des documents s'échelonnant sur une bonne douzaine d'années, de 1165 à 1178, on perçoit mieux la durée et le déroulement de la crise que traversa l'Ordre de Sempringham. Les documents parvenus jusqu'à nous, de par leur teneur même, en impliquent de façon certaine un nombre important d'autres, aujourd'hui perdus. Ils émanaient des instances locales et de la Curie romaine: mandements et mandats concernant les juges délégués et les membres de l'Ordre en la personne du Maître; suppliques d'évêques, abbés et prieurs du royaume; suppliques des différents prieurés sous le couvert du Maître; privilèges

---

[35] Foreville, 108-9 — 'Cum per Lincolniensem episcopatum transirem'. Le légat qui assista au concile de Northampton (26 janvier 1176) dut traverser le diocèse de Lincoln dans le courant du mois (cf. Eyton, 198).
[36] Cheney, 53-5, 56.

pontificaux adressés à Gilbert, puis à Roger, en leur qualité de 'grand prieur', pour chacune des maisons de l'Ordre.

Ainsi, est mieux perçue et mieux circonscrite la révolte des frères lais qui engendra de graves perturbations et menaça l'existence même de l'Institut gilbertin. Les maisons doubles, menacées, furent sauvegardées et rentrèrent dans leurs privilèges à l'issue de la crise. Celle-ci fut maîtrisée grâce à la constance de Gilbert dans son propos initial, et le caractère *sui generis* de l'Ordre fut maintenu contre vents et marées.

APPENDIX I

MS, BL, Cott. Cleop. B I, Lettre 3, ed. Foreville, 102-3

fo 92v   Epistola regis Henrici ad dominum papam pro sancto Gileberto.

Dilectissimo domino et patri spiritali A[lexandro], Dei gratia summo pontifici, H[enricus] eadem gratia rex Anglie, *et cetera*, salutem cum summa devotione debitum obsequium.

Vestre diligenter supplicamus paternitati, quatinus pro Dei amore et nostro/
fo 93 interventu, aures benignas adhibeatis universis scriptis episcoporum et aliorum virorum religiosorum quibus magnifice comm[e]ndant personam et sanctitatem venerabilis viri Dei magistri G[ileberti] de Sempingham, et singularem fructum utriusque sexus quem fecit in domo domini, et juxta eorum testimonium et deprecationem petitionem illius executionem mandare dignemini, precipientes rebellibus ipsius ordinis conversis et omnibus [aliis] professionis domorum de Sempingham ut inviolabiliter observent professionem et votum suum sicut privilegio vestro et predecessorum vestrorum sanccitum est et eximie confirmatum; et si obedire contempserint, placeat sanctitati vestre precipere episcopis in quorum diocesi prefatus vir Dei habet domos suas, ut eos, auctoritate vestra, coherceant obedire per omnia voto et professioni sue, secundum tenorem privilegii vestri et predecessorum vestrorum.

Vestre etiam discretioni in veritate que Deus est notificamus quod rebelles illi graviter perturbaverunt totum ordinem et gravem jacturam fecerunt domibus ordinis, furtim asportando possessiones earum, et in factis eorum nichil est nisi furor quia magistrum ordinis et plures canonicorum suorum, per quos integritas religionis ibi viget, vel jam ejecissent a domibus ordinis vel neci tradidissent, nisi timuissent nos
fo 93v et alios fundatores domo/rum qui nullatenus sustineremus ipsos laicos dominari in elemosina nostra, nec moniales alienari a custodia magistri G[ileberti] de Sempingham et canonicorum suorum, quorum provisione et doctrina, usque in presentiarum, satis mirabiliter floruit imparum vita et totius ordinis status. Nec volumus vos latere quod ipsi perversi nobis dedissent trecentas marcas argenti, si sustinuissemus eos dominari ad libitum et canonicos eliminari a domibus, quibus voto et professione tenentur; sed non ausi sumus, tam pro metu Dei, quam pro reverentia vestri privilegii et predecessorum vestrorum, quibus ordinis corruptores anathematis vinculo innodantur, eis in tanta et tam maligna favere stultitia quia nobis constat, si in hoc assensum preberemus, quod totius ordinis excidium hinc proveniret. Quod ne ullomodo contingat, sanctitas vestra, malignantibus medullitus resistat.

APPENDIX I

MS Bodl. Libr. Digby 36, lettre 10, ed. Knowles, x, 483-4

Letter x. *The king to the pope* (1)

Littere regie ad papam pro sancto Gilleberto.

Dilectissimo domino et patri spirituali Alexandro dei gratia summo pontifici H[enricus] eadem gratia rex Anglie et cetera. Uestre diligenter supplicamus paternitati quatinus pro dei amore et nostro interuentu aures benignas adhibeatis uniuersis scriptis episcoporum et aliorum uirorum religiosorum, quibus magnifice commendant personam et sanctitatem uenerabilis uiri dei magistri Gilleberti de Sempyngham et singularem fructum utriusque sexus quem fecit in domo domini, et iuxta eorum testimonium et deprecationem petitionem illius executioni mandare dignemini, precipientes rebellibus ipsius ordinis conuersis et omnibus aliis professionis domorum de Sempyngham, ut inuiolabiliter obseruent professionem et uotum suum sicut priuilegio uestro et predecessorum uestrorum est sancitum et eximie confirmatum, et si obedire contempserint placeat sanctitati uestre precipere episcopis, in quorum diocesi prefatus uir dei habet domos suas, ut eos auctoritate uestra coherceant obedire per omnia uoto et professioni sue secundum tenorem priuilegii uestri et predecessorum uestrorum. Uestre etiam discretioni in ueritate que deus est significamus quod rebelles illi grauiter perturbauerunt totum ordinem et grauem iacturam fecerunt domibus ordinis furtim asportando possessiones earum, et in factis eorum nichil est nisi furor, quia magistrum ordinis et plures canonicorum suorum, per quos integritas religionis ibi uiget, uel iam eiecissent a domibus ordinis uel neci tradidissent, nisi timuissent nos et alios fundatores domorum, qui nullatenus sustineremus ipsos laicos dominare in elemosina nostra, nec moniales alienari a custodia magistri Gilleberti de Sempyngham et canonicorum suorum, quorum prouisione et doctrina usque in presentiarum satis mirabiliter floruit ipsarum uita et totius ordinis status. Nec uolumus uos latere quod ipsi peruersi nobis dedissent ccc marcas argenti si sustinuissemus eos dominari ad libitum et canonicos eliminari a domibus quibus uoto et professione tenentur, set non ausi sumus tam pro metu dei quam pro reuerentia uestri priuilegii et predecessorum uestrorum, quibus ordinis corruptores anathematis uinculo innodantur, eis in tanta et tam maligna fauere stultitia. Quia nobis constat si in hoc assensum nos preberemus, quod totius ordinis excidium hinc proueniret, quod ne ullo modo contingat sanctitas uestra malignantibus medullitus resistat.

Proinde obnixe rogamus quatinus ordinem prefatum faciatis inuiolabiliter obseruari secundum quod a prefato magistro Gilleberto prestitutus est et a uobis confirmatus. Si enim quod deus auertat, contigerit licitis quorundam conatibus maximeque rusticorum et conuersorum illorum laicorum, qui et ante conuersionem suam ascripticii glebe fuerunt, institutionem prefati ordinis immutari ut, quod absit, dissolute uiuere incipiant, firmissime sciatis quod et nos et barones nostri possessiones et dominia nostra que eisdem domibus contulimus ob eorundem religiosam conuersationem et sanctum propositum eodem ordine mutato retrahemus. Que enim ob causas prefatas prenominatis domibus collata sunt, causis eisdem cessantibus licite poterunt, ut credimus, reuocari. Et si ordinem prefatum secundum primam institutionem a uobis et predecessoribus uestris approbatam et firmatam debito rigore feceritis obseruari, nos, quod ad secularem iustitiam nostram pertinet, eum pro posse nostro manutenebimus, et personas illius ordinis in maximo honore et reuerentia, sicut habere consueuimus, et exactiori, si fieri poterit, diligentia uenerabimus. Hec, et que alia prefatis domibus expedire credimus, nuntiis nostris magistro J. archidiacono Cicestrie et magistro O. clerico secretius intimauimus, ut uobis ea fideliter exponant et super his nobis consilium uestrum reportent. Ualeat, &c.

APPENDIX II

MS BL Cott. Cleop. B I, Lettre i2, ed. Foreville, 105-6

Epistola regis ad papam pro sancto Gileberto.

A[lexandro] domino pape, Henricus rex Anglie, *et cetera*.

Sanctitati vestre gratias quanta possumus devotione referimus pro magistro G[ileberto] de Sempingham et fratribus et conventibus ejusdem ordinis quod eos sub protectione vestra suscepistis et eundem ordinem, autentico scripto, confirmastis quod quia eorum quieti et paci paterna affectione providetis. Noverit autem sanctitatis vestre discretio quod certissime credimus eos debite et devote in domibus suis domino ministrare et se in exterioribus ita [gerere] ut conversatio illorum Deo et hominibus merito credatur acceptabilis, unde circunstantium tam clericorum quam laicorum, gratiam non modicam meruisse noscuntur, et ob hoc solum in oculis nostris et nostrorum gratiam et favorem non modicum promeruerunt. Innotescat autem vestre serenitati quod prenominatus magister ordinis, quamvis debilitatem fo 100 corporis incurrerit, animi tamen constantiam et robur/ nullatenus relaxavit, immo quanto fervore et zelo in fortiori etate ordinem prestatum regebat, tanto adhuc, ut credimus, id ipsum satagere non cessat, nec ad idem regimen in regno nostro idoneor posse inveniri.

Et quoniam quidam ex fratribus dissolutius vivere, et ordinis primam institutionem infringere nituntur, movet nos non modicum et eos qui in domos prefatas elemosinarum suarum largitiones contulerint. Proinde, obnixe rogamus quatinus ordinem prefatum faciatis inviolabiliter observari, secundum quod a prefato magistro prestitutus est et confirmatus a vobis. Si enim, quod Deus avertat, contigerit licitis quorumdam conatibus et maxime rusticorum et conversorum laicorum, et qui ante conversionem suam ascriptitii glebe fuerunt, institutionem prefati ordinis immutari ut, quod absit, dissolute vivere incipiant, firmissime sciatis quod et nos et barones nostri, possessiones et domania nostra que eisdem domibus contulimus, ob eorumdem religiosam conversationem et sanctum propositum, eadem, ordine mutato, retrahemus. Que enim, ob causas prefatas, prenominatis domibus collata sint, causis eisdem cessantibus, licite poterunt, ut credimus, revocari. Et si ordinem prefatum secundum primam institutionem a vobis et predecessoribus vestris approbatam et fo 100v firmatam, debito rigore feceritis observari, nos quod ad secularem/justitiam nostram pertinet, eum pro posse nostro manutenebimus, et personas illius in maximo honore et reverentia, sicut habere consuevimus, exactiori si fieri poterit diligentia venerabimur. Hec et que alia prefatis domibus expedire credidimus, nunciis nostris magistro J[ordano], archidiacono Cicestrie, et magistro O., clerico, secretius intimavimus ut vobis ea fideliter exponant et super his nobis consilium vestrum reportent.

APPENDIX II

MS Bodl. Libr. Digby 36, lettre 9, ed. Knowles, xi, 485-6

Lettre XI. *The king to the pope* (2)

Littera domini regis Anglie gratiosa ad dominum papam.

Alexandro pape etcetera Henricus rex Anglie et cetera. Sanctitati uestre gratias quanta possumus deuotione referimus pro uenerabili uiro magistro Gilleberto de Sempyngham, canonicis et monialibus et omnibus conuentibus eiusdem ordinis, quod eos sub protectione uestra suscepistis et eundem ordinem auctentico scripto confirmastis, et quod eorum quieti et paci paterna affectione prouidetis. Nouerit autem sanctitatis uestre discretio quod certissime credimus eos debite et deuote in domibus suis domino ministrare, et se in exterioribus ita gerere ut conuersatio illorum deo et hominibus merito credatur acceptabilis. Uerum circumstantium tam cleri--corum quam laicorum gratiam non modicam meruisse noscuntur, et ob hoc solum in oculis nostris et nostrorum gratiam et fauorem non modicum promeruerunt. Innotescat autem serenitati uestre quod prenominatus magister G[illebertus], quamius debilitatem corporis incurrerit, animi tamen constantiam et robur nullatenus relaxauit, immo quanto feruore et zelo in fortiori etate ordinem prefatum regebat, tanto adhuc idipsum satagere non cessat nec ad idem regimen in regno nostro credimus idoneor posse inueniri,

quem ignis diuinus ita inflammauit ut magne multitudinis uirorum et mulierum animos in dei amore succenderet, et ipsius plantationis institutor primus fieret et inuentor. Per illum enim deus multa et magna et usque ad eius tempora inaudita operatus est [deus] in medio terre nostre. Et licet teneamur omnibus religiosis et ecclesiasticis uiris parmam regie protectionis impendere, multo fortius et attentius illos protegere cogimur et fauere quos in regno nostro Anglie et de gente nostra primo sancte religionis normam originaliter nouimus suscepisse ad dei laudem et uniuersalis ecclesie gloriam et decorem. Ualete.

APPENDIX III

MS BL Cott. Cleop. B I, Lettre 7, ed. Foreville, 97

*[Epistola Rogeri Eboracensis archiepiscopi ad Alexandrum papam.]

Domino pape A[lexandro], Rogerus Eboracensis [archi]episcopus et H[ugo] Dunelmensis episcopus.

Juxta formam quam in scripto parvitati nostre dedit sullimitas vestra, in causa processimus que inter magistrum G[ilebertum] de Sempingham et fratres ejus vertebatur, et quidem quod ad provinciam nostram de facili expedivimus. *Unica quippe domus est in Eboracensi diocesi in qua canonici et conversi cum monialibus, infra eadem septa que quidem ampla sunt, sed seorsum, ut fama publica est, honeste habitant*; in qua nec jusjurandum nec aliud quippiam contra primam [professionem] predictus magister ab ipsis exegerat; nullum eorum carcerali deputavit custodie; neminem eorum excommunicaverat; sed omnes in ea vocatione manserant in qua ab eo vocati fuerant. Precepimus itaque ei ut canonicos a monialibus, juxta formam mandati vestri, separaret, quod libens concessit.

De litteris quoque vestris, quas universo ordini illi direxistis, quas ipse de falso notasse dicebatur, nichilominus solliciti fuimus, et diligenter quesivimus cur eas falsitatis arguisset, cum nec in scriptura, nec in dictamine, nec in bulla aliqua falsa nota appareret. Ipse vero constanter negavit quod nec eas receperat nec viderat. Et fo 96v quoniam fratres ad hoc convincendum non satis instructi venerant, ad / voluntatem eorum dies prorogata est. Veniente autem die, ego Rogerus archiepiscopus, immo servus vester, quoniam dominus Dunelmensis ex necessaria causa absens fuit, accitis abbatibus et prioribus et aliis viris prudentibus maturi consilii, devotum mandato vestro obsequium exhibui; et quoniam eadem die fratres predicti in eorum probatione, que proposuerant, omnino defecerunt, hii qui in diocesi nostra morantur, circa quos sicut dictum est nichil contra primam professionem et ordinis institutionem innovatum fuerat, absque ulla murmuratione, jam dictum magistrum in patrem et ipse eos in filios benigne suscepit, supplices dumtaxat preces porrigentes, quatinus pauca temperaret, quibus sopitis, non solum extra, sed intus pacem perfectissimam affuturam esse firmiter asserebant; in quibus temperandis, nec mandato vestro nec consilio magistrum credimus defuturum. Reliquos quoque qui extra nos positi sunt, in osculo, sicut vir mansuetus est, non minus benigne recepit, preter solum Oggerum, qui cornua peccatorum assumens, nec ad fratrum suorum lacrimas motus, nec ad commonitionem abbatum et priorum qui nobis assistebant vel nostram redire voluit, nisi sepedictus magister ad arbitrium ejus novas in ordine suo conderet institutiones.

fo 97   Superest igitur, domine, / quatinus innocentem et per quem Deus multa et magna et usque ad tempus ejus inaudita operatus est in medio nostri, mansuetudo consoletur apostolica, ut qui jam in diebus suis processit, nature debitum in brevi redditurus pacifice esse carcere mortis hujus egredi possit; nec patiamini ipsum ab his conculcari qui non que religionis sunt querentes, sed sua, imitari pro voto suo querunt *magistros prurientes auribus* (II *Tim.* IV, 3).

APPENDIX III

MS BL Cott. Cleop. B I, Lettre 6, ed. Foreville, 96

95v   *Epistola R[oberti Lincolniensis] episcopi [ad Alexandrum papam.]

Sanctissimo patri et domino A[lexandro], Dei gratia summo pontifici, minimus suorum R[obertus] eadem gratia [Lincolniensis] ecclesie episcopus, salutem et debitam in omnibus et per omnia obedientiam.

Audivimus et dolemus quod quedam sinistra significata sunt sanctitati vestre *de domibus illis* que subjecte sunt regimini magistri G[ileberti] de Sempingham, videlicet quod canonici et fratres et moniales simul habitent. Sed longe aliter se res habet: seorsum enim habitant, seorsum comedunt, et ita ab invicem sunt segregati, quod nulli canonico, vel fratri, pateat aditus ad moniales. *De domibus autem illis quas in diocesi nostra habet*, certissime audemus asserere quod honestissime et religiosissime reguntur. Vir siquidem prefatus suave olentis opinionis est, et dominus suis providere omnimodis intendit. Si vero longe separarentur canonici et fratres a monialibus, sicut ad suggestionem quorumdam vos precepisse accepimus, *non possent stare domus ille*; advocati namque qui canonicis et monialibus illis possessiones suas,
96 pietatis intuitu, concesserunt, nullatenus sustinerent, sed facillima sumpta occasione, libentur eis subtraherent quicquid / benigne prius ipsis impenderant. Valete.

---

* Nous soulignons dans l'une et l'autre lettres (en italique) l'état des maisons doubles: une seule dans l'archidiocèse d'York, plusieurs dans le diocèse de Lincoln.

THE LETTERS OMITTED FROM ANSELM'S COLLECTION OF LETTERS

Walter Fröhlich

The writing of letters and the gathering of such letters in large letter-collections is one of the striking features which distinguish intellectual life of the eleventh and twelfth centuries from those immediately preceding and following. This activity blossomed forth from the numerous schools which were attached to the monasteries and cathedrals of western Europe.

In the Middle Ages the writing of letters was closely linked to the writing of verses for teaching purposes. Both exercises were conscientiously practised; they were expressed by the same verb 'dictare' which can be rendered as either 'to write according to dictation' or 'to write poetry'. Thus, as C. Erdmann conclusively demonstrates, the writing of letters became an important and self-conscious genre of literary composition.[1] It provided a means of expression for the culture and the learning of the writers. Yet the letters themselves also have an intrinsic importance in relation to the significance and purpose of their subject matter. Many letters, therefore, acquired a twofold value derived from their form and their content.

Among the most important letter-writers were the teachers and scholars of the monastic and cathedral schools. Their learning, displayed in their writings, made them well-known so that a great number of these teachers were promoted to abbacies and episcopal sees and thus also occupied important political positions.[2]

One of these teachers and scholars was Anselm, a native of Aosta, monk, prior and abbot of Bec until 1093 and then archbishop of Canterbury until his death in 1109. In reply to a letter from Warner, a novice of Christ Church Canterbury, Anselm sent a brief piece of spiritual advice in 1104 (Anselmi Epistola, = AEp, 335). He added that if Warner wished for more profound counsel on the monastic way of life he should look up an earlier letter which he had written to a Dom Lanzo when the latter had been a novice (AEp 37). The letter to Warner was written while Anselm was spending his second exile in Lyon. The letter to Lanzo, prior of the Cluniac house of St Pancras at Lewes 1077-1107, was sent while Lanzo was still a novice at Cluny some thirty years before.

It seems unlikely that Anselm would have expected Warner to search for that particular letter among numerous miscellaneous manuscripts but rather that he would

---

[1] Carl Erdmann, *Studien zur Briefliteratur Deutschlands im 11. Jahrhundert*, Leipzig 1938; the same, *Briefsammlungen*, in Wilhelm Wattenbach — Robert Holtzmann, *Deutschlands Geschichtsquellen im Mittelalter, Teil II*, Darmstadt 1967, 415-22; see also *The Letters of Peter the Venerable*, ed. Giles Constable, Harvard Hist. Studies, 78, Harvard 1967, 1-12; the same, *Letters and Letter-Collections*, in *Typologie des Sources du Moyen Âge occidental*, fasc. 17, Turnhout 1976.

[2] For a selection of promoted scholars see *The Letters of St Anselm*, transl. Walter Fröhlich, Kalamazoo, in the press, Introduction.

be able to find it in the library of his monastery, the cathedral priory of Christ Church Canterbury, in the codex containing the collection of Anselm's letters. For Anselm had assembled a collection of his letters which he enlarged and rearranged over a number of years.[3]

From the evidence available it appears that Anselm, in reply to enquiries and requests from various people, started collecting letters he had written from about the early 1070s. No letter written by him before 1070 has been preserved. His motive for collecting his early letters — those written while he was prior and abbot of Bec — seems to have been on account of their moral content of exhortatic and spiritual advice rather than for their literary form. Business matter and day-to-day information were almost totally excluded and entrusted to the oral report of the bearer of the letter.[4] Anselm's collection of his early letters, with a few exceptions, contains only his outgoing correspondence.[5]

Anselm's correspondence covering his archiepiscopal period comprises 328 items. It contains not only the outgoing letters but also some he received as well as some letters between third parties.[6] In those letters written while he was archbishop of Canterbury the emphasis of the contents shows a shift from pastoral advice to political problems of church reform, Anglo-Norman statecraft and the struggle for supremacy in the 'corpus christianorum'. Thus the character of the collection changed from being a compilation of letters valued for their moral content to that of letters dealing with state affairs of the utmost political importance.

The final part of this collection seems to contain all letters bearing upon the renewed outbreak of the primatial controversy between the metropolitan sees of Canterbury and York which took place in the autumn and winter 1108 and spring and summer 1109. Thus yet again the character of the collection was changed. It acquired the character of a register of the archbishop's correspondence.

The first part of Anselm's collection of letters — those while he was prior and abbot of Bec — passed through three stages. The oldest manuscript containing the first stage is British Library, MS Cotton Nero VII (henceforth referred to as N), since it is the only manuscript that styles Anselm merely as prior and abbot of Bec. It contains 99 letters on 142 pages. Some pages are missing at the end but the letters on these lost pages can be reconstructed from London Lambeth Palace,

---

3 The following summary is based on André Wilmart, 'La destinataire de la lettre de S. Anselme sur l'état et les voeux de religion', *Revue Bénédictine* (=*RB*) 38, 1926, 331-4; the same, 'Une lettre adressée de Rome à S. Anselme en 1102', *RB* 40, 1928, 262-6; the same, 'La tradition des lettres de S. Anselme, lettres inédites de S. Anselme et de ses correspondants', *RB* 43, 1931, 38-54; Franciscus Salesius Schmitt, 'Zur Überlieferung der Korrespondenz Anselms von Canterbury, Neue Briefe', *RB* 43, 1931, 224-38, reprinted in *Anselmi Opera Omnia* (=*AOO*) ed. F. S. Schmitt, 6 vols, Edinburgh 1946-1963 and Stuttgart 1968. André Wilmart, 'Une lettre inédite de S. Anselme, à une moniale inconstante', *RB* 40, 1928, 319-32; F. S. Schmitt, 'Zur Entstehung der handschriftlichen Briefsammlungen Anselms von Canterbury', *RB* 48, 1936, 300-17 = *AOO* 154*-171*; the same, 'Die Chronologie der Briefe Anselms', *RB* 64, 1954, 176-207 = *AOO* 172*-203*; the same, 'Die unter Anselm veranstaltete Ausgabe seiner Werke und Briefe, Die Codices Bodley 271 und Lambeth 59', *Scriptorium* 9, 1955, 64-75 = *AOO* 226*-239*; Walter Fröhlich, 'Die Entstehung der Briefsammlung Anselms von Canterbury', *Historisches Jahrbuch* 100, 1980, 457-66; the same, 'The genesis of Anselm's collection of letters', *American Benedictine Review* 35, 1984. The opinion maintained in these articles is at variance to that of Richard William Southern, *Saint Anselm and his biographer*, Cambridge 1963, 67-8n, 238n.

4 See e.g. Anselmi Epistola (= AEp) 4, 5, 14, 22, 66, 68, 89, 121, 124, 126, 132.

5 Anselm sent 138 letters; he received 8 letters; one letter names Anselm neither as writer nor as addressee.

6 Anselm is the author of 234 letters, the recipient of 76 letters and neither of both in 18 letters.

MS 224 (M).[7] The latter is an autograph of William of Malmesbury who had copied Anselm's works and letters into this manuscript and had used N for the purpose.

The letters in N do not follow any strict chronological order, their only division being the letters written as prior and those written as abbot of Bec. This division is provided by a rubric after letter N 69 (= AEp 87) at the bottom of fol. 94r: 'Hactenus continentur epistole domni Anselmi abbatis, quas fecit donec prior Beccensis fuit. Quae vero iam deinceps sequuntur, egit postquam abbatis nomen et officium suscepit'. As this rubric is written on an erasure it must be the work of the original scribe or his immediate corrector and not that of a later copyist.[8] This points to the fact that the scribe or his corrector knew Anselm only as abbot of Bec and not yet as archbishop of Canterbury. The rubric at the beginning of the collection of Anselm's letters supports this: 'Incipit liber epistolarum domni Anselmi abbatis.' This rubric separates Anselm's letters from the letters of Lanfranc which are collected in the first part of N. Both collections appear to have been written by the same hand. This consideration is supported by the fact that two letters (AEp 30, 31) from Archbishop Lanfranc (one to Prior Anselm and one to his nephew Lanfranc at Bec) are excluded from Anselm's collection since they are already among the collection of Lanfranc's letters.

The date for the compilation of this first stage of Anselm's letter collection is provided by AEp 145 sent to Abbot Ralph of Séez congratulating him on his promotion in 1089. This letter is not to be found in N but it can be assigned to N on the evidence of M. Since the itinerary of Abbot Anselm shows no absence of the abbot of Bec from his monastery in 1089 it would seem that Anselm's first collection of his letters was assembled and written into N at Bec under Anselm's supervision and assistance.[9] The death of Archbishop Lanfranc on 26 May 1089 and the compilation of a collection of his letters could have been the incentive to do this some time in 1090. Anselm's letter to his former pupil Maurice in 1085 (AEp 104) points to the probability that Anselm had been thinking about collecting his letters for some time, for this letter closes: 'We are still waiting for our letters which Dom Maurice is supposed to have sent us'.

Barely two years later Anselm was engaged on improving the first stage of his letter collection. In autumn 1092 (AEp 147) he informs Prior Baldric and the community of Bec about the delay of his return to Bec due to King William's refusal to grant him leave to do so. He asks: 'Send me the Prayer to St Nicholas which I wrote and the letter which I had started writing against the propositions of Roscelin; and if Dom Maurice has any other letters of ours which he has not yet sent, send them as well.' It would appear that he intended using this period of enforced leisure to improve the first collection of his letters and thus required all the letters which had been collected at Bec since the compilation of N to be sent to him in England. He improved the rough chronology of N — which had only divided the letters into those of the prior and those of the abbot — by rearranging all the letters in their proper order. He also inserted in their correct order five of the letters to Maurice which

---

[7] AEp 88 = M 63; AEp 96 = M 69/70; AEp 102 = M 1; AEp 112 = M 17; AEp 113 = M 10; AEp 120 = M 79; AEp 130 = M 47; AEp 131 = M 46; AEp 132 = M 58; AEp 134 = M 57; AEp 140 = M 15; AEp 144 = M 16; AEp 145 = M 75; AEp 146 = M 74.

[8] See Neil Ripley Ker, *The English Manuscripts in the Century after the Norman Conquest*, Oxford 1960, 50-1.

[9] For the itinerary see Walter Fröhlich, *Die bischöflichen Kollegen Erzbischof Anselms von Canterbury*, Diss. München 1971, 191-9; now in Letters of St Anselm.

had meanwhile been returned to him. Abbot Anselm's enforced stay in England took place in the wake of his third inspection tour of the English cells and estates of Bec for which he had set out on 26 August 1092.[10] Having accomplished the purpose of his journey he spent the autumn and winter 1092-1093 with his friend Abbot Gilbert Crispin at St Peter's, Westminster, waiting for the king's leave to return to Bec. Therefore the second edition of his letters was most likely executed at Westminster during this period.

The best example of this second stage of Anselm's letter collection is to be found in the first part of his collection in Cambridge, Corpus Christi College MS 135 (E_1). Having thus been gathered and compiled in two stages by Anselm himself — in 1090 at Bec and 1092/93 at Westminster — this collection of the letters of the prior and abbot of Bec developed differently in Canterbury and Bec. They are the collections of Anselm's letters to be found in London Lambeth Palace, MS 59 (= L) written at Canterbury and in Paris Bibliothèque Nationale, MS 14762 (= V) written at Bec, forming L_1 and V_1 and representing the third stage of the first part of the Anselmian letter collection. L_1 and V_1 differ from N and E_1 and from each other by the addition of further letters and in the chronological sequence of the letters which they contain. L_1 contains 132 letters while V_1 comprises 156 of which 27 are duplicates.

The earliest collection of Anselm's letters written as archbishop of Canterbury from 6 March 1093 to 21 April 1109 is to be found in the second part of L (= L_2) since all other manuscripts containing letters of the archiepiscopal period depend upon this part of L. The collection in L_2 comprises 257 letters. They were compiled by Anselm himself during another period of enforced leisure. From December 1103 to September 1106 he was banished from the Anglo-Norman realm because of the dispute about investitures between King Henry I and Pope Paschal II. Anselm spent most of this, his second exile, with his friend Archbishop Hugh of Lyon. During this time also, he directed the production of a final edition of his works and letters. Following Anselm's instructions (AEp 334, 379) this task was conscientiously and meticulously carried out by the scribe Thidricus at Christ Church Canterbury. The fruits of Thidricus' labours are the magnificent manuscripts Oxford Bodleian, Bodley 271, containing Anselm's philosophical and theological works, and London Lambeth Palace MS 59 comprising his letters. After Anselm's return to Canterbury in September 1106 his letter collection acquired the character of a registry into which new letters were copied. Soon after Anselm's death an appendix — L_a — was added to L_1 and L_2. On thirty-one pages L_a contains a miscellany of letters, tracts, poems and other documents.[11] A number of the letters in L_a are referred back to the collec-

---

10 For Anselm's journeys to England in 1079, 1086 and 1092 see Marjorie Chibnall, 'The Relations of St Anselm with the English Dependencies of the Abbey of Bec 1079-1093', *Spicilegium Beccense*, Paris 1959, 521-30; the same, *Le domaine du Bec en Angleterre au temps d'Anselme*, Paris 1984/5.

11 L_1 and L_2 cover fol. 1r to fol. 160v, line 3 of right column. They are most carefully written with very few mistakes. L_a comprises fol. 160v to 190r. It is split into two parts by nine and a half empty pages. The first part of L_a consists of a letter (L 390), a tract on 'velle', a deathbed confession, a sermon on the bliss of eternal life, three tracts on 'aliquid' and 'facere', on 'de potestate' and on different modes of 'causa', two poems in praise of Anselm, the covering letter for Anselm's work 'Cur Deus Homo' to Urban II, another letter (L 391), the canons of the synods of London of 1102 and 1108 and finally seven other letters (L 392, 393, 394, 395, 396, 397, 398). The remaining folios after the gap of nine and a half empty pages contain, in a different hand, a miscellaneous collection of writings as follows: two letters (L 399, 400), two tracts on 'velle', one a repetition of those written before the gap, a repetition of the deathbed confession, another letter (L 401), a draft of a part of Anselm's tract 'De concordia', Anselm's epitaph on

tion of L_2 by symbols and instructions in the margin.[12] Two poems in praise of Anselm are also to be found in L_a. The second of these is introduced by the following rubric: 'Item versus de eodem praesulis Anselmi quem nuper obisse dolemus'. If 'nuper' is understood as 'recently', just as Anselm himself had used it e.g. in AEp 104, it appears that L_a was written shortly after Anselm's death on 21 April 1109, but that L_1 and L_2 were written during his lifetime.

The Bec tradition of part I of Anselm's letter collection of V_1 took over part II of the collection of L_2 in order to form V_2 without taking cognizance of possible duplications of letters or the need for inserting letters of the Bec tradition into the Canterbury tradition.

At the end of this brief survey of the genesis of the collection of Anselm's letters the following stemma may sum up the relationship of the main manuscripts containing this collection.

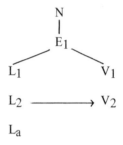

The final edition which Anselm made of his letters is to be found in L. It comprises 389 letters. The most recent modern edition of Anselm's works and letters by F. S. Schmitt contains 475 letters. In his edition Dom Schmitt excluded a considerable number of spurious letters which had found their way into the collection by various means during the course of centuries.[13] Indeed, had Anselm kept all the letters written to him requesting a reply, his collection would have been much larger still since in at least 120 letters he refers to some written supplication as the cause for his written reply.[14]

In all there are therefore some 206 letters — 86 items from Dom Schmitt's edition and 120 items referred to — that did not find their way into L. This would amount

Hugh, a fragment of a tract on the presence of God in the Blessed Sacrament, a distich of two lines, a legal document and a repetition of the first poem in praise of Anselm. For a detailed account see Walter Fröhlich, 'The Genesis of the Collection of St Anselm's Letters', *American Benedictine Review* 1984. There are thirteen letters in L_a: L 390 = AEp 193; L 391 = AEp 411; L 392 = AEp 331; L 393 = AEp 212; L 394 = AEp 255; L 395 = AEp 202; L 396 = AEp 200; L 397 = AEp 440; L 398 = AEp 207; L 399 = AEp 471; L 400 = AEp 472; L 401 = AEp 469; L 402 = AEp 475. L 399, L 400 and L 401 are duplicating L 388, L 389 and L 387 which are the last entries into L before L_a was added.

[12] These letters are referred into L_2: L 390, L391, L 392, L 393, L 394, L 398.

[13] F. S. Schmitt, 'Die echten und unechten Stücke der Korrespondenz Anselms von Canterbury', *RB* 65, 1955, 218-27 = *AOO* 204*-212*.

[14] See e.g. AEp 4, 6, 9, 10, 11, 12, 13, 15, 17, 23, 24, 35, 36, 38, 40, 42, 43, 45, 46, 52, 53, 57, 58, 60, 61, 65, 73, 77, 80, 83, 85, 87, 88, 97, 100, 109, 113, 118, 121, 132, 138, 147; 148, 161, 162, 163, 164, 166, 173, 175, 186, 187, 191, 192, 204, 209, 218, 223, 232, 233, 246, 247, 250, 254, 262, 263, 264, 292, 293, 294, 298, 299, 300, 301, 305, 307, 315, 316, 319, 320, 322, 323, 327, 328, 329, 330, 331, 333, 334, 343, 345, 347, 348, 349, 355, 356, 357, 361, 363, 374, 375, 376, 379, 395, 399, 406, 407, 413, 415, 416, 417, 418, 419, 421, 425, 432, 433, 440, 447, 451, 457, 458, 460.

to about 30 per cent of the items of Anselm's total correspondence or nearly 53 per cent as compared to the collection entered into L. For this reason it seems obvious that Anselm carefully selected from the mass of his correspondence and diligently compiled a collection of the letters he considered worth preserving.

Between the 389 letters of L — Anselm's final collection of his correspondence — and the 475 letters of the recent Anselmi Opera Omnia in which Dom Schmitt included all known items of Anselmian correspondence, there is a difference of 86 letters.[15] Why were they not included in L? Was L purely a random selection or did Anselm omit these letters because he regarded them as unworthy of preservation or unfitting for the purpose of his final collection?

A detailed examination of these omitted letters will attempt to provide clues and reasons for their omission and may point to Anselm's method and intention in compiling his collection.

The eighty-six letters not to be found in L can be split into two groups: twelve date from the period while Anselm was prior and abbot of Bec, the remaining seventy-four to the time of his archiepiscopal pontificate.

The first group of twelve letters omitted from L all date from Anselm's time as prior and abbot of Bec.[16] One is received from, and all the others are sent to, ecclesiastics — including two to Archbishop Lanfranc and two to Pope Urban. Ten of these letters deal with pastoral problems and contain advice to abbots and other monks on how to deal with excommunicated persons, with married priests or with secretly penitent priests. Anselm also intercedes with heads of monasteries on behalf of other monks and advises monks on their day-to-day problems. These letters were most likely omitted from L because of their relative unimportance, their purely local relevance, their rather lenient treatment of sinning priests which clashed with Anselm's rigorous attitude of later years, or because of some criticism Anselm may have made or demonstrated with regard to Archbishop Lanfranc.

The two letters sent to Pope Urban (AEp 126, 127) deal with Bishop Fulk of Beauvais who had been a monk of Bec. Abbot Anselm had consented to his uncanonical promotion by appointment of King Philip I of France in 1088. Having gained pardon for his uncanonical promotion from Pope Urban, and having been reinstated as Bishop of Beauvais, he was unable to administer his diocese for various reasons. In AEp 126 Anselm begs Urban's help for Fulk and in AEp 127 he implores the pope secretly to relieve Fulk of the burden of episcopal office which he is too weak to bear. He ends this letter: 'If it pleases you I wish and beg that this letter be for your eyes alone.' It seems likely that this embarrassing affair caused the exclusion of these letters from L. A third letter dealing with this problem — written when Anselm was archbishop of Canterbury — AEp 193, was also omitted from L, probably for the same reason. The positive suppression of these letters is confirmed by evidence supplied by the MS itself. There would have been enough space for both letters on fol. 54 of L. The folio between the present folios 53 and 54: that is to say, the original fol. 54 bearing these two letters has been removed, probably following

---

15 These are AEp 18, 26, 27, 63, 64, 65; 88, 123, 124, 126, 127, 145; 148, 150, 151, 152, 155, 159, 163, 164, 165, 166, 168, 169, 172, 173, 174, 175, 176, 177, 178, 179, 181, 183, 184, 190, 195, 204, 205, 208, 209, 215, 216, 224, 225, 226, 239, 282, 284, 304, 305, 310, 337, 348, 351, 352, 362, 363, 365, 366, 367, 373, 398, 407, 437, 438, 439, 442, 453, 454, 456, 457, 468, 459, 460, 470, 473 and the ten letters from La: AEp 193, 200, 202, 207, 212, 255, 331, 411, 440, 475. See footnote 11 above.
16 AEp 18, 26, 27, 63, 64, 65; 88, 123, 124, 126, 127, 145.

Anselm's instructions. AEp 193, also omitted from L, was later added as the first item in L$_a$.[17]

The seventy-four letters written when Anselm was archbishop of Canterbury and which are not to be found in L, are too numerous to be examined individually. These letters can be divided into nine groups which will account for fifty-seven of them while seventeen will be left undiscussed.

1. There is a large batch of nineteen letters which were all sent to the monks of Bec as a community or to individual members of it.[18] Some were forwarded via Bec to other individuals i.e. to Bishop Gilbert of Evreux (159), Countess Ida of Boulogne (167) and Archbishop Hugh of Lyon (176). According to Dom Schmitt this is why they were preserved in V, forming the Bec tradition of Anselm's letter collection.[19] It does not, however, answer the question why they were not preserved in L at Canterbury since they were written there. Having collected his letters for some ten years up to that time and having compiled them into N of 1090 and the later E$_1$ in 1092/93, Anselm almost certainly kept drafts and copies of the letters he sent to his monastery following his investiture as archbishop of Canterbury on 6 March 1093.

A review of the subject matter of these letters may provide some clue to the reason for their omission from L. A few were written in reply to the widespread gossip about Anselm's cupidity for the archbishopric (156, 159, 160, 164). This gossip seems to have been common in and around Bec, in the diocese of Evreux and in the whole duchy of Normandy. Anselm saw himself repeatedly forced to protest his innocence and lack of cupidity when he travelled to England in summer 1092 and to emphasise his surprise at being made archbishop in March 1093 by King William II, by the clergy and people, the bishops and barons of the Anglo-Norman kingdom (148). In their persistent demand for him to accept the burden of archiepiscopal office he perceived the will of God which he was obliged to obey. Despite Anselm's assurances a number of the community of Bec were not convinced and refused their consent to his relinquishing the abbatial office in order to accept the archbishopric of Canterbury (150, 155). They pointed out that they were bound to him in obedience and he to them for ever. Anselm replied that his obedience to God transcended his commitment to the community but on the other hand he demanded their obedience in accepting his choice in the election of his successor. Moreover, he expected their continued obedience to him for the rest of his life, even after the election of a new abbot. In fact, the monk Boso, disregarding the authority of the new abbot, obediently followed Anselm's call to Canterbury (174, 209).

In order to assure that his nominee was elected as abbot of Bec, Anselm suggests a candidate in AEp 157 which is included in L. However two letters in which he assures the duke's consent as well as the king's protection (164) and the help of an old friend (163) for the election of his protegé are missing from L. Did he suppress these in order to conceal the extent of his interference? His demands in this connection contravene the Rule of St Benedict which does not require any bond of obedience between an abbot and members of the community after the abbot's departure from the monastery, but which postulates the free election of a new abbot by the members of the community. The long-drawn-out procedure of electing William of

---

[17] This letter fills four lines above and six lines below the margin as well as the usual writing area of two columns of 31 lines on fol. 160v and spills five lines right across into the bottom margin of fol. 161r.

[18] AEp 148, 150, 151, 152, 155, 163, 165, 166, 173, 174, 178, 179, 205, 209.

[19] See *AOO* 156*-162*.

Beaumont as Anselm's successor, from August to October 1093, amply demonstrates the community's resentment at Anselm's intrusion in this matter.

Anselm's exclusion of these letters from L could point to the fact that he felt his image might be damaged by their publication, or the realisation that his too-frequent refutations of greed for the archbishopric might raise suspicion that he did indeed protest too much!

2. The next group of eight letters which are not preserved in L are written to Bishop Osmund of Salisbury and various members of convents in his diocese: two to Gunhilda, daughter of King Harold and nun at Wilton (168, 169), two to Abbess Eulalia of Shaftsbury (183, 337), one to the nun M., the daughter of Earl Richard of Clare (184) and three to Bishop Osmund (177, 190, 195).[20] At first sight it is surprising that these letters to nuns were not entered into L. They abound in advice and encouragement to persevere step by step towards the celestial kingdom by leading a good life as a spouse of Christ, abandoning the secular world of sin and misery. Yet Anselm's first letter to Bishop Osmund in spring 1094 might hold the reason for their exclusion.

Anselm intimates to the bishop of Salisbury that pastoral care and canon law ought to have moved him to act in regard to a certain 'filia perdita'. The lady here referred to is Eadgyth, 'filia regis Scotorum'. Eadgyth was the daughter of Malcolm, king of Scotland and Margaret, the kinswoman of Edward, of the true royal family of England, and niece of Edgar the Atheling.[21] She had possibly come to England with her aunt Christina in 1086. In 1093 both were at Wilton where Christina was a nun. King Malcolm had never intended his daughter to become a nun. In fact, since she was at the marriageable age of about fifteen she played an important part in his political plans and was to be married to Count Alan Rufus, lord of Richmond and most powerful baron in the north of England. This planned marriage came to nothing, however, since Alan Rufus became involved with the nun Gunhilda, whom he abducted from her convent in Wilton, and he died on 4 August 1093. His brother, Count Alan Niger, who succeeded him not only in his estates but also in his matrimonial plans also died soon after this.[22] The nun Gunhilda seems to have returned to Wilton as she was later remembered with honour there.[23]

The proposal of marriage with Eadgyth, then known as Mathilda, was taken up by King Henry I in 1100 as a calculated political move. In order to open the way for the planned marriage Anselm had to conduct a complicated procedure to prove that Mathilda/Eadgyth had never been a nun although she had worn the veil. For his part in the investigation Anselm was harshly criticised. Eadmer reports that many people maligned Anselm, saying that he had not kept the path of strict right in this matter.[24] After Mathilda's marriage to King Henry on 11 November 1100 Anselm

---

[20] According to F. S. Schmitt AEp 177, 183, 184, 190, 195 form a small local collection preserved on folios 67 and 68 in Cambridge, Trinity College Ms B. I. 37, see F. S. Schmitt, 'Zur Überlieferung der Korrespondenz Anselms von Canterbury', *RB* 43, 1931, 230-8; AEp 337 is in M and AEp 168 and 169 in Trier, Stadtbibliothek MS 728; see also André Wilmart, *RB* 38, 1926, 331-4, footnote 3.

[21] ASC 1100.

[22] See David C. Douglas, *William the Conqueror*, London 1964, 267-9, 426.

[23] See 'William of Malmesbury', *Vita Wulfstani*, ed. R. R. Darlington, Camden Society, 3rd series, 40, 1928, 34.

[24] Eadmer 121.

became her spiritual advisor. A large number of letters bear witness to their relationship thereafter.[25]

Having referred to this lady as a 'filia perdita' in the early stages of his pontificate this letter may have been embarrassing for Anselm when he enjoyed the queen's close friendship in later years. Moreover, the inclusion of this letter and those connected with it might have stirred the sleep of dormant critics and blown about the dust of past scandals. Such considerations would explain the omission of these eight letters from L.

3. The complete collection of Anselm's letters contains fifty-four which name King Henry or Queen Mathilda as sender or recipient. Eight of these, which not only bear the names of the king or queen but also that of Pope Paschal II as sender or receiver, are omitted from L.[26]

King Henry started this correspondence in January 1101 by congratulating Pope Paschal on his promotion (215). He offered friendship, obedience and the payment of Peter's Pence as his predecessors had done. In return he expected to hold his kingdom unimpaired like his predecessors. At the end of the same year he requested the pallium for Archbishop Gerard of York from the pope (221). In reply Paschal praised Henry for the good beginning of his reign and admonished him to abstain from investitures for the sake of the liberty of the Church (224). The pope demonstrated by the authority of Holy Scripture and the Fathers that the right of investiture of bishops and abbots belonged to the Church and not to kings. He promised to grant the king whatever he asked for provided he gave up investitures (216).

In November 1103, after the failure of the four embassies to Rome in order to obtain a mitigation of the papal decrees on lay investiture and the homage of clerics, the pope resumed direct relations with the king, congratulating him on the birth of his first-born son and heir William. He once more admonished the king to abandon investitures (305). A year later Paschal assured Henry of his care for his salvation. He informed him that he was retaining his messengers until the following Lenten synod (1105) so that his queries on homage and investiture might be answered according to the will of God. He chided the king for having sent Anselm into exile once more and also for having despoiled him of his possessions. The pope praised the king, however, because the decrees of the Westminster Council of 1102 were being implemented (348). A few months later — January/February 1105 — the pope admonished the king for the third time not to despise the Church, to receive Anselm back according to the papal decrees and to allow Anselm to publish them, to protect the Church in her lawful liberty and to give up his evil advisors, two of whom he was planning to excommunicate (351). At the same time the pope urged Queen Mathilda to persuade her husband to abandon investitures and to obey the will of God so that he might not lose what God had given him. He warned her about the king's evil advisors and their imminent excommunication (352). These letters represent the preserved correspondence between the king/queen and the pope. They are all omitted from L. Other letters included in L hint at even further items of this correspondence which have not yet come to light.[27]

The fact that the pope's correspondence with King Henry and Queen Mathilda is excluded from L recalls Anselm's letter to Thidricus in 1105 in which he replies

---

[25] AEp 242, 243, 246, 288, 296, 317, 320, 321, 323, 346, 347, 384, 385, 395, 400, 406; see also F. S. Schmitt, *RB* 43, 1936, 231-4.
[26] AEp 215, 216, 221, 224, 305, 348, 351, 352.
[27] See e.g. AEp 315, 318, 323, 368.

to the latter's enquiry thus: 'Litteras quas quaeris regis ad papam, non tibi mitto, quia non intelligo utile esse, si serventur' (379). This letter to Thidricus seems most likely to refer to the latter's work of compiling the collection of the archbishop's letters and copying them into L. This work had been going on since about 1105. While Anselm was forced to suffer his second exile he sent these instructions to Thidricus who obediently followed them by omitting all but one of the items (323) of the correspondence between the king, the queen and Pope Paschal II from L.[28]

This correspondence was not entirely suppressed, however, since six of these eight letters are to be found in a separate integral collection of twenty-three letters from Christ Church Canterbury.[29] The pope's cautious negotiations with the king and his lenient treatment of him while Anselm was suffering the hardship of exile for having upheld the pope's decrees might well be the reason for Anselm's exclusion of this correspondence from L.

4. Also missing from L are the two letters from the pope (282) and Cardinal John (284) of December 1102. Paschal reminded Anselm of the condemnation of simony by the Council of Bari and restated his advice on married priests and deacons. Cardinal John thought it necessary to encourage Anselm to defend the right of the Church against the king and the false bishops. In view of the second exile which Anselm was suffering because of his defence of the liberty of the Church in England and the propagation of its reform these letters must have irked him somewhat, which would explain their exclusion from the main collection of his letters.[30]

5. A small batch of three very short letters representing the correspondence between Bishop Lambert of Arras and Anselm is also omitted from L. In the first of these letters Anselm asked Lambert for safe conduct for a papal cleric through his diocese (437). In reply Lambert enquired about Anselm's health and sent greetings to Dom Baldwin (438). Anselm replied very briefly that he was healthy in body but suffering from growing weakness (439).

Anselm's contacts with Flanders and Arras in particular had been intensive ever since Girard, the moneyer of Arras, and Baldwin had entered the monastery at Bec.[31] Bishop Lambert, together with the exiled Anselm, was present at the synod of Rome in 1099 when Urban pronounced sentence of excommunication on 'all lay persons who conferred investitures of churches, all persons accepting such investitures from their hands and all persons who consecrated to the office of any preferment so given'.[32] Moreover, during his stay in Rome Anselm, in the face of some

---

[28] R. W. Southern, *St Anselm and his biographer*, Cambridge 1963, 68 n is of different opinion. He holds that 'there is not the slightest reason to think that this letter AEp 379 refers to the making of this or any other collection of letters'. In his judgement R. W. Southern merely relied on palaeographic evidence, see Walter Fröhlich, 'The Genesis of Anselm's collection of letters', see footnote 3.

[29] This is British Library, MS Add. 32091; for a description of the manuscript see Walter Holtzmann, *Papsturkunden in England*, vol. 1, Berlin 1930/31, 166-7, 221-31. The letters are AEp 216 = Add. 5; AEp 224 = Add. 10; AEp 305 = Add. 16; AEp 348 = Add. 17; AEp 351 = Add. 18; AEp 352 = Add. 19; AEp 215 and 221 are preserved in *Quadripartitus*, ed. Felix Liebermann, Halle 1892, 151-2.

[30] They are preserved: AEp 282 = M 83, AEp 284 = Add. 12.

[31] See AEp 14, 15, 23, 96, 164; 124, 151, 223, 284, 339, 349, 367, 371, 377, 378, 390, 397, 430, 438, 462; 86, 180, 248, 249, 298.

[32] Eadmer 114. Anselm sent three Paschal-letters AEp 222, 281, 353 to Lambert. These papal letters to Anselm are in accordance with the decrees of Urban's synod of 1099 and represent Paschal's hard line on investitures. Anselm included them into L as L 162, L 226 and L 287 and sent copies of them to Flanders. They were incorporated into a collection of canonical material

opposition, had helped to secure papal promotion of John, the archdeacon of Arras, to the see of Térouane. Anselm and the bishop of Arras had become close friends as Anselm's letter of summer 1103 to Dom Conus, included in L, testifies (285).

The final expression of the intimate friendship between Anselm and Lambert can be perceived in the fact that after Anselm's death the monks of Christ Church Canterbury sent the late archbishop's personal manuscript of his works to Arras where it is still kept.[33] Despite this close connection with Arras these three short letters were omitted from L, probably because of their triviality.

6. Shortly after the Council of Westminster at Whitsun 1108 Anselm wrote to Pope Paschal requesting confirmation for the Council's decision to divide the diocese of Lincoln and to create a new bishopric of Ely (441). The see was to be established at the abbey of Ely and the monks were to assist the bishop as cathedral chapter.[34] Paschal's letters to King Henry and Archbishop Anselm granting and confirming the creation of the new see of Ely and the nomination of Hervey of Bangor as first bishop are not included in L. These four letters (457, 458, 459, 460) were all issued at Troia on 21 November 1108. Allowing at least eight weeks for a winter journey from Troia near Foggia in southern Italy to England they would not have been delivered until January or February 1109 after work on manuscript L had been completed and it was being copied in its turn. They might not even have arrived before Anselm's death in April. They were never incorporated into any copy of the Anselmian letter collection.[35]

7. Another group of five more letters is missing from L. These letters are part of the correspondence dealing with the renewed outbreak of the primatial controversy between Canterbury and York following the promotion of Thomas of Beverley to the see of York after the death of Archbishop Gerard on 27 May 1108.

The whole correspondence on this issue numbers thirteen letters, eight of which are in L.[36] Three of the missing letters are from Thomas, the elect of York, and the Chapter of York to Anselm at Canterbury. They dispute the archbishop's right to demand a profession of obedience from the elect before his consecration at the primate's hands (453, 454, 456).[37] Another letter (470) from the king to Anselm requests him to defer the consecration of the elect of York until Easter 1109 so that after his return to England he himself might settle the case between the two metropolitans.[38] Since the letters from York demonstrate the York opinion in this dispute and the king did not side wholeheartedly with the claim of Canterbury it would seem likely that the open and veiled threats to the primatial claim of the

---

of the bishopric of Térouane in the second half of the twelfth century being letters 11, 12 and 13 therein. Max Sdralek dealt with the material in *Wolfenbüttler Fragmente*, Münster 1891, 55-9. It seems very unlikely that Lambert received more than these three letters otherwise they would have been entered into this collection, see also *Councils and Synods*, ed. Dorothy Whitelock, Martin Brett, Christopher N. L. Brooke, Oxford 1981, vol. i, 658, 660.

[33] Arras, Stadtbibliothek MS 484, catalogue nr. 805; see *AOO* 91*-94*, 213*.

[34] AEp 441 = L 370.

[35] They are 6210, 6211, 6212, 6213 in P. Jaffe, S. Löwenfeld, *Regesta Pontificum Romanorum*, vol. i, Leipzig 1885.

[36] AEp 443 = L 367; AEp 444 = L 368; AEp 445 = L 369; AEp 455 = L 376; AEp 464 = L 382; AEp 465 = L 383; AEp 471 = L 388 and again in L$_a$, L 399; AEp 472 = L 389 and again in L$_a$, L 400.

[37] They are in *Hugh the Chanter, the history of the Church of York 1066-1127*, ed. Charles Johnson, Oxford 1961, 19 = AEp 453; 20 = AEp 454; AEp 456 = Eadmer 204.

[38] AEp 470 = Eadmer 205.

archbishop of Canterbury were the grounds for the omission of these letters from the final edition of Anselm's letters in L. Therefore it is surprising that Anselm's letter to Rannulf of Durham, representing the Canterbury point of view in this controversy (442), is also missing from the collection.[39] In this letter Anselm states that Turgot, the elect of St Andrews in Scotland, could not be consecrated by anybody but the archbishop of Canterbury as long as Thomas, the elect of York, had not received his consecration at Canterbury.

8. Five of the thirteen letters which constitute the correspondence with Archbishop Gerard of York are omitted from L.[40] The first of these (255) was written by Gerard to Anselm after the Council of Westminster 1102. He informed Anselm that clerics were spurning the statutes of the Council and sought his help against those who evaded the canons through sophistry. He also confessed a sin of simony he had once committed. This letter demonstrated Gerard's zeal for church reform and his personal repentance.

However, after the return of Gerard and the bishops of Norwich and Chester from Rome in summer 1102 the relationship between Anselm and Gerard deteriorated considerably. The royal envoys delivered a report on their negotiations with Pope Paschal about the mitigation of the decrees forbidding lay investiture which was vehemently contradicted by Anselm's messengers. The pope refuted the bishops' report as a lie and excommunicated the royal envoys and anybody who had received investiture or had consecrated those thus invested since August 1102. Gerard caused further disagreement when, at the king's command, he was prepared to consecrate the recently invested bishops of Winchester, Hereford and Salisbury after Anselm had refused their consecration on the ground of the papal decrees of 1099, confirmed by Paschal in 1101 and 1102.[41] The letter from Paschal to Gerard in spring 1105 (354) reprimanding him for his wrongdoing and for not having been a support to Anselm is indeed included in L. Gerard's reply (362), which is not included in L, points out that the papal charge was based on false reports and that he had always favoured Anselm's cause. In summer and winter 1105/6 Gerard sent two letters to Anselm informing him that since he had found the truth he and many others would be obedient to the archbishop (363) and admitting that he now perceived the danger of lay investiture (373) he begged Anselm's prayers to assist him in his good intentions. In spring 1108 Gerard sought Anselm's help at the recommendation of Pope Paschal (440). These last four letters, demonstrating Gerard's conversion to the pope's and Anselm's position on investiture and his renewed harmony with the pope are missing from L. They and the letter of 1102 are all favourable to Gerard.

The remaining seven letters of this correspondence which are included in L create a negative image of Archbishop Gerard of York as a wicked, bickering and obstinate man. Only one letter of late 1105 somewhat mitigates this picture: in this together with other bishops, Gerard beseeched Anselm to return to England and promised him their help (386).

It would appear that Anselm omitted this correspondence with Gerard, his ecclesiastical opponent in the investiture dispute, even though it might have improved the bad impression conveyed by the other letters of Gerard's correspondence retained

---

[39] AEp 442 = M 102.
[40] AEp 238, 250, 253, *255*, 256, 283, 326, 354, *362, 363, 373*, 386, *440*. Those in italics are omitted from L. They are preserved: AEp 255 = L 394; AEp 362, 363, 373, = *Quadripartitus* 155-9; AEp 440 = L 397.
[41] See AEp 216, 219, 222, 224, 281.

in L. This must support the feeling that there was method in Anselm's omissions. Was the injury inflicted by Gerard's behaviour and actions during the controversy still rankling?

9. Three more items in the list of omitted letters level harsh criticism at Anselm for his prolonged absence from the see of Canterbury and the Church of England due to his second exile from December 1103 to September 1106.[42] A member of the community of Christ Church Canterbury, possibly Prior Ernulf himself, informed the archbishop about the increase of evil caused by his long absence from England (310). He declared that Anselm's absence was unbearable and stated that his presence was essential to any improvement. He entreated him urgently to return to England to resume his duties. Another anonymous person judged the long-drawn-out quarrel between King Henry and Archbishop Anselm as nothing but the illusion of diabolic tricks and complained that it was causing the destruction of the whole Church of the English. He blamed all the misery in England on Anselm's failure to return (365). Moreover, in a long poem Gilbert Crispin, abbot of Westminster and Anselm's friend, displayed to the absent archbishop the evils which had invaded the Church of England because of the pastor's absence and beseeched Anselm to return to his flock (366). Apart from these three voices there were many people who did not understand the reason for Anselm's refusal to return to England. Even after the agreement of L'Aigle between king and archbishop on investiture and homage (21 July 1105) Anselm delayed his return because he had not yet received the pope's endorsement to the compromise agreed upon there, nor his explicit permission to absolve excommunicated persons and to associate with them, even though he was aware that the English churches were suffering cruel treatment because of his absence. In their ignorance of the dealings between the pope, the king and the archbishop, a number of Anselm's friends, his episcopal colleagues (386, 387) and many other people also criticised the absent archbishop and informed him that his absence was causing more evil than good.[43] Since in Anselm's eyes this criticism was unjustified, it would appear that he excluded these letters in order not to mar the image of himself which he wanted to convey and preserve.

This survey of letters omitted from L has thus covered the contents of sixty-nine of the missing eighty-six letters.[44] Why did Anselm omit certain letters from the final edition of his letter collection in L? Apart from those omitted for their triviality or lack of general interest, the intention of these omissions on the one hand appears to suggest that everything was suppressed which might have caused embarrassment (criticism of Lanfranc, the case of Bishop Fulk of Beauvais, Anselm's part in arranging the king's marriage with Eadgyth/Mathilda) or revive criticism of Anselm's supposed cupidity for the wealthy archbishopric or of his long absences from England. Moreover, such letters which might have challenged Anselm's claim to be the sole advocate and protagonist for the reform and freedom of the Church (Henry, Gerard) and the mighty defender of the primatial claim of Canterbury were also omitted.

On the other hand, in the compilation of the last edition of his letters Anselm seems to have wished to supply a compendium of his thoughts on a great variety of spiritual matters as well as his ideas and the concepts underlying his disagreements with the kings of the Anglo-Norman realm on the issues of the 'usus atque leges'

[42] AEp 310, 365, 366.
[43] See Eadmer 162, 167, 171; AEp 386, 387.
[44] The following letters were not dealt with: AEp 181, 200, 202, 204, 207, 208, 212, 225, 226, 239, 255, 304, 331, 367, 398, 407, 411, 473.

and lay investiture as well as church reform and the primatial claim of Canterbury over York.

More important still, the letter collection displays Anselm as a faithful monk and ardent soldier of Christ who devoted his life totally to God and His service. He appears as a zealous labourer in creating a loving and truly Christian community of monks and as an active reformer of the Church of God in unity with the pope and in agreement with papal ordinance. Thus he set the example of the impeccable Christian prelate whose faultless public conduct was to serve as a model and a precedent for others to act in the same way. The image of his behaviour was intended to create binding customs and eventually good laws. Anselm's letter collection was to be a manual of examples for his own time and for the future.

Therefore manuscript L containing this letter collection is a monument to Anselm's righteousness and firm demeanour as a churchman vigorously pursuing the demand for 'libertas et reformatio ecclesiae' and defending the Church of God resolutely in the face of threats and isolation as well as personal suffering and disadvantages. From the survey of the letters omitted from this MS it would appear that Anselm took great care to suppress any correspondence which would have damaged the picture of himself which he intended for posterity.

WAR AND DIPLOMACY IN THE ANGLO-NORMAN WORLD THE REIGN OF HENRY I

C. Warren Hollister

It has long been understood that the institutional and constitutional history of medi-eval England was shaped by the fiscal demands of war and diplomacy. As in the later Middle Ages[1] so also in the Anglo-Norman era, the development of the royal admin-istration is, in J. O. Prestwich's words, 'intelligible only in terms of the scale and the pressing needs of war finance'.[2] Thus, the familiar administrative innovations of the Norman kings — exchequer, vice-regency courts, justices in eyre,[3] and much else — served the needs of a royal policy that was directed primarily toward military expansion or defence, a policy that required pensions to allies, diplomatic bribes, and massive outlays for military wages and the construction and expansion of castles. The immense scope of Anglo-Norman castle building has been made clear by Jean Yver, Derek Renn, and R. Allen Brown.[4] And recent studies by Marjorie Chibnall and J. O. Prestwich have disclosed the impressive size and decisive importance of the Anglo-Norman military household or *familia regis*, a rapid-deployment force of many hundreds of paid warriors who accompanied the king or garrisoned his strong-holds.[5]

Given that military expenses stimulated the precocious growth of Anglo-Norman government, two related points will be argued in this paper. First, issues of war and peace were of such overriding importance to the Norman kings as to shape royal policy not only in the area of fiscal administration but in a great variety of other areas as well. Second, and I am aware of the anachronism, war and peace in the Anglo-Norman world occurred in a predominantly 'international' context, by which I mean that they depended far less on the turbulent barons and feudal rebellions so dear to our older textbooks than on relations among kingdoms and major princi-palities. Although baronial rebellions were indeed a continual threat, it has not always been fully appreciated that many of them, increasingly as one moves from the eleventh century into the twelfth, occurred in the context of international politics.

---

[1] See, for example, M. H. Keen, *England in the Later Middle Ages*, London 1973; Michael Prestwich, *The Three Edwards: War and State in England, 1272-1377*, New York 1980; G. L. Harriss, *King, Parliament and Public Finance in Medieval England to 1369*, Oxford 1975.
[2] J. O. Prestwich, 'War and Finance in the Anglo-Norman State', *TRHS*, 5th ser. iv, 1954, 19-43.
[3] The profits of justice constituted about ten per cent of all English royal revenues in AD1130: Judith Green, 'Praeclarum et Magnificum Antiquitatis Monumentum: The Earliest Surviving Pipe Roll', *BIHR* lv, 1982, 16.
[4] Jean Yver, 'Les châteaux forts en Normandie jusqu'au milieu du XIIe siècle', *Bulletin de la Société des Antiquaires de Normandie*, liii, 1955-1956, 28-115; André Chatelain, *Donjons Romans des Pays d'Ouest*, Paris 1973; D. F. Renn, *Norman Castles in Britain*, 2nd edn, London 1973; R. Allen Brown, *English Medieval Castles*, 3rd edn, London 1976.
[5] J. O. Prestwich, 'The Military Household of the Norman Kings', *EHR* xcvi, 1981, 1-35; Marjorie Chibnall, 'Mercenaries and the *familia regis* under Henry I', *History* lxii, 1977, 15-23.

The general pattern of political interaction between major power centres is well known. Kate Norgate long ago traced in meticulous detail the prolonged conflicts between Anjou, Blois, Normandy and England, and Walther Kienast provided a masterful account of political relations between the kings of medieval France and Germany together with their major princes.[6] More recently, David Bates and Elizabeth Hallam have provided valuable studies of relations among the French territorial principalities, while David Douglas emphasised the point some years ago that William the Conqueror's path to Hastings was cleared by the deaths, in 1060, of King Henry I of France and Count Geoffrey Martel of Anjou.[7] In later years, when France and Anjou regained political coherence, the Conqueror and his successor William Rufus fought often, and not always successfully, against these powers.[8]

Nevertheless, the defence of the Anglo-Norman dominions has proven less absorbing to historians of our century than to the Norman kings. Neither our current interest in social history nor our traditional interest in national history has encouraged us to linger over the campaigns of English monarchs in France. But when we do attempt to interpret the policies of Anglo-Norman kings in the light of their interests rather than our own, a number of seemingly unrelated events begin to shift focus.

Two of the most celebrated issues in the history of the Anglo-Norman Church, for example, reached their climax and resolution amidst the two greatest military crises of Henry I's reign. The English investiture controversy was resolved in 1105-1106, precisely the years of Henry I's all-out campaigns to conquer Normandy. And the Canterbury-York dispute achieved its greatest intensity and its resolution during the years 1118-1120, when Henry's defence of Normandy against the most formidable coalition of his reign ended in a treaty with France which, but for the subsequent disaster of the White Ship, might well have ensured peace for the next generation.

The best contemporary witnesses of these two ecclesiastical crises, Eadmer of Canterbury and Hugh the Chantor of York,[9] were aware of Henry's concurrent military-diplomatic activities, but dimly so. Their attention was riveted on the affairs of their respective churches and archbishops. Modern church historians have acknowledged the relationship between the ecclesiastical controversies and Henry's wars but without entirely appreciating the paramount importance of these particular wars to the fate of the Anglo-Norman monarchy. It seems clear, however, that although Henry was very interested in both ecclesiastical disputes, he would have viewed them as altogether secondary to his conquest of Normandy in 1105-6, his political survival in 1118-1119, and the recognition of his lordship over Normandy through an international peace settlement in 1120.

[6] Kate Norgate, *England under the Angevin Kings*, 2 vols, London 1887, vol. i; Walther Kienast, *Deutschland und Frankreich in der Kaiserzeit (900-1270): Weltkaiser und Einzelkönige*, 2nd edn, 3 vols, Stuttgart 1974-1975: an excessive degree of ethnic-nationalistic ideology does not rob this work of its value; Michel Bur, *La formation du comté de Champagne, v. 950-v. 1150*, Nancy 1977, who discusses 'La politique des blocs princiers . . .': 290; and J.-F. Lemarignier, *Recherches sur l'hommage en marche et les frontières féodales*, Lille 1945, 34-72.

[7] D. C. Douglas, *William the Conqueror*, London 1964, 173-5; David Bates, *Normandy before 1066*, London 1982, 65-85; Elizabeth Hallam, 'The King and the Princes in Eleventh-Century France', *BIHR* liii, 1980, 143-56. See also the important articles by Robert Fossier, Marcel Pacaut, K. F. Werner, and Lucien Musset in *Les principautés au moyen âge: Communications du Congrès de Bordeaux en 1973, revues et corrigés*, Bordeaux 1979, 9-59.

[8] Douglas, 211-44.

[9] Eadmer; Hugh the Chantor, *The History of the Church of York, 1066-1127*, ed. Charles Johnson, London 1961.

Operating on this premise, let us first re-examine the Canterbury-York dispute in the years between 1118 and 1120. It is likely that Henry I had no strong convictions about the quarrel. He would have found it, in Frank Barlow's words, inconvenient and embarrassing.[10] It has been said that the Norman kings supported Canterbury over York because of their fear of northern separatism,[11] but in Henry's time, when the north was peaceful and relations with Scotland downright affectionate, there can have been no such fear. Nevertheless, for all his skill at equivocation and creative delay, Henry could not forever evade his responsibility to decide between the primacy of Canterbury and the autonomy of York. To review briefly, Thurstan, on his election to the archbishopric of York in 1114, had refused to profess obedience to Ralph d'Escures, archbishop of Canterbury. Ralph responded in the usual way by refusing to consecrate Thurstan. Under intense pressure from both sides Henry decided for Canterbury, probably because an opposite decision would have earned him more and stronger enemies. After four years of inconclusive manoeuvering, both archbishops were in Normandy where the king was fighting his war. In autumn 1119, Henry permitted Thurstan to visit the papal court which was then touring France. Pope Calixtus II consecrated Thurstan, seemingly to Henry's surprise and against his wishes. Henry thereupon prohibited Thurstan's return to England or Normandy. Thurstan stayed with the papal court, and in March 1120 Calixtus, on the verge of returning to Italy, granted him a written and sealed privilege — a papal bull — permanently exempting archbishops of York from the profession to Canterbury. Calixtus gave Thurstan another bull threatening an interdict on England and the suspension of Archbishop Ralph. At this, Henry relented and, after some further delay, readmitted Thurstan to his see.[12]

Let me now place these events in the context of Henry's military and diplomatic struggles. In 1115, shortly after the quarrel between the archbishops commenced, and immediately after obtaining oaths of fealty from the Norman magnates to his son and heir, William Adelin, Henry I tried to bribe Louis VI of France to make a formal concession of Normandy to William and accept his 'profession' for the duchy.[13] Louis would in effect have been renouncing Henry's nephew and enemy, William Clito, whose counter-claim served as the focal point of all opposition to Henry's rule. After some indecision Louis refused, and his refusal resulted ultimately in all-out war. By early 1118 Henry was engaged in a desperate campaign against the combined forces of Louis VI, Baldwin VII of Flanders, Fulk V of Anjou, and an ominous and growing number of rebellious Normans. There may well have been times when Henry would have regarded his contending archbishops as a pair of flies buzzing around the head of a gladiator fighting for his life. In December 1118, when Hugh the Chantor reports an exchange of icy words between Archbishops Ralph and Thurstan, other sources record the greatest defeat of Henry's career at the battle of Alençon.[14]

---

[10] Frank Barlow, *The English Church, 1066-1154*, London 1979, 41.

[11] Most recently, and with qualifications, by Mary Cheney in her important article, 'Some Observations on a Papal Privilege of 1120 for the Archbishops of York', *Journal of Ecclesiastical History* xxxi, 1980, 430.

[12] For a full account see Donald Nicholl, *Thurstan Archbishop of York (1114-1140)*, York 1964, 57-74, which must now be supplemented by Cheney, 'Papal Privilege of 1120', 429-39.

[13] *Liber Monasterii de Hyda*, ed. Edward Edwards, RS 1866, 309; see, more generally, C. Warren Hollister, 'Normandy, France, and the Anglo-Norman *Regnum*', *Speculum* li, 1976, 225-7.

[14] Hugh the Chantor, 60; Orderic, vi, 206-8; *Gesta consulum andegavorum: additamenta*, in *Chroniques des comtes d'Anjou et des seigneurs d'Amboise*, ed. Louis Halphen and René

Archbishop Thurstan, with his attractive blend of holiness and sophistication, was an old friend of Henry's — a veteran of the royal chapel and brother of one of Henry's most ardent supporters in the Norman war, Auduin bishop of Evreux. And Thurstan alone among the Anglo-Norman episcopate enjoyed the affection of Louis VI.[15] This fact may cast some light on Thurstan's otherwise mysterious reply in spring 1119 to Henry's entreaty that he return to England. 'If I stay here until you also return', Thurstan responded, 'I may be able to be of some use to you'.[16] Later in the year, after the decisive Anglo-Norman victory at Brémule, Henry let Thurstan depart for the papal court. The Canterbury sources state that Thurstan promised to refuse papal consecration whereas Hugh the Chantor denies it.[17] Whatever the case, Calixtus consecrated Thurstan at Reims, and according to Hugh the Chantor, Thurstan immediately began working through his friend, Cardinal Cuno of Praeneste, to urge Pope Calixtus to confer with Henry and to do all in his power to arrange the peace with France that Henry so desired.[18] The conference between Henry and Calixtus occurred a month later, in November 1119.[19] Chagrined by Thurstan's consecration without the profession, Eadmer reported a widespread opinion that Thurstan 'could never have presumed to behave as he did in so great a matter had he not noticed that the king was a willing party to it'.[20] Some evidently believed that Henry and Thurstan had an understanding from the beginning, which is possible but unlikely. It is true that Thurstan's consecration was irrelevant to Henry's interests though disastrous to Canterbury's, and that Henry's real advantage lay in appearing to back Canterbury stalwartly while availing himself of Thurstan's diplomatic talents. But in accepting papal consecration Thurstan was defying Henry's will, and even the most astute monarchs can lose their tempers on such occasions. Henry seems to have done so when he banished Thurstan from the Anglo-Norman dominions.

In spring 1120, immediately after obtaining the papal bull threatening England with an interdict and Archbishop Ralph with deposition, Thurstan visited Countess Adela of Blois and her son, Count Theobald II, Henry's nephew and military ally. Adela was Henry's favourite sister, Thurstan's spiritual daughter, and one of the most prudent politicians of her era. According to Hugh the Chantor's eyewitness report, Thurstan 'did not entirely conceal from them what he had done and what he carried'. News of the interdict threat reached Henry, but the papal letter itself was never presented to him; it was later preserved in the church of York as a memento of the victory.[21] Thereafter, Thurstan avoided the company of Louis VI 'out of prudence', because there was still strife between Louis and Henry,[22] but through the mediation of Cardinal Cuno the exiled archbishop is reported to have taken great pains to procure a peace between the two kings, 'being the man on the Norman side in whom Louis had the most confidence'.[23]

Thurstan's itinerary during the weeks following his visit to Adela suggests shuttle diplomacy. He immediately sought out Cardinal Cuno, then returned to confer with the countess while Cuno spent Easter (18 April) with Louis VI at Senlis. Two days

Poupardin, Paris 1913, 155-61.

15 Hugh the Chantor, 65.   16 Hugh the Chantor, 65.

17 Hugh the Chantor, 68-9; Eadmer, 255, followed by John of Worcester, *Chronicle*, ed. J. R. H. Weaver, Oxford 1908, 14.

18 Hugh the Chantor, 75.   19 Hugh the Chantor, 76-80; Orderic, vi, 282-90.

20 Eadmer, 257; cf. Nicholl, 64.   21 Hugh the Chantor, 91-2, 102-4.

22 Hugh the Chantor, 92.   23 Hugh the Chantor, 97.

after Easter, Thurstan again met with Cuno at Dammartin and then returned to Adela to help arrange for her entry into religious life, while at the same time contacting Henry through messengers.[24] A meeting was then arranged between Cuno and Henry on 30 May at the castle of Vernon on the Norman frontier, where Henry agreed to restore Thurstan to York provided that he would delay his return until Henry had squared matters with Canterbury.[25] Shortly thereafter the peace between Henry and Louis was ratified, and on essentially the terms that Henry had offered in 1115 before the war commenced. One must not permit the subsequent catastrophe of the White Ship to obscure the fact that the peace of 1120 was a dazzling diplomatic triumph for Henry I. And Simeon of Durham agreed with Hugh the Chantor that Thurstan had played the central role in the negotiations.[26] Without inferring deeper secrets than the sources disclose, I will only suggest that the papal interdict, leaked but never delivered, was not intended as a serious threat (for Calixtus, battling with the emperor and his antipope, needed Henry's support) but as a shield with which Henry could — and did — deflect the wrath of Canterbury when he permitted Thurstan to assume his archbishopric without the profession.[27] As the Anglo-Saxon chronicler observed, 'Archbishop Thurstan of York was reconciled to the king through the pope, and came into this country and received his bishopric, though it was very displeasing to the archbishop of Canterbury'.[28] It also seems unlikely that a person as deeply involved in the politics of her age as Adela of Blois would have taken the veil until the terms of a mutually acceptable peace between her son, her brother, and the king of France had been arranged.

Fifteen years earlier, the English investiture compromise was achieved under oddly similar circumstances: the threat of a major ecclesiastical sanction and the mediation of Adela of Blois, against the background of a full-scale military campaign. In 1105-6, Henry was directing all his efforts toward the conquest of Normandy from his bumbling older brother, Robert Curthose. Unlike the Canterbury primacy issue, the papal prohibition of lay investiture and the homage of prelates seized Henry's full attention. They were direct challenges to royal customs that Henry defended on the principle of good stewardship.[29] Pope Paschal retreated early from his opposition to homage,[30] but on the matter of investiture Henry and Paschal seemed equally intransigent. At the papal court at Rome in November 1103, Henry's envoy, William Warelwast, declared (according to Eadmer) that 'the king of the English will not, even at the loss of his kingdom, allow himself to be deprived of the investiture of churches', to which the pope replied, 'not even to save his life will Pope Paschal ever permit such a right with impunity'.[31] As a consequence of this impasse, Anselm,

---

[24] Hugh the Chantor, 92-3.

[25] Hugh the Chantor, 95-7.

[26] Simeon of Durham, *Opera Omnia*, ed. Thomas Arnold, 2 vols, RS 1882-1885, ii, 258; cf. *De gestis regum*, ii, 496 on the Peace of 1120: 'Veruntamen tam splendidae et excogitatae pacis serenum, tam omnium spes in speculam erectas, confudit humanae sortis varietas'.

[27] At Christmas, 1120, Henry explained to Archbishop Ralph and his suffragan bishops the consequences of not readmitting Thurstan: 'Intelligens archiepiscopus sagittam hanc prius in se infigi, episcopi vero ignominiam regi reputantes in regno suo Chriscianitatem interdici, ut eum revocaret et concesserunt et consiliati sunt': Hugh the Chantor, 100.

[28] *ASC*, AD 1120.

[29] See Henry I's letter to Paschal II: *Sancti Anselmi Cantuariensis Archiepiscopi Opera Omnia*, ed. F. S. Schmitt, Edinburgh 1946-61, v, ep. 215.

[30] R. W. Southern, *St Anselm and his Biographer*, Cambridge 1963, 171-4.

[31] Eadmer, 153. Both positions were overstated, as subsequent events disclosed.

no longer able to function in cooperation with both king and pope, went into exile at Lyons.[32]

He re-emerged suddenly a year and a half later and headed northward with the announced intention of excommunicating Henry I. At that precise moment Henry was engaged in his first full scale military campaign in Normandy, which he justified as an effort to save the Norman Church from the violence and anarchy permitted by Robert Curthose's misrule.[33] Amidst spreading rumours of the excommunication threat, and perhaps because of it, Henry's army suffered defections and his campaign halted.[34] Thereupon, through the mediation of the prudent Countess Adela, with whom Anselm discussed his excommunication plan during a long stopover at the court of Blois, Henry met Anselm at Laigle in south-eastern Normandy and negotiated a settlement. Henry retained the right to receive homage from his prelates but surrendered on the central issue of investiture.[35] In 1106 Paschal ratified the settlement, freeing Anselm to return to Canterbury and Henry to complete his conquest of Normandy.[36]

From this sketch, which radically condenses a controversy about which much has been written and much argued, it should be clear that Henry I yielded investitures because he valued Normandy more. Anselm had moved against him at the critical moment, and with the duchy at stake Henry gave in.[37] Anselm's own motive is much less clear, because of the extraordinarily murky explanations provided by Eadmer and by Anselm himself.[38] Perhaps he acted when he did for reasons unconnected with the Norman war, and his timing was a piece of good luck. Professor Sally Vaughn, on the other hand, has argued that Anselm deliberately struck at Henry when he was most vulnerable,[39] and I believe she is correct. Anselm was a great theologian and spiritual adviser; he was also a person of considerable experience in political affairs. He had spent all but the first three years of a long ecclesiastical career in important administrative offices – as prior and abbot of Bec, and, since 1093, as archbishop of Canterbury. He was acquainted with the policies and hopes of both Robert Curthose and Henry I and had twice assumed major military responsibilities in the defence of England against cross-channel invasion threats.[40] During

---

[32] Eadmer, 154-7. As Anselm and William Warelwast neared Lyons on their homeward trip, William told Anselm that Henry would receive him in England only if Anselm renounced the papal ban on lay investiture. Unwilling to ignore a direct papal command, Anselm settled in Lyons.

[33] Orderic, vi, 60-4, 86, 96, 284-6.

[34] Eadmer, 166; Orderic, vi, 78. According to Eadmer, Anselm's threat had prompted many to turn against a sovereign not too well loved.

[35] Eadmer, 166; *Vita Anselmi*, ed. R. W. Southern, Oxford 1962, 134-5; *Anselmi Opera*, ep. 388. Anselm was fully aware of the terms of the compromise (ep. 389); he regarded the settlement as 'so badly needed and so clearly right' (ep. 369) and asked the monks of Canterbury to pray that such concord might be effected between pope and king that he could be reconciled with both (ep. 376).

[36] *Anselmi Opera*, epp. 402, 428, 433; Eadmer, 182-4.

[37] Southern, *Anselm*, 176-7; Barlow, *English Church*, 299; Sally N. Vaughn, 'St Anselm and the English Investiture Controversy Reconsidered', *Journal of Medieval History* 6, i (1980): 73-6. It has often been said that in yielding investitures, Henry I relinquished little or no real power. Anselm himself had pointed this out in a letter to Henry's chief adviser, Robert count of Meulan: (*Anselmi Opera*, ep. 369); and Hugh the Chantor, 14, repeats the point.

[38] Eadmer, 163-4; *Anselmi Opera*, ep. 388.

[39] Vaughn, 'St Anselm', 73-6.

[40] In 1095, in the face of a cross-channel invasion threat, William Rufus had given Anselm the military command of southern England: *Anselmi Opera*, epp. 191-2; and Anselm had brought

his exile of 1103-1106, Anselm remained in close touch with England;[41] on one occasion he wrote to his friend William Giffard, bishop elect of Winchester, urging him not to betray a Norman castle to Henry as many others were doing.[42] It is difficult to believe that Anselm could have been unaware of the effect of his excommunication threat on Henry's Norman war. More probably, Anselm did not really intend to excommunicate Henry in 1105 any more than Calixtus II intended to lay England under interdict in 1120. Anselm would surely have realised as clearly as Henry did that the resolution of the English investiture controversy was inseparable from the campaign to conquer Normandy and reunify the Anglo-Norman dominions – a goal that Anselm warmly supported once the investiture issue was resolved.

During the twenty-nine years of Henry I's rule in Normandy, from his triumph over Curthose at Tinchebray in 1106 to his death in 1135, his overriding priority was the defence of his Anglo-Norman dominions, through peaceful diplomacy if possible, and⋅ the maintenance of order within them. Historians have credited Henry with maintaining the peace in England but not in Normandy where, as an American writer put it, he was afflicted with 'almost incessant warfare', and, according to a French writer, he battled 'ceaselessly and without definitive success against his perpetually rebelling barons'.[43] But a closer review of the narrative sources and their chronologies suggests that the peace of Henry's duchy was broken only twice – in the period around 1117-19 and in 1123-24 – and that Normandy enjoyed relative tranquillity for all but two or three years of his twenty-nine year rule.[44] Suger of Saint-Denis remarked that in c.1118 Louis VI invaded a land long accustomed to peace. Orderic Vitalis reported that in December 1135, just after Henry's death, Geoffrey of Anjou found abundant provisions in Normandy 'after a long peace under a good prince', and William of Malmesbury praised Henry for maintaining a peace such as Normandy had never before known, even in the days of William the Conqueror.[45]

Nevertheless, Henry's lordship of Normandy was challenged periodically by the hostile coalition of France, Anjou and Flanders, fighting on behalf of Robert Curthose's son, William Clito. It was challenged not only in the war years of 1117-19 and 1123-24 but on other occasions when Henry was obliged to use all his diplomatic talents to keep Normandy free of military violence – in 1109-13 when Louis VI vainly demanded Henry's homage, and again in 1127-28 when Louis installed William Clito as count of Flanders.

In view of these later conflicts, Henry's conquest of Normandy in 1105-1106

---

his knights to Henry I's army and camped with them in the field during Curthose's invasion of 1101: Eadmer, 127. On this last occasion Anselm threatened to excommunicate Curthose and used all his powers of persuasion to convince Henry's magnates to remain loyal to their king. Eadmer (127) went so far as to claim that without Anselm's intervention, Henry 'ea tempestate perdidisset jus Anglici regni'.

[41] E.g. *Anselmi Opera*, epp. 330, 337, 355, 357; he continued to attend to Canterbury affairs while in Lyons: epp. 331, 358-60.

[42] *Anselmi Opera*, ep. 322; cf. *ASC*, AD1104.

[43] Charles W. David, *Robert Curthose, Duke of Normandy*, Cambridge, Mass. 1920, 180; Josèphe Chartrou, *L'Anjou de 1109 à 1151*, Paris 1928, 7.

[44] C. Warren Hollister and Thomas K. Keefe, 'The Making of the Angevin Empire', *Journal of British Studies* xii, 1973, 4 and n.10.

[45] Suger, *Vie de Louis VI le Gros*, ed. Henri Waquet, Paris 1964, 184-6; Orderic, vi, 472; *De gestis regum*, ii, 476.

was marked by two rather odd circumstances. First, he accomplished the conquest without hindrance from France or Anjou. He evidently purchased the neutrality of the French monarchy, and in 1105 Geoffrey Martel — eldest son of Fulk IV of Anjou, who had associated him in the governance of the county — was leading a contingent in Henry's army alongside Elias count of Maine. Count Elias withdrew from the campaign around the time that Anselm, his friend and spiritual adviser, was threatening to excommunicate Henry I but returned in 1106 to lead the decisive charge at Tinchebray.[46] The second oddity is that after Tinchebray Henry I, a political realist not given to acts of self-defeating sentimentality, took pity on the three-year-old William Clito, and placed him under the protection of Elias of Saint-Saens, Curthose's son-in-law and devoted follower, whose chief castle was dangerously close to Normandy's north-eastern frontier.[47]

These two oddities can perhaps be explained by the fact that a fundamental shift of long-range consequence was occurring just then in the policies of both France and Anjou — a revival of royal and comital authority which, although gradual, underwent a sudden acceleration with the accessions of Louis VI in 1108 and Fulk V of Anjou in 1109.[48] Both these princes pursued energetically the goals which their fathers had sought only half-heartedly: the extension of control over castles — the all-important instruments of military and administrative authority — and the tightening of bonds of vassalage with their aristocratic subordinates through oaths of homage and fealty. French historians have viewed these policies as efforts to replace the banal authority inherited from the Carolingians, which had been in a state of advanced decay in the Ile de France since the 1030s and in Anjou since about 1060, with new, vertical lines of authority in the form of a feudal hierarchy.[49] Dr Elizabeth Hallam, in discussing the emergence of both the idea and reality of social hierarchy in later eleventh-century France, noted the close connection between the growth of Capetian feudal power and a new, aggressive attitude on the part of Louis VI on the royal lands and beyond them. Olivier Guillot, echoing Louis Halphen, noticed a similar and concurrent process occurring in Anjou.[50]

It would have been difficult for Henry I to foresee in 1106 the surge of French royal authority that began in 1108, or the parallel surge that followed Fulk V's accession in 1109.[51] Although Henry's affectionate treatment of William Clito involved

[46] Orderic, vi, 68, 78, 88-90; cf. *La chronique de Morigny (1095-1152)*, ed. Léon Mirot, 2nd edn, Paris 1912, 21; Suger, 106; *De gestis regum*, ii, 480. Geoffrey was killed in battle in May, 1106, well before Henry's return to Normandy for the campaign that culminated in his victory at Tinchebray: Chartrou, 3; on Elias's relationship to Anselm see *Anselmi Opera*, ep. 466.
[47] Orderic, vi, 92.
[48] Compare J.-F. Lemarignier, *Le gouvernement royal aux premiers temps capétiens (987-1108)*, Paris 1965, Éric Bournazel, *Le gouvernement capétien au XIIe siècle, 1108-1180*, Limoges 1975; Elizabeth M. Hallam, *Capetian France, 987-1328*, London 1980, 91-7, 111, 114-19; Chartrou, 26 and ff.; Louis Halphen, *Le comte d'Anjou au XIe siècle*, Paris 1906, 133-205; Olivier Guillot, *Le comte d'Anjou et son entourage au XIe siècle*, 2 vols, Paris 1972, i, 124, 352, 428-34.
[49] See in particular Guillot, i, 431-4, and for a valuable summary, Hallam, 'Kings and Princes in Eleventh-Century France', 143-56.
[50] Hallam, *Capetian France*, 95; Halphen, 203-4; Guillot, i, 433-4; cf. Karl Ferdinand Werner, 'Kingdom and Principality in Twelfth-Century France', in *The Medieval Nobility*, ed. Timothy Reuter, Amsterdam 1978, 266-7.
[51] I am using the word 'accession' loosely, to describe their acquisition of full authority over their dominions. Both men had earlier shared their fathers' titles and authority, yet the policy shifts occur just after their fathers' deaths. See Chartrou, 4; Achille Luchaire, *Louis VI le Gros: annales de sa vie et de son règne*, Paris 1890, 289-93 and no. 8.

a risk, it would have seemed a small one at a time when the great princes of France smiled benignly while Henry reforged the Anglo-Norman state. But Louis VI, immediately after his father's death, demanded Henry's homage for Normandy, along with the homage of other princes of France, and the neutralisation of two of Henry's frontier castles on the Norman bank of the Epte, Bray-et-Lû and, more importantly, the great stronghold at Gisors — both of which, according to Suger, Henry held in violation of an earlier agreement.[52] It is characteristic of Louis VI's lifelong policy that his initial hostilities with Henry I should result from demands involving castles and an act of homage. But Henry too was avidly interested in castles and homages and offered Louis neither. The two kings met in March, 1109,[53] at Neufles-St-Martin on the Epte, Louis having plundered and burned on the way the French holdings of Henry I's chief adviser, Robert count of Meulan.[54] The meeting resulted in an uneasy two-year truce followed by two years of war in France and Maine.[55]

Meanwhile Fulk V became sole count of Anjou on his father's death in 1109, and inherited Maine *jure uxoris* in 1110 on the death of Count Elias, Henry I's friend and *fidelis*. Unlike Elias, Fulk V rejected Henry's suzerainty over Maine and refused to do him homage for it.[56] Robert II count of Flanders joined the coalition against Henry but died soon afterwards of an injury incurred while campaigning with Louis VI. Indeed, several of the military and diplomatic confrontations between Henry and Louis were affected dramatically by the strange coincidence that four consecutive counts of Flanders — Robert II, Baldwin VII, Charles the Good, and William Clito — suffered violent deaths at crucial moments; but that is another story.

During the truce after the meeting at Neufles (1109-11), Henry in England and Louis in France attended to other matters while apparently encouraging one another's magnates to plot rebellion. In 1111 the struggle flared into open warfare — all of it outside Normandy — followed by a general peace settlement early in 1113 on terms altogether favourable to Henry.[57] That he was able to keep Normandy at peace during these years and win a triumphant settlement is both noteworthy and intriguing. His manoeuverings during these years are well worth examining, for they exemplify early twelfth-century diplomacy at its best. Henry won allies by means of bribes, intrigues and strategic marriages, and he discouraged potential rebels with the aid of a remarkably alert intelligence system. Orderic credits Henry with being so thoroughly familiar with secret plots against him as to astonish the plotters, and he observes

---

[52] Suger, 102-6. Gisors was built as a ducal castle during William Rufus's occupation of Normandy; afterwards Robert Curthose seems to have granted it as a fief to its ducal castellan, Theobald Pain (Orderic, v, 308, 309 n.3), who apparently held it at the time of Tinchebray but returned it to the ducal authority soon afterwards at Henry's urging and perhaps for a price (Suger, 102: Theobald Pain relinquished the castle to Henry 'tam blandiciis quam minis'). From the time that he assumed the governance of Normandy, it was Henry's policy to resume control of previously ducal lands and castles granted away by Curthose (Orderic, vi, 94). Suger's account of the conflicts between the two kings in and after 1109 is badly garbled, but it remains possible that Henry's negotiations with the French monarchy with respect to his conquest of Normandy included a promise not to restore Gisors to ducal control. On Louis' demand for homages, see Hollister, Anglo-Norman *Regnum*, 223 and n.121.

[53] Or just possibly April: Luchaire, no.72.

[54] Robert was count of Meulan in the French Vexin, lord of the Beaumont lands in Normandy, and earl of Leicester: see Sally N. Vaughn, 'Robert of Meulan and Raison d'Etat in the Anglo-Norman State, 1093-1118', *Albion* x, 1978, 352-73.

[55] Hollister, 'Anglo-Norman *Regnum*', 223-4.

[56] *ASC*, A D 1110.

[57] Hollister and Keefe, 'Making of the Angevin Empire', 7-8.

elsewhere, in connection with the quarrels of 1109-1113, that Henry swept away the designs of his enemies like cobwebs and crushed them without shedding the blood of his own men.[58]

Following Orderic's hints, one can reasonably suspect that this sweeping of cob-webs was exemplified by the singular abundance of arrests and forfeitures of Anglo-Norman magnates during the troubled years between 1109 and 1113. In 1110, as the Anglo-Saxon chronicler reports without explanation, Henry disseised and exiled William Malet, William Bainard, and Philip of Braose, the last-named being restored in 1112. At about the same time, 1110 or shortly thereafter, Roger of Abitôt, sheriff of Worcestershire and constable of Worcester castle, was deprived of his lands because, as William of Malmesbury explains, with headlong madness he ordered the assassin-ation of a royal official.[59] At about the same time (1109-c.1114) Robert of Lacy was deprived of his honour of Pontefract, while in Normandy Henry ordered the arrest of William Clito, who narrowly escaped capture at Saint-Saens and fled into exile with his guardian, Elias.[60] In 1112 Henry arrested and imprisoned Robert of Bellême and exiled William count of Evreux and William Crispin, restoring these last two magnates in the peace settlement of 1113.[61] The international implications of these moves are suggested by Orderic's assertion that Robert of Bellême was at the time of his arrest serving as an envoy of King Louis VI,[62] and by the kinship ties that linked William Crispin and William of Evreux with Amaury de Montfort and his nephew, Fulk V of Anjou. William of Evreux spent his exile in Anjou, and William Crispin would later turn up in Louis VI's army at Brémule.[63]

Conversely, Henry worked during these years to win the support of magnates in the dominions of his enemies. 'Many of the nobles of Maine', Orderic writes, 'went over to Henry's side, and after doing fealty surrendered their castles to him.'[64] One noble family from Maine may have been won over, or subsequently rewarded, by Henry's grant of the forfeited Lacy honour of Pontefract to Hugh of Laval.[65] Hugh was the uncle and guardian of Guy IV, heir to the Laval estates in Maine, and one piece of evidence suggests that Guy of Laval, perhaps through Hugh's intercession, may have married an otherwise unknown bastard daughter of Henry I's named Emma.[66] Another of the royal daughters was wed at an undiscoverable date to

---

[58] Orderic, vi, 100, 176.
[59] On William Malet, William Bainard and Philip of Braose see *ASC*, AD1110, 1112; Huntingdon, 237, adds that the three men had wronged the king but does not elaborate. On Roger of Abitôt's fall see *De gestis pontificum*, 253, and *The Cartulary of Worcester Cathedral Priory (Regester I)*, ed. R. R. Darlington, Pipe Roll Society, London 1968, xxv, 26-7. The most probable date for Roger's fall is 1110; it cannot have occurred after 1114 but might conceivably be associated with Henry's Welsh campaign of May-June 1114. On Henry's arrests during this period, see RaGena DeAragon, 'The Growth of Secure Inheritance in Anglo-Norman England', *Journal of Medieval History* viii, 1982, 385.
[60] W. E. Wightman, *The Lacy Family in England and Normandy, 1066-1194*, Oxford 1966, 66-7, 243-4 (Wightman recognises the international context of Henry's dealing with the honour of Pontefract); Orderic, vi, 162 and n. 4, 164.
[61] *ASC*, AD1112; Orderic, vi, 178, 180.
[62] Orderic, vi, 188 and n.5, 256, 344.
[63] Orderic, vi, 180, 198, 236-8.
[64] Orderic, vi, 176-7; Marjorie Chibnall's translation.
[65] Wightman, 66-7. Wightman inclines toward a later date (1114-1118) for Hugh's acquisition and associates it with the hostilities of 1116-1119. The honour may have been in royal hands for an appreciable time between Robert's forfeiture and Hugh's arrival: Wightman, 243-4.
[66] Bertrand de Broussillon, *La maison de Laval, 1020-1605*, i, 1895, 79: '. . . on prétend même que l'abbaye de Clermont aurait conservé longtemps une tombe sur laquelle on lisait: EMMA

Roscelin vicomte of Maine and lord of Beaumont-le-Vicomte.[67] The winning of friends in Maine may well have been on Henry's mind when in 1111 he raised Geoffrey Brito, dean of Le Mans cathedral and a favourite of the late Count Elias, to the archbishopric of Rouen.[68] And if Henry did not instigate the rebellion of 1112 in Anjou, he was at least convenienced by the fact that it diverted Fulk V's military resources at the height of the international conflict.[69]

Meanwhile, between 1111 and 1113 King Louis VI was contending, not always successfully, with the largest rebellion of his reign. Henry I's closest friend, Robert count of Meulan, whose county in the French Vexin had been pillaged by Louis in 1109 and again in 1110, settled scores in 1111 by seizing and plundering Paris.[70] In the same year the young Theobald of Blois, perhaps on the advice of his mother Adela, broke with Louis and allied himself with Henry.[71] By 1112 a remarkably large number of French magnates had joined Theobald in an uprising against Louis. The coalition included Lancelin of Bulles lord of Dammartin, Payn of Montjai, Ralph of Beaugenci, Milo of Brai vicomte of Troyes, Hugh de Crecy lord of Château-fort, Guy de Rochefort, Hugh count of Troyes, and Hugh du Puiset, supported, Suger adds, by an army of Normans.[72] Orderic describes Louis at this time as being too much occupied to disturb the king of England by invading Normandy.[73]

Meanwhile, Henry was winning other allies against France by marrying or be-trothing royal offspring to important neighbouring princes. Two such alliances can be dated firmly to the months immediately preceding the peace of 1113. The be-trothal early in 1113 of Henry's son, William Adelin, to Matilda daughter of Fulk V drew Anjou from the French into the Anglo-Norman orbit (as would their marriage in 1119, and the betrothal and marriage of the Empress Maud to Geoffrey count of Anjou amidst the Flemish succession crisis of 1127-28).[74] Similarly, the union between Henry's natural daughter Maud and Conan III of Brittany almost certainly occurred just before the peace of 1113 and was intended, as Orderic explains, to establish a bond of peace between the Anglo-Norman monarch and the Breton ducal house.[75]

Henry married a number of his bastard daughters to neighbouring princes across the Norman frontiers,[76] and although none except the marriage of Maud and Conan can be dated securely, it is likely that other such marriages were also designed to win allies during periods of conflict with France and Anjou. We have already touched on the marriages or possible marriages of Henry's daughters to Roscelin of Beaumont-

ANGLORUM REGIS FILIA DOMINAQUE LAVALLENSIS'. The author dismisses this tradition on the grounds that Robert of Torigny excludes 'Emma' from his list of Henry I's daughters, but the list is by no means complete. Emma is absent from the list of Henry's illegitimate daughters in GEC, xi, Appendix D, 112-21.

[67] GEC, xi, Appendix D, 116; Orderic, vi, 444 and n.3.·

[68] Orderic, v, 236; vi, 172. I am indebted to David S. Spear for the suggestion. Hugh the Chantor, 82, 89, hints that Archbishop Geoffrey was involved in the negotiations of 1119-1120 between Thurstan of York, Louis VI, and the papal curia.

[69] Chartrou, 27.

[70] Luchaire, nos. 72, 103, 111. The episode might possibly be dated 1110; Luchaire favours 12 March 1111.

[71] Luchaire, nos. 117, 121.

[72] Luchaire, no.134; Suger, 146-8.

[73] Orderic, vi, 176-8.

[74] Hollister and Keefe, 'Making of the Angevin Empire', 14 and n.62.

[75] Orderic, ii, 352; vi, 174 and n.4, 180.

[76] Hollister and Keefe, 'Making of the Angevin Empire', 5-6.

le-Vicomte and Guy of Laval. Another shred of evidence is to be found in a letter of Ivo bishop of Chartres to King Henry protesting the betrothal of one of Henry's daughters to Hugh fitz Gervase of Châteauneuf-en-Thymerais.[77] The letter can be dated loosely by the death of Ivo of Chartres late in 1116, and the fact that Gervase of Châteauneuf was in arms against Henry during the war of 1111-1113.[78] It looks' very much as though the marriage plan that Ivo blocked was intended to draw the family of Châteauneuf into the Anglo-Norman alliance network in connection with the peace of 1113, and that it exemplified the same policy that brought about William Adelin's betrothal to Matilda of Anjou and Maud's to Conan of Brittany.

Not only in 1109-1113 but in later years as well, diplomatic marriages and baronial conspiracies and rebellions tended to coincide with hostilities between Henry, Louis, Fulk, and the luckless counts of Flanders. Viewed in the context of international war and diplomacy, the conventional portraits of Henry I as a menacing, avaricious monarch who arrested and disinherited his barons arbitrarily, and of Louis VI as one who devoted his life to taming the royal principality through constant warfare against the castellans, require a degree of modification. As one browses through Luchaire's annals of Louis VI with a chronology of international politics in mind, one is struck by the close correlation between the rebellions of Louis' castellans and other vassals and his wars with Henry I.[79] An oft repeated example of Louis' persistent struggles with what used to be called 'robber barons' of the Ile de France is his capture and destruction of the castle of Le Puiset on three separate occasions. Intriguingly, the occasions can be dated to the war years of 1111, 1112, and 1118, and on the second of them Louis was able to take the castle only after the departure of five hundred Norman knights who had been assisting in its defence.[80]

Not every French rebellion occurred during the years when Louis and Henry were at war. Public order was less firmly established in Louis' dominions than in Henry's, where the correlation of Norman rebellions and international wars is absolute. But it is during the years of peace that we are apt to find Louis engaged in distant expeditions, such as his campaigns in Auvergne in 1122 and 1126.[81] Returning from the first of these, Louis could regard himself as 'triumphant over all his enemies and in possession of a glorious peace'.[82] Similarly in Anjou under Fulk V and Geoffrey le Bel, there is a tendency (but only that) for rebellions to coincide with wars against Henry I. That the correlation is not accidental is suggested by the complaint of an Angevin chronicler that Henry I was in the habit of buying the support of Angevin barons.[83] The 'turbulent magnates' who loom so large in traditional interpretations of the period are by no means figments of historians' imaginations. But just as the

---

[77] *Patrologia* clxii, cols 265-6.

[78] Orderic's reference to the hostilities between Gervase and Henry I (vi, 176) can be dated 1112 and occurs in the context of the larger conflict involving Fulk V of Anjou, Louis VI, and Theobald of Blois. Gervase's wife, Mabel, was a niece of Henry I's enemy, Robert of Bellême. Their son Hugh married Aubrée, sister of Waleran count of Meulan c.1123, to seal a military alliance between Hugh and Waleran against Henry I in connection with the general hostilities of 1123-1124: Orderic, vi, 332 and note 2.

[79] Luchaire, nos. 75, 76, 87, 103, 108, 111, 114, 117, 134, 220, 236, 246, 262, 420.

[80] Suger, 162 and, more generally, 158-68; Luchaire, nos. 114, 134, 236.

[81] Luchaire, nos. 318, 369.

[82] Luchaire, no. 324.

[83] Chartrou, 27-33. Of the nine years in which Chartrou dates Angevin rebellions – 1109, 1112, 1115, 1118, 1123, 1124, 1129, 1130, and 1135 – five are years of warfare with Henry I (1112, 1118, 1123, 1124, 1135). On Henry's policy of buying the support of Angevin barons, see *Gesta consulum andegavorum*, 68.

powerful frontier-lord Robert of Bellême, Henry I's premier baronial troublemaker, ended his political career in the service of Louis VI, and Amaury de Montfort, Robert of Bellême's successor on Henry's little list, was an adviser of Louis VI and uncle of Fulk V, so also were Louis VI's hated foes, Hugh du Puiset and Thomas of Marle, allied at crucial moments with Henry I. Thomas of Marle, whose savagery toward defenceless victims and malicious torturing of prisoners are so vividly described by Suger and Guibert of Nogent,[84] is reported by Walter of Thérouanne to have joined the opposition to William Clito's rule in Flanders in 1127-28 in a coalition designed by Henry I.[85]

The Norman rebellion of 1123-24 provides a useful case study of the interplay between domestic and international politics. Henry of Huntingdon ascribes the revolt to a quarrel between Henry I and his young magnate Waleran of Meulan over some undisclosed issue, and provides no hint that the ensuing hostilities had an international dimension.[86] Orderic Vitalis provides a fuller and more plausible explanation: Amaury de Montfort count of Evreux, being angered at the activities of unscrupulous royal officials in his county, persuaded his nephew, Fulk V of Anjou, to betroth his daughter Sibylla to William Clito and grant the county of Maine as her marriage portion until Clito could recover Normandy from Henry I. Amaury then persuaded Waleran of Meulan and other magnates to rebel in Clito's behalf.[87] Although Orderic's criticism of unscrupulous officials is a topos that runs back to the publicans of the Gospels and beyond, it is not difficult to believe that Amaury, a wealthy and powerful magnate with extensive holdings on both sides of the Norman frontier, could resent the spread of the Anglo-Norman government across his county. Indeed, the castle of Evreux itself had for several years been occupied by a royal garrison.[88] But further information, from the *Anglo-Saxon Chronicle*, makes it clear that Orderic's explanation is romanticised and misleading. The problem must be traced back to the marriage in 1119 of William Adelin and Matilda, daughter of Fulk V of Anjou, and William Adelin's death the following year in the wreck of the White Ship. Fulk V was just then journeying to Jerusalem, and Henry kept Matilda at his court in England until Fulk returned to Anjou and had his daughter brought home.[89] The marriage had been intended to seal a lasting peace, and Fulk had agreed to grant Maine to William Adelin as a marriage portion, to be held of Anjou. William's death broke the seal and raised the issue of Maine once again. Fulk sent messengers to Henry's Christmas court at Dunstable in 1122 to discuss the return of Matilda's dowry, but early in 1123, probably in February, they departed in anger, having failed to persuade Henry to give it back.[90] The following September, Orderic tells us, Amaury, Waleran and others met to plot their rebellion.[91]

---

[84] Suger, 30-2, 172-80, 250-4; Guibert de Nogent, *Histoire de sa vie (1053-1124)*, ed. Georges Bourgin, Paris 1907, 177-9, 198-9; cf. Huntingdon, 308-10 (*De contemptu mundi*).
[85] Walter of Thérouanne, 'Vita Karoli Comitis', *MGH* xii, 557. The coalition included Baldwin of Hainaut, William of Ypres, Godfrey of Louvain (Henry I's father-in-law), and Stephen of Blois count of Boulogne.
[86] Huntingdon, 245.
[87] Orderic, vi, 332.
[88] Orderic, vi, 278; William the Conqueror and his successors claimed the right to place their garrisons in private castles at will: C. H. Haskins, *Norman Institutions*, Cambridge, Mass. 1918, 282 ('Consuetudines et Iusticie', c. 4).
[89] *ASC*, A D 1121; Chartrou, 13-16.
[90] *ASC*, A D 1123; *De gestis regum*, ii, 498.
[91] Orderic, vi, 334.

It is not to be supposed that Henry's break with Anjou was a product of the royal avarice; indeed, he tried to cheer the departing messengers with gifts.[92] As Simeon of Durham informs us, the dowry consisted not of money but of lands, towns and castles,[93] and they were presumably in Maine. Simeon does not identify them, but Robert of Torigny provides the names of many castles built, strengthened or garrisoned by Henry I, and among them are three major castles in Mayenne in northern Maine: Ambrières, Gorron, and Châtillon-sur-Colmont, all of which were in Henry's hands at his death in 1135.[94] He might well have alleged ancient claims to them – Ambrières was first fortified in 1054 by William the Conqueror[95] – and it looks very much as though they were committed to Henry at the time of his son's marriage and were still garrisoned by his knights in 1123. Robert of Torigny may be providing a further hint when he reports objections from various quarters to Henry's habit of dealing with castles across the Norman frontiers as if they were his own, strengthening them with walls and towers.[96]

The narrative sources, concentrating on the insurrection in Normandy, are all but silent on warfare with Anjou. Simeon of Durham alone mentions military operations on the frontier of Maine, involving William Clito and Fulk V, and he provides no details, while the Anglo-Saxon chronicler alludes even more vaguely to Henry's hostilities in 1124 with Louis, Fulk, and his own Norman landholders.[97] Louis' involvement is suggested by the presence of French knights and magnates, including the king's kitchener, in the garrisons of Waleran of Meulan's Norman castles of Pont-Audemer and Beaumont.[98] And Henry's warfare in Anjou may be echoed in the record of an accord between the family of Thomas of St John and the abbey of Mont-Saint-Michel c.1124 stating that the parties came to terms at Argentan, in King Henry's presence, after Thomas's return from captivity at Gorron.[99] Thomas of St John had fought in Henry's behalf during the Tinchebray campaign of 1106, and in 1118 his brothers, Roger and John, were the hand-picked commanders of Henry's garrison at La Motte-Gautier-de-Clinchamp, a former Bellême castle in Maine.[100] Thomas of St John had probably been commanding a body of knights in Henry's pay – perhaps Breton mercenaries[101] – when he was seized by the Angevins and Manceaux and incarcerated at Gorron. He may, indeed, have been in charge of

---

[92] *ASC*, AD 1123.

[93] Simeon, ii, 267.

[94] *The Chronicle of Robert of Torigni*, in *Chronicles of the Reigns of Stephen, Henry II, and Richard I*, ed. Richard Howlett, 4 vols, RS 1884-1889, iv, 107, 128, described as Norman castles taken by the Angevins following Henry's death in 1135. Alençon may also have been at issue: Hollister and Keefe, 'Making of the Angevin Empire', 10.

[95] Robert Latouche, *Histoire du comté du Maine pendant le Xe et le XIe siècle*, Paris 1910, 31, 61.

[96] Jumièges, 310.

[97] Simeon, ii, 274; *ASC*, AD 1124.

[98] Orderic, vi, 340, 342.

[99] *Regesta*, ii, no. 1422.

[100] Orderic, vi, 84, 194, and notes; Jacques Boussard, 'Thomas de Saint-Jean-le-Thomas et l'abbaye du Mont-Saint-Michel', in *Droit privé et institutions régionales: Études historiques offertes à Jean Yver*, Paris 1976, 87-96; on the family, see GEC, xi, 340-6. Thomas served c.1111 as co-sheriff of Oxfordshire; he appears to have crossed to Normandy with the king in 1123: *Regesta*, ii, nos. 1400-1401, 1418.

[101] The St John brothers' Norman *caput* was at Saint-Jean-le-Thomas in the Cotentin, and they were important tenants of Mont-Saint-Michel, from which area Henry is said to have often recruited Breton mercenaries: Marjorie Chibnall, 'Feudal Society in Orderic Vitalis', *ante* i, 1978, 47; *De gestis regum*, ii, 478; cf. Chibnall, 'Mercenaries and the *Familia Regis*', 21.

the castle's defence and captured as a result of a successful Angevin siege, for if his captors had moved him it would likely have been to a more secure rear base.

The victory of Henry's military household over the rebels in March and April, 1124, was accompanied by related events of international scope. In July or August, the Emperor Henry V, by the counsel of his father-in-law Henry I, led a large-scale military expedition against Reims.[102] It came too late to help Henry I, who had already restored order to Normandy, though advance rumours of the emperor's project may have discouraged Louis VI from involving himself more directly in the Norman-Angevin hostilities. Whatever the case, the imperial expedition was an utter failure. The Germans turned back, overawed by the size of Louis VI's army, perhaps intimidated by the *oriflamme* banner of Saint-Denis and, just possibly, terrified by an eclipse of the sun.[103]

In the meantime, through complex negotiations between Henry I and the papal curia, Clito's marriage to Sibylla of Anjou was annulled on grounds of consanguinity, very narrowly interpreted, and Henry rewarded the papacy for its good service by permitting Cardinal John of Crema to exercise full legatine powers in England in 1125.[104] As in 1105, Henry was prepared to diminish slightly his control of the English Church when the diplomatic stakes were high, and as in 1120 he was prepared to do so at Canterbury's expense.

International politics clearly overarched the Norman rebellion of 1123-24 no less than the Norman rebellion of 1118-19, the French rebellion of 1111-13, and the epoch-making Flemish rebellion of 1128 against William Clito — during which Henry kept Clito's enemies in his pay and squeezed the Flemish textile towns with a boycott of English wool.[105]

Louis VI had rendered only indirect support to the Norman rebels in 1123-24, and when he installed Clito in Flanders in 1127 and backed him militarily in 1128, Henry's response was similarly indirect — if perhaps more effective. The two kings had not been at blows since 1119, and at Clito's death in 1128 even their shadow boxing ceased. During the seven-year peace of 1128-35 Louis and Henry did not meet, nor were they linked by any known feudal relationship.[106] But both recognised

---

[102] Suger, 218-30; Luchaire, no. 349 and references.

[103] Henry V's expedition cannot be dated precisely. Luchaire, in reviewing the evidence, concludes that it occurred sometime after 25 July and before the end of August, pointing out that Henry V was at Worms on 25 July and that several contemporary writers place the invasion in August. Luchaire further points out that Lambert de Waterlos, writing a generation later, places the expedition *intrante mense augusto* but gets the year wrong; and that, according to the *Auctarium Laudunense*, Henry V withdrew on 14 August. The solar eclipse of 11 August 1124 would have been visible from Reims at about noon (though the path of totality lay to the north of France): Theodor R. von Oppolzer, *Canon of Eclipses (Canon der Finsternisse)*, tr. by Owen Gingerich, New York 1962, 222-3 and Chart 111; Galbert of Bruges reports that the eclipse, even though partial, was an awesome occurrence signifying an oncoming calamity: *Histoire du meurtre de Charles le Bon*, ed. Henri Pirenne, Paris 1891, 5.

[104] Helene Tillmann, *Die päpstlichen legaten in England bis zur Beendigung der Legation Gualas (1218)*, Bonn 1926, 27-30; Sandy B. Hicks, 'The Anglo-Papal Bargain of 1125: The Legatine Mission of John of Crema', *Albion* viii, 1976, 301-10; cf. Martin Brett, *The English Church under Henry I*, Oxford 1975, 45-7; Barlow, 109.

[105] Walter of Thérouanne, 557; Galbert of Bruges, 146-7; *Recueil des historiens des Gaules et de la France*, ed. Martin Bouquet and others, 24 vols, Paris 1738-1904, xv, 341; Gaston Dept, *Les influences anglaise et française dans le comté de Flandre au début du XIIIe siècle*, Ghent 1928, 18ff.; F. L. Ganshof, 'Les origines du concept de souveraineté nationale en Flandre', *Revue d'histoire du droit*, xviii, 1950, 144, 146 n. 4.

[106] Hollister, 'Anglo-Norman *Regnum*', 231.

Innocent II in the papal schism of 1130, and both received him at their courts. In May, 1131, Henry met Innocent II at Rouen in a glittering international assemblage that included Peter the Venerable abbot of Cluny, Bernard of Clairvaux, and, interestingly, Louis VI's chief adviser, Suger of Saint-Denis.[107]

From Suger's own writings, and those of his biographer, William of Saint-Denis, it becomes clear that the father of Gothic architecture was also a French royal envoy to the Anglo-Norman court, visiting Henry frequently and working for peace. Suger had earlier served as provost of the Saint-Denis dependency of Berneval on the Norman coast where he had been generously treated at Henry I's tribunals.[108] Although he later became Louis VI's counsellor and panegyrist, he always remained friendly toward Henry.[109] William of Saint-Denis describes Suger as being on the most intimate terms with the Anglo-Norman monarch, mediating for him with Louis VI to arrange bonds of peace, and frequently coming and going between the two courts.[110] In a letter to Count Geoffrey and the Empress Matilda after Henry's death, Suger himself recalls the honour and love which 'the glorious King Henry' always showed him, running to greet him on both his public and secret visits, and entrusting him with confidential peace negotiations with the king of France.[111] Suger credits himself with settling many wars and intrigues between the two kings, and with having had a hand in every peace negotiation during the final twenty years of Henry's reign. He offers to do the same service to Maud and Geoffrey – if they will keep their hands off Berneval as the good King Henry had done.[112]

Apart from the mere record of his presence at Henry's court in 1131, Suger's diplomatic activities have left no trace in contemporary sources. One faint hint can perhaps be found in a charter of Louis VI issued at Saint-Denis in 1120, sometime before August 3, disclosing that the king was in the company of his queen, his chief household officials, and Cardinal Cuno of Praeneste, Archbishop Thurstan's friend and fellow peace weaver.[113] Suger was not yet abbot, but he was a monk of Saint-Denis and was doubtless among those present. We are left to wonder whether they were negotiating the peace of 1120.

Again, Thomas Waldman and Elizabeth A. R. Brown recently discovered, in a section of a Queen's College Oxford manuscript containing materials that clearly originated at Saint-Denis, a genealogy demonstrating the relationship between an unnamed daughter of Henry I and Hugh fitz Gervaise of Châteauneuf.[114] The genealogy has been copied verbatim from the aforementioned letter of Ivo of Chartres that blocked the projected marriage alliance of c.1113. This letter appears in full, along with some of Ivo's other letters, in a collection of Saint-Denis materials in the Bibliothèque Nationale which contains the bulk of the known writing of William

---

[107] *Regesta*, ii, no.1691 n. (Suger did not attest for Henry I but witnessed a concurrent papal letter); Denis Bethell, 'English Black Monks and Episcopal Elections in the 1120s', *EHR* lxxxiv, 1969, 692; *Regesta Pontificum Romanorum*, ed. P. Jaffé, J. Loewenfeld *et al.*, i, Leipzig 1885, no.7472: Innocent II, at Rouen on 9 May, 1131, confirms the privileges and possessions of Saint-Denis at the request of Abbot Suger.

[108] Suger, 'De administratione', in *Oeuvres complètes de Suger*, ed. A. Lecoy de la Marche, Paris 1867, 184-6: Suger was provost of Berneval from 1107 to 1109.

[109] E.g. Suger, 14, 98-102.

[110] William of Saint Denis, 'Sugerii Vita', *Oeuvres complètes de Suger*, 384.

[111] Bouquet, xv, 520.

[112] Similarities between the passages in Suger's letter and William's 'Vita' suggest that William wrote the letter at hand.

[113] Luchaire, no. 289.

[114] Queen's College ms. 348, fol. 48.

of Saint-Denis and the only surviving copies of Suger's later letters.[115] Clearly, Ivo's campaign against politically significant 'incestuous' marriage alliances was followed with keen interest at Saint-Denis in Suger's time. Whatever bearing this may have on Suger's own activities, his service as mediator between Henry I and Louis VI suggests that international diplomacy, both public and clandestine, was a livelier enterprise than the better known narrative and record sources would lead us to believe.

That Normandy and England both suffered widespread violence in the years after Henry I's death might suggest that Henry's peace was a mere oasis, an aberration of no lasting importance. But with the eventual victory of the house of Anjou over Stephen of Blois for the Anglo-Norman succession, Henry I's policy of domestic peace was reestablished and enlarged, and with such success as to make Stephen's reign the aberration.

Yet the 'Angevin Empire' radically reshaped the old Anglo-Norman political world. The unifying concept of the *gens Normannorum*, which G. A. Loud has shown to have been both vigorous and long established in the years of Henry I, began to fade amidst the multitude of principalities ruled by the early Angevin kings.[116] And the vision of a unified, distinctive Anglo-Norman polity, which crystallised under Henry I to the point that one optimistic contemporary could speak of a 'regnum Norman-Anglorum', dimmed in Stephen's reign and all but vanished in Henry II's.[117] With King John's 'triumphs' (as some appear to interpret them), the Angevin dominions dissolved into a new political order more closely resembling the *regnum Franciae* and *regnum Angliae* of later times.

But as Karl Ferdinand Werner has persuasively argued, the road from the Carolingian state to the 'modern' state 'leads through the compact territories of northern France to the great powers of England and France which developed out of them'.[118] The Anglo-Norman era marked the zenith of the older power centres which would be the building blocks of Henry II's 'empire' and Philip Augustus's vastly expanded kingdom, but were still virtually autonomous in the days of Henry I and Louis VI. These two monarchs did much to increase the cohesion of their dominions, as did the dukes and counts who allied with them or fought them. And their achievements in administrative organisation and domestic peacekeeping, of such fundamental significance to the history of Europe,[119] were shaped by the demands of warfare and diplomacy within an international political order soon to be transformed.

---

[115] BN lat. 14192: for this reference I am again indebted to T. Waldman and E. A. R. Brown.

[116] G. A. Loud, 'The "Gens Normannorum" – Myth or Reality?' *ante* iv, 1981, 104-16, 204-9.

[117] John LePatourel, *The Norman Empire*, Oxford 1976; Hollister, 'Anglo-Norman *Regnum*'.

[118] Werner, 'Kingdom and Principality', 276; cf. 263-4.

[119] For a stimulating general analysis see Joseph R. Strayer, *On the Medieval Origins of the Modern State*, Princeton 1970, and more briefly, 'The Historical Experience of Nation-Building in Europe', in *Medieval Statecraft and the Perspectives of History: Essays by Joseph R. Strayer*, Princeton 1971, 341-8.

THE INTRODUCTION OF KNIGHT SERVICE IN ENGLAND*

J. C. Holt

The *cartae baronum* submitted to King Henry II in 1166 are a curiously neglected source in English history. Edited by Thomas Hearne in 1728[1] and by Hubert Hall in 1896[2] they were one of the bases of J. H. Round's paper on the Introduction of Knight Service published in 1891.[3] Yet they have not been re-examined systematically in recent discussions of Round's famous thesis. Perhaps Round has seemed to squeeze them dry. Perhaps the *cartae* have not seemed particularly relevant to the lines which have been followed by Round's critics, for they provide only ancillary evidence in the debate about local 'continuity' between thegnly and knightly estates, and, since they were composed a century after the Norman Conquest, they seem to leave room for the argument that the quotas of knight-service of the late twelfth century arose, not artificially from some act of government, but through gradual growth in the century following the Conquest. Yet the *cartae*, with the Pipe Rolls, are the fundamental source for this whole field of study. They establish the size of many quotas of military service, whether by direct statement or by permitting computation; they illustrate the attitudes both of the Crown and its tenants-in-chief towards military service; and they lead to questions about military service to which there is still no satisfactory answer. It is with the *cartae*, therefore, that this paper is first concerned.

Round's chief concern was to correlate the *cartae* with the information on scutage in the Pipe Rolls of Henry II. The present objective is to correlate the information of both the *cartae* and the Pipe Rolls with the history of feudal tenements. For it is obvious enough that the military burdens laid on the tenants-in-chief of the Crown were bound to bear the mark of forfeiture, escheat, marriage, sale and all the other accidents, genealogical, economic, and political, which might befall in the descent of a great estate. Round was not concerned with this within the context of his argument, and for good reason; for he set out to refute the notion that the military service of the Norman period 'developed in unbroken continuity from Anglo-Saxon obligations'.[4] To that end the establishment of the existence of an unrelated, artificial system of military tenure was sufficient; and he scarcely paused to consider whether that apparently artificial system might itself be a result of gradual growth, not over the years of the Conquest itself, but in the century which followed. The

* I am indebted to Professor C. Warren Hollister and Professor T. K. Keefe for commenting on an earlier version of this paper.
[1] *Liber Niger Scaccarii*, ed. Thomas Hearne, Oxford 1728.
[2] *The Red Book of the Exchequer*, ed. H. Hall, RS 1896.
[3] 'The Introduction of Knight Service into England', *EHR* vi, 1891, 417-43, 625-45, vii, 1892, 11-24; reprinted in J. H. Round, *Feudal England*, London 1909, 225-314 from which all references below are taken.
[4] Round, 234.

evidence to the contrary, which placed responsibility firmly on the shoulders of William the Conqueror, seemed to him both clear and certain. However, Round had rejected 'continuity' through the front door only to leave the back unbarred; for a historian approaching the evidence of the Pipe Rolls and the *cartae* independently will at once be struck by the number of examples which do not seem to fit Round's hypothesis, either because the service seems to be random, quite unrelated to the units of fives and tens on which Round's arguments depended, or because the tenant-in-chief does not seem to know what his quota was.[5] Now it is these instances which underpin the argument that quotas emerged gradually in the century following the Conquest.[6] Round noted some of them, but asserted that they 'are quite insufficient to overthrow the accumulated array of evidence on the other side and some of them are, doubtless, capable of explanation'.[7] This is the starting point of the present argument.

The *cartae* are not easy to deploy effectively. Some of the barons who made returns seem to have been uncertain about what was required. Henry II had apparently asked three questions:[8]

1. How many knights were enfeoffed by the death of Henry I? (The old enfeoffment.)
2. How many knights have been enfeoffed since the death of Henry I? (The new enfeoffment.)
3. How many knights remain on the demesne? That is how many knights was the tenant-in-chief to supply from his own resources in order to fulfil the service quota or *servitium debitum*?

A number of barons confused the second and third questions by recording that the new enfeoffment had taken place on the demesne, and a few confused the old enfeoffment in 1135 with the service due. Disentangling such misunderstandings is relatively easy where the transcripts of the *cartae* in the Black Book and the Red Book of the Exchequer present the whole or most of the original text. In many cases, however, they simply include lists of fees under the formal headings of old enfeoffment, new enfeoffment and demesne, categories which may be misleading in view of the confusion revealed by some of the complete returns.

There is one further essential difficulty which cannot be circumvented. The *cartae* only reveal the service quota if it was directly stated or if it exceeded the sum of the old and new enfeoffment; in the latter case it can be calculated by simple addition of the old and new enfeoffment and service due on the demesne. Where there is no statement of the quota, and no genuine service recorded on the demesne, then the quota cannot be computed from the *cartae*. In some cases it can be established from the payments of scutage recorded in the Pipe Rolls of 1159, 1161, 1162 and 1165. But if that proves impossible then it is unlikely to be established at all, since later scutages were based not on the quota, but on the new or old enfeoffment. There are nearly forty tenancies-in-chief, numbering five knights' fees or more, where the sum of the old and new enfeoffments either exceeds, or coincides with, the quota

---

[5] H. G. Richardson and G. O. Sayles, *The Governance of Medieval England*, Edinburgh 1963, 88-90.

[6] In addition to Richardson and Sayles, see Frank Barlow, *William I and the Norman Conquest*, London 1965, 107-9; D. J. A. Matthew, *The Norman Conquest*, London 1966, 127-8.

[7] Round, 257.

[8] Round, 236-46; F. M. Stenton, *The First Century of English Feudalism*, 2nd edn, Oxford 1961, 137-9.

and where no service is stated to have lain on the demesne. They include the earl-
doms of Arundel, Cornwall, Gloucester, Buckingham, Norfolk and Clare, and the
great honours of Port, Belvoir, Wallingford and Eye.

In some of these cases it may be that the old or the total enfeoffment approxi-
mates to or coincides with the quota.[9] There is also a handful of examples where
later evidence seems to provide a hint of what the quota had been; for instance, in
1213 Earl Roger Bigod fined with King John to secure a reduction of service from
125¼ knights, a figure based on the old enfeoffment which was the usual basis of
assessment for the Bigod fee, to sixty,[10] which is a typical figure for the larger
honours established in the generation of the Norman Conquest. But all this is infer-
ence, and in all that follows, at least as regards the analysis of quotas, almost all these
baronies have been left out of account. The random service which they rendered
does not disprove Round's hypothesis; nor does it give support to some alternative
argument that quotas arose from the gradual accumulation of precedent. In these
cases there is no evidence that quotas had ever been established; it is equally true
that if they had, the information would not reveal them.

The remaining baronies, totalling some 150, may be categorised in two different
ways. The first may be defined by the quota, which is represented either by a small
number, up to five, or by multiples of fives and tens, or by some quite random number. Now there is no need to found the decimal quotas in Round's *constabularia*.
What matters is that such quotas must in general represent an arbitrary system of
service. Precedents do not accumulate in fives and tens. Anglo-Saxon tenements of
five hides certainly survived into the Norman period; some, a few, became knight's
fees;[11] but no convincing argument has yet been produced to equate the decimally
based quotas of the Norman period with the decimally arranged hides or the duo-
decimally arranged carucates of the Anglo-Scandinavian kingdom.[12] There is no
satisfactory escape from the conclusion that the decimal quotas were imposed. The
random quotas in contrast could simply have grown. Indeed one of the objects of
this paper is to show how they grew.

A second, more complex set of categories is concerned with the history of the
tenancies-in-chief simply as property. Some baronies enjoyed a relatively smooth
passage from the Conquest to the reign of Henry II, descending directly in the male
line, undisturbed by political disaster or the fortunes of civil war, unaffected by the
financial consequences of excessive enthusiasm for the Crusade, monastic endowment, lavish building, or the accumulation of estates. Some baronies had a more
chequered history, broken by division among heiresses or the succession of a collateral, or a disputed claim sometimes coinciding with civil war. Some escheated to
the Crown, temporarily or permanently, because of default of heirs or the treason
of the tenants. Many baronies of the twelfth century were not at first tenancies-
in-chief at all; they began as undertenancies of the great lordships of the Norman

---

[9] The knights' fees reported from the honour of Eye in 1166 totalled 80, but there is nothing
in the return to indicate that that was the *servitum debitum* (*Red Book*, 411).

[10] *Pipe Roll 13 John*, 2.

[11] Marjory Hollings, 'The Survival of the Five-Hide Unit in the Western Midlands', *EHR* lxiii,
1948, 453-87.

[12] See the difficulties encountered by Hollings, 475-60 and by John, 158-9, and the comments
thereon of J. O. Prestwich, 'Anglo-Norman Feudalism and the problem of continuity', *Past and
Present* 26, 1963, 43-4. Compare the comment of Helena M. Chew, *The English Ecclesiastical
Tenants-in-Chief and Knight Service*, Oxford 1932, 6-7 on F. W. Maitland, *Domesday Book and
Beyond*, Cambridge 1897, 160.

period — Mortain, Bayeux, Montgomery, Lancaster — and emerged as holdings in chief only when the mesne lordship had disappeared through reversion to the Crown. Others were late creations, established long after the influences which had determined the initial pattern of enfeoffment had lost impetus. Others were Marcher lordships and hence had special, localised military functions. Yet others were reconstituted holdings, motley concoctions manufactured out of bits and pieces from other estates.

These categories have been distinguished more sharply than a close examination of individual estates might sometimes warrant. Nevertheless, artificial though they are, they established a point of great importance. The less disturbed the descent of an estate the more likely it is to have a decimal quota. The more difficult its descent, the less likely it is to have a decimal quota. The decimal quota goes with the normal, the random with the abnormal. This contrast is by no means obvious from a casual glance at the known *servitia*, for the decimal quotas come from baronies which illustrate almost the whole range of 'accidents' affecting the descent and homogeneity of feudal tenancies. It is only when approached through the history of the tenancies that it stands out sharply and clearly.

Much the largest single group of baronies with known quotas descended relatively undisturbed as tenancies-in-chief in the male line from the time of the Domesday Survey to the reign of Henry II. Of these, nearly thirty in all, the Vere barony of Hedingham paid scutage on thirty-one fees in 1162[13] and the Giffard barony of Elston (Wiltshire) apparently owed a quota of nine;[14] all the rest had decimal quotas.[15] Of the Domesday tenancies-in-chief with known quotas which descended unimpaired in the female line, a group of fifteen, only three had random quotas in 1166; the Peche barony of Great Bealings or Great Thurlow (Suffolk) returned twelve,[16] the barony of Aveley (Essex) seven and a half[17] and the Marmion barony of Tamworth probably twelve;[18] all the rest had decimal quotas.[19] Of the Domesday tenancies-in-chief with known quotas which descended unimpaired and without dispute through collaterals, a relatively small group of three, there was no exception to the general pattern.[20] Even where rebellion led to escheat, and the temporary or final dispossession of a family, an honour was still likely to return a decimal quota so long as it was not dismembered. Hence the Lacy honour of Pontefract was assessed

---

[13] *Pipe Roll 8 Henry II*, 71. Compare *Pipe Roll 14 Henry II*, 39, *Pipe Roll 6 Richard*, 37, *Pipe Roll 13 John*, 124. The total of fees returned in 1166 was 29 1/8 (*Red Book*, 352-3).

[14] *Pipe Roll 8 Henry II*, 14, *Red Book*, 245.

[15] Benington, Blankney, Cainhoe, Cavendish, Caxton, Crich, Eton, Hastings, Craon, Helion Bumpstead, Horsley, Kentwell, Norton, Pleshey, Poorstock, Rayne, Richard's Castle, Rothersthorpe, Stafford, Tarrington, Tattershall, Thoresway, Tutbury, Weedon, West Dean, Whitchurch, Wolverton, Wormegay.

For convenience of reference, here and throughout, I have used the classification of I. J. Sanders, *English Baronies: a study of their origin and descent 1086-1327*, Oxford 1960.

Limitation of space prevents me from including a full apparatus. I have restricted detailed references to particular cases or to supplementing information both on the descent of estates and military service which is summarised in Sanders.

[16] *Red Book*, 366-7.

[17] *Red Book*, 353; *Pipe Roll 14 Henry II*, 38.

[18] *Pipe Roll 11 Henry II*, 18. On the origins of the Marmions as lords of Tamworth see GEC, viii, 505-6. The descent of Tamworth probably also involved collateral succession.

[19] Blagdon, Brattelby, Chipping Warden, Dudley, Hockering, Hooton Paynel, Kempsford, Malton/Alnwick, Lewes, Nether Stowey, Okehampton, Trowbridge.

[20] Bywell, Castle Cary (?), Monmouth. But see also Tamworth in n.18 above. Okehampton also descended to collaterals as well as through heiresses. See GEC, iv, 308-9.

at sixty,[21] and so also were the Mowbray honour of Thirsk[22] and the great fee of Tickhill,[23] all of which underwent escheat in the century after the Conquest. Holderness, confiscated in turn by the Conqueror, by Rufus and by Henry I, nevertheless retained its integrity and rendered a service of twenty knights in 1168.[24] In all, more than twenty baronies out of a total of nearly thirty which escheated temporarily to the Crown, or which seem to have suffered some unexplained break in descent and yet retained their unity, returned a decimal quota on performed service equivalent to a decimal quota.[25] As a group they are less uniform than those which descended easily in the male line, but the decimal quota was nevertheless preponderant.

The main source of random quotas lay elsewhere. Most important of all in terms of numbers are those baronies of the late twelfth century, nearly fifty in all, which had emerged from undertenancies of the great lordships of the first Norman settlement. In many instances direct continuity between the initial undertenancy and the later barony can be demonstrated without much difficulty, both as regards the holding and its tenancy. The same is sometimes true of the service, and hence this, when it emerges as a 'baronial' quota in the relative light of day of the late twelfth century, reflects the policies of the early tenants-in-chief rather than of the Crown. The most obvious instance is that of the 'fees of Mortain' which were assessed by the Exchequer at two-thirds of a normal fee.[26] They cannot have been anything but the creation of Robert, Count of Mortain, or of his son, William. Many of them, indeed the majority, carried decimal quotas.[27] This is also true of some of the Shropshire baronies which were first established by Roger of Montgomery, or by his son Robert of Bellême.[28] In contrast, only a few of the Kentish baronies which originated in fiefs held of Odo, Bishop of Bayeux, returned a decimal quota: the Talbot/Mountchesney barony of Swanscombe, which owed thirty,[29] the baronies of Chilham and Patricksbourne, each of which owed fifteen[30] and the Arsic barony

---

[21] For the breaks in the descent of Pontefract see W. E. Wightman, *The Lacy Family in England and Normandy*, Oxford 1966, 66-73. For the quota see *Red Book*, 421-4.

[22] I take the 60 fees *de antiquo feodo* to stand for the *servitium* (*Red Book*, 420). On the descent of Thirsk and its associated lordships see *Charters of the honour of Mowbray*, ed. Diana E. Greenway, London 1972, xxi-xxiv.

[23] *Pipe Roll 7 Henry II*, 38, *Pipe Roll 8 Henry II*, 34. On the descent of the honour see *The Cartulary of Blyth Priory*, ed. R. T. Timson, Thoroton Society, Record Ser. xxvii, xxviii, 1973, cxv-cxl.

[24] For the confiscation and descent of the lordship see Barbara English, *The Lords of Holderness 1086-1260*, Oxford 1979, 6-16; for the *servitium*, see *Pipe Roll 14 Henry II*, 90, *Pipe Roll 18 Henry II*, 62.

[25] Returning decimal quotas in 1166 or performing decimal service apparently equivalent to the quota: Barnstaple, Bourn, Bradninch, Cogges, Curry Malet (?), Great Weldon, Great Torrington, Holderness, Little Dunmow, Little Easton, Odell, Patricksbourne, Pontefract, Shelford, Southoe, Stansted Montfichet, Stanton le Vale, Thirsk, Tickhill, Totnes(?), Winterbourne St Martin. Apparently carrying non-decimal quotas: Berkhamstead, Cottingham, Haughley, Salwarpe, Lavendon. In the case of Haughley there may have been a quota of 50. The enfeoffment of 80 in the honour of Eye could possibly coincide with a quota.

[26] *Red Book*, 232; Sir Paul Vinogradoff, *English Society in the eleventh century*, Oxford 1908, 52-4; C. Warren Hollister, *The Military Organisation of Norman England*, Oxford 1965, 44-6.

[27] Cardinham (20 fees of Walter Hay, *Red Book*, 261), Chiselborough 10, Hatch Beauchamp 20, Odcombe 15. For further comment on the fee of the Surdeval family see below, pp. 96-7.

[28] Castle Holgate probably 5 (*Red Book*, 275), Cause 5, Wem probably 5 (*Book of Fees*, 144).

[29] *Red Book*, 195-6.

[30] *Red Book*, 191-2, 197; and probably also Peverel of Dover (*Pipe Roll 33 Henry II*, 209).

of Cogges which owed ten.[31] The remaining quotas were either three, or a multiple of three, or some apparently quite random number.[32] In all these cases, what determined the pattern of enfeoffment initially is now largely lost to view, but the tendency of the pattern to vary from one honour to another is clear and beyond question: the obvious conclusion is that the Norman tenant-in-chief was himself responsible. It is not impossible, of course, that the service was adjusted when such an undertenancy became a tenancy-in-chief. But, if so, it is apparent that such an intrusion was insufficient to eradicate the characteristic features of the fees of Mortain, for example, and it is likely in general that neither William Rufus nor Henry I would want, or be in a position to re-order the service of tenants who sided with them against the great rebel lords. As a category, therefore, this group of baronies is of considerable interest. It reflects the remarkable loyalty of the undertenants to the Crown and the increasing security of tenure which their loyalty achieved.[33] It also suggests that these quotas at least were established at an early date: before Odo's final forfeiture of 1088 for the tenancies of his barony, before 1102 at the very latest for the baronies which stemmed from the honour of Roger of Montgomery and before 1104, in some cases probably earlier, for the fees of Mortain.[34]

This group of baronies is partly overlapped by another: the Marcher lordships. The records of the late twelfth and early thirteenth centuries reveal the existence along the northern and Welsh borders of estates graced with the title and status of baronies from which military service was *sui generis*, designed to meet the special circumstances of border warfare. The Northumbrian baronies were created in the main by Henry I; a few may have originated before 1100, either in grants from Rufus or as undertenancies of the Norman earldom of Northumbria.[35] Styford and Mitford had a quota of five; Bywell returned sometimes five, sometimes thirty;[36] the rest carried random quotas, all of them except the Vesci barony of Alnwick which returned twelve, of less than five.[37] The pattern is similar further west in Cumbria. Here all the early holdings, whether established by the first lord of Cumbria, Ranulf Meschin, or by Henry I, were held by the render of cornage; it was only gradually in the course of the twelfth century and in the reign of John that this was converted to knight-service, and then the quotas were small and random.[38] Some of the Welsh Marcher lordships likewise lay outside any formal pattern. At Wigmore, in the late thirteenth century, the Mortimers claimed to hold by the service of two knights in time of war in Wales and of one knight in time of war in England.[39] At Oswestry in 1166 the fitz Alans held by the service of ten knights *in exercitu et chevalcia* within the county of Shropshire and, 'as the old men testify' of five knights outside the county.[40]

[31] *Pipe Roll 7 Henry II*, 26.
[32] Allington probably 3 (*Red Book*, 197). Chatham either 12 or 14 (*Pipe Roll 11 Henry II*, 106, *Red Book*, 191), Folkestone probably 21 (*Red Book*, 615-16), Pont probably 12 (*Red Book*, 618), West Greenwich probably 24 (*Red Book*, 617). The above figures largely depend on the castle-guard owed at Dover. For Ros, in contrast, there is a firm statement of 7 (*Red Book*, 197).
[33] For further comment see J. C. Holt, 'Feudal Society and the Family in early medieval England; I. The Revolution of 1066', *TRHS* v, 32, 209-12.
[34] For further discussion of some of the tenancies of Mortain see below, p.103.
[35] William E. Kapelle, *The Norman Conquest of the North*, London 1979, 191-200.
[36] *Red Book*, 437-8; *Pipe Roll 8 Henry II*, 52, *Pipe Roll 14 Henry II*, 172, *Book of Fees*, 201.
[37] *Book of Fees*, 200-3. The figures here depend on the returns to the Inquest of 1212.
[38] J. C. Holt, *The Northerners*, Oxford 1961, 91-2; Kapelle, 212; *Book of Fees*, 197-9.
[39] *Cal. I.P.M.*, iv, 235.   [40] *Red Book*, 274.

Baronies which were originally under-tenancies and the Marcher lordships account for a very large proportion of the random quotas of service. The remainder come largely from baronies which escheated for a time to the Crown and from baronies which were seriously reconstructed. True, an escheated barony might retain a decimal quota if there were no serious delapidation. But any estate which did not descend in the direct line of adult heirs was to some degree at risk. Estates which underwent wardship or descended through heiresses or through collaterals, and even more those estates which escheated through default of heirs or treason, were vulnerable, a prey to litigation, to the greedy eye of powerful neighbours, most of all to the Crown's exercise of patronage. Consider the fate of the Domesday holding of the Picard, Arnulf de Hesdin, which Round touched on in his paper on the origins of the Stewarts.[41] Arnulf's sons died without heirs; one was probably hanged by Stephen at Shrewsbury in 1138; and the estates, centred on Wiltshire and Gloucestershire, were divided respectively between two daughters, Maud and Aveline. A quota, either for Maud's portion or the whole estate, was still recorded under Henry II; it was assessed at forty in 1165.[42] Even so, Maud's grandson, Pain of Montdoubleau, submitted a confused *carta* in 1166: seven fees of the honour had got into the hands of Geoffrey de Vere during the reign of Henry I; Earl Patrick of Salisbury had received twenty fees in marriage with Pain's aunt, and had also taken a further fee by war which was now in the hands of Alfred of Lincoln.[43] Indeed it would be quite impossible to construct a quota for this barony but for the assessment of 1165. For the other portion of the estate which Aveline took by marriage to the fitz Alans of Oswestry, there is no such saving evidence. In 1166 William fitz Alan returned a *carta* which is among the most insistent and idiosyncratic in distinguishing between the enfeoffment and the quota. Nevertheless, in accounting for his Wiltshire fee all he could do was to list knights fees, which totalled eight and a half, and then add: 'We are not certain what service is owed to the King from this holding which belonged to Arnulf de Hesdin'.[44] Yet a quota there must in all probability have been for the other division of Arnulf's Domesday holding still carried one. The obvious conclusion to be drawn from William's *carta* is that it was no longer possible to trace it. It is also noteworthy that William fitz Alan expected an estate which he defined by reference to its Domesday tenant, dead before the end of the eleventh century, to have carried one.

Other baronies present similar stories. William son of Reginald de Ballon's was but briefly reported in his *carta* in language still reflecting the pathos of the dispossessed:

> William son of Reginald performs the service of one knight from his demesne. Hamelin de Ballon, his grandfather, was enfeoffed of the old feoffment to perform the aforesaid service. He has been deprived of Great Cheverell on the order of the lord king and of the honour of Abergavenny for which he owes service, if the lord king so pleases. He has no-one enfeoffed of the new enfeoffment.[45]

The estates of Roger of Berkeley were undergoing similar decomposition. Berkeley itself had just been lost to Robert fitz Harding. In his *carta* Roger reported two and a half fees of the old enfeoffment on which some of the service had been lost. He then added five fees and a number of hides from which further service had

[41] *Studies in Peerage and Family History*, London 1907, 116.
[42] *Pipe Roll 11 Henry II*, 74.   [43] *Red Book*, 297-8.
[44] *Red Book*, 274.   [45] *Red Book*, 281.

been lost; some of these were in dispute with Maurice son of Robert fitz Harding.[46] From this report the Exchequer plumped for a service of seven and a half fees in 1168 and subsequent assessments.[47] What it had been earlier it is impossible to say. Robert fitz Harding, in contrast, the new tenant with a clear commitment and a clean sheet, reported a quota of five for the honour of Berkeley in 1166.[48] The delapidated barony is one side of the coin; the reconstituted barony the other.

These two groups, especially the reconstituted baronies, are much the most illuminating of all. Up to a certain point it was possible for the Norman kings to act on a *tabula rasa*, to construct baronies from the lands of English tenants, from the royal demesne and from escheated estates of rebels, and to impose an artificial, decimal quota. After that point this became difficult if not impossible, for the escheats were occupied by enfeoffed knights owing specified amounts of service established by their dispossessed lords. The dividing line between the two, the point of balance, came in the reign of Rufus and Henry I, especially in the decade straddling the battle of Tinchebrai of 1106. This is well illustrated from the history of a number of Lincolnshire and Yorkshire baronies which were reaching their final form at this time. The Paynel fee, for example, was a conglomerate estate which included considerable additions to the lands which Ralph Paynell held at the time of Domesday Survey: in Lincolnshire, lands previously held by the Lacys which in 1086 had formed part of the barony of Odo of Bayeux, forfeited in 1088; and fees which Richard de Surdeval held of the honour of Robert, Count of Mortain.[49] Both these acquisitions probably came to Ralph by marriage.[50] Despite these diverse origins, and despite the complicated division of the barony among the Paynels it seems quite certain that the *servitium* came to the artificial total of forty-five in the 1160s: fifteen the responsibility of Robert de Gant;[51] fifteen the responsibility of William Paynel of Hooton Paynel;[52] and fifteen apparently already divided by 1124 between Hugh Paynel of West Rasen and Fulk Paynel of Drax.[53] How was such a total figure reached? It can scarcely be accepted as an accidental accumulation. It must therefore be that either the service due on the Paynel Domesday fief, plus the service on the new acquisitions, happened to come to forty-five, which seems too much of a coincidence; or the original service due on the 1086 holding was forty-five and the later additions carried no additional service, a process of augmentation which occurred in the case of some knights' fees, but at first sight seems most improbable in this case because of the extent of the additional tenancies; or the whole service of the Paynel fee was recast after the acquisition of the Lacy and Surdeval estates and their conversion to tenancies-in-chief following the forfeiture of Odo of Bayeux and the Counts of Mortain.

This last hypothesis requires us to accept a projection of the atmosphere of the Conquest into the period 1088-1106, with the King still constructing great fiefs and his leading subjects still ready to accept heavy feudal service. However, this can have

---

[46] *Red Book*, 292-3.
[47] *Pipe Roll 14 Henry II*, 123; *Pipe Roll 18 Henry II*, 121.
[48] He nevertheless reported that he was unable to obtain service from manors and fees still held by Roger of Berkeley (*Red Book*, 298).
[49] *Early Yorkshire Charters*, vols i-iii, ed. W. Farrer, Edinburgh 1914-16; vols iv-xii, ed. C. T. Clay, Yorkshire Archaeological Society, Record Ser., Extra Ser., 1935-65, vi, 56-62.
[50] *Early Yorkshire Charters*, vi, 4.
[51] *Early Yorkshire Charters*, vi, 33-4.
[52] *Early Yorkshire Charters*, vi, 41-2.
[53] *Early Yorkshire Charters*, vi, 8, 19.

been achieved only so long as there was the possibility of a clean sweep, only so long as the estates in question were not already in the possession of tenants holding by precise amounts of military service. If such tenants were firmly established then the perpetuation or establishment of an artificial quota would obviously be much more difficult. Compare the Paynel fee with the barony of Bourne which was granted by Henry I to Baldwin fitzGilbert de Clare within a decade or so of the point at which the Paynel barony was reaching its final form. Bourne included estates drawn from at least three Domesday fiefs, those of Oger the Breton, Godfrey of Cambrai and Baldwin the Fleming.[54] It could only have produced a conveniently round number of knights, if the lands had hitherto carried no service, or if the original service was now overridden, or if by coincidence the service came to a round figure. In fact it did not. The service of Bourne was $10^1/8$. That $^1/8$ does not simply represent a near miss at ten. $10^1/8$ is not only the service recorded in the 1166 return for the barony but also the service for which scutage was consistently charged thereafter.[55] In this instance assessment in round numbers was abandoned; instead the service was determined by the amount already due on the various fiefs which were thrown together to form the barony, plus any later enfeoffment. All this finds confirmation in the unusually diffuse and irregular *carta* which Hugh Wake submitted for his barony in 1166. Instead of accepting the usual distinction between old feoffment and new feoffment and service in demesne, he seems to have followed categories of his own: first the fees existing in the barony when it was created and secondly the subsequent feoffments of his predecessors, William de Rollos and Baldwin fitz Gilbert, and himself. The sum total was the service due. 'This is the service,' he submitted, 'whereby my predecessors in their day served King Henry I who gave them the lands and I owe you, as the lord who gave them to me, the service of my body when you wish to take it.'[56] This is quite different from the Paynel fee. Here the *servitium* is derived from the original and later constituents of a fief; there the *servitium* was apparently imposed on those constituents.

Neither the Paynel nor Bourne fees stand as isolated examples. On the side of Paynel there is also Trussebut. This barony consisted largely of the Domesday holding of Erneis de Burun. But Geoffrey fitz Pain, the tenant in the early twelfth century, held further lands in Beckering, Riby and elsewhere in Lincolnshire, some if not all of which were derived from the estates of Roger of Poitou forfeited in 1102.[57] The fee then was conglomerate in structure. Yet the *servitium* of the Trussebut fee was almost certainly 15 and if not that then 10.[58] Again the Brus fee comprised numerous lands in Yorkshire which were still the lands of the King in 1086, many more where Robert de Brus succeeded Robert Count of Mortain, many more still where Brus succeeded the Count's tenant, Richard de Surdeval, and also the small Domesday holding of William Taillebois in Lincolnshire:[59] once again a conglomerate structure, yet the service of the Brus fee was indubitably 15.[60] Other fees followed the pattern

---

[54] *The Lincolnshire Domesday and the Lindsey Survey*, ed. C. W. Foster and T. Longley with intr. by F. M. Stenton, Lincoln Record Society xix, 1924, 162-4, 173, 196-7; *Facsimilies of early charters from Northamptonshire collections*, Northamptonshire Record Society iv, 1930, 19-20.
[55] *Pipe Roll 14 Henry II*, 64; *Pipe Roll 2 Richard*, 90; *Pipe Roll 3 John*, 7, 9.
[56] *Red Book*, 378-80.
[57] *Early Yorkshire Charters*, x, 23-7.
[58] *Pipe Roll 11 Henry II*, 50; *Pipe Roll 14 Henry II*, 90; *Early Yorkshire Charters*, x, 8.
[59] *Early Yorkshire Charters*, ii, 16-19; *Lincolnshire Domesday*, 197, *Book of Fees*, 166.
[60] *Pipe Roll 14 Henry II*, 90; *Red Book*, 434.

suggested by the example of Bourne. The Ros barony of Helmsley originated in the grants which Henry I made to Walter Espec, again from the forfeited estates of Robert Count of Mortain.[61] This was concurrent with the foundation of the Brus barony; indeed Robert Brus and Walter Espec were closely associated figures in the administration of the northern counties at this time. Yet while the Brus fee appears to have had an artificial *servitium*, the Ros fee certainly had not. The feoffment in 1166 was $5^{23}/24$ *de veteri* and $2^{1}/3$ *de novo*. Scutage was usually charged on $5^{3}/4$.[62] Nor was the Crown the only influence at work recasting the structure and service of tenancies-in-chief. The 1166 *carta* of the honour of Mowbray reveals yet another possible development. Here the knights of the honour presented the awkward number of 88 enfeoffed knights, but added that 60 were *de antiquo feodo* and that 28 had been added by Nigel d'Albini from the demesne.[63] Nigel acquired the barony in the reign of Henry I c.1109. But for the long memory of the knights of the honour we should not know what the original service had been or that the change of ownership had been accompanied by, or had led during Nigel's lifetime to, a considerable increase in the number of fiefs.

The consequences of forfeiture, accumulation and reconstitution were unpredictable. However, they contributed to many of the random *servitia* which appear in 1166. The honour of Miles of Gloucester, combining lands held in the previous generation by Walter of Gloucester and Bernard de Neufmarché, along with acquisitions from both Stephen and Matilda, returned 17 *de veteri* and $3^{3}/4$ *de novo* fees.[64] Cottingham, the remnant of the Stuteville estates seized after the capture of Robert de Stuteville before Tinchebrai and only restored to the family under Stephen, carried a quota of 8.[65] Marshwood, first established for the Mandevilles by Henry I, returned a quota of 11 plus some fractions of fees and one fee of Mortain.[66] In one important case the process whereby the random quota was achieved is clearly recounted. William d'Aubigny's *carta* runs as follows:[67]

This is the holding of William d'Aubigny, butler of the Lord King, of the gift of Henry [I] who gave him fifteen knights of the fee of Corbuchon. And later he gave him a fee of ten enfeoffed knights of the land of Roger Bigod with the daughter of Roger Bigod of his own hand. And later he gave him the service of Ralph son of Godric of twelve knights; and the service of Alfred de Athelburgo of two knights; and of Picot de Bavent of one knight; and the fee of Reiner *Sine Averio* of one knight; and the fee of William de Musterville of one knight.

These totalled 42 fees. William then outlined his father's and his own enfeoffments. As it happened the grand total, including the 10 fees held in mesne tenure of the Bigod fee, came to 75. That is a useful reminder that a decimal quota could sometimes be achieved at random, for this barony clearly originated in a succession of grants of enfeoffed knights. That could scarcely produce a decimal quota other than at second-hand or by accident.

[61] *Early Yorkshire Charters*, x, 143-5.
[62] *Red Book*, 432-3, 490; *Pipe Roll 6 Richard*, 163; *Pipe Roll 8 Richard*, 185.
[63] *Red Book*, 420, 490.
[64] David Walker, 'The "Honours" of the Earls of Hereford in the Twelfth Century', *Transactions of the Bristol and Gloucestershire Archaeological Society* lxxix, pt ii, 1960, 174-211; *Red Book*, 293-4.
[65] *Early Yorkshire Charters*, ix, 5, 70-6; *Red Book*, 429.
[66] *Red Book*, 219.   [67] *Red Book*, 397-8.

Such an analysis of the relation between the quotas and the descent of baronies establishes one certain and central point: the decimal quotas were the more ancient. To dig down through the layers of evidence deposited by disturbed tenancies, to shift to one side the peculiar services of the Marcher baronies, to recognise that some layers in the record are the work not of the Crown but of tenants-in-chief, is to strip and lay bare the remains of a structure, much of it still surviving in 1166 in clear detail, in which quotas were based on a decimal system; that is on an artificial system, on an arbitrary system. Change was from the artificial to the random, not from the random to the artificial. Change occurred when something happened to disturb the normal descent of tenancies; and it was likely to occur only when that happened. If the hypothesis of gradual growth involves the view that there was some kind of debate about the service-quotas in the course of the twelfth century, either within baronies, or between barons and the Exchequer, a debate whereby in the end, through the accumulation of precedents, many quotas were settled on a decimal basis, then some evidence must be produced to establish a trend which seems to run clean against the demonstrable consequences of tenurial disturbance and quite contrary to the Exchequer's determination, from 1166 onwards, to move away from artificial quotas towards some more realistic assessment based on the number of knights enfeoffed. The obvious conclusion to be drawn from the evidence is that the quotas were mostly known and fixed by the end of the eleventh century at the latest.

There are other routes to the same end. The instances collected by Round of barons who in 1166 claimed tenure *a conquestu*[68] ought perhaps to be left out of the count; for these assertions are balanced on the other side by statements that quotas were unknown, or were confirmed only by reference to juries of knights of the fee; and in the last resort what these soldiers said either way is not certain evidence. But the division of their estates is. Between 1145 and the accession of Henry II the lands of William Paynel of Drax were divided between the two sons of his first marriage on the one hand, and his daughter by a second marriage and her husband, Robert de Gant, on the other. Despite opposed political allegiances, which led to conflicting grants by Stephen and Henry of Anjou, and despite the fact that one half was subsequently subdivided unequally between the two sons, each half returned the same quota of 15 in 1166.[69] Sometime before 1100 Joel of Totnes was established by William Rufus in the honour of Barnstaple. When Joel died before 1130 his lands descended to a childless son and then to two daughters married respectively to Henry de Tracy and Philip de Briouze. In 1165 their sons each accounted for the service of 25 knights.[70] William de Rames, lord of Rayne in Essex, who died before 1130, left his estates to two sons, Robert and Roger. Robert died without issue before 1142 and the lands were reunited, but when Roger died before 1159 they were split up once again. In 1159 each half of the original barony accounted for 9½ fees, but as each enjoyed a reduction of half a knight the quota of each half must have been 10, which one half had in fact returned in 1166.[71] Hardouin de l'Escalerie, the Domesday tenant of Caxton, Cambridgeshire, divided

[68] Round, 295-6.
[69] *Early Yorkshire Charters*, vi, 19, 32-3.
[70] *Pipe Roll 31 Henry I*, 153; *Pipe Roll 11 Henry II*, 80.
[71] J. H. Round, *Geoffrey de Mandeville*, London 1892, 399-404; *Pipe Roll 5 Henry II*, 5; *Liber Niger*, i, 240, which is superior to *Red Book*, 356-7.

his lands between two sons. In 1166 his grandsons each returned a quota of 15.[72] In all these cases only three explanations seem possible. One is that the quotas of the separate fragments of these baronies happened to coincide. A second is that equal quotas were imposed subsequently to the division of the baronies. A third is that an existing quota was divided when an estate was partitioned, and there can be little real doubt that this last is the most satisfactory explanation. If so, then the Paynel quota must have been settled before 1154; the Barnstaple quota, certainly, and the Rayne quota, probably, before 1130; and the quota for Caxton within a few years of the end of the eleventh century. The acquisition of the lands of heiresses provides evidence less strict in its implications, but pointing to the same conclusion. The *carta* which William de Roumare returned in 1166 made no distinction between the honour of Bolingbroke, the lands of the heiress Lucy, on the one hand, and the patrimony of the Roumare family in Hampshire and Wiltshire on the other. These estates had long been associated for Lucy's second husband, Roger son of Gerald de Roumare, who brought them together, died c.1097.[73] Yet in 1159 and in 1162 the Roumare patrimony was assessed separately at 20 fees.[74]

All this seems to lead on to a ready acceptance of Round's great thesis of 1891. But it is not quite so easy, for at the very core of Round's case there lay a simplification at once unacceptable and inaccurate. It is contained in his statement:

> I hold that . . . [the tenant-in-chief's] military service was in no way derived or developed from that of the Anglo-Saxons, but was arbitrarily fixed by the king, from whom he received his fief, irrespectively both of its size and of all pre-existent arrangements.[75]

It is clear from the context that Round was not referring to any king, but to William the Conqueror. His statement was aimed in determined fashion against the notion of 'continuity', but it also conveyed the impression that the Conqueror, at one and the same time and in one and the same act, established both a barony and its service quota, and that impression has been a pervading influence ever since Round wrote. The difficulty, of course, is that although a quota might be established in a moment the honour to which it was attached could not. One of the curiosities of the historiography of Anglo-Norman feudal tenures is that this problem was recognised or at least dimly perceived long ago. Few apparently now read Stubbs' *Constitutional History* on the introduction of knight-service, yet the sixth edition of volume 1 appeared in 1897, six years after Round's famous paper, and Stubbs overcame his episcopal responsibilities and defied the onset of academic encrustation to the extent of making three amendments to the existing text. The first referred to Round's paper and accepted his distinction between the 'exaction of military service' and the 'carving out of the land into knights' fees'. The second amounted to a cautious acceptance of Round's main point:

> The early date at which the due service (debitum servitium) of feudal tenants appears as fixed goes a long way to prove that it was settled in each case at the time of the royal grant.

But that concession to the new view was followed immediately by a third amendment

---

[72] *Curia Regis Rolls*, v, 139-40; *Red Book*, 367-9.
[73] GEC, vii, 743-4.
[74] *Pipe Roll 5 Henry II*, 47; *Pipe Roll 8 Henry II*, 36.
[75] Round, 261.

to the old text — '*It must not however be assumed that this process was other than gradual.*'[76] Maitland also sank a probe into this central vagueness at the heart of Round's argument. He, like Stubbs, was convinced in principle, and agreed that 'We have good reason to believe that the Conqueror when he enfeoffed his followers with tracts of forfeited land defined the number of knights with which they were to supply him'. But he added a prescient footnote:

> This we regard as having been proved by Mr Round's convincing papers . . . Sometimes when land came to the king by way of escheat and was granted out, new terms would be imposed on the new tenant; but, in the main, the settlement made in the Conqueror's day was permanent.[77]

That note, properly pursued, would have started several important questions to which Round's hypothesis gives rise. For the situation which he imagined, in which an honour created in its entirety was bestowed on a baron in return for a specified amount of military service, can have occurred but rarely. The land which the Conqueror used to endow his followers came to his disposal in successive lots: in 1066 the old royal estates of the Anglo-Danish royal house, the possessions of the family of Godwin and the lands of those who had fought and lost at Hastings; in 1069-71 the midland and northern estates of Earls Edwin and Morcar and their followers; in 1075 the East Anglian properties of Ralph Guader. Even along the southern English littoral, in Sussex, where the first baronies were established between 1067 and 1070, Mr Mason has convincingly demonstrated that there was extensive subsequent readjustment.[78] Further north the great baronies were built up even more obviously by miscellaneous acquisition. Count Alan of Brittany cannot have received many of his estates in Yorkshire before the fall of Earl Edwin in 1071; it is unlikely that he received the Lincolnshire and Norfolk estates of Ralph the Staller before the rebellion of Ralph Guader in 1075; the honour of Richmond was of composite origin.[79] So also was the honour of Chester. As recorded in Domesday it was a hotch-potch, made up of lands which had been held not only by English predecessors — Harold, Earl Siward, Earl Edwin, and Eadnoth the Staller, but also by Frenchmen — Walter of Dol, Ralph de Beaufou; and indeed in one estate Walter of Dol had been preceded in King William's time by Walter of Caen. As William Farrer noted, 'it is improbable that Earl Hugh obtained all the lands that he held in 1086 at the same time'.[80] Nor did the process of accretion end in 1086. It was continued after 1088 by the escheat and redistribution of the estates of Odo of Bayeux and of some of the lands of Robert, Count of Mortain; in 1095 by the escheat of the lands of Robert de Mowbray; and these were but the first of successive deprivations and redistributions continuing until after Tinchebrai. All this left its mark. The Bigod fee in Suffolk included manors which Roger Bigod had held of Odo of Bayeux at the time of Domesday.[81] So also did the Lacy fee in Yorkshire

---

[76] W. Stubbs, *Constitutional History of England*, 6th edn, Oxford 1897, i, 284-5. Cf. 4th edn, 1883, i, 284-5.
[77] F. Pollock and F. W. Maitland, *History of English Law*, Cambridge 1898, i, 258, 259n.
[78] J. F. A. Mason, *William the First and the Sussex Rapes*, Historical Association, Hastings and Bexhill Branch, 1966, 13-16.
[79] *Early Yorkshire Charters*, iv, 2, 94-5, 117; *Lincolnshire Domesday*, 63-8; *Domesday Book*, ii, 144, 147, 148b; VCH *Norfolk*, ii, 10, 17; GEC, ix, 568-74; x, 783-4.
[80] W. Farrer, *Honors and Knights' Fees*, ii, London 1924, 5-6.
[81] VCH *Suffolk*, i, 392-3.

and other counties.[82] The Mowbray fee included over 100 carucates in Yorkshire, Lincolnshire and Nottinghamshire which Gilbert Tison had held at the time of the Survey.[83] Lands held by Erneis de Burun in 1086 are later found in the Mowbray, Trussebut and Paynel fees;[84] all three lordships had decimal quotas in 1166.

How were the decimal quotas established for such conglomerate baronies? There seem to be four obvious hypotheses. The first is that estates, as they were combined and redistributed during and after the Conqueror's reign, already carried service which happened in combination to produce decimal quotas. That demands excessive faith in coincidence; moreover, when such a process can be observed in the late twelfth century it clearly had the opposite effect of producing random quotas. A second possibility is that the quotas were not established until the end of the process of territorial agglomeration, and this too is unconvincing. There is clear evidence, too well known to require further discussion here, that William the Conqueror had imposed quotas on ecclesiastical tenants-in-chief by 1070/72.[85] Moreover, there appears to be no obvious explanation of why we should allow Rufus and Henry I to impose arbitrary quotas, but not William. Yet again the territorial flux did not cease at any one point in time. There was no occasion when Rufus or Henry could assume that all was at last ship-shape and ready for the establishment of the neat, artificial system much of which still survived in 1166. Finally, the process led increasingly away from decimal towards random quotas; this stage had already been reached when Henry I began to enfeof William d'Aubigny, his butler.[86]

This leaves two possibilities. One is that nothing was done to change the quota when new estates were added to an honour. The other is that the quota was recast, either in the Conqueror's time or later, as additions or changes were made to the estates of an honour, but recast within the system of arbitrary, decimal figures. These hypotheses are not mutually exclusive. Policy must have depended on the King's relations with a particular tenant-in-chief, perhaps on the size of a barony and its existing quota, on whether the accretion of estates came suddenly or as a more continuous trickle, on whether the lands were enfeoffed or not. Hence it is reasonable to assume in any particular case that the quota may have been either maintained or recast.

The evidence on this matter is very fragile. The first hint comes from two episcopal baronies: Thetford/Norwich, which has been carefully examined by Miss Dodwell;[87] and London, which was discussed by Round.[88] In each case the baronies carried decimal quotas, of forty and twenty respectively; and for Norwich the quota can be shown to have been established before 1111-13. In each case the Domesday Survey listed considerable acquisitions made by divers and sometimes devious means between 1066 and 1086, one at least of which in the case of Thetford/Norwich can scarcely have been held as a tenancy-in-chief before 1075.[89] In each case the acquisitions were listed separately from the other episcopal holdings. Those of Thetford/Norwich

---

82 *Early Yorkshire Charters*, iii, 123, 125; Whiteman, 31-2.
83 *Early Yorkshire Charters*, xii, 19-23.
84 *Charters of the Honour of Mowbray*, xxii-xxiii; *Early Yorkshire Charters*, vi, 57; x, 23-4.
85 The importance of the writ to Aethelwig, abbot of Evesham, which Round, 303-4, rightly emphasised, is not seriously diminished by Richardson and Sayles, 64-5.
86 See above, p.98.
87 Barbara Dodwell, 'The Honour of the Bishop of Thetford/Norwich in the late eleventh and early twelfth centuries', *Norfolk Archaeology* xxxiii, pt 2, 1963, 185-99.
88 VCH *Essex*, i, 339.
89 Eccles was recorded in Domesday Book as a tenancy held of Earl Ralph; Dodwell, 186.

are headed *terra de feudo*; those of London *feudum episcopi*.[90] Whatever is made of this, it seems clear that the Domesday commissioners were conscious of the problem created by territorial accretion, and in these cases they seem to be settling it by stating that the acquisitions were part of, not separate from, the service quota. An alternative, less acceptable hypothesis would be that these acquisitions *were* the whole fee, but this does not tally with the pattern of subenfeoffment. The gains were considerable. In the case of Thetford/Norwich Miss Dodwell noted that 'they radically altered the balance of properties ...' and since they lay in south-east Norfolk 'cannot but have facilitated the later move [of the diocesan centre] to Norwich'.[91] But, whichever hypothesis is adopted, there is nothing definite to show whether territorial accretion affected the quota in these instances or not.

Some further light is shed on the problem by the break-up of the lands of Robert and William of Mortain, for their enfeoffments might still survive as small 'fiefs of Mortain' in the late twelfth century. It is certain that some of their estates in the north, which never seem to have been restored after Robert's rebellion of 1088, were incorporated in other baronies without any apparent effect on the quota or the rate at which fees were charged.[92] In many southern counties, in contrast, these accretions tended to figure as fees of Mortain additional to a separate quota charged at the full rate, and it may well be significant that charters to the monastery of Marmoutiers demonstrate that William of Mortain still had control of some of his Dorset estates in 1104-6.[93] The different treatment of the Mortain estates may then reflect the date at which they escheated: the earlier escheats being incorporated in existing or revised *servitia*; the later escheats leaving the characteristic increments to *servitia* in the form of fees of Mortain.

This problem is probably incapable of any general solution. However, it matters less than a more obvious point which Round's argument obscured. Whatever view is taken of the perpetuation or reconstruction of the original quotas it is clear that Rufus and Henry I still had the capacity to establish considerable territorial agglomerations, either *ab initio* or through reconstruction, which carried decimal quotas. The last obvious examples are the Redvers barony of Plympton which must have been established by 1107 and the Brus barony of Skelton which originated at about the same time. The first probably and the second certainly were assessed at fifteen knights.[94] Moreover, it seems probable that the main reason for moving away from such assessments toward random quotas is not to be found in any deliberate change in royal policy but in the fact that estates available for redistribution to deserving supporters were encumbered with sitting tenants. Now if this is so it necessarily reflects on the *rationale* behind the whole system. It has been argued with increasing force in the last two decades, most convincingly of all by J. O. Prestwich, that the Norman kings relied on long-term military service for pay and other rewards and that the service quotas were an unreal basis for the muster of an effective fighting

---

90 *Domesday Book*, ii, 11, 193.
91 Dodwell, 187.
92 *Early Yorkshire Charters*, ii, 11, 16, 19; vi, 57-8.
93 *Cal. Docs. France*, 1209.
94 On Skelton see above, p.97. The 15 owed from Plympton was the recognised service and apparently included Christchurch and the Isle of Wight, *Book of Fees*, 74. At the end of the twelfth century scutage was also paid on 45 fees which were not recognised, *Pipe Roll 6 Richard*, 171; *Pipe Roll 1 John*, 199. It may be that the break in the tenure of the honour in the reign of Stephen lies behind the discrepancy, GEC, iv, 309-12.

force.[95] What then was their function? It might easily be imagined that the Conqueror introduced the system simply because he could not conceive of land held freely on any other terms, and it is this escape-route which the present argument necessarily closes. For if, as Round argued, the quotas were established by the Conqueror, it follows that the quotas must have been reconsidered and confirmed or readjusted, and in some cases established *ab initio* by Rufus and Henry I. And few would be ready to accept the hazardous hypothesis that not just one, but all three, were acting in unquestioning, purposeless, absence of mind.

At this point the Pipe Rolls provide an invaluable cross-bearing. At first sight they seem to fit into a neat scheme in which tenants-in-chief either paid scutage or not, and in which the scutage was calculated *pro rata*, on the quota up to 1166 and thereafter on the old or new enfeoffment. The system of the Normans was apparently still in working order. But there is a difficulty, serious enough to wreck such a neat reconstruction. The implication of the Pipe Roll evidence is that men paid their full scutage, or none at all, and hence that they served with their full quota or not at all. Now there are many entries of quittances on only a part of the service due, but these are usually allocated to under-tenants, who had presumably given their service; indeed some of these under-tenants were themselves tenants-in-chief and can be shown on such occasions to have received quittances in that capacity also. But, these cases apart, the Pipe Rolls scarcely ever reflect the ordinary accidents of military organisation and campaigning. The record never mentions tenants-in-chief charged just on one or two fees, representing tenants who lay sick abed or had important engagements elsewhere. Now that must mean that the impression of the Pipe Rolls is unreal and unacceptable. And that in turn means that service in the field must have been acquitted not necessarily by the precise quota but by a reasonable turn-out acceptable to the King and his Marshal; and what that amounted to must have depended on many other factors: the interest of the tenant-in-chief in military matters, the period for which he and his men were ready to serve, and so on. In short, the earliest Pipe Rolls at first hide, but in fact imply, that feudal obligations were met as they were later, in the late twelfth and early thirteenth centuries, when service in the field was not precisely related to the quota or to the old or new enfeoffment.

If these arguments are correct they help to explain an unusual feature of the *cartae* of 1166. A considerable number of tenants-in-chief expressed ignorance of their quotas or reported some difficulty in establishing what it was: that they had had to enquire, for example, from juries or from the ancient men of the fee. In some cases these difficulties can be directly related to the history of the tenancy, but not in all. Earl Patrick of Salisbury reported his enfeoffment and quota of forty knights after enquiring from 'his honest and ancient men';[96] the 'ancient men' of the barony of Little Dunmow likewise informed Walter fitz Robert that his quota was fifty;[97] and Geoffrey de Mandeville consulted with the men of his fee to establish that his quota was sixty.[98] These statements, otherwise difficult to explain, fall into place if it is accepted that service need not have been performed at the level prescribed by the quota. For the common feature of the *cartae* quoted above is not that these

---

[95] J. O. Prestwich, 'War and Finance in the Anglo-Norman State', *TRHS*, 5th ser., 4, 19-43. Since feudal tenants often served for diverse forms of reward quite apart from their due service I have deliberately avoided the word 'mercenary'.

[96] *Red Book*, 239-40.

[97] *Red Book*, 348.

[98] *Red Book*, 347.

men had not served; if their absence from the earlier accounts from 1159 to 1165 can be taken at its face value, they had; but that they had not paid scutage. And if the payments of sums assessed against the knight's shield was the main practice keeping the quota alive, then it is probable that these men, and others who served regularly, had not been required to remember their quotas for a very long time. There need be no wonder that the memories of the ancients had to be searched.

Nothing has bedevilled the discussion of military service in Anglo-Norman England so much as the peculiar nature of the *cartae* and the related Pipe Roll evidence. In one aspect they are a living record, a revelation of a system of financial assessment still being hammered out and refined. In another aspect they are dead, an archaeological deposit left by the tenurial history of the previous century. The reality of the one should not be confused with the unreality of the other. The *cartae* were drawn up at a time when the pattern of enfeoffment was changing. Henry II continued old established quotas, but he never attempted to establish new baronies with large decimal quotas. Berkeley, with a quota of five, was an example from the first years of the reign and was probably determined by the fact that it had formed part of an already established barony. For the rest, Henry II was satisfied with small *servitia* which rarely exceeded one knight. Admittedly by this time, there was less opportunity for the Crown to redistribute property in the large-scale lavish manner of Rufus and Henry I. But Henry II made no obvious attempt to follow earlier practice, and the small baronies and quotas of his reign are better associated with the later enfeoffments of Richard and John. At least that was so in England. In Ireland it was different, for Henry II was to Ireland as the Conqueror had been to England, and Henry, who never established a single new barony with a quota of more than five in England, imposed a quota of a hundred on Leinster, sixty on Limerick, sixty on Cork and fifty on Meath.[99] At the same time the Norman aristocracy, heavily engaged in conspicuous expenditure on more comfortable stone-built castles in England, reverted to raising motte and baileys by the dozen in the newly subject land across the Irish sea.[100] The old system was dead, but could be resuscitated very rapidly if the circumstances required. And, as in England earlier, so in Ireland the system soon became unreal, overlain by scutage and paid service within not much more than a generation of the first settlement.

What then was the system? Is system even the right word? It seems to have amounted simply to this: that when, or perhaps before, the Conqueror in England or Henry II in Ireland granted large estates to their followers they wanted some guarantee that the recipients would contribute towards the successful maintenance of the conquest. Hence the imposition of quotas. Was it 'when' or 'before'? In Ireland it was 'when'; quota and endowment coincided. In England the quota could have come first, to be matched by territorial endowment as and when it became available. That is consistent with the indications that decimal quotas survived territorial accretion. There is no need to follow Round in imposing the practices of the twelfth century, in which specified service was performed for precisely defined tenure, on the crucial years immediately after the Conquest. The English quotas were large in comparison with those in Normandy, or in the case of Ireland in comparison with Henry II's enfeoffments in England, not because William was more powerful as king

99 J. Otway-Ruthven, 'Knight Service in Ireland', *Journal of the Royal Society of Antiquaries of Ireland*, lxxxix, 1959, 1-15.
100 H. G. Leask, *Irish Castles and Castellated Houses*, Dundalk 1964, 6-11: G. H. Orpen, *Ireland under the Normans*, Oxford 1911, i, 338-43; ii, map.

than as duke, or simply because Henry II wanted to bring the Norman adventurers in Ireland to heel, but because of the greater urgency in newly conquered lands. There is little to suggest that either William I or Henry II expected their vassals to stand in serried ranks of fives and tens to be told off by numbers from the right; military urgencies were likely to be too immediate for such strict accounting. At this preliminary stage too, as regards the conquest of England, there can have been little serious intention of using an army so raised for war on the continent; nor was there much possibility yet of exploiting the quotas as fiscal assessments. These emphases came in later generations, the result first of the wars among William's sons and then of the wide ranging interests of the Angevin kings. If the rigid accountancy of the late twelfth-century Exchequer is transferred from scutage to service and then from late twelfth-century service to late eleventh-century service the system looks woefully illogical and unsatisfactory. How could men serve both as tenants-in-chief and under-tenants, for example? And how could they fight in the field and defend their castles at one and the same time? But the system in its origin was real enough if viewed as a simple, rough-and-ready practical response to the hazards of conquest.

SCANDINAVIAN INFLUENCE IN NORMAN LITERATURE OF THE ELEVENTH CENTURY

Elisabeth M. C. van Houts

The purpose of this article* is to trace the possible use of Scandinavian sources and, on a more general level, to discuss Scandinavian influences on Norman literature of the eleventh century. Such a survey will enable us to prove or disprove the now commonly accepted notion that the rupture in political and economic relations between Normandy and Scandinavia after c.1025 self-evidently meant a break in the cultural contacts between those areas. It has also been argued that the breakdown in Norman-Scandinavian relations from that time onwards reflected the attitude of the Normans; feeling and acting like Frenchmen they ignored completely their Viking background. I hope to show that although this view might hold true for political and institutional history it needs revision in so far as cultural aspects are concerned.

The first two authors whose work I shall discuss are Garnier of Rouen who wrote a Latin poem, or rather satire, against the Irishman Moriuth; and Dudo of Saint-Quentin, author of the first history of the Norman dukes. Let me begin with the poem about Moriuth.[1]

Some time before the year 1000 the Irish poet Moriuth and his wife were captured by the Vikings and taken away separately. As prisoner, Moriuth was chained and taken by boat to a slave-market outside Ireland. During this most unpleasant trip the Vikings made him their laughing-stock. The poor poet happened to be very hirsute — but with a bald head: a physiognomy which caused the Vikings much fun. The *Dani* standing around him ridiculed his wolflike appearance; they urinated on his head and played other nasty tricks on him. It certainly must have been a relief for Moriuth when the Vikings delivered him at the Northumbrian town of Corbridge, where the Irishman was sold as a slave to a monastery of nuns. His hell would soon change into heaven: he told them he was a poet and thus he entertained the nuns,

* I am most grateful to Dr David Abulafia and Dr Anna Sapir Abulafia, who, once again, corrected my English, and to Dr Diana E. Greenway without whose kind assistance the finishing touch to this article would not have been realised. I also wish to acknowledge the financial assistance of the British Academy and the Netherlands Organization for the Advancement of Pure Research (Z.W.O.).

[1] 'Satire de Garnier de Rouen contre le poète Moriuth (X-XIe siècles)', ed. H. Omont, *Annuaire-Bulletin de la Société de l'Histoire de France* xxxi, 1891, 193-210. L. Musset, 'Le satiriste Garnier de Rouen et son milieu (début du XIe siècle)', *Revue du Moyen Age Latin* x, 1954, 237-67. B. Leblond, *L'accession des Normands de Neustrie à la culture occidentale (X-XIe siècles)*, Paris 1966, 182-3, 279-81. J. Campbell, 'England, France, Flanders and Germany, some comparisons and connections', *Ethelred the Unready. Papers from the millenary conference*, ed. D. Hill, Oxford 1970 [BAR, British Series, 59] 255-70, esp. 261. M. Lapidge, 'Three Latin poems of Aethelwold's school at Winchester', *Anglo-Saxon England*, i, 1972, 85-145, esp. 101-3. L. Musset, 'Rouen et l'Angleterre vers l'an mil', *Annales de Normandie* xxiv, 1974, 287-90.

but not only with his self-made verses. Despite his baldness he was able to seduce more than one nun, but unfortunately he overreached himself. His advances were turned down and he was chased from the convent. From that moment, his wandering life led him from one slave-market to another in search of his lost Irish wife. In the end he found her in Vaudreuil, a place not far from Rouen, where she worked as a slave in a spinning-mill. At the intercession of no less a person than Duchess Gunnor, to whom Moriuth had turned for help, she was bought free. The Irish couple decided to settle down in Rouen and Moriuth took up his career as a poet. But his new Rouen colleagues thought his poems to be of a less than inferior quality. One of them, Garnier of Rouen, wrote a satire against him, and this Latin poem is the source for our knowledge of Moriuth's life.

In plain and often obscene words Garnier depicts a not very flattering portrait of Moriuth. He alternately refers to him as a hairy monster, a wolf or a goat. Yet this poem, at times funny but also obscure, gives us an enormous amount of information about the wandering life of an Irishman who, on his way to search for his wife, crossed Northern Europe. Twice on his trip he was captured by the Vikings and twice he escaped from their hands. He might also have had earlier experiences with Vikings in the time before he was captured. I do not think it unlikely that Moriuth originated from the coastal areas of Ireland, which were heavily populated by Scandinavians.[2] The occasional contacts between Moriuth and Vikings, or Scandinavian people in general, might underlie some of Moriuth's pagan practices described by Garnier.

According to Garnier the Irish poet consulted the pagan gods three times during his long search for his wife to ask them where she might be. The first time was just after he was chased from the nunnery in Corbridge, when, acting like an augur, he consulted the intestines of a woodpecker. Later on, while Moriuth was wandering through *Saxonia* he did the same thing. This time however he used not a (black) bird, but a young girl, whom he had sacrificed to his gods. After his arrival'in Rouen he asked their help a third time.[3] These pagan rituals are strongly reminiscent of Viking sacrificial ceremonies and, as I have already indicated, may point to a mixed Hiberno-Scandinavian background of Moriuth.[4]

Yet another conclusion may be drawn from Garnier's poem, namely that in about 1000 Rouen was both a commercial and a literary centre, closely in contact with the British Isles and Scandinavia. The poem *Contra Moriuth* written in the Norman capital can be profitably compared to a form of dialogue widely attested in especially Norse and Irish vernacular literature, namely the *flyting*. In his discussion of similar poems to the ones Garnier wrote Dr Lapidge draws attention to the vernacular

---

[2] F. Henry, *Irish Art during the Viking invasions 800-1200 A D*, London 1967, gives a useful account of the Scandinavian settlement in Ireland. See also: Th. D. Kendrick, *A history of the Vikings*, London 1930, 274-99. D. O. Corrain, *Ireland before the Normans*, Dublin 1972, 80-110.

[3] 'Satire de Garnier contre Moriuth', ed. Omont, vv 145-50, vv 189-202, vv 269-70.

[4] See for Scandinavian religion and sacrificial rites: L. Musset, *Les peuples Scandinaves au Moyen Age*, Paris 1951, 33-8. J. de Vries, *Altnordische Religionsgeschichte*, i, Berlin 1956, 2nd edn, 406-38. H. Kuhn, 'Die Religion der nordischen Völker in der Vikingerzeit', *I Normanni e la loro espansione in Europa nell'alto Medioevo*, Spoleto 1969 (Settimane di Studio del Centro Italiano di Studi sull'alto Medioevo, 16) 117-29, esp. 121-2. G. Jones, *A history of the Vikings*, Oxford 1968, 315-34. E. O. G. Turville-Petre, *Myth and Religion of the North. The religion of ancient Scandinavia*, London 1964, 236-63. A. P. Smyth, *Scandinavian Kings in the British Isles, 850-880*, Oxford 1977, 201-24. P. H. Sawyer, *Kings and Vikings*, London-New York 1982, 131-43.

flytings which are often violent *invectivae*. Although the poem against Moriuth has not been written in the form of a dialogue it certainly is a dialogue between Garnier and Moriuth, two rival poets. In this context I wish to stress the important fact that *flytings* and Latin poems more or less belonging to that genre are not to be found elsewhere outside Normandy, the British Isles and Scandinavia, thus proving the close literary links between these areas.[5]

According to Garnier's poem against Moriuth, not only slaves but also those of a 'higher social' level of society knew tales like the one about Moriuth. In this case at least three persons were informed about him: his colleague Garnier, Duchess Gunnor,[6] who bought Moriuth's wife free, and her son Robert Archbishop of Rouen, to whom the poem was dedicated. It is probable that they were not the only people who knew about Moriuth. Other colleagues of Garnier and Moriuth as well as people connected with the ducal court might have been familiar with the fate of Moriuth and his wife. A person who belonged to both categories and therefore might have been well informed was, of course, Dudo of Saint-Quentin.[7] Professor Musset has convincingly shown that both Garnier and Dudo belonged to the same literary school of Rouen and probably knew each other. In any case Dudo's functions as ducal chaplain and chancellor are well known.[8] Garnier included contemporary Viking stories and, as far as pagan rituals are concerned, tales of what were probably Scandinavian sacrificial rites. Is Dudo an equally reliable source when he describes Viking and Scandinavian practices in his account of the Norman past and present?

Dudo of Saint-Quentin, a Vermandois himself and thus a French immigrant in Normandy, probably finished his history of the Norman dukes before 1015.[9] His main informant was Radulf of Ivry, half-brother of Duke Richard I who commissioned Dudo to write a history of the ducal house. Richard and Radulf had the same mother, Sprota, who was of Breton origin. Dudo included passages on pagan sacrificial rituals similar to the ones which Garnier described. He wrote about the Vikings sacrificing human blood to their war-god Thor and about their priest consulting the intestines of an ox to know beforehand the outcome of the next Viking raid.[10] Although we have to be cautious not to rely too much on Dudo's political history, we may follow his account in so far as it depicts Scandinavian customs. Hardly anyone would now doubt his statements about Rollo dividing land among his *fideles* by way of the *funiculus*.[11] Nor do scholars doubt the veracity of Dudo's account of Rollo's trick to divert a French attack near Chartres. According to Dudo, Rollo told his men to slaughter all the horses and other animals in order to use their corpses to build a *castrum*. The French approaching this animal castle did not dare to attack it, afraid

5 Lapidge, 'Three latin poems', 98-9.
6 See for the identification of the *domina comitissa* ('Satire de Garnier contre Moriuth', ed. Omont, vv 237-9): Musset, 'Le satiriste Garnier de Rouen', 252.
7 Musset, 'Le satiriste Garnier de Rouen', 247-8.
8 M. Fauroux, 'Deux autographes de Dudon de Saint-Quentin', *Bibliothèque de l'Ecole des Chartes* cxi, 1953, 229-34.
9 See for Dudo of Saint-Quentin also: G. Huisman, 'Notes on the manuscript tradition of Dudo of Saint-Quentin's *Gesta Normannorum*', below, 122-35.
10 Dudo, 129-30.
11 Dudo, 171. J. Yver, 'Les premières institutions du duché de Normandie', *I Normanni e la loro espansione in Europa nell'alto Medioevo* (see above, note 4), 299-366, esp. 321 note 52. D. Douglas, 'The rise of Normandy', *Time and the Hour. Some collected papers of D. C. Douglas*, London 1977, 97 (originally published in *Proceedings of the British Academy* xxxiii, 1947, 101-31). See for a more sceptical opinion D. Bates, *Normandy before 1066*, London 1982, 22.

as they were of such a barbaric scene.[12] Another example is the berserker passage. Even Prentout, one of Dudo's most severe critics, had to admit that there might be some truth in the description of William Longsword and thirty of his followers acting like berserkers while taking an oath with a great deal of noise and thus performing the Scandinavian *vapnatak*.[13]

Concerning the veracity of such tales we have to bear in mind that Dudo, like Garnier, wrote at a time when some of the grandchildren of the first permanent settlers in Normandy were still alive (e.g. Duke Richard and his half-brother Radulf of Ivry). They recounted memorable events from the heroic past, which inevitably would contain pagan Scandinavian reminiscences. Dudo included these in his account knowing that they could be corroborated by contemporary accounts from people in direct contact with Scandinavians, whether they were Vikings or tradesmen. Indeed, it can be deduced from Dudo's work that he used eyewitness accounts by contemporary Scandinavians. In Book IV Dudo relates how Duke Richard I asked the Danes' assistance in his struggle against the alliance of the French king and Thibald of Chartres.[14] The Danes came and together with Duke Richard they defeated the French enemy. After the victory Duke Richard persuaded the Danes to let themselves be baptised in Rouen. Those of them who preferred their own pagan religion were expelled from Normandy and went to Spain.[15] There, according to Dudo, they raided the coastal areas, conquered eighteen towns and fought a battle (the battle of Lisbon in 966) against the Spanish *rusticani*. For this account Dudo used a record of an eyewitness:[16] 'On the third day (after the battle) the Vikings returned to the battlefield and while they turned the dead to disrobe them, they saw that those parts of the bodies of the black Ethiopians which had touched the ground were whiter than snow, whereas the other parts (of the bodies) had kept their original (black) colour'. Dudo then continues — and I stress this point because it is one of the few prose passages in which Dudo addresses himself directly to his readers — 'I wonder how the dialecticians, who with regard to the *accidens* (black) for raven and Ethiopian consider the two to be inseparable, will explain this now that they know (lit. see) that it has changed (namely parts of black bodies being white)'.[17] Obviously we have here a description of an encounter between Vikings and people of darker skin than the Scandinavians. They might have been Saracens, whom the Vikings thought to be entirely dark skinned, like Negroes, and not only dark in those parts of the body exposed to the sun, i.e. the face and hands. Scandinavian saga-literature testifies to this widespread Viking belief about Saracens.[18]

---

12 Dudo, 165. H. Prentout, *Etude critique sur Dudon de Saint-Quentin et son Histoire des premiers ducs Normands*, Paris 1916, 191, 195.
13 Dudo, 190. Prentout, *Etude critique*, 300-1. Yver, 'Les premières institutions', 313 note 34.
14 Dudo, 276.
15 Dudo, 287.
16 Dudo, 287-8: *Tertio namque die campum praelii Northmanni repetentes, mortuosque, ut induviis eos privarent, vertentes, repererunt partes corporum nigellorum Aethiopumque terrae finitimas atque incumbentes nive candidiores; reliquum vero corpus pristinum colorem servans intuiti sunt.*
17 Dudo, 288: *Sed mirum mihi quid super hoc characterizabunt dialectici, qui quum accidens corvo Aethiopique categorizant inseparabile esse, hic mutatum vident.*
18 Dudo might have heard this story told to him either in Scandinavian or French in which the word *Blámenn* for blue men (read black men) was translated as *Aethiopes*, the common Latin word for Negroes. *Blámenn* was the common name for Saracens. See R. Dozy, 'Les Normands en Espagne', *Recherches sur l'histoire et la littérature de l'Espagne pendant le Moyen Age*, ii, Leyde 1869, 304-5. Prentout, *Etude critique*, 387-8.

I have discussed this passage because of the fact that Dudo used an eyewitness account which is most probably of Scandinavian origin. And it is also interesting to note Dudo's curiosity as to how the dialecticians will deal with a philosophical axiom which is found to be contradicted by a practical example.

Concerning the use of Scandinavian sources of information in the first quarter of the eleventh century, it has often been pointed out that c.1025 some Scandinavian was still spoken in Normandy.[19] We know of quite a few Scandinavians coming to Normandy as well as of direct contacts between Duke Richard II and Scandinavian kings and Vikings.[20] In 1003 the Danish king Svein Forkbeard paid a visit to Duke Richard II in Rouen and both concluded a treaty of alliance and mutual assistance.[21] At about the same period the Norman duke negotiated with the Vikings who kept Emma, the vicountess of Limoges, prisoner for nearly three years. Thanks to the duke's interference she was freed from the hands of the Vikings.[22] Shortly before 1014 the Norwegian Viking Olaf, who later became King of Norway and the first Norwegian martyr, arrived in Normandy to stay for about one season. He was baptised by Archbishop Robert in Rouen.[23] About ten years later Olaf's Icelandic skald, Sigvatr and his friend Berg, also visited Rouen.[24] From these contacts we may conclude that direct communication and therefore direct exchange of information, either literary or not, existed between Normandy and the Scandinavian countries. These relations were based on a mutual Scandinavian background still considered as being in existence in both areas.

The third quarter of the eleventh century, and especially the decade after the Conquest of England was a fruitful time for Norman literature and historiography.[25] Three major works were written in that period and all three of them bear evidence of Scandinavian influences. I will begin with the *Carmen de Hastingae Proelio*.[26]

In this Latin poem the burial of King Harold after the Battle of Hastings is described as a purely Viking funeral. At the end of the battle-day Harold's dismembered body was ordered by Duke William to be brought back to his camp. When Harold's mother arrived to ask for her son's body in exchange for its weight in gold, the duke became furious. He swore that he would rather give Harold the custody of the harbour. To fulfil this threat the duke ordered Harold's body to be buried under a heap of stones on top of a cliff as *custos littoris et pelagi*, guardian of the shore

[19] L. Musset, *Les invasions. Le second assaut contre l'Europe chrétienne (VII-XIe siècle)*, Paris 1971, 2nd edn, 267. Bates, *Normandy before 1066*, 20-1.
[20] L. Musset, 'L'image de la Scandinavie dans les oeuvres Normandes de la période ducale (911-1204)', *Les relations littéraires Franco-Scandinaves au Moyen Age*, Paris 1975 (Bibliothèque de la Faculté de Philosophie et Lettres de l'université de Liège, 208) 193-215, esp. 198-200. Bates, *Normandy before 1066*, 37.
[21] Jumièges, 80. M. Fauroux, *Recueil des actes des ducs de Normandie (911-1066)*, Caen 1961, 23.
[22] *Adémar de Chabannes, Chronique*, ed. J. Chavanon, Paris 1897, 166-7.
[23] Jumièges, 85-7. See also below, 119.
[24] 'Sigvatr, Vestrfararvisur', ed. Finnur Jonsson, *Den Norsk-Islandske Skjaldedigtning*, Copenhague-Christiana 1912-16, 4 vols, i, 241-3; ii, 226-8; translation: *Heimskringla, history of the kings of Norway by Snorri Sturlason*, transl. L. M. Hollander, Austin 1964, 436. See also J. Adigard de Gautries, *Les noms de personne en Normandie de 911 à 1066*, Lund 1954, 69-70.
[25] E. R. Labande, 'L'historiographie de la France de l'Ouest aux Xe et XIe siècles', *La Storiografia altomedievale*, Spoleto 1970 (Settimane etc. 17, see note 4), 751-91, esp. 760-3. A. Gransden, *Historical writing in England c.550 to c.1307*, London 1974, 92-104.
[26] I consider this poem to have been written not long after 1066. See for a discussion on the historicity of the Carmen: R. H. C. Davis, L. J. Engels, *et al.*, 'The Carmen de Hastingae Proelio: a discussion', *ante* ii, 1-20.

and the sea.[27] The two editors of the *Carmen* and Professor Jäschke have commented on this passage and they stress the fact that what is described here as a pagan funeral is a common Viking-Germanic practice of Northern Europe.[28] Viking kings often were buried near the sea, either on land or in sunken ships. With regard to the *Carmen*, Jäschke lays weight on the relationship between the burial-mound (the heap of stones) and the king's mound (a heap of stones, a small hill or some other ground on a higher level) in Germanic societies. Both mounds were often combined and played an important part in the inaugural ceremonies of new kings. A person became king while seated on the grave of his predecessor. In this case the author of the *Carmen* describes a Germanic-Viking ceremony by which William the Conqueror becomes king at the same spot where and at the same moment when his predecessor is buried.[29] A partially verbal echo of the *Carmen* version of Harold's burial can be found in William of Poitiers' *Gesta Guillelmi*. After William of Poitiers has written about Duke William's refusal to hand over Harold's body he says: 'it is said by way of mockery that the duke rather would install him (Harold) as *custos littoris et pelagi*, guardian of the shore and the sea, a post which he (Harold) had occupied before in better days'.[30]

This story which was known to the author of the *Carmen* and William of Poitiers[31] clearly reveals Scandinavian influence, but because it is connected with England we might look for the source of this tale in Scandinavian England rather than Normandy.

Of the three post-1066 Norman historiographers William of Jumièges is the historian most influenced by Scandinavian legend, not directly from the North but indirectly via England. He mentions Scandinavian involvement in Normandy, for which he often is our only continental contemporary source, and he includes Scandinavian sources; but he also presents certain facts from a Scandinavian point of view.

Already in the first book of the *Gesta Normannorum Ducum* (*GND*), concerning the coming of the Vikings in the ninth century, he introduces a completely different story from that of his predecessor and main source of information, Dudo of Saint-Quentin. Whereas this author concentrates on his hero Hastingus, who seems to be the personification of several Scandinavian leaders in Normandy,[32] William of Jumièges gives prominence, not to the Franco-Scandinavian Hastingus, but to the Anglo-Scandinavian Björn Ironside. According to William after the battle of Fontenoy (841) an internally divided kingdom of France lay open to barbarian pagans from outside. Among the first to come was Björn Ironside, son of King Lothbroc.[33] This

---

27 *Carmen*, vv 573-92, 36-8.
28 *Carmen*, xliii-xlv. K. U. Jäschke, *Wilhelm der Eroberer. Sein doppelter Herrschaftsantritt im Jahre 1066*, Sigmaringen 1977 (Vorträge and Forschungen, 24), 39-52. Both give examples for similar rites. See also J. M. Boberg, *Motif-index of early Icelandic literature*, Copenhague 1966, 226, 255-6.
29 Jäschke, *Wilhelm der Eroberer*, 46-8.
30 *Gesta Guillelmi*, 204.
31 This is the only Scandinavian reminiscence in William of Poitiers' work, apart from a few possible references to old Norman (or Scandinavian?) law on 38, 64 and 118; a reference to Ireland as a country where Danes are still living occurs on 238.
32 F. Amory, 'The Viking Hasting in Franco-Scandinavian legend', *Saints, Scholars and Heroes. Studies in medieval culture in honour of Charles W. Jones*, ed. M. King, W. Stevens, ii, Minnesota 1979, 269-86.
33 Jumièges, 5-6: *Quo tempore pagani, cum Lotbroci regis filio, nomine Bier Costae quidem ferreae, procurante ejus expeditionem Hastingo, omnium paganorum nequissimo, a Noricis seu Danicis finibus eructuantes, maritima littora incolentes continuis cladibus vexaverunt, civitates diruentes atque abbatias concremantes. Qui vero iste Lothbrocus, vel ex cujus stirpe oriundus*

king, executing the laws of his ancestors, forced his son Björn by lot into exile together with his tutor Hastingus and a multitude of *iuvenes* from his country which, according to William, has to be situated in *Noricis seu Danicis finibus*.[34] Björn acquired his nickname Ironside because of his invulnerability, which is explained by William as follows:[35] 'And therefore he was called Ironside, because, when his shield did not protect him and when he stood unarmed in the battlefield, he, invulnerable, despised whatever force or arms, for his mother had him infected with very strong magic poison.' Concerning Björn's career William tells that after ravaging France for thirty years Björn and Hastingus went to the Mediterranean in order to conquer Rome. The instigator of the plan was the ambitious Hastingus who wanted his *dominus* Björn to become emperor.[36] What followed however was not the sack of the eternal city, but the conquest of Luna,[37] a town on the coast not far from Pisa, taken by mistake because the Vikings thought that it was Rome. After this conquest Björn and Hastingus returned north separately. Björn, whom William calls *totius excidii signifer exercituumque rex*, returned to his native country, suffered shipwreck, losing most of his ships and barely reached a harbour in England.[38] From there he went to Frisia where he died.[39] His tutor Hastingus had returned straight to France, where he made peace with the French king and received the custody of Chartres.[40] We have here a combination of two stories: one about Hastingus going to Luna, as told by Dudo, and another, unknown, about Björn Ironside, son of King Lothbroc.

I do not intend to examine in detail the historicity of Björn Ironside and his father Lothbroc, but I must discuss our knowledge of the legend of these Vikings in order to trace the source of William's information. This is all the more necessary because William of Jumièges is the first written authority to mention Lothbroc and Björn Ironside.

It has long since been a point of discussion whether William's Lothbroc is the same as the Scandinavian hero depicted in the famous thirteenth-century Ragnar Lodbrocsaga. Particularly during the first decades of this century my compatriot

---

extiterit, libet subscribere posteris.
[34] Jumièges, 8-9: *Quae denique lex per multorum tempora regum inconvulsa mansit, quo adusque Lothbrocus rex de quo supra prelibavimus, patri in regno successit. Is etiam rex, patrum legibus excitus, cum ingenti juvenum agmine, sorte cogente, filium, nomine Bier Costae ferreae, a suo abdicat regno, cum ejus pedagogo Hastingo, per omnia fraudulentissimo, ut, peregrina regna petens, exteras sibi armis adquireret sedes.*
[35] Jumièges, 9: *Qui ideo Costa ferrea vocabatur, quia, nisi clipeus ei obiceretur, inermis in acie stans, armorum vim quamcumque sperneret illesus, vehementissimis matris ejus veneficiis infectus.*
[36] Jumièges, 15: *His atque hujuscemodi calamitatum malis, ut prelibavimus, Galliis non absque piaculo quorumlibet per triginta fere annorum spatium lugubre detritis, Hastingus, dominum suum ad altiora cupiens provehere, de imperiali diademate cum agmine complicum cepit attentius tractare. Postremo inito consilio, velivolum permeantes mare, Romam deliberant clandestina irruptione obtinere.*
[37] Jumièges, 15: *Sed nimia exorta tempestate, ad urbem Lunis devolvuntur, vento impellente, quae pro sui decore hoc vocabatur nomine.* See for a discussion of the famous Luna expedition: Prentout, *Etude critique*, 53-7. R. H. C. Davis, *The Normans and their myth*, London 1976, 54-5.
[38] Jumièges, 16-17: *Nam Bier, totius excidii signifer, exercituumque rex, dum nativum solum repeteret, naufragium passus, vix apud Anglos portum obtinuit, quampluribus de suis navibus submersis.*
[39] The phrase immediately following the word *submersis* does not occur in Marx' edition. It runs as follows: *Indeque Fresiam petens, ibidem obiit mortem.*
[40] Jumièges, 17.

Dr Jan de Vries made an exhaustive study of the extant versions of the Ragnar Lothbrocsaga and its sources.[41] His work became a point of departure for later scholars studying the transmission and the historicity of this Scandinavian saga. De Vries was over anxious not to use the saga as a reliable source for Scandinavian history from the eighth century onwards. Setting aside the saga, he concluded that in the ninth century two famous Viking kings existed: Lothbroc and Ragnar. The careers of both these kings were later conflated into that of one legendary hero: Ragnar Lothbroc. Whereas Lothbroc was the father of his far more famous sons Ivar, Ubba and Halfdan, who were active, and later became well known, in the British Isles, Ragnar was a different person. His latinised name *Reginherus* was found in French contemporary annals describing the Viking attack on Paris in 845. His son was, on this argument, the Viking Bern or Berno mentioned in French sources as being the leader of a group of Vikings raiding the Seine area in about 855-858. According to scholars belonging to the 'school of De Vries'[42] William of Jumièges, knowing the French-Norman *Reginherus* and *Berno*, invented the Ragnar Lothbroc saga which we find in the *GND*;[43] and so laid the base for the thirteenth-century Scandinavian Ragnarssaga.

Another line of argument represented by Steenstrup, Vogel and Loomis was recently taken up by Smyth.[44] These scholars identify the *Ragnall* known from Irish sources, the *Lothbroc* from English sources and the French *Reginherus* as one and the same ninth-century historical person; a point of view which is doubtful because of the scanty historical evidence. Smyth's book however can be profitably used as far as the growth of the legend of Lothbroc from the mid-eleventh century onwards is concerned.

Let us now return to William of Jumièges and the fact that he is the oldest known written authority to mention the name Lothbroc. About two decades later Adam of Bremen, who wrote c.1088, calls Lothbroc's son Ivar the most cruel of all Vikings, while referring to him as Ivar son of *Lodparcus* and thus betraying his knowledge of the name Lothbroc. Adam explicitly mentions his source of information, namely

---

[41] *Volsungasaga ok Ragnarssaga Lodbrókar*, ed. M. Olsen, Copenhague 1906-1908 (Samfund til ud givelse af gammel Nordisk Litteratur, 36). Translated in *Thule, altnordische Dichtung und Prosa*, Jena 1926, no. 21, 139-99. J. de Vries, 'Die Entwicklung der Sage von den Lodbrokssöhne in den historischen Quellen', *Arkiv för Nordisk Filologi* xliv, 1928, 117-63. Idem, 'Die historischen Grundlagen der Ragnarssaga Lodbrókar', *Arkiv för Nordisk Filologi* xxxix, 1923, 244-74. Idem, 'Die ostnordische Überlieferung der Sage von Ragnar Lodbrók', *Acta Philologica Scandinavica* ii, 1927, 115-49. Idem, 'Die westnordische Tradition der Sage von Ragnar Lodbrók', *Kleine Schriften*, Berlin 1965, 285-330 (originally published in 1928). Idem, 'Die Wikingersaga', *Romanische Monatsschrift* xv, 1927, 81-100. In these articles De Vries followed and developed the arguments of G. Storm, *Kritiske Bidrag til Vikingetidens Historie* (i, Ragnar Lodbrok og Gange-Rolv), 1878, 34-129, 193-200.
[42] De Vries in turn was followed by (among others) Jones, *A history of the Vikings*, 212-15 and most recently by R. W. McTurk, 'Ragnarr Lodbrók in the Irish Annals?', *Proceedings of the seventh Viking Congress Dublin 15-21 August 1973*, ed. B. Almquist and D. Green, London 1976, 93-123.
[43] See for a discussion of the relevant passages in William of Jumièges' *GND*: De Vries, 'Die Entwicklung', 130-5 and De Vries, 'Die historische Grundlagen', 254-6.
[44] J. C. H. R. Steenstrup, *Normannerne*, Copenhagen 1876-82. W. Vogel, *Die Normannen und das Frankische Reich bis zur Gründung der Normandie (799-911)*, Heidelberg 1906 (Heidelberger Abhandlungen zur Mittleren und Neueren Geschichte, 14) 104-5, 113-15, 409-12. G. Loomis, 'Saint Edmund and the Lodbrok (lothbroc) legend', *Harvard Studies and notes in Philology and Literature* xv, 1933, 1-23. Smyth, *Scandinavian Kings*, 17-35, 263-6.

a *Gesta Francorum*, a still unidentified French history.[45] The next author knowing the name of Lothbroc is the anonymous writer of the *Annals of St Neots* writing in the second quarter of the twelfth century at Bury St Edmund's in East Anglia. Among the events described under the year 878 it is said that one of the *spolia* captured after the battle between King Alfred and an unnamed brother of Ivar and Halfdane (sons of Lothbroc) was a magic raven banner. The banner was said to have been woven by three daughters of *Lodebrochi*, sisters of Ivar and Ubba.[46] The first combination of the names Ragnar and Lothbroc occurs in the so-called Islendingabók of Ari Thorgilsson, who wrote in Iceland in the period between 1122 and 1133.[47] Like Adam of Bremen he refers to Ivar as son of Lothbroc, whom he calls Ragnarr Lodbrók.[48] It is important to note that the literary written identification of Ragnar and Lothbroc was made in Iceland in the early twelfth century. From the same area stems the oldest known written evidence of Björn's name in Scandinavia. It occurs in the skaldic poem *Hattalykill* written in about 1145 by the Icelandic skald Hallr and Jarl Rögvaldr, a skald from the Orkneys. Björn is mentioned as son of Ragnar Lothbroc together with the 'English' sons of this Viking sagahero.[49] So far we have traced the early written tradition of the names of both Ragnar Lothbroc and his son Björn Ironside. The history of both, as told by William of Jumièges, closely resembles that of the Hiberno-Norse version of the saga as described in the so-called *Fragmentary Annals of Ireland*.

The *Fragmentary Annals* were written in the mid-eleventh century under the patronage of the Osraige dynasty. The work displays considerable knowledge of the Vikings of the south-east of Ireland. Dr Radner, the editor of this text, convincingly argues that is is based on reliable contemporary sources from the late ninth and tenth centuries.[50] According to this chronicle, shortly before the fall of York in 867 Ragnall and his three sons were expelled from Scandinavia to the Orkneys. The two eldest sons, unnamed, left their father and youngest brother and went on a Viking raid to England and France. Inspired by ambition, however, they decided to go farther south to the Mediterranean. They attacked the coastal areas of Spain and

---

[45] *Adam von Bremen, Gesta Hammaburgensis ecclesiae pontificum*, ed. B. Schmeidler, W. Trillmich, in: Quellen des 9. und 11. Jahrhunderts zur Geschichte der Hamburgischen Kirche und des Reiches, Berlin 1961, 208: *Crudelissimus omnium fuit Inguar, filius Lodparchi, qui christianos ubique per supplicia necavit. Scriptum est in Gestis Francorum.*

[46] *The Annals of St Neots and the Vita Prima sancti Neoti*, edd. D. N. Dumville and M. Lapidge, Cambridge 1984, s.a. 878: *Ibique acceperunt spolia non minima. In quo etiam acceperunt illud vexillum quod Reafan nominant. Dicunt enim, quod tres sorores Hynguari et Hubbae, filiae videlicet Lodebrochi, illud vexillum texuerunt, et totum paraverunt illud uno meridiano tempore. Dicunt etiam, quod in omni bello ubi praecederet idem signum, si victoriam adepturi essent, apparet in medio signi quasi corvus vivens volitans; si vero vincendi in futuro fuissent, penderet directe nihil movens. Et hoc saepe probatum est.*

[47] *Islendigabok*, ed. J. Benediktsson, Reykjavik 1968 (Islenzk fornrit, 1) 4. Translation by W. Baetke, *Thule* (see note 41) no. 23, Jena 1928, 44.

[48] Both most probably used the *Passio sancti Edmundi*, written by Abbo of Fleury and based almost exclusively on English sources: ed. M. Winterbottom, *Three Lives of English Saints*, Toronto 1972, 67-87, esp. 78-9.

[49] *Hattalykill*, ed. E. A. Kock, in: *Den Norsk-Isländska Skaldediktungen*, Lund 1946, i, 239-49, verse 9a. See for this poem De Vries, 'Die westnordische Tradition', 286-9. Smyth, *Scandinavian kings*, 80-1.

[50] *Fragmentary Annals of Ireland*, ed. and translated by Joan N. Radner, Dublin 1978, xxii-xxv. See for the validity of this source Smyth, *Scandinavian kings*, 61-7. McTurk, 'Ragnarr Lodbrók', 106-9. F. T. Wainwright, 'Ingimund's Invasion', *EHR* ccxlvii, 1948, 145-69, esp. 146-9 and 154-6.

North Africa, but after some time one of the sons tired of their raids and wanted to return home. On their way back through the Strait of Gibraltar many Vikings were slain and part of the fleet was shipwrecked. The two sons luckily escaped and returned to Ireland.[51] Attention has been drawn to important similarities between this account and that of William of Jumièges.[52] Both mention a Viking raid to the Mediterranean by a son or sons of Ragnall/Lothbroc. The two texts stress the ambition which led them to the Mediterranean. On their way back it is said in both sources that part of the fleet was shipwrecked. The texts do not agree as far as the places of return are concerned. The *Fragmentary Annals* mention Ireland, whereas William of Jumièges let Björn return first to England and then to Frisia. It is obvious that we have here two versions of basically the same story of Ragnar Lothbroc's son(s) ambitiously going on a Viking raid to the Mediterranean.

Two more elements in William of Jumièges' version of the Ragnar Lothbroc saga seem to derive from an Anglo-Scandinavian source. The motif of magic invulnerability, as implied by Björn's nickname, can be found in many Scandinavian sagas. It often concerns, as in Björn's case, magic protection given to Vikings by women, either mothers, sisters or wives. Examples can be found in the Völsunga saga and the Ragnar Lothbroc saga: Sigmund the Völsung was helped by his spae-wife to be immune against weapons; he had a magic sword once given to him by the god Odin; Ragnar Lothbroc got a magic shirt from his wife Aslaug and his daughters are said to have woven a magic raven banner which brought the bearer victory. Stories like these were widely circulated through the British Isles and Scandinavia from the eleventh century onwards.[53] The other motif to be discussed is that of the Frisian connection of Ragnar Lothbroc's sons.[54] William of Jumièges tells us that Björn went to Frisia and died there. This tale seems to derive from the same tradition transmitted in Northumbrian histories, like the *Historia de sancto Cuthberto* (tenth-century)[55] and the *Annales Lindisfarnenses et Dunelmenses* (twelfth-century) according to which Ubba was a *dux Fres(c)ior/num*. The *Annales* also contain the story that Halfdan, Ubba and Ivar invaded East Anglia with an army consisting of, among others, Frisians.[56]

Let me sum up my findings concerning William's place in the development of the Ragnar Lothbroc saga. 1. Written knowledge of the name Lothbroc points to

[51] *Fragmentary Annals*, ed. Radner, 118-20.
[52] McTurk, 'Ragnarr Lodbrók', 106-9. Smyth, *Scandinavian kings*, 61-7.
[53] Smyth, *Scandinavian kings*, 36-53, esp. 42-5 and Appendix II (The raven banner in Devon, 878) on 269-70. A discussion on magic banners in Anglo-Saxon history can also be found in: *Encomium Emmae Reginae*, ed. A. Campbell, London 1949 (Camden 3rd series, 72) 96-7. Boberg, *Motif-index*, 54-93 (magic), esp.: 64 (magic clothes), 65 (magic weapons), 70 (magic shirt gives invulnerability), 87 (many examples of magic invulnerability).
[54] See for the Frisian connection Vogel, *Die Normannen*, 411-12. McTurk, 'Ragnarr Lodbrók', 120 and Smyth, *Scandinavian kings*, 51. Pritsak thinks mistakenly that Frisia is an error of translation of the Old Norse *Gardar* meaning Rus' and not Frisia. According to Pritsak's interpretation Björn went to that part of Eastern Europe which was later known as Rus' and which is to be identified with Aldeigjuborg, see: O. Pritsak, *The Origin of Rus'*, vol. i, *Old Scandinavian sources other than the saga's*, Cambridge (Mass.) 1981, 164-82, esp. 167-8, 177-8 and 583.
[55] *Historia de Sancto Cuthberto*, ed. Th. Arnold, *Symeonis monachi opera omnia*, i, London 1882, RS, 196-214, esp. 202 (*Ubba dux Fresciorum*) 204 (*Ubba dux Fresonum*). See for the date of this text *EHD* i, 129, and Gransden, *Historical writing*, 76-7.
[56] W. Levison, 'Die "Annales Lindisfarnenses et Dunelmenses" kritisch untersucht und neu herausgegeben', *Deutsches Archiv* xvii, 1961, 447-506, esp. 475, 484 s.a. 855: ... *Paganorum exercitus, scilicet Dani et Frisones, ducibus Halfdene, Ubba et Inguar applicant in insula Scepeige.*

an Anglo-Scandinavian tradition known in Jumièges (c.1070/1071), Hamburg (c.1088), East Anglia (early twelfth century) and Iceland (1122-1133). 2. Björn's name is found before 1150 in two sources, the *GND* and the skaldic poem *Hattalykill* (c.1145). Both seem to derive from a common source.[57] 3. Björn's Mediterranean trip in the *GND* shows striking resemblances with the *Fragmentary Annals* pointing to a common Anglo-Scandinavian source known in the British Isles. 4. Björn's magic invulnerability is a Scandinavian saga-motif. 5. Frisia in connection with Ragnar Lothbroc's sons was known in Jumièges (c.1070/1071) as well as in Northumbria from the tenth century onwards. Taking these elements together we may conclude that it is more likely that William of Jumièges found his Ragnar Lothbroc version in an Anglo-Scandinavian source, than that he invented the story as Dr De Vries and others thought he had done.[58] William of Jumièges, however, is the *auctor intellectualis* of the combination between Dudo's Hastingus story (known in France and Normandy at the beginning of the eleventh century) and the Ragnar Lothbroc saga known in the British Isles from at least the eleventh century onwards.[59]

There are more passages in the *GND* of William of Jumièges which show Scandinavian influence. The mysterious *Haigroldus rex Daciae*, mentioned by Dudo of Saint-Quentin, who is said to have come from Denmark to Normandy in order to assist Duke Richard I in his struggle against the French king, is identified by William of Jumièges as being King Harold (Bluetooth) of Denmark (941-988).[60] According to the author of the *GND* Harold was expelled from Denmark by his son Svein and came to Normandy to ask the Norman duke for help. He received the Cotentin where he was allowed to stay to reinforce his army. While staying in Normandy he later repaid his debt with an alliance with the Norman duke against Louis IV of France. This part of the story is obviously based on Dudo, whereas the reference to the dissension between King Harold and his son Svein derives from another, probably Scandinavian, source of information. Apart from William of Jumièges only two other eleventh-century sources seem to know about the struggle for power in Denmark. Both the author of the *Encomium Emmae* (c.1040) and Adam of Bremen (c.1088) relate the exile of the Danish King Harold Bluetooth by his son Svein Forkbeard.[61] They were better informed than William stating that Harold went to the Slavs and not to Normandy.[62] Both Dudo and William of Jumièges mistook the temporary

---

[57] Whereas I have not found traces of knowledge of the *GND* in Scandinavia before c.1180, when Theodoricus used the *GND* for his *Historia de antiquitate regum Norwegiensium*, it is very unlikely that the poem *Hattalykill* has been influenced by William of Jumièges' story. A common source would be the most plausible explanation.

[58] The combination of the two stories as found in the *GND* might have influenced the development of the thirteenth-century Ragnarssaga into its most elaborate form. The incorporation of the *Luna*-expedition in the Scandinavian Ragnarssaga might have taken place some time after 1180 from which moment onwards the *GND* were known in Scandinavia.

[59] I have not found any trace of a Norman (oral) tradition concerning Ragnar Lothbroc and Björn Ironside before the time of William of Jumièges.

[60] Jumièges 41, 53, 57, 66-7. That William of Jumièges obviously had in mind Harold Bluetooth is proved by his reference to Harold's son Svein (Forkbeard), see for this identification J. Adigard des Gautries, *Les noms de personne en Normandie de 911 à 1066*, Lund 1954, 68-9. For a historical commentary on both Dudo's and William's account see Ph. Lauer, *Le règne de Louis IV d'Outremer*, Paris 1900, appendix v, 287-92. Prentout, *Etude critique*, 359-61.

[61] *Encomium*, ed. Campbell, 1-li, 8-10. *Adam of Bremen, Gesta*, ed. Schmeidler-Trillmich, 260-2.

[62] As far as we know Harold Bluetooth never went to Normandy. See Musset, *Les peuples Scandinaves*, 83 note 4. Jones, *A history of the Vikings*, 127-30.

Viking leader of Bayeux in about 945 for his royal contemporary namesake Harold (Bluetooth).[63] Considering the fact that only a mainly English source like the *Encomium* and a German historian like Adam, who got his information directly from Svein's grandson, knew about the dissension between Harold and Svein, William of Jumièges must have taken his information from an Anglo-Scandinavian source.

Another passage in the *GND* concerning Scandinavian affairs speaks about the early career of Olaf, the later king and first martyr of Norway.[64] William of Jumièges is our only non-Scandinavian source to name Olaf and to tell us about his Viking raids in France. His account shows striking resemblance to the contemporary skaldic verses made by Sigvatr.[65] He was an Icelandic skald living at the court of the later King Olaf from 1015 onwards.

Sigvatr's poem entitled *Viking verses* is the most important source for our knowledge of Olaf's Viking career. It was written shortly after 1015 when Sigvatr came to Olaf's court. Thanks to the fact that his skaldic verses were incorporated in later sagas (e.g. the saga collection known as the *Heimskringla* of Snorri Sturlason), they have come down to us. It is remarkable that the poetry is hardly ever used as a source on Norman history, for the poem of Sigvatr agrees with the *GND* in its account of Olaf raiding the coast of Brittany. According to William of Jumièges, Olaf, together with his unidentified companion *Lacman rex Suauorum*, was asked by Richard II for assistance against Odo of Chartres. Before a battle was fought Olaf and *Lacman* attacked the coast of Brittany, defeated the Bretons by trickery, captured the castle of Dol and returned to Rouen. The trick used by the Vikings to win the battle against the Bretons consisted of digging trenches in the battlefield. The trenches were narrowed on the surface in order not to be noticed at first sight. As soon as the Breton cavalry entered the battlefield the horses stumbled and before the battle had actually started the Breton cause was lost.[66] The skaldic poetry of Sigvatr does not mention this trick. It does, however, refer to the capture of the castle of Dol, at least if we are allowed to identify William's Dol with the skald's *Hól*.[67] According to Sigvatr, Olaf went further south and also attacked the coast of Aquitania where he won a battle against William V of Aquitania.[68] For this we do have independent evidence in the Chronicle of Adémar of Chabannes (c.1030), where it is said that the Vikings got their victory by cunning.[69] According to Adémar, who does not seem to know Olaf, the Vikings dug trenches in the battlefield during the night. They covered these with sods so that the next morning the horses of the Aquitanians immediately broke their legs when they fell into the pits. William's story that Olaf,

---

63 See most recently Bates, *Normandy before 1066*, 13-14.
64 Jumièges, 85-7. See for Olaf's early career especially *Encomium*, ed. Campbell, 76-82. E. O. G. Turville-Petre, *The heroic age of Scandinavia*, London 1951, 140-6. Jones, *A history of the Vikings*, 375.
65 See for Sigvatr: Jan de Vries, *Altnordische Literaturgeschichte*, i, Berlin 1964 (Grundriss der Germanischen Philologie 15), 253-8. E. O. G. Turville-Petre, *Scaldic poetry*, Oxford 1976, 77-87. Sigvatr's *Vikingavísur* (*Viking verses*) are edited in: *Den Norsk-Islandske Skjaldedigtning*, ed. Finnur Jonsson, i, 223-8; ii, 213-16. A translation can be found in *Heimskringla, History of the kings of Norway by Snorri Sturlason*, translated by L. M. Hollander, Austin 1964, 245-64. A partial translation of Sigvatr's poetry has been given in *EHD* i, 332-41 and A. Campbell, *Skaldic verse and Anglo-Saxon history*, London 1971, 3-16.
66 Jumièges, 85-6.
67 Sigvatr, *Vikingavísur*, ed. Finnur Jonsson, ii, 215 (translation Heimskringla, 257: At Hól he broke the high-on headland towering-stronghold).
68 Sigvatr, *Vikingavísur*, ed. Finnur Jonsson, ii, 215 (translation Heimskringla, 257).
69 *Adémar de Chabannes, Chronique*, ed. Chavanon, 176.

returning from his raids, stayed in Normandy and was even baptised by Archbishop
Robert, is not to be found in the skaldic verses. William tells us that Olaf returned
to Norway and was betrayed and murdered by his own people (1030). He calls Olaf
king and martyr and depicts him as now enlightening his people with his miracles
and virtues. By saying this William of Jumièges is one of the earliest sources to refer
to Olaf's martyrdom, holiness and miracles.[70] William must have got his information
about Saint Olaf either by way of England or directly from Norway.

There remains to be discussed one point of similarity between the *GND* and the
skaldic poetry about Olaf by Sigvatr and his colleague Ottar the Black, that is the
story according to which Olaf had assisted Cnut in his struggle to get the throne of
England after his father Svein died in 1014.[71] This is not true. We do know that
Olaf played a rôle in the Danish conquest of England in the years 1009-11. Professor
Campbell in his edition of the *Encomium Emmae* suggests that already during Olaf's
lifetime people confused Olaf's early career at the side of Thorkill in 1009-11 with
the campaign of Cnut three years later. Chronologically it is absolutely impossible
for Olaf to have been able to accompany Cnut to or in England: because in the
course of the year 1014 Olaf had returned to Norway to become king. Campbell
concludes that early Norse confusion is to be blamed for the mistake made by the
skalds, William of Jumièges and Adam of Bremen. It is remarkable that none of the
English sources associates Cnut and Olaf in 1014.[72] I would like to argue that, with
regard to Olaf's career, William of Jumièges, together with the skaldic poets, represents the Scandinavian and not the English point of view. In this context we have
to bear in mind that Olaf's skald Sigvatr and his friend Berg did visit Normandy in
1025-26.[73] During their visit they might possibly have told their version of the
story of Olaf's Viking career, a version which might have lingered on in Normandy
until the time of William of Jumièges.

I have pointed out elsewhere the ambivalence of the *GND* concerning the political
relations between England and Normandy before 1066.[74] Especially William of
Jumièges' account of Duke Richard II's attitude towards England is predominantly
pro-Danish and anti-English, or better, anti-King Ethelred. It is against this background that I drew attention to two more Scandinavian elements in the *GND*. The
first one concerns William's description of what seems to be a Scandinavian marriage
by seizure, that of Cnut and Emma in 1017. The Christian celebration, according
to William, followed a few days later.[75] The second is the possible blood-brother
relationship depicted in the *GND* between Duke Robert the Magnificent and the
Aethelings, Edward and Alfred, while staying in Normandy during their period of
exile.[76]

One source closely connected to the *GND* remains to be discussed, namely one

---

[70] B. Dickins, 'The cult of S. Olave in the British Isles', *Sagabook of the Viking Society* xii,
1937-45, 53-80. See for Normandy Musset, 'L'image de Scandinavie', 198.

[71] Ottar the Black was also a poet of Olaf's court. See De Vries, *Altnordische Literaturgeschichte*,
i, 237-9. *EHD* i, 332-41. Campbell, *Skaldic Verse*, 3-16.

[72] *Encomium*, ed. Campbell, 79-80.

[73] See above, note 24.

[74] E. M. C. van Houts, 'The political relations between Normandy and England before 1066
according to the Gesta Normannorum Ducum', *Actes du Colloque International du CNRS, nr.
611: Etudes Anselmiennes* (forthcoming 1984). See also Campbell, 'England, France, Flanders',
(note 1), 259-60.

[75] Jumièges, 82-3.

[76] Jumièges, 109.

of the anecdotes incorporated in the B-redaction of the *GND* describing the alleged visit of Duke Robert the Magnificent to the Byzantine emperor in 1035.[77] This story was written at an unknown time in the eleventh century.[78] It contains three motifs which long since have been regarded as belonging to a common Norman-Scandinavian literary stock. They are the mule with the golden horseshoes, the ban on buying or selling firewood and the use of walnuts as fuel. Together or separately these motifs occur in stories about Normans or Scandinavians who go to Southern Italy or Byzantium, the most famous of whom are Robert, Duke of Normandy, Harold Hardrada of Norway and the Norse Sigurd the Jerusalem Traveller.[79] No one yet has been able to show the exact literary (inter-) dependence between these tales. It is obvious however that they stem from the same literary tradition found in Normandy, Scandinavia and Southern Italy in the eleventh and early twelfth centuries.

In this paper I have shown that Norman historiography in particular betrays Scandinavian influence. This is all the more remarkable because the other main form of literature, hagiography, widely produced in Normandy, does not in the least present the same picture. From the abundance of eleventh-century hagiographical texts only one contains a possible Scandinavian reminiscence. The *Miracula sancti Audoeni*, written shortly after 1047, refer to the name *Ros* in the Bessin implying a vague notion of Vikings once called *Ros*.[80] Can we conclude any more from this search for Scandinavian traditions in Norman literature?

The authors living in the first quarter of the eleventh century described in their works Scandinavian elements which had survived the past and which could be corroborated by direct contemporary contacts with Scandinavians. Part of the tales imported during this time may have lingered on in Normandy, for example the account of Olaf's early career as described in the skaldic poetry of Sigvatr. In the second half of the eleventh century most of the 'new' information about the Viking past or Scandinavian relations in recent times derived from England. The introduction of fresh Scandinavian motifs in the work of William of Jumièges must be seen against the background of the cultural exchange between his monastery of Jumièges and England since the period 1042-50/1052. Robert Champart, former abbot of Jumièges and later (arch-) bishop in England, paved the way for the incorporation of Anglo-Saxon and Scandinavian motifs in sculpture and manuscript-illumination which

---

[77] Jumièges, 112-13.
[78] E. M. C. van Houts, *Gesta Normannorum Ducum, een studie over de handschriften, de tekst, het geschiedverhaal en het genre*, Groningen 1982, 102.
[79] C. H. Haskins, *Norman institutions*, Cambridge (Mass.) 1918, 267-9. R. Louis, 'Les ducs de Normandie dans les chansons de geste', *Byzantion* xxviii, 1958, 391-412, esp. 391-402. See most recently G. Loud, 'The "Gens Normannorum" – myth or reality?', *ante* iv, 104-16, esp.115.
[80] *Miracula sancti Audoeni*, ed. J. Richard, in: *Les miracula composés en Normandie au XIe et XIIe siècle*, Paris 1975 (unpublished thesis of the Ecole des Chartes, see *Positions des Thèses*, Paris 1975, 183-9) 39: *Est locus infra Baiocensem diocesim quatuor a Cadomo milibus distans, quem certis de causis veteres coloni Ros appelari maluerunt, in hoc ecclesia* ... See also the edition of the *Miracula* in the *AASS* Aug. iv, 836. I am most grateful to Dr J. Richard who kindly let me consult his unpublished thesis.
See for R(h)os as a name for Vikings: Musset, *Les invasions*, 269-70. T. Lewicki, 'L'apport des sources arabes médiévales (IXe-Xe siècles) à la connaissance de l'Europe centrale et orientale', in: *L'Occident et l'Islam nell'alto Medioevo*, Spoleto 1965 (Settimane . . ., 12), 461-85, esp. 479. C. Joret, 'Les noms de lieu d'origine non romane et la colonisation Germanique et Scandinave en Normandie', *Millénaire Normand 1911*, ii, Rouen 1913, 97-160 does not discuss the place name R(h)os.

originated in Jumièges.[81] Once started about the middle of the eleventh century this exchange was reinforced after 1066. Last year Dr Maylis Baylé showed us how during the late eleventh century Scandinavian architectural elements were imported into Normandy from England.[82] The Scandinavian literary reminiscences in the *Carmen*, William of Poitiers' *Gesta Guillelmi* and, above all, the *GND*, point to Anglo-Scandinavian literary or oral sources, more than to a persisting Norman-Viking tradition. The fact remains however that in Normandy, just as in England, in the eleventh century, Scandinavian saga motifs were incorporated in literature, thus proving that the Normans still paid cultural and literary tribute to their Scandinavian past.[83]

[81] See my 'Political relations' (see above, note 74) and M. Baylé, 'La sculpture du XIe siècle à Jumièges et sa place dans le décor architectural des abbayes normandes', *Aspects du Monachisme en Normandie (IVe-XVIIIe siècles)*, ed. L. Musset, Paris 1982, 75-90, esp. 82-90. The interest in Scandinavian literary saga motifs mainly existing in Jumièges in the second half of the eleventh century is negatively proved by the absence of similar (or the same) motifs in the historical parts of works like the *Inventio et miracula sancti Vulfranni* (written at Saint-Wandrille c.1060), the *Libellus de revelatione, edificatione et auctoritate Fiscannensis monasterii* (written at Fécamp c.1090-95) and *De statu huius ecclesiae* (Coutances) *ab anno 836 ad 1093* (written at Coutances shortly after 1093).

[82] M. Baylé, 'Interlace patterns in Norman romanesque sculpture: regional groups and their historical background', *ante* v, 1-20, esp. 8-20.

[83] This conclusion contradicts Musset's statement that in Normandy no Scandinavian literary influence can be found in the tenth and eleventh centuries. See his 'Le satiriste Garnier de Rouen', 237-8.

NOTES ON THE MANUSCRIPT TRADITION
OF DUDO OF ST QUENTIN'S *GESTA NORMANNORUM*

Gerda C. Huisman

Two years before he died duke Richard I of Normandy commissioned Dudo of St Quentin to compose a work describing 'the customs and deeds of the Norman land and also the laws introduced by his grandfather Rollo'. Dudo, canon and since 1015 dean of the chapter of St Quentin, had been a frequent visitor at the ducal court since he first came to Normandy in 986/7. After Richard I died in 996 his son and heir Richard II and his half-brother Raoul d'Ivry asked Dudo to continue writing his Norman history.[1] The completed work is known as *De Moribus et Actis Primorum Normanniae Ducum*. This title is a rephrasing of Dudo's own words in his dedicatory letter to bishop Adalbero of Laon, and was first used by André Duchesne when he published the text in his collection of Norman historiography. When a second edition appeared in 1865 the editor, Jules Lair, had kept this long title.[2] However, those manuscripts which supply a title call the work *Gesta Normannorum* or *Historia Normannorum*. Two eleventh-century manuscripts of Dudo's work explicitly call the text *Gesta Normannorum*. The entry for a codex containing a *Gesta Normannorum* in the twelfth-century library catalogue of Fécamp can be identified with one of the surviving manuscripts of Dudo's work. Therefore I propose to replace the long and certainly not original title invented by Duchesne with *Gesta Normannorum*.[3]

Much has been written about Dudo's abilities and faults, both as historian and as writer, and judgments have not always been favourable.[4] I do not now wish to

---

* I gratefully acknowledge the financial assistance in preparing and presenting this paper given by the Netherlands Organization for the Advancement of Pure Research (Z.W.O.) and the British Academy.

1 Dudo, 119-20, 295.
2 Dudo, 119: *ut mores actusque telluris Normannicae, quin etiam et proavi sui Rollonis, quae posuit in regno jura describerem.* A. Duchesne, *Historiae Normannorum Scriptores Antiqui*, Lutetiae Parisiorum 1619, 51-160; Jules Lair, *De Moribus et Actis Primorum Normanniae Ducum Auctore Dudone Sancti Quintini Decano*, Caen 1865 (Mémoires de la Société des Antiquaires de Normandie, 3e série, tome iii).
3 MS Berne, Burgerbibliothek Bongars 390: at the end of Dudo's text (the only text in the codex) in a contemporary hand *hec sunt gesta normannorum*; MS Cambridge, UL Mm. 5.17: at the end of Dudo's text (the only text in the codex) *Explicit liber normannorum vel gesta eorum*; MS Cambridge, CCC 276 has an overall title for the codex *Historia Romanorum et Normannorum* on the first flyleaf, written in a twelfth (?)-century hand; MS London, BL Cotton Claudius A vii *historia normannorum* on the second flyleaf, and on f.1r *hystoria normannorum* on the first line after the opening words of book i *Totius namque molis*; MS London, BL Cotton Nero D viii on f.1r *Incipit historia normannorum.* For the catalogue of Fécamp, see note 23.
4 The most recent evaluations are to be found in Eleanor Searle, 'Fact and Pattern in Heroic History: Dudo of St Quentin', *Viator* 15, 1984; David Bates, *Normandy before 1066*, London 1982, xiv-xvi, 10-15; R. H. C. Davis, *The Normans and their Myth*, London 1976, 50-62; Barbara Vopelius-Holtzendorff, *Studien zu Dudo von Saint-Quentin, dem ersten Geschichts-*

	11th century	12th century	13th century	15th century	16th century	17th century	dedicatory letter	poems	complete text	additional version
(Alençon, Bibliothèque Municipale 20)			x				?	?	?	?
Antwerp, Museum Plantin-Moretus 17.2		x					x	x		
Berlin, Deutsche Staatsbibliothek Phillipps 1854	x						x	x	x	x
Berne, Burgerbibliothek Bongars 390	x								x	
Cambridge, Corpus Christi College 276	x						x	x		
Cambridge, University Library Mm. 5. 17		x							x	x
Douai, Bibliothèque Municipale 880		x					x			
Leiden, Universiteitsbibliotheek Voss. Lat. F. 47					x		x		x	
London, British Library Cotton Claudius A xii		x							x	x
London, British Library Cotton Nero D viii			x				x	x	x	x
London, British Library Harley 3742				x			x		x	
London, British Library Royal 13. B. xiv		x					x	x	x	x
Oxford, Bodleian Library R. James 28						x	–	–	–	–
Paris, Bibliothèque Nationale n.a.l. 1031		x								
Rouen, Bibliothèque Municipale Y 11	x						x	x	x	(x)

Fig. 1   Manuscripts of Dudo of St Quentin, Gesta Normannorum

enter into this particular debate, but I propose to discuss some problems concerning the study of the manuscripts which contain Dudo's *Gesta Normannorum*. As my study is still in progress this paper necessarily must be read as an interim report with some hypotheses and conclusions which are still tentative. I begin with a discussion of the editions of the *Gesta Normannorum*. This is followed by some remarks on the manuscripts in general and by a discussion of each manuscript. Because the collation of the manuscripts has not yet been finished or evaluated it is too early to present a discussion of the textual relationships between the manuscripts, but some lines in a future stemma can be drawn already from the material presented here.

In the introduction to his collection of Norman historians Duchesne mentions that he used two manuscripts for the editing of Dudo's work. One of these still survives and is now in East Berlin (see checklist of manuscripts, Fig. 1). The whereabouts of the second manuscript, which Duchesne borrowed from François d'Amboise, are unknown today. All we know about the codex is this owner's name and that it did not contain the nearly eighty poems which are interspersed through the text in a number of manuscripts.

Lair's principal goal was the rehabilitation of Dudo's work as a reliable historical source, and he was much less interested in the manuscript tradition of the text. He knew of ten manuscripts, seven of which he collated for the edition. The three manuscripts he did not use are MS Oxford, Bodleian Library, Coll. R. James 28, an historical summary written in the seventeenth century citing only two short fragments from Dudo's work; MS Berne, Burgerbibliothek Bongars 390 and MS Leiden,

schreiber der Normandie, 987-1015, Göttingen 1967 (unpublished dissertation).

Universiteitsbibliotheek Voss. Lat. F. 47 (see pp.125, 127). Unfortunately MS Alençon, Bibliothèque Municipale 20, an early thirteenth-century copy of the *Gesta Normannorum*, was consumed in the fire when Lair's house burnt down.[5]

In his description Lair provided summary information on the manuscripts known to him. This information is reduced to the contents of the codices, an approximate dating by centuries and the mentioning of the presence or absence of the poems. There is no attempt at a coherent survey of the manuscript tradition. Lair considered all the texts to be defective. Therefore he found it impossible to base an edition on one particular manuscript. Instead he chose the best readings in whatever manuscript he found them.[6] Comparison of Lair's critical apparatus with the manuscripts he consulted shows his many inaccuracies: faulty readings, attributions of variants to the wrong manuscripts, readings not found in any manuscript and omissions of significant variants.[7]

To the list of manuscripts known to Lair five more can now be added: MS Antwerp, Museum Plantin-Moretus 17.2; MS Cambridge, University Library Mm. 5. 17; MS London, British Library Harley 3742; MS London, British Library Royal 13. B. xiv; MS Paris, Bibliothèque Nationale n.a.l. 1031. The existence of MS Paris, BN n.a.l. 1031 was known to Lair only through an entry in the seventeenth-century catalogue of the abbey Ter Duinen (see p.126). In the last century this manuscript was in the possession of Sir Thomas Phillipps at Middlehill, just like the manuscript now kept in East Berlin, which Lair did consult.

Figure 1 shows several characteristics of the manuscripts. Of the fourteen manuscripts no less than ten are to be dated to the eleventh and twelfth centuries: MS Berne, Burgerbibliothek Bongars 390 to the first half of the eleventh century; MS Rouen, Bibliothèque Municipale Y 11, MS Berlin, Deutsche Staatsbibliothek Phillipps 1854, and MS Cambridge, Corpus Christi College 276 to the second half of the eleventh century; MS Cambridge, UL Mm. 5. 17. c.1100; MS Paris, BN n.a.l. 1031 c.1110; MS London, BL Royal 13. B. xiv, MS Antwerp, Museum Plantin-Moretus 17.2, MS Douai, Bibliothèque Municipale 880, and MS London, BL Cotton Claudius A xii later in the twelfth century; MS London, BL Cotton Nero D viii was written during the thirteenth century; MS Alençon BM 20 (now lost) was also dated to the thirteenth century; MS London, BL Harley 3742, was written c.1445; and MS Leiden, Universiteitsbibliotheek Voss. Lat. F. 47 in the sixteenth century.

Four manuscripts survive incomplete: MS Douai, BM 880 breaks off in the middle of book III, halfway through the first column on a page; MS Antwerp, Museum Plantin-Moretus 17.2 and MS Paris, BN n.a.l. 1031 break off at the end of book III, in both cases because of the loss of several leaves; MS Cambridge, CCC 276 ends

---

[5] For Lair's descriptions of the manuscripts, see Dudo, 105-11. For MS Alençon, BM 20, see also Elisabeth M. C. van Houts, *Gesta Normannorum Ducum: een studie over de handschriften, de tekst, het geschiedwerk en het genre*, Groningen 1982, 199-200.

[6] Dudo, 111-12.

[7] A very small number of examples must suffice here: Dudo, 123 n.c: contrary to Lair's assertion, the two poems are not divided by a blank line; Dudo, 125 the poem to Raoul d'Ivry: Lair comments on *le plus grand désordre* in which this poem is printed in Duchesne (from MS Berlin, DSB Phillipps 1854), but the irregularity is that ll. 1-3 have been copied between ll. 20 and 21; Dudo, 129 l. 2: *superficiem ejus* this reading only in MS Douai, BM 880, MS Paris, BN n.a.l. 1031 *om.*, the other MSS read *terram*; Dudo, 129, l.15: *profusus* all MSS read *protensus*; Dudo, 133 n.1: the marginal gloss in MS London, BL Cotton Claudius A xii reads *Qualiter astingus dolose finxit se baptizari et christianum fore*; Lair observed the double ending (see p.131) occurring in several manuscripts only in MS London, BL Cotton Nero D viii (Dudo, 299).

suddenly near the end of book IV, halfway through the second column on the page.

Most of the manuscripts originate from Normandy or England: e.g. MS Berlin, DSB Phillipps 1854 from Fécamp; MS Paris, BN n.a.l. 1031 from St Wandrille; MS Rouen, BM Y 11 from Jumièges; MS Cambridge, CCC 276 from St Augustine's, Canterbury. An exception is MS Douai, BM 880 which probably was written in the monastery of Anchin, near Douai. Due to lack of clues it is difficult to locate MSS Berne, Burgerbibliothek Bongars 390; London, BL Cotton Claudius A xii, London, BL Royal 13. B. xiv; London, BL Cotton Nero D viii; Cambridge, UL Mm. 5. 17; Antwerp, Museum Plantin-Moretus 17.2; and Leiden, UB Voss. Lat. F. 47 precisely.

A division of the manuscripts in groups including or omitting the poems sets apart MSS Berne, Burgerbibliothek Bongars 390; Cambridge, University Library Mm. 5. 17; Douai, Bibliothèque Municipale 880; London, British Library Cotton Claudius A xii; London, British Library Harley 3742; and Paris, BN n.a.l. 1031, which offer only the prose text, from MSS Berlin, DSB Phillipps 1854; Cambridge, CCC 276; London, BL Cotton Nero D viii; London, BL Royal 13. B. xiv; Antwerp, Museum Plantin-Moretus 17.2; Rouen, BM Y 11; and Leiden, UB Voss. Lat. F. 47, which do present the poems. The six manuscripts without the poems nevertheless do contain two, three or four of them. The first poem is a vituperation of Hasting in book I, included in MSS Berne, Burgerbibliothek Bongars 390; Cambridge, UL Mm. 5. 17; Douai, BM 880; London, BL Cotton Claudius A xii; London, BL Harley 3742; and Paris, BN n.a.l. 1031.[8] A speech by the English king *Alstemus* to Rollo to thank him for coming to his assistance, is copied in MSS Berne, Burgerbibliothek Bongars 390; Cambridge, UL Mm. 5. 17; Douai, BM 880; London, BL Harley 3742; and Paris, BN n.a.l. 1031.[9] A prayer from Rollo asking God to end the tempest preventing him from sailing back to France appears in the same five manuscripts.[10] The poem on the occasion of the reunion of Rollo with his son William, in book III, is found only in MSS Berne, Burgerbibliothek Bongars 390 and London, BL Cotton Claudius A xii.[11] According to Lair MS Alençon, BM 20 also included two poems.

Of the ten manuscripts dating from the eleventh and twelfth centuries five contain the prose text but omit the poems and the dedicatory letter to bishop Adalbero of Laon (MS Douai, BM 880 omits the letter, but contains the poems). Therefore it seems as if very early in the history of the text two redactions were in existence. (I have found no trace of an independent appearance of the poems.) The four manuscripts with only the prose text are MSS Berne, Burgerbibliothek Bongars 390; Cambridge, UL Mm. 5. 17; Paris, BN n.a.l. 1031; and London, BL Cotton Claudius A xii. MS Berne, Burgerbibliothek Bongars 390 was in the sixteenth century in the library of Pierre Daniel of Orléans, who had acquired many French manuscripts, a.o. from Normandy.[12] A Norman origin of this manuscript therefore is not immediately to be excluded, but the codex itself does not offer specific information on date or provenance. The script is difficult to date more precisely than to the first half of the eleventh century. The initial letters are very plain and hardly have any decoration

8 Dudo, 130: *Hic sacer atque ferox . . .*
9 Dudo, 148: *Prosapia pollens, gestorum lumine fulgens . . .*
10 Dudo, 149: *O Deus omnipotens, coelestia lumine complens . . .*
11 Dudo, 182: *Gaudebant ambo, genitus quidem honore paterno . . .*
12 J. R. Skinner, *Catalogus Codicum Manuscriptorum Bibliothecae Bernensis*, ii, Bern 1770, 158-9; H. Hagen, *Catalogus Codicum Bernensium (Bibliotheca Bongarsiana)*, Bern 1875, 360. For Pierre Daniel see K. A. de Meyier, *Paul en Alexandre Petau en de geschiedenis van hun handschriften*, Leiden 1947, 58-61.

at all. This manuscript is of special value to the study of the text tradition of Dudo's *Gesta Normannorum* as it offers a link between the manuscripts with and those without the poems: signs which look like paragraph marks occur in nearly every place in the text where other manuscripts have a poem. These marks have been written by the scribe. This may indicate a connection with an earlier manuscript of the prose redaction, in which the places where poems were to be inserted had been marked as preparation for a composite copy of the prose text with the addition of the poems (and the dedicatory letter).

The two initials in the text of Dudo suggest that MS Cambridge, UL Mm. 5. 17 is of Norman origin. Further dates on its history are lacking. On the first page of Dudo's text a later hand has written *Iste liber est beati*, but this unfinished ex-libris is not very helpful.[13]

MS Douai, BM 880 once belonged to the library of the Benedictine monastery of Anchin, near Douai. Anchin and the nearby abbey of Marchiennes formed a cultural centre in the twelfth century, one of the leading figures being the historian Andrew of Marchiennes.[14] Therefore the presence of a copy of Dudo's *Gesta Normannorum* in the library of Anchin is not surprising. The handwriting of the manuscript can be dated to the late twelfth century. As far as Dudo's text is concerned, this is one of the few manuscripts including the dedicatory letter to bishop Adalbero of Laon, while at the same time omitting the poems. Two other copies, MS London, BL Harley 3742 and MS Leiden, UB Voss. Lat. F. 47 offer this same combination.

The history of MS Paris, BN n.a.l. 1031 can be traced back to its place of origin, St Wandrille, via the libraries of Sir Thomas Phillipps and the abbeys of Ter Duinen and Ter Doest in Flanders. The manuscript itself was unknown to Lair, though it was in the Phillipps library where Lair did consult the manuscript now MS Berlin, DSB Phillipps 1854. However, he mentions an entry in the seventeenth-century catalogue of the Cistercian monastery of Ter Duinen, in a collection of Belgian library catalogues published in 1641.[15] This entry reads: *Historia de Hagno, de Rollone, et Willelmo ducibus Normannorum, cum Tractatu de naturis animalium, incerti authoris*. The first part of this entry fits MS Paris, BN n.a.l. 1031 perfectly: the manuscript contains only the first three books of the *Gesta Normannorum*. The last leaf of the last gathering and probably also a number of gatherings with book IV are now lost. The identification of this manuscript with the catalogue entry is confirmed by a now nearly illegible inscription on the first page which reads: *Abbatiae Thozanae*, of the abbey of Ter Doest; in 1624 Ter Doest was incorporated in its mother-convent Ter Duinen. The treatise on the nature of animals is now lost. The same catalogue entry has recently been discussed in connection with the discovery of the original copy of the *Annals of St Wandrille*, written in the first decade of the twelfth century at St Wandrille. This manuscript of the *Annals* was found in MS The Hague, Koninklijke Bibliotheek 128 E 14. Previously they were known only in a seventeenth-century copy made *ex codice membraneo antiquo abbatiae Dunensis*,

---

[13] *A Catalogue of the Manuscripts Preserved in the Library of the University of Cambridge*, Cambridge 1861 (repr. 1980), iv, 322-3.

[14] *Catalogue général des manuscrits des bibliothèques publiques des départements*, Paris 1878, vi, 635-6. For Andrew of Marchiennes, see K. F. Werner, 'Andreas von Marchiennes und die Geschichtsschreibung von Anchin und Marchiennes in der zweiten Hälfte des 12. Jahrhunderts', *Deutsches Archiv* 9, 1952, 402-63.

[15] Th. Phillipps, *Catalogus Librorum Manuscriptorum*, Middlehill 1873 (nr. 8171). The catalogue of Ter Duinen is printed in A. Sanderus, *Bibliotheca Belgica Manuscripta*, Lille 1641 (repr. 1969), i, 150-207.

qui fuit antea abbatiae Thozanae. In this MS the *Annals of St Wandrille* were preceded by a history of the dukes of Normandy. The handwriting of these two manuscripts, MS Paris, BN n.a.l. 1031 and MS The Hague, Koninklijke Bibliotheek 128 E 14, bears such a close resemblance that the MSS were almost certainly written by the same person. This gives us an origin for MS Paris, BN n.a.l. 1031 in St Wandrille, and an approximate date, contemporary with the date of the *Annals,* c.1106-11.[16]

The *Gesta Normannorum* in MS London, BL Cotton Claudius A xii was written in England in the twelfth century. Dudo's work is bound together with fifteenth-century historical material from Bury St Edmunds.[17] The Dudo part, however, does not show enough evidence to enable us to settle for Bury as the place of its origin.

Around 1445 John Norfolk, a fellow of All Souls College at Oxford, wrote MS London, BL Harley 3742, in which he copied among other texts Dudo's *Gesta Normannorum.* This copy is remarkable for its extraordinary great number of spelling mistakes, caused probably by a bad or badly written exemplar.[18]

The latest known copy of Dudo's work is in MS Leiden, UB Voss. Lat. F. 47, written in France in the sixteenth century.[19]

The MSS Rouen, BM Y 11; Berlin, DSB Phillipps 1854; Antwerp, Museum Plantin-Moretus 17.2; Cambridge, CCC 276 and London, BL Royal 13. B. xiv all include the poems and the dedicatory letter to Adalbero of Laon. MS Rouen, BM Y 11 once was part of the library of Jumièges.[20] It is probable that the part of this manuscript which contains the *Gesta Normannorum* is a product of the scriptorium of Jumièges. Considering the script, it could be dated to the second half of the eleventh century. This manuscript is notable for the numerous blank spaces unevenly distributed through the book, seemingly without any specific reason. Lair suggests that these blanks were meant for miniatures, but this is difficult to accept. Very few Norman manuscripts are decorated with a full series of miniatures, and no historical text is known to have one. For instance, of the Norman manuscripts of William of Jumièges' *Gesta Normannorum Ducum* only MS Rouen, BM Y 14 has one historiated initial.[21] The location of the blank spaces in the text does not show any pattern. Sometimes they follow after the completion of a paragraph; sometimes half a line is left blank even when the sentence is not yet finished; at other times a blank follows on phrases

[16] J. P. Gumbert, 'Un manuscrit d'Annales de Saint-Wandrille retrouvé', *Bibliothèque de l'Ecole des Chartes* 136, 1978, 74-5.

[17] *A catalogue of the Manuscripts in the Cottonian Library Deposited in the British Museum,* London 1802, 191; N. R. Ker, *Medieval Libraries of Great Britain,* London 1964[2], 20.

[18] *A Catalogue of the Harleian Manuscripts in the British Museum,* London 1808, ii (repr. 1973), 57; M. B. Parkes, *English Cursive Book Hands 1250-1500,* London 1969, plate 6(i); Andrew G. Watson, *Catalogue of Dated and Datable Manuscripts in the Department of Manuscripts, the British Library,* London 1979, nr. 784 and plate 477; Van Houts, *Gesta Normannorum Ducum,* 198-9.

[19] K. A. de Meyier, *Codices Vossiani Latini, Pars I Codices in folio,* Leiden 1973, 99-100.

[20] *Catalogue général des manuscrits des bibliothèques publiques de France* i, Rouen 1886, 293-4; Van Houts, *Gesta Normannorum Ducum,* 195-6, the opening page of the manuscript is published in Davis, *Normans and their Myth,* 48.

[21] Manuscripts produced in Normandy usually are decorated with initials; only a few manuscripts have miniatures and then mostly as frontispieces. A full series of miniatures is to be found in the Mont St Michel Sacramentary (MS New York, Pierpont Morgan Library 641). See Alexander, *Norman Illumination,* 85, 127-72; and François Avril, 'La décoration des manuscrits dans les abbayes bénédictines de Normandie au XIe et XIIe siècles', *Ecole des Chartes. Positions des thèses* 1963, Paris 1964, 21-8. For a description of MS Rouen, BM Y 14, see Van Houts, *Gesta Normannorum Ducum,* 213-15.

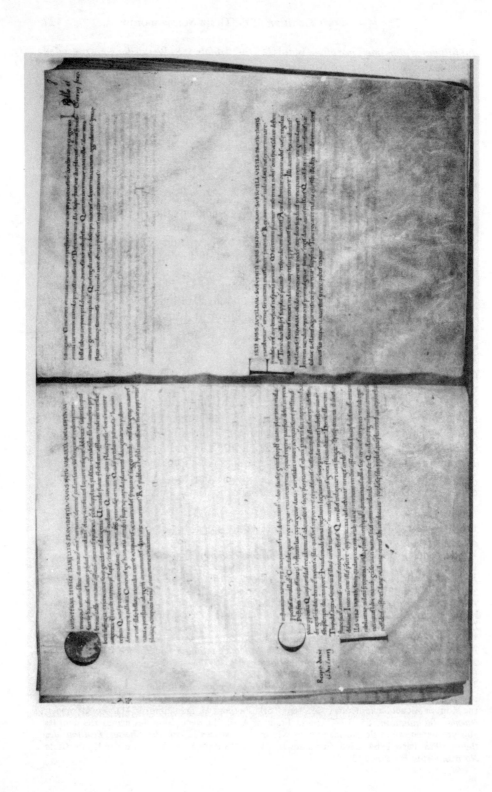

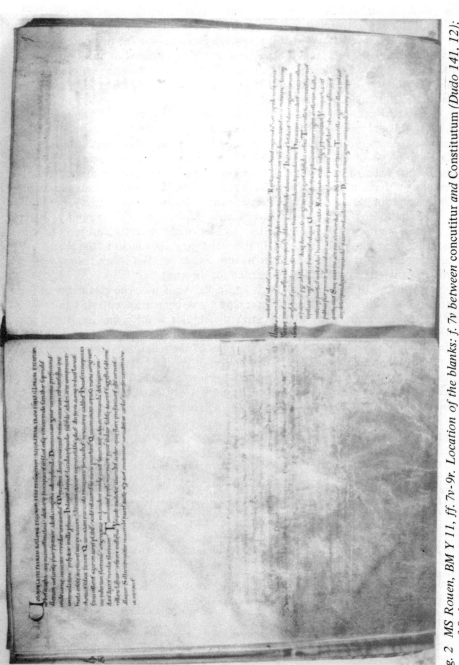

Fig. 2 *MS Rouen, BM Y 11, ff. 7v-9r. Location of the blanks: f. 7v between* concutitur *and* Constitutum (*Dudo 141, 12*); *f. 8r between* unanimes *and* Ferte (*Dudo 142, 2*); *f. 8r after* inquit (*Dudo 142, 14*); *ff. 8v-9r between* equiperis *and* vicibus (*Dudo 142, 31*).

like *Rollo inquit*, and the speech starts immediately after the blank (see Fig. 2).[22] Comparison of the text with the edition and with other manuscripts shows that it is complete. I have not yet found a satisfying explanation for this phenomenon. I suggest that in the exemplar of MS Rouen, BM Y 11 a number of blank spaces was present for a reason obvious there (for example because of holes in the parchment), and that the scribe of MS Rouen, BM Y 11 has tried to copy these blank spaces as faithfully as he could.

The twelfth-century inventory of the library of Fécamp mentions a *Gesta Normannorum*. This entry is to be identified with MS Berlin, DSB Phillipps 1854, which has at the end a poem in praise of Fécamp and its abbot John (very likely John of Ravenna, abbot of Fécamp 1028-78). Dr Alexander argues convincingly that the manuscript was written at Mont St Michel during the third quarter of the eleventh century.[23] Maybe it came to Fécamp as a gift, or it was borrowed and never returned. The manuscript has a sort of title page with a large initial and decorative script.

MS Cambridge, CCC 276 bears a shelfmark of St Augustine's Canterbury, where it was also written, probably in the last decades of the eleventh century.[24] It ends suddenly, near the end of book IV. In this manuscript the rubrics to the poems give the complicated names of the metres used in the poems. The poems themselves are written with letters smaller than those used for the prose.

MS London, BL Royal 13. B. xiv is an English book too. The irregularity of the script makes it difficult to date.[25] It must have a close connection with MS Cambridge, CCC 276 because both manuscripts have the rubrics to the poems explaining the different metres used. Moreover, to the poems addressed to the Muses (at the beginning of book IV) an explanation of the names of the Muses and their etymologies is added as a marginal gloss in MS Cambridge, CCC 276.[26] This gloss is repeated in MS London, BL Royal 13. B. xiv, where it is more or less incorporated in the text: the manuscript is in two columns and the gloss is written as one column next to a column of poetry. Attention is drawn to the gloss by an outline around it and

---

[22] Blank spaces occur on 28 of the 128 pages of Dudo's text: 4r, 6r, 7v, 8rv, 9rv, 28rv, 29rv, 31rv, 32v, 33r (the whole page is blank), 35rv, 37r, 38rv, 39v, 40v, 41r, 42v (the whole page), 43r (the whole page), 44r, 45r, 47v (62v, erasure, see p.131).

[23] Valentin Rose, *Die Handschriften-Verzeichnisse der Königlichen Bibliothek zu Berlin. Zwölfter Band. Verzeichniss der Lateinischen Handschriften* i, Berlin 1893, 315-16; Alexander, *Norman Illumination*, 40, 235. The catalogue of Fécamp is printed in *Catalogue général* i, xxiv-xxvi, and discussed in Geneviève Nortier, *Les bibliothèques médiévales des abbayes bénédictines de Normandie*, Paris 1971, 10-11; Betty Branch, 'Inventories of the libraries of Fécamp from the eleventh and twelfth century', *Manuscripta* 23, 1979, 159-72. Nortier identifies *Gesta Normannorum* with the work of Dudo of St Quentin, while Branch supposes it to be a copy of William of Jumièges' *Gesta Normannorum Ducum*, because Mont St Michel did have a William of Jumièges but not a Dudo: 171 n.24.

[24] N. R. Ker, *Medieval Libraries*, 41; M. R. James, *A Descriptive Catalogue of the Manuscripts in the Library of Corpus Christi College Cambridge*, Cambridge 1912, ii, 38-9; Alexander, *Norman Illumination*, 28 n.2, 40; Anne Lawrence, 'Manuscripts of Early Anglo-Norman Canterbury', *Medieval Art and Architecture at Canterbury before 1220*, The British Archaeological Association Conference Transactions for the year 1979, v, 1982, 101-11.

[25] George F. Warner and Julius P. Gilson, *British Museum Catalogue of Western Manuscripts in the Old Royal and King's Collection*, ii, 99.

[26] The gloss from MS Cambridge, CCC 276 is printed in Dudo, 210. The incomplete words can be restored from MS London, BL Royal 13. B. xiv: *Clio* repperit; *hoc* autem; *polimn*eme. The last two lines, *Urania . . . facio* are not to be found in MS London BL Royal 13. B. xiv.

rubricating lines over the words. This would indicate that MS London, BL Royal 13. B. xiv was copied, directly or indirectly, from MS Cambridge, CCC 276.

MS Antwerp, Museum Plantin-Moretus 17. 2 seems to me to be another English manuscript, written in the twelfth century. It is incomplete at the end because of the loss of a number of leaves. This manuscript shows at the head of the poems the same rubrics indicating the metres used in the poems as appear in MSS Cambridge, CCC 276 and London, BL Royal 13. B. xiv. Another feature which this manuscript has in common with MS Cambridge, CCC 276 is the smaller handwriting used for the poems.[27]

The thirteenth-century manuscript London, BL Cotton Nero D viii is one of the most carefully executed manuscripts among those containing Dudo's *Gesta Normannorum*. It includes also the A-redaction of William of Jumièges' *Gesta Normannorum Ducum*, which follows immediately upon Dudo.[28] There is no clear separation between the two texts, except for an initial which does not differ from other initials used for the marking of chapters. The F-redaction of the *Gesta Normannorum Ducum* follows upon the A-redaction. This combination of Dudo's text with the A-redaction of William's work also occurs in MSS London, BL Harley 3742 and Rouen, BM Y 11, but in this last one the *Gesta Normannorum Ducum* is written by another, later, scribe in a separate part of the codex.[29]

At the end of his work Dudo describes the funeral of duke Richard I and the opening of the grave on the next day by the duke's brother Raoul d'Ivry and his men. They smell the sweet odour of sanctity and find the body *quasi vivi hominis*. Afterwards a chapel was built above the tomb.[30] MS London, BL Cotton Nero D viii tells this story twice: immediately before this passage as it is printed in the edition another version in slightly different words is given. MSS Berlin, DSB Phillipps 1854 and Cambridge, UL Mm. 5. 17 have this same feature, as well as MSS London, BL Royal 13. B. xiv and London, BL Cotton Claudius A xii. The scribes of the last two manuscripts, however, only wrote the 'second' version (which appears first!). In MS Rouen, BM Y 11 the other version was originally inserted, too, but it has been erased. (This is, incidentally, the only blank space in the manuscript that can be explained.) MSS Berne, Burgerbibliothek Bongars 390; Leiden, UB Voss. Lat. F. 47; and London, BL Harley 3742 give the text as printed in the edition. The remaining manuscripts are incomplete. MS Cambridge, CCC 276 ends just where the addition would begin.[31]

---

[27] J. Denucé, *Catalogue des manuscrits – Catalogus der handschriften Museum Plantin-Moretus*, Antwerpen 1927, 154-6.

[28] *A Catalogue . . . Cottonian Library*, 238-9; Van Houts, *Gesta Normannorum Ducum*, 196-8.

[29] Van Houts, *Gesta Normannorum Ducum*, 195, 199.

[30] Dudo, 298-9.

[31] MS London, BL Cotton Nero D viii has inserted between *suo desiderio* and *Quis tam ferreum* (Dudo, 298 ll. 21-2): *Tandem prerumpitur lugens populus. corpusque ab episcopis et a fortioribus iuxta rapitur. sepulcroque cum magno eiulatu mancipatur. extimploque saxo cooperitur. Sequenti nanque die sepulccrum rodulfo comite aperiente ingens ex eo manauit flagrantia. uincens odor opobalsama. inuenit omnia eius membra quasi uiui hominis. et inde manauit odor suauior flagrantia terebintine. et balsami. afflans illorum olfactum Denique super tumbam construxerunt mire pulcritudinis capellam. basilice protense amplitudinis mirabiliter innexam. illicque allatus columpnis mirifice. et tumba colitur cum xpisto in gloria resurrecturus. Complens nanque cursum huius fragilis uite dux magnus ricardus. obijt anno ab incarnatione domini nostri ihesu xpisti. Nongentisimo nonagesimo sexto.* MS London Royal 13. B. xiv has this same insertion. Like MS London, BL Cotton Nero D viii it continues with *Quis tam ferreum* and then ends the prose part of the text with *honore sub magno*. This is followed by the final poem *O Fiscanne*. MS

Fig. 3 The origin of the disorder in the poem Praesul amande in MS London BL Cotton Nero D viii

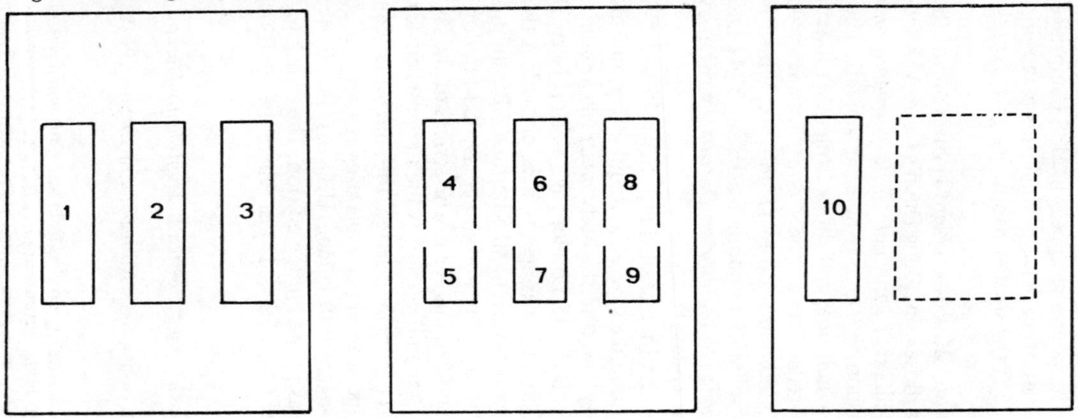

3a Stage I

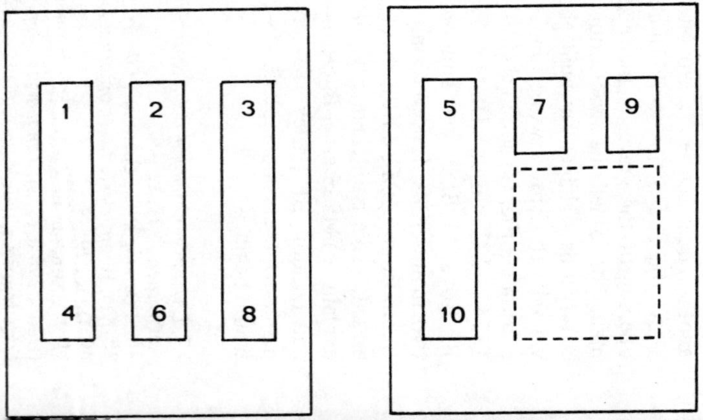

Sequence of verses		
Ed. Lair		MS BL Cotton Nero D viii
1.	1- 18	1.	1- 18
2.	19- 36	4.	55- 65
3.	37- 54	2.	19- 36
4.	55- 65	6.	74- 83
5.	66- 73	3.	37- 54
6.	74- 83	8.	92-102
7.	84- 91	5.	66- 73
8.	92-102	10.	111-130
9.	103-110	7.	84- 91
10.	111-130	9.	103-110

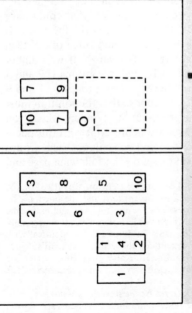

3c Stage III, MS London BL Cotton
Nero D viii

The mingling of prose and poetry in Dudo's *Gesta Normannorum* posed several problems for scribes. Some of them did no more than write out the words without distinguishing between prose and poetry. Others found solutions for the lay-out which are pleasing to the eye and make it easier for the reader to find his way through the book. In MSS Rouen, BM Y 11 and Berlin, DSB Phillipps 1854 after some pages the scribes gave up writing consistently in verses and wrote the poems out in long lines: the poems are marked by rubrics only. The scribes of MSS Cambridge, CCC 276 and Antwerp, Museum Plantin-Moretus 17.2 used a more refined technique: the poems are written in smaller script than the one used for the prose parts, which gives a very elegant appearance to the books.[32]

The scribe of MS London, BL Cotton Nero D viii, however, did the most careful planning. He went to great pains to justify the lines, by writing wide-spaced and elongated letters. This is especially striking in the poems, where the varying length of the verses demanded a lot of measuring to reach these results. Therefore it was a surprise to find great disorder in the succession of verses in one of the poems. This poem counts 130 lines in the edition (MS London, BL Cotton Nero D viii has an extra verse 81a).[33] MS London, BL Cotton Nero D viii gives these in the following sequence (the numbering of verses is taken from the edition): (1) 1-18, (4) 55-65, (2) 19-36, (6) 74-83, (3) 37-54, (8) 92-102, (5) 66-73, (10) 111-30, (7) 84-91, (9) 103-10 (see Fig. 3). It seems unlikely that an attentive person like the scribe of this manuscript would have caused such a mess. In one of the earlier copies something must have gone wrong. I have tried to make a reconstruction of what could have happened. Fig. 3 shows that in MS London, BL Cotton Nero D viii the poem is divided in ten groups: three groups of eight, three of eleven and three of eighteen verses, and one group consisting of the original twenty last verses. If we number these groups, as they appear in the edition, from 1 to 10 then the groups 1, 2 and 3 have eighteen verses each; groups 4, 6 and 8 have eleven verses; groups 5, 7 and 9 have eight verses and group 10 has twenty verses. I suppose that the solution must lie in this symmetrical division. The order of the groups in MS London, BL Cotton Nero D viii is 1-4-2-6-3-8-5-10-7-9. If we assume a manuscript with this poem written in three columns, with groups 1, 2 and 3 forming one column each, groups 4+5, 6+7 and 8+9 in three columns of eighteen verses on the following page and

London, BL Cotton Claudius A xii ends just like MS London, BL Cotton Royal 13. B. xiv. MS Cambridge, CCC 276 ends with *concrepabat pro uocibus ululantium*, and the poem *O Fiscanne*. In MS Rouen, BM Y 11 the rest of the line after *desiderio*, seven full lines, and half a line before *Quis tam ferreum* are erased. Fragments of not fully removed letters confirm that originally the insertion had been written on these lines. MS Berlin, DSB Phillipps 1854 is identical with MS London, BL Cotton Nero D viii in the final part, except for the year of Richard's death, which is given as *millesimo secundo*. MS Cambridge, UL Mm. 5.17 also gives 1002. After the end of the inserted passage the rest of the page is blank. *Quis vero . . . millesimo secundo* is written on the next folio.

32 Generally, the scribes of the manuscripts of Dudo's *Gesta Normannorum* are not very consistent in their lay-out of the 78 poems inserted in the text. Sometimes the poems are written in verses with one verse per line, at other times the verses are copied out consecutively on the full line, so that only the rubrics distinguish the poems from the prose text. To give a few examples: in MS London, BL Royal 13. B. xiv 6 poems only are not written in verses. In MS Berlin, DSB Phillipps 1854 the poems in books I and II are all written in verses; in books III and IV only 4 poems are written in verses, the others in long lines. In MS Cambridge, CCC 276 all the poems are copied in verses. In MS London, BL Cotton Nero D viii all poems except 10 are copied in verses. MS Rouen, BM Y 11 has in book I 6½ poems in verses, none in verses in book II, in book III 7 poems in verses and in book IV the poems are all in long lines.

33 Dudo, 127-8: *Praesul amande*. L. 81A: *Et monachilis*.

the final twenty verses on the third page, this would appear as is shown in Fig. 3a. On the second page of the poem something caused a break or a division between the eleventh and twelfth lines of each column. This could be, for instance, a fault in the parchment, which forced the scribe to leave some extra space between these lines. Next to the last twenty lines on the third page enough space was left for the subsequent poem which, incidentally, has twenty verses too. The next step occurred when this copy was used as an exemplar. The new scribe observed several 'blocks' of verses. Maybe he did not understand the text sufficiently well, maybe he merely copied it automatically. However this may be, on a leaf with a writing space larger than the one used in his model, the scribe copied groups 1, 2 and 3 and groups 4, 6 and 8 as pictured in Fig. 3b, then proceeded to the next page for groups 5, 7 and 9. Finally group 10 was copied beneath group 5. This resulted in columns of twenty-eight or twenty-nine lines. The twenty-line poem following upon the problematic one fits nicely next to group 10. The third phase is that the components $1+4$, $2+6$, $3+8$ and $5+10$ are seen as belonging together and are copied in just that order. This results in the sequence of the groups as 1 - 4 - 2 - 6 - 3 - 8 - 5 - 10 - 7 - 9, as it appears in MS London, BL Cotton Nero D viii (see Fig. 3c). It is of no consequence that this third copy has a different lay-out, with four instead of three columns.

This survey of the manuscripts in which Dudo of St Quentin's *Gesta Normannorum* survives is primarily meant to present material additional to the information provided by Lair in his edition. It is as yet too early to provide a full discussion of the textual history or a comprehensive view of the manuscript tradition. Some tentative conclusions, however, can be formulated.

1. The addition of five manuscripts to the ten known to the last editor, and the observation that his edition is far from accurate in its details, argue for the desirability of a new edition.

2. The fact that so many manuscripts survive from the eleventh and twelfth centuries (ten in all), of Norman as well as of English origin, indicates that Dudo's *Gesta Normannorum* was still being read after William of Jumièges wrote his *Gesta Normannorum Ducum*. The assumption that Dudo's work was fairly soon superseded by William's must therefore be rejected.

3. The absence of the poems and of the dedicatory letter to Adalbero of Laon in five of the eleventh and twelfth-century manuscripts (and in two eleventh-century ones) may indicate that the prose text was composed as the original version, and that after 1015 (when he could style himself as dean of St Quentin) Dudo expanded his work with poems and a dedicatory letter. This hypothesis puts the date of the original version between 996, the year of duke Richard I's commission, and before 1015; and the date of the second redaction after 1015.

THE ARCHITECTURAL IMPLICATIONS
OF THE *DECRETA LANFRANCI*

Arnold William Klukas

A medieval church building was first and foremost a space in which to perform the sacred drama of the Christian liturgy. Structure, scale, and decoration were all subordinate to the cultic requirements of Mass and Divine Office. Art historians have traditionally studied medieval buildings in terms of their stylistic or formal relationships to other buildings, presumably because of their deep-rooted visual orientation and because most liturgical historians from whom they might gain insights into the functional requirements of these buildings have been concerned primarily with words rather than with actions, with similarities of texts rather than with their performance content. Thus the primary *raison d'être* of a medieval church has been ignored.

It is my concern to study liturgical actions and relate those actions to the physical structures which housed them. The major difficulty with this approach, particularly in the Romanesque period of European architecture, is the paucity of information about liturgical practice. Furthermore, few extant churches have preserved their pre-fourteenth-century liturgical arrangements. Only in England are we fortunate enough to have well-documented evidence of both liturgical practice and architectural plans from the Romanesque period, and thus it is to England that I have turned in my study of how architectural forms were built to accommodate liturgical requirements in the Romanesque period.

In such a study it is most useful to have well-documented information as to the liturgical practices before as well as during the period in question. By noting the changes which occurred between the two and then examining the buildings which were designed to house them, one can be reasonably sure that certain architectural anomalies or peculiarities resulted from liturgical requirements rather than from stylistic inspiration or from the whim and fancy of the master mason. The *Regularis Concordia*, written by St Ethelwold for the Council of Winchester (c.970), preserves for us the customs of Anglo-Saxon England which endured to the Norman Conquest in all of England and well beyond the Conquest in certain monastic houses. The *Decreta Lanfranci*, composed by Archbishop Lanfranc for his priory of Christ Church, Canterbury (c.1070), details the customs which the new Norman archbishop wished to implement for his new English subjects. A comparison of the cultic actions required in these two documents allows us to distinguish families of liturgical requirements with resultant architectural requirements (for liturgical families see Appendix I). These architectural requirements can be correlated with the architectural formulae displayed in Lanfranc-related buildings as opposed to those buildings in which more traditional Anglo-Saxon customs endured.

Two problems immediately emerge when we begin to investigate the architecture of post-Conquest England. From the liturgical point of view we must overcome the assumption clearly articulated by A. W. Clapham in regard to Norman architecture:

> The Anglo-Norman churches of the first generation after the Conquest form
> a nearly homogeneous class of building which is indivisible into geographical
> schools and is in most of its structural features a reproduction of the Norman
> Romanesque of the Continent.[1]

In reality Clapham's view greatly oversimplifies the architectural and liturgical evidence and thus overlooks the liturgical diversity which occurred on both sides of the Channel. In Normandy at least three distinctly different liturgical traditions co-existed before the Conquest so that the traditions which the Normans brought with them to England were not at all uniform.[2] The liturgical diversity in England became even greater, with churches using Norman, Lotharingian or native Anglo-Saxon customs – or even mixing them together. We must therefore clearly distinguish, if at all possible, the liturgical family to which each individual monastic house was related. Secondly, much of medieval architectural history has been based on the assumption promulgated most eloquently by Viollet-le-Duc that all medieval buildings were the technically progressive experiments of their master builders. This rationalist approach was an expression of Viollet-le-Duc's own anti-clerical pro-democratic prejudices[3] and consequently it ignores the role of the patron, i.e. the liturgists and iconographers, to stress the structural designs of the masons.

Once having passed beyond these two underlying prejudices, one still faces many individual pitfalls on the road to a liturgical reinterpretation of Romanesque architecture. So often the buildings which best preserve their Romanesque appearance are accompanied by a frustrating lack of primary liturgical documentation. Furthermore, some of the most detailed manuscripts from this period refer to buildings which have been so rebuilt or altered over the years that nothing remains of their Romanesque interior arrangements. For example, for St-Étienne de Caen, a major extant building, little liturgical documentation has been preserved while, on the other hand, several primary liturgical documents survive for St-Wandrille where nothing remains of the Romanesque church. While enduring these frustrations in gathering evidence one still must be careful not to state too emphatically that particular liturgical functions demanded specific spatial arrangements. Often there is more than one architectural solution. For example, a procession can just as easily be performed by means of an ambulatory with radiating chapels (such as Battle Abbey) or by means of a straight path across the chord of an apse (such as St Albans Abbey). Thus, one must proceed with care and patience; but in spite of the difficulties, I believe that this liturgical approach can be of great assistance to those who wish to understand the context of architecture in post-Conquest England.

Three specific things can be learned from such a liturgical reinterpretation. First of all, if we group buildings by their patrons rather than by their mason's lodges, liturgical relationships should be manifest in parallel formal arrangements. For example, the English buildings most closely connected to Normandy in liturgy (Canterbury Cathedral) should most closely resemble Norman prototypes (St Étienne

---

[1] A. W. Clapham, *English Romanesque Architecture, Vol. 2: After the Conquest*, Oxford 1930, 19.

[2] A. W. Klukas, *Altaria Superioria: The function and significance of the tribune-chapel in Anglo-Norman Romanesque*, Pittsburgh 1978, 151ff.

[3] Eugene Viollet-le-Duc, *Dictionnaire raisonné de l'architecture française du XIe au XVIe Siècle*, Paris 1875, 10 volumes.

de Caen). Secondly, having ascertained the particular liturgical family to which a certain building belonged, we can, with the appropriate archaeological evidence, more fully reconstruct its internal arrangements. Finally, we can discover the rationale for certain architectural formulae which have hitherto puzzled architectural historians.[4] For example, Anglo-Norman buildings with features unknown in Normandy, such as the aisled transepts and western transepts evident in Winchester, Ely and Bury, can be explained by reference to Anglo-Saxon liturgical traditions.[5]

Archbishop Lanfranc composed a customary for his newly rebuilt monastic cathedral at Canterbury sometime after 1070. It is now known as the *Decreta Lanfranci*. The *Decreta* is certainly the most detailed and well-preserved set of rubrics we have from Romanesque England. Of the fifteen houses which used the *Decreta*, nine church buildings are extant enough today for us to discuss the relationship of their formal characteristics to their common liturgical source. In presenting this study I will first discuss the content of the document, outline its observance at Canterbury Cathedral Priory, ennumerate its architectural implications, and finally relate those implications to the architectural solutions actually evident in the nine extant buildings which functioned under its influence.

The *Decreta Lanfranci*, or *Monastic Constitutions of Lanfranc*, survive in six manuscript copies of which the Durham Cathedral Chapter Library Ms. B. iv. 24 is the earliest and most complete.[6] The preface to the *Decreta* states that Lanfranc wrote them for the use of Henry, the former prior of Christ Church, Canterbury, when Henry went to Battle as its abbot in 1096.[7] These observances were not newly invented for Henry at Battle, rather they were Lanfranc's organised compilation of the observances he had instituted at Christ Church.

It seems certain that Lanfranc intended his *Decreta* to be a model for other monastic houses in England, and without question Lanfranc intended to enforce what observances he thought worthy upon all those under his authority. Lanfranc was first and foremost a monk, and as a monk he considered poverty, chastity and obedience to be the essential foundation for all monastic life. Liturgy must be performed under the vow of obedience, i.e. a monk must humbly accept what observances his superiors considered appropriate. Indeed, Lanfranc states:

> All such [rubrical] arrangements, once they have been settled for their subjects
> by superiors, cannot without blame be violated by those whose whole life is
> one of obedience.[8]

Lanfranc considered much of what he found at Canterbury to be wanting, in particular he felt that the liturgical life of his monks must be brought into accord with the most advanced thinking on the Continent. Lanfranc clearly states that he

---

[4] For example Clapham, *After*, notes that axial western towers (page 38) and large crypts (page 64) were not characteristic of Normandy.

[5] See my 'Winchester, Ely, Canterbury and the continuity of Anglo-Saxon litergical tradition in post-Conquest England', in *Congrès Anselmiennes de Bec*, Paris 1983.

[6] The *Decreta Lanfranci* (hereafter the *Decreta*) is available in two editions by David Knowles, *The Monastic Constitutions of Lanfranc*, Oxford 1953, and *Decreta Lanfranci Monachis Cantuariensibus Transmissa* which is volume iii of *Corpus Consuetudinum Monasticarum*, gen. ed. Dom K. Hallinger, Siegburg 1967. As the 1953 edition is more readily available to English-speaking readers we shall refer to it in the text.

[7] David Knowles and C. N. L. Brooke, eds, *The Heads of Religious Houses, England and Wales, 940-1216*, Cambridge 1972, 29.

[8] *Decreta*, 2.

had compiled his Canterbury customs from the most honoured monastic houses of his time:

> We send you the customs of our monastic life which we have compiled from the customs of those monasteries which in our day have the greatest prestige in the monastic order.[9]

The monks of Christ Church did not view Lanfranc's compilation of the best Continental customs with the same respect. Indeed Lanfranc was confronted with open rebellion and had to take harsh measures to enforce these new customs. One of Lanfranc's own letters allows us to see his struggles with his monks:

> I pleaded that the language was unknown to me and that the native races were barbarous, but to no avail ... I accepted the appointment, I arrived, I took office. Now I endure so many troubles and vexations every day — such hardness of heart, greed and dishonesty — that 'I am weary of my life'.[10]

Eadmer, the Christ Church chronicler and author of Lanfranc's biography, saw Lanfranc's relationship to his monks in a somewhat different light:

> ... Lanfranc, as an Englishman, was still somewhat green, and some of the customs which he found in England had not found acceptance with him. So he changed many of them, often with good reason, but sometimes simply by the imposition of his own authority.[11]

Canterbury had taken a significant part in the monastic revival of tenth-century England.[12] Its liturgical observances had been those of the *Regularis Concordia* and closely tied to Winchester — but all of this was swept away by Lanfranc. Indeed Edmund Bishop sees Lanfranc as intentionally setting out to eradicate the traditional customs and replace them with a simplified observance. Bishop speaks of Lanfranc's abolition of Anglo-Saxon saints from the Christ Church calendar and Lanfranc's eradication of the Anglo-Saxon offices of the Virgin:

> The Office of the blessed Virgin is nowhere mentioned in Lanfranc's Statutes for Canterbury Cathedral for Benedictines, which in more than one particular prescribe the contrary to older English customs in a way so express as to show that his directions are aimed at them in a prohibitory sense.[13]

It is certain, then, that Lanfranc intended to abolish the Anglo-Saxon traditions which he found in the English communities under his jurisdiction. But what did he intend to put in their place? Lanfranc introduced an attitude towards observance which he had learned at Bec, an attitude that favoured austerity in customs and simplicity in language.[14] Lanfranc did not impose the customs of Bec as such upon

9 *Decreta*, 1.
10 *Lanfranc's Letters*, Letter No. 1, lines 19-27 (1083), 31-3.
11 R. W. Southern, ed., *The Life of St Anselm . . . by Eadmer*, Oxford 1962, 50-1.
12 See A. Robinson, 'The Early Community of Christ Church, Canterbury', *Journal of Theological Studies* 27, 225-40; David Knowles, *The Monastic Order in England . . . 940-1216*, Cambridge 1963, Appendix iii, 696; and Christopher Hohler, 'Some Service Books of the Later Saxon Church', *Tenth Century Studies*, ed. David Parsons, London 1975, 73.
13 E. Bishop and A. Gasquet, *The Bosworth Psalter*, London 1908, 28, notes the pre- and post-Conquest Calendars of Christ Church; E. Bishop, 'On the origins of the Prymer', *Liturgica Historica*, Oxford 1918, 227 explains the deleted offices of the Virgin.
14 Dom Anselm Hughes has shown that while Lanfranc's *Decreta* were not synonymous with

England. His *Decreta* are closely bound to the Bec customs known to us but are an extension of those customs as they were modified by Lanfranc's experience as an abbot and archbishop. Lanfranc composed his *Decreta* anew, for in his preface to the *Decreta* he addresses the work to Henry, former prior of Christ Church and a monk at both Caen and Bec with Lanfranc, and tells him that he drew what was best from 'many sources'. Early in our own century Rose Graham indicated that while Bec was certainly the primary source for Lanfranc, he also drew from several other sources, notably the Cluny customary composed by Bernard in 1067[15] (for a comparison of the *Decreta* with Bec and Cluny see Appendix I). Dom David Knowles confirms Dr Graham's assumption in his own study of the *Decreta* and points out that Lanfranc ignores the *Regularis Concordia* completely.[16]

But why should Lanfranc have been so anti-Saxon? The answer lies both in the reform policies advocated by Pope Gregory VII, who wished to bring the English Church into line with Continental views of organisation and observance,[17] and in the personality of Lanfranc himself. Lanfranc had been trained as a lawyer and gained fame as a teacher of dialectic. His well-known debate with Berengar of Tours showed Lanfranc's own scholarly interest in original sources, authentic texts, and logical arguments.[18] Lanfranc shunned poetic allusions and dramatic figures of speech.[19] The elaboration of language and the dramatic elements in the *Regularis Concordia* were in opposition to the very principles of his scholarly method. The texts of the Anglo-Saxon service-books were not the modern revised Gallican text used in Normandy, the calendar was cluttered with saints unknown outside England and dubious in character, and the multiplication of offices had obscured the original organisation of the hours of prayer required by St Benedict. Thus Lanfranc as a scholar and lawyer could not tolerate what he found in the observances characterised by the *Regularis Concordia*. He could see no other solution than to replace the Anglo-Saxon customs altogether.

Lanfranc did not have the authority to impose his *Decreta* upon every monastic house in England. Benedictine houses were autonomous institutions which jealously guarded their privileges and traditions from episcopal and royal usurpation. Indeed chroniclers record instances of outright rebellion in several Benedictine houses when new customs were introduced. The infamous case of the murder of several Saxon

---

Bec customs, they were closely tied to Bec, see *The Bec Missal*, London 1963, vii-viii. The sole surviving manuscript containing the customs of Bec was written between 1290-1310. As it is a revision of two previous customaries it seems to indicate that the earliest version was close to Lanfranc's *Decreta*. For this customary and a discussion of the problems surrounding it see *Consuetudines Beccenses*, ed. M. P. Dickson, *Corpus Consuetudinum Monasticarum*, iv, Siegburg 1967. Of the austerity of the Bec customs Dickson says, liii:

> ... nous en relevions une note d'austerité qui témoigne de leur vrai sens. Le moine du Bec qui, dans la première moitié du XIIe siècle, se plaint du mépris des Cisterciens à l'égard de son abbaye affirme que celle-ci connaît, en dépit de quelques advocissements apportés quant à la nourriture et au vêtement, des rigueurs que nul fondateur n'aurait voulu imposer ...

[15] Rose Graham, 'The relation of Cluny to some other movements of Monastic Reform', *Journal of Theological Studies* 15, 1914, 184. For Bernard's customary see M. Herrgott, ed., *Vetus Disciplina Monastica*, Paris 1926.

[16] David Knowles, *Decreta Lanfranci, Corpus Consuetudinum Monasticarum* III, xvii-xviii.

[17] A. Hughes, *The Bec Missal*, vii.

[18] See R. W. Southern, 'Lanfranc of Bec and Berenger of Tours', *Studies in Medieval History Presented to F. M. Powicke*, Oxford 1948, 27-48.

[19] See Margaret Gibson, *Lanfranc of Bec*, Oxford 1978, 39 for a discussion of Lanfranc as a scholar and writer.

monks at Glastonbury will be sufficient evidence: Thurstan, the new Norman abbot of Glastonbury, was a monk under Lanfranc at St-Étienne de Caen and demanded that his monks observe the Caen customs. They refused, and in his anger he ordered his Norman body-guards to shoot their arrows at the monks in choir as they were singing the forbidden offices. King William removed Thurstan from office for a while, but Thurstan was to return to Glastonbury at a later date — to the dismay of the community.[20]

Lanfranc did not approve of Thurstan's use of violence, but Lanfranc's own treatment of the recalcitrant monks at St Augustine's, Canterbury, where Lanfranc did have the right of appointment, was not without violence. The monks at St Augustine's refused in 1087 to accept the appointment by Lanfranc of Guido, a monk of Christ Church, as their abbot. After two years of bitter reaction against Guido and the *Decreta* which he had brought with him, Lanfranc demanded that the monks submit. They refused and Lanfranc then imprisoned the English prior Alfwin and the monks who supported him, and then publicly flogged the other rebel-monks before sending them to other houses. Lanfranc died before the issue was finally settled by the replacement of the entire St Augustine's community with monks from Christ Church, who accepted Guido and his *Decreta*.[21] Lanfranc claimed that he had the right as patron to act as he did at St Augustine's, but he could not claim that right at other houses.

By the middle of the twelfth century fifteen houses were following some form of Lanfranc's *Decreta*, but in each case the acceptance of the *Decreta* was due to the initiative of the abbots of these communities rather than because of a uniform policy for all of England promulgated from the archbishop. We have mentioned the circumstances under which both Canterbury houses accepted the *Decreta*. Prior Henry, for whom the *Decreta* were originally composed, moved to Battle Abbey in 1096 as its abbot and introduced Lanfranc's observances upon his arrival.[22] This created little difficulty because the Battle community was composed of French monks brought from Marmoutier at the time of Battle's foundation. When Gilbert Crispin, Lanfranc's disciple and friend from Bec, was appointed abbot of Westminster Abbey c.1085 he introduced the *Decreta*, and indeed the customs of Abbot Ware (1258-63) show a heavy reliance at Westminster upon the *Decreta* almost two hundred years after its first introduction.[23] By 1140 Westminster had acquired a cell, Great Malvern Priory, as a bequest from Great Malvern's founder. Great Malvern would thereafter have followed Westminster customs, although no books survive to confirm that probability.[24]

---

[20] *De gestis pontificum*, 197 and Knowles, *Monastic*, 114-15.

[21] The most detailed account of this controversy is found in the 'Acts of Lanfranc', *EHD* ii, 631-5. See also Knowles, *Monastic*, 115-17; and A. J. MacDonald, *Lanfranc*, London 1926, 245-50.

[22] For a discussion of which houses accepted Lanfranc's *Decreta* see J. A. Robinson, 'Lanfranc's monastic constitutions', *Journal of Theological Studies* 10, 1909, 375-88. For Battle see 383.

[23] For Westminster see Robinson, *Journal of Theological Studies* 10, 1909, 378; Robinson, *Gilbert Crispin, Abbot of Westminster*, Cambridge 1911, 28; Knowles, *Monastic*, 123; and J. Wickham Legg, *Missale ad usum Ecclesie Westmonasteriensis*, London 1897, III, vi; E. M. Thompson, *Customary of the Benedictine Monasteries of St Augustine, Canterbury and St Peter, Westminster* ii, London 1904, iii, vii-ix.

[24] For the history of the priory see M. M. C. Calthorp, 'Priory of Great Malvern', in VCH *Worcestershire* ii, London 1906, 136. The hermit Aldwin, without the consent of the Bishop of Worcester, granted the house to Westminster Abbey at his death in 1140. William of Malmesbury, *De gestis pontificum*, 285-6, speaks of a close connection between Bishop Wulfstan and

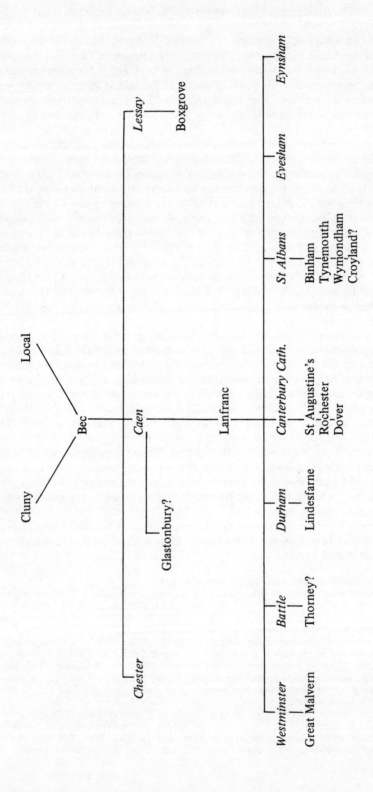

Fig. 1 The liturgical lineage of the Bec/Lanfranc customs

Paul of Caen, nephew of Lanfranc, enforced the *Decreta* at St Albans when he became abbot there in 1077 and Matthew Paris records this fact, saying that Paul was strict in his observance of the *Decreta* as well as wise in its interpretation.[25] Loyalty to the observances of the *Decreta* must have continued into Matthew Paris' own day, for Dr Hartzell has shown the strong connection of the chant found in a St Albans breviary to that known at Bec.[26] St Albans' several dependencies, Tynemouth, Binham, and Wymondham, accepted the customs of their mother house. Matthew Paris records a fourth priory at Croyland when he mentions that Godfrey, former prior of St Albans, brought the St Albans customs with him when he went to Croyland in 1138;[27] the remaining service books of Croyland, however, do not show such St Albans influence.[28] Because of this ambiguity we will omit Croyland from our discussion.

Rochester Cathedral Priory was founded by Bishop Gundulf, suffragan bishop to Lanfranc, as a cell of Christ Church, Canterbury.[29] The service books and observances were to be the same in both houses, and manuscript evidence bears this out; the script and contents of books known to be from Rochester are nearly identical to those of Christ Church.[30] Christ Church established another cell at St Martin's Priory, Dover.[31] Although the house could claim a foundation during the reign of King Eadbald (c.640) it was not refounded as a priory of Christ Church until 1139, or sixty years after Lanfranc's death when Christ Church's customs had changed considerably.

When Walter of Cerisy, former chaplain to Lanfranc, became abbot of Evesham in 1077 he introduced the *Decreta* and followed Lanfranc's example in ridding the Evesham calendar of all but its most important Anglo-Saxon saints.[32] Walter put all the Anglo-Saxon relics to a trial-by-fire; all those saints whose earthly remains survived

Aldwin; another source as recorded in *Monasticon* iii, 447, tells of an early and continuous Westminster connection.

[25] Matthew Paris, *Gesta Abbatum S. Albani* I, i, 52: 'Ista quoque Paulus abbas, vir religiosus et elegantur litteratus, et in observantia ordinis regularis rigidus et prudens . . . et facta est ecclesia sancti Albani quasi schola et disciplinaris observantiae per totum regnum Angliae . . . attulerat namque secum consuetudines Lanfranci et statuta monastica a domina papa merito approbata conscripta . . .'

[26] For a discussion of the musical and liturgical traditions at St Albans see D. H. Turner, 'The Crowland Gradual', *Ephemerides Liturgicae* 74, 1960, 168-74; K. D. Hartzell, 'An Unknown English Benedictine Gradual of the 11th Century', *Anglo-Saxon England* iii, Cambridge 1975, 131-44.

[27] Matthew Paris, *Gesta Abbatum S. Albani*, ed. Riley, RS 28, vol. v, I, 121: 'Qui [Godfridus] ordinem huius domus, cum consuetudinibus, ibidem constiuit observari.'

[28] See Turner, 'The Crowland Gradual', 170.

[29] For the history of Rochester see *Textus Roffensis*, ed. T. Hearne, Oxford 1720, 143-5; H. Wharton, *Anglia Sacra*, London 1691, i, 327-94; and 'Vita Gundulfi', *Patrologiae series Latina*, ed. J. P. Migne, Paris 1844-64, clix, 820. An excellent discussion of Gundulf's life is by R. A. L. Smith, *EHR* 57, 1943, 257-72.

[30] See C. R. Dodwell, *The Canterbury School of Illumination*, Cambridge 1954, 119: 'The script of the Rochester books is very close to that of Christ Church. In one or two books it is indistinguishable from it . . . the illumination of books which were definitely written at Rochester is largely derived from that of Christ Church.'

[31] St Martin's Priory, Dover, did possess a copy of the *Decreta* which is datable by its script to c.1150. See Knowles, *Decreta*, xxiii. By the time of its foundation in 1139, Christ Church, Canterbury, had begun a major rebuilding of its east end to provide for a more elaborate liturgy than Lanfranc had authorised. St Martin's was built to accommodate these newer customs.

[32] See *Chronicon Monasterii de Evesham*, ed. W. D. Macray, London 1863, 96. See also Knowles, *Monastic*, 124 and Knowles, *Decreta*, xxiii.

the flames were retained in the calendar and the rest were deleted. Eynsham Abbey in Oxfordshire, after a troubled and unsettled period from the Conquest until 1094, was refounded by Bishop Remigius of Lincoln upon the Lanfranc *Decreta*. One of the few extant twelfth-century copies of the *Decreta* was written for Eynsham, and the thirteenth-century customs of Eynsham show that the influence was maintained.[33]

The final houses which were organised according to Lanfranc's *Decreta* were the cathedral priory at Durham and its cell at Lindisfarne. Bishop William of St-Calais had received the assistance of Lanfranc and Gilbert Crispin in his reorganisation of the house at Durham.[34] Bishop William is known to have sent a request to Lanfranc for a copy of the *Decreta* and the Cathedral Chapter at Durham still possesses the book which Lanfranc sent. It is labelled *Consuetudines Dorobornenses*, i.e. *Canterbury Customs*.[35] The *Decreta* were certainly the basis of the Durham customs, and we know that Durham's priory at Lindisfarne followed the observances of its mother house. Two other copies of the *Decreta* were possessed by cathedrals, but it is certain that the copies known to have been at Worcester and Hereford were placed in their libraries rather than used in their chapter houses.[36]

We thus arrive at a total of nine abbeys and cathedral monasteries and at least six priories which submitted to Lanfranc's *Decreta* (Fig. 1). These fifteen houses shared the common inheritance which Lanfranc had learned at Bec, an inheritance which stressed orderly observance, lucid language, and austerity in ritual. The customs which Lanfranc initiated at Christ Church, Canterbury were not received with equal approbation in all these fifteen houses. We have seen that they caused open rebellion at St Augustine's, and at Croyland and Christ Church the customs did not long outlive their author. Be that as it may, the *Decreta* which Lanfranc composed and introduced to England presented a new approach to liturgical observance unknown to the native Anglo-Saxon observances. Unlike the laboured and elaborate stipulations of the *Regularis Concordia*, the *Decreta Lanfranci* were simple and orderly, the outcome of an ordered and scholarly mind that preferred purity of language to poetic allusions and simplicity of performance to dramatic ritual. The *Decreta* must have seemed very foreign to England, but its influence on liturgical observances there was far reaching and enduring. Let us now turn to the architectural implications of the *Decreta* as were evident in Canterbury Cathedral in Lanfranc's time.

Lanfranc began the rebuilding of his cathedral soon after his arrival in 1070, and brought with him his wide experience in the ordering of the liturgical and administrative activities of William the Conqueror's newly founded abbey of St-Étienne de Caen.[37] The structural parallels between St-Étienne and Canterbury are striking (Figs 2 and 3). As at Caen the west end of Canterbury terminated as a twin-towered

---

33 The twelfth-century copy of the *Decreta* is now Bodleian MS 435; the thirteenth-century Eynsham customs have been edited by Antonia Gransden as *The Customary of the Benedictine Abbey of Eynsham in Oxfordshire, Corpus Consuetudinum Monasticarum* ii, Siegburg 1963; for the history of Eynsham see *Monasticon* iii, 7-10 and Knowles, *Monastic*, 124.

34 This is recorded by Symeon of Durham, *Opera*, ed. T. Arnold, London 1882, i, 119-22.

35 This manuscript is now listed as Durham Cathedral Library MS B. IV. 24. This book is mentioned in an inventory of 1392 where it is listed as being in the 'Spendement' – the treasury under the dormitory. For further details see Robinson, 'Lanfranc's', 382. Archdale King also comments on the strong dependence of the observances of Durham upon Canterbury, see *Liturgies of the Past*, London 1959, 303.

36 See Robinson, 'Lanfranc's', 383.

37 See Gibson, *Lanfranc*, 98 ff.

façade that opened directly to the nave interior without a porch or narthex. In both the eight-bay nave opened to a crossing covered by a lantern tower. In both the transept arms terminated in bridges which opened into the upper floor of each transept apse. In both the solid walls of the three-bay presbytery terminated in an apse, creating an external apse-echelon plan of five chapels. In both the elevations were similar: a three-storey elevation with a full tribune. The only divergence between the two buildings is that Canterbury had a crypt under its choir and Caen did not.[38] The crypt at Canterbury points to the functional differences between the two churches: St-Étienne was an abbey that had the duke of Normandy as its patron, Canterbury was an abbey but also functioned as the metropolitan cathedral of all England, the repository of national saints and kings, and as a church closely tied to the English monarchy. Canterbury's multiplicity of functions required a more complicated structure.

Recent archaeological work at Canterbury has revealed more than has hitherto been known about Lanfranc's cathedral,[39] and provides us with the opportunity of reconstructing the liturgical arrangements of the interior as outlined in the *Decreta*. Additional information about altar dedications and shrine locations not mentioned in the *Decreta* can be added from other primary sources, chiefly those of Eadmer and Gervase.[40] Lanfranc's observances are monastic, specifically Benedictine, and served an observant community of at least sixty brethren[41] but, as Lanfranc notes in his preface, the customs had to serve also the metropolitan cathedral of the primate of all England. Monastic liturgy is primarily introspective and exclusive, while cathedral liturgy must be explicit and inclusive. Lanfranc says:

> We have added a few details, and have made certain changes, particularly in the ceremonies of certain feasts, considering that they should be kept with greater solemnity in our church by reason of the primatial see which is there.[42]

Lanfranc accepted the fact that splendour was a necessary aspect of a cathedral's public display, even if contrary to monastic piety.[43] What concerns us here is not the origin of the text of the *Decreta*, but the practical implications, e.g. processional routes, altar placements, access for pilgrims, etc. In other words, how did Lanfranc

---

[38] For the reconstruction of Lanfranc's plan for Canterbury see R. Gem, 'The Significance of the Eleventh-century Rebuilding of Christ Church and St Augustine's . . .', *Medieval Art and Architecture at Canterbury*, [British] Archaeological Association Transactions, 4, London 1982, 1ff. A slightly different reconstruction is provided by Frank Woodman, *The Architectural History of Canterbury Cathedral*, London 1981, 23ff. For the reconstruction of St-Étienne de Caen see V. Ruprich-Robert, *L'église Ste-Trinité et l'église St-Étienne à Caen*, Caen 1864; G. Bouet, 'Analysis architectural de l'abbaye de St-Étienne de Caen', *Bulletin Monumental* 31, 1865, 417ff; E. Lambert, *Caen, roman et gothique*, Caen 1935; Eric Carlson, *The Abbey Church of Saint-Étienne at Caen in the Eleventh and Early Twelfth Centuries*, doctoral dissertation for Yale University, 1968; and the excavation reports of the east end in 'Excavations at St-Étienne, Caen (1969)', *Gesta*, 10, 1971, 23-30.

[39] See H. J. A. Strik, 'Remains of the Lanfranc Building . . .', *Medieval Art and Architecture at Canterbury*, 22ff, especially Fig. 3 which shows the reconstructed crypt plan.

[40] R. Willis, 'The Architectural History of Canterbury Cathedral', *Architectural History of Some English Cathedrals*, Chicheley 1972 [1845], 1-141, gives a nearly complete translation of Gervase's account of the cathedral before the fire of 1174 (32-62), and excerpts the descriptions of Eadmer (1ff).

[41] Eadmer, *Epistolae ad Glastonienses*, Migne, *Patrologiae*, clix, 805: 'Sexagenariam quantitem ascenderat.' Knowles, *Monastic*, 714, suggests that by 1090 the community had grown to 100.

[42] *Decreta*, 1.

[43] Gibson, *Lanfranc*, 166 comments upon his rich gifts to the cathedral sacristy.

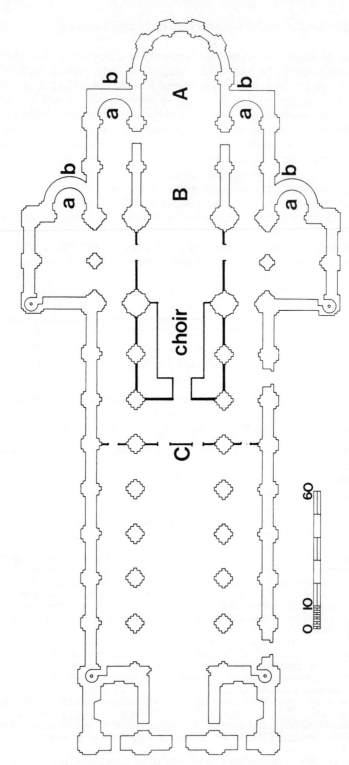

Fig. 2   St Étienne de Caen. Reconstructed liturgical plan (see p.168 for the key used for liturgical furnishings)

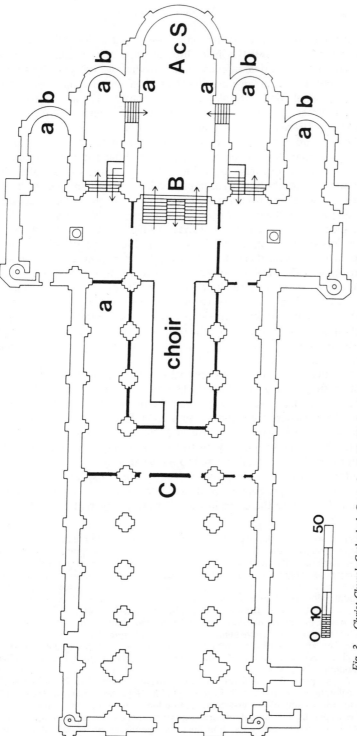

Fig. 3   Christ Church Cathedral, Canterbury. Plan (after Strik) and reconstructed liturgical arrangements

choreograph his attitudes towards monastic observances in his cathedral?

The *Decreta* is clear about the major liturgical foci of the interior: a high altar at the east end, [44] a matutinal or choir altar[45] to the west of the high altar and yet east of the monk's stalls, a large crucifix[46] over the entrance into the choir from the nave, and an axial door at the west end of the nave.[47] The other altars and their placement are of secondary importance to this fixed arrangement of interior fittings (see Fig. 3). The *Decreta* explains how these various foci are interrelated when it outlines the standard processional route for the community:[48] (1) enter the church through the west door (2) halt before the crucifix above the choir entrance with a station (3) enter the choir, bow to the high altar, and return to the stalls. This processional route at Canterbury was accomplished by the community using the cloister south range and west gate to arrive at the west door. Forming two columns at the font, the community walked the length of the nave up to the rood screen. The screen was called such because the top of the screen formed the base of the great crucifix, or rood, which visually dominated the nave. At the centre of this screen was an altar open to the laity, dedicated to the Holy Cross. Flanking this altar were two doors that allowed the two columns of monks to go through the screen and then regroup to enter the single choir door under the pulpitum. The pulpitum was one bay east of the rood screen and backed up against the monks' stalls. The pulpitum, if it followed the standard form, provided a spacious platform above the tops of the western choir stalls and was used for the reading of the Gospel on feastdays, as well as for other purposes. Once through the pulpitum the monks bowed to the high altar and re-entered their stalls.

At Canterbury the pulpitum was probably attached to the fourth pair of nave piers west of the crossing (see Fig. 3). The monks' stalls occupied the remaining eastern bays of the nave. Screens on the north and south sides of the crossing cut off the monks' enclosure from the transept arms. Pilgrims who wished to visit the relics deposited in the crypt would have to go through two sets of gates: the first in the nave south aisle in alignment with the rood screen (the north aisle was blocked at its eastern end by a chapel dedicated to the Virgin), and then pass through a gate on the south side of the crossing to traverse the lantern space and enter the axial stairs down to the crypt. Pilgrims could see, but were rarely allowed access to the shrines and altars above the crypt in the presbytery. The matutinal altar probably

[44] *Decreta*, 65 states that the two altars stood near each other in the presbytery: 'Pridie ante has festiuitates parentur duo Presbyterii altaria, presbyterium, et chorus.' The Good Friday adoration of the cross indicates that the matutinal and high altars were at the same level, that is above the crypt, and that the high altar was elevated several steps above the matutinal altar with enough space between them to allow for prostrations, 40: 'Tunc duo sacerdotes, quibus cantor iusserit, induti albis accedant ad crucem, quae debet esse praeparata et cooperta ad altare matutinale . . . duo leuitae in albis stantes ad gradus ante altare maius.'

[45] The provision of a matutinal altar between the high altar and choir seems to have originated at Cluny. It is also called the *altare minus*, see Knowles, *Decreta*, 4 n.

[46] *Decreta*, 16: 'ante crucifixum stationem faciant'. For a detailed discussion of the development and characteristics of roods and rood screens see Aymer Vallance, *Greater English Church Screens*, London 1947, 1-13.

[47] *Decreta*, 16: 'per maiores monasterii portas introeant . . .' The *Regularis Concordia* requires an additional station at the font, see T. Symons, ed., *The Monastic Agreement*, Oxford 1953, 48.

[48] *Decreta*, 16: 'exeant ad processionem, cantore incipiente antiphonam Aue gratia, et alias si necesse fuerit; per maiores monasterii portas introeant, ante crucifixum stationem faciant. Finito cantu, quem inceperant, cantore statim incipiente antiphonam Cum inducerent, canentes chorum intrent . . . et missam celebrent.'

stood above the crypt entrance in the first bay of the presbytery. The high altar stood two bays east of the matutinal altar and was flanked by altars containing the relics of St Elphege (on the north) and St Dunstan (on the south).[49] The *Decreta* does not mention any side altars other than the altar in honour of the Virgin on the north side of the nave.[50] We know from other sources the locations and dedications of most of the altars extant in Lanfranc's day. In the north transept arm the apse nearest the cloister was appropriately dedicated to St Benedict.[51] This was the first altar the monks saw when entering the cathedral. The apse in the south arm of the transept was dedicated to St Michael.[52] Altars were also placed in the eastern ends of the presbytery aisles but their dedications do not survive.

The terminal bridges of the transept arms also held relics and altars. The relics of St Bregwin[53] were stored in the bridge of the north arm; the tribune above the north aisle of the presbytery was dedicated to St Blaise.[54] The chapel in the upper apse of the transept south arm was dedicated to All Saints.[55] The bridge of the south transept arm held the relics of St Wilfrid.[56] This enumeration of side altars gives us a sum total of at least ten side altars within the monastic enclosure. As many of the monks were also priests, and therefore under the obligation to say at least one daily mass, several side altars were necessary.[57] Masses had to be said after daybreak but before noon, and as the morrow mass at the matutinal altar was sung at about 9.00 a.m. (in summer) and the high mass at about 11.00 a.m. (in summer) there was little time left available for private masses.[58] With about two hours of open time in a community of thirty or more priests at least ten side altars would be required.

Canterbury Cathedral had two liturgical requirements that diverged from St-Étienne de Caen and were not usual in other monastic houses either, and hence not mentioned in the *Decreta*. The first was the requirement of an archiepiscopal *cathedra*, or bishop's chair. The archbishop was also the abbot of the Christ Church community and as such had the right to a seat in the monks' stalls. But as archbishop he also required a seat to express his episcopal functions. No record of Lanfranc's *cathedra* remains, but it most probably stood in the apse of the presbytery behind the high altar.[59]

---

49 In the *Instructio Noviciorum*, Corpus Christi College, Cambridge MS 441, printed in Knowles, *Decreta*, 134-49 the novice is told to bow first to the altar of St Elphege, to the left of the high altar, bow to the high altar, and then bow to the altar of St Dunstan. See especially page 149.

50 *Decreta*, 12: 'In nocte dominicae natiuitatis signa primum pulsentur . . . Dicta oratione incipiat cantor antiphonam O beata infantia. Quam canentes eant ad altare sanctae Mariae, et ibi dictis matutinis de omnibus sanctis uadant in dormitorium.' Since the monks say this on the way to the dormitory the Lady altar must be adjacent to the cloister door in the west wall of the north transept. Eadmer also mentions an oratory of St Mary in the north aisle of the nave.

51 Eadmer, in Willis, *English Cathedrals*, i, 40.

52 Eadmer, in Willis, *English Cathedrals*, i, 39.;

53 Gervase, in Willis, *English Cathedrals*, i, 16.;

54 Eadmer, in Willis, *English Cathedrals*, i, 40.;

55 Eadmer, in Willis, *English Cathedrals*, i, 29.

56 Gervase, in Willis, *English Cathedrals*, i, 16-17.

57 See Otto Nussbaum, *Kloster, Priestermonch und Privatmesse*, Bonn 1961.

58 See Knowles, *Decreta*, xv, for a discussion of the liturgical horarium. He notes that the *Decreta* is somewhat unusual in not providing a specific time in the morning for private masses to be said. See also Knowles, *Monastic*, 448 ff for a full description of a monastic day.

59 This problematic placement is visually difficult, for the *cathedra* would be hardly visible behind the high altar, but it seems liturgically correct from eleventh-century practice. For a detailed discussion of this problem see C. S. Phillips, 'The Archbishop's three seats in Canterbury Cathedral', *Antiqs. Journ.* 29, 1949, 26-36.

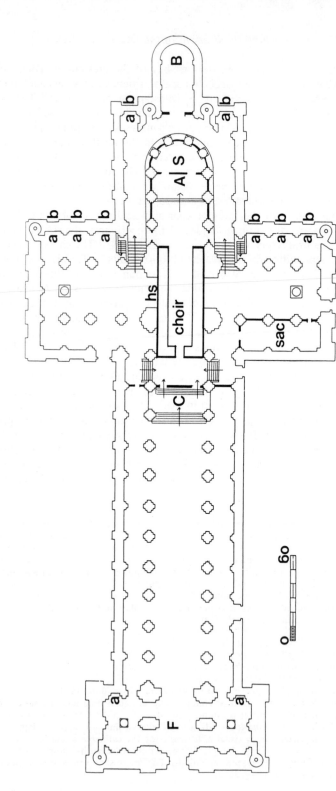

Fig. 4   Cathedral of St Swithun and SS. Peter and Paul, Winchester. Reconstructed liturgical plan

The second architectural requirement for Canterbury was not unknown to other monastic houses (St Augustine's, for example) but was unusual to the degree to which Canterbury was placed in its embarrassment of riches — that is the proper disposition of its numerous relics. As we have already seen Lanfranc was loathe to recognise all the Anglo-Saxon saints whose relics were preserved at Canterbury. Which relics should be venerated and which should not? Furthermore, to what extent should the laity have access to the veneration of these relics? Lanfranc's *Decreta* are silent on these questions, but the silence of the *Decreta* does suggest that the crypt, under the presbytery, was not available to the monks. Even as the nave was used by the monks only to process to their enclosure, so also the crypt was open to pilgrims and thus was considered outside the enclosure. St-Étienne de Caen had few relics and no need to accommodate pilgrims, hence the major difference between Caen and Canterbury is this difference in function. The fact that Lanfranc's east end was soon pulled down to provide an enlarged choir and crypt[60] indicates that Lanfranc's crypt had not adequately provided for this function.

But how unusual was the Canterbury arrangement from other churches in England? An obvious contrast can be made with the monastic cathedral of Winchester which was also begun soon after the Conquest. Winchester's new Norman bishop and prior were unusually generous in their acceptance of pre-Conquest traditions, as outlined in the *Regularis Concordia*.[61] The new cathedral at Winchester (Fig. 4), begun in 1079, was a third again larger than Lanfranc's new cathedral. Unlike Canterbury, where Lanfranc and his *Decreta* emphasised new Continental ways, Winchester emphasised its Anglo-Saxon past. The evidence for this conscious desire for continuity is plentiful. King William enlarged the old royal palace across from the west front of the Old Minster and continued to celebrate the Easter ceremonial crown-wearing in the cathedral.[62] Indeed, all the old Saxon kings and bishops who had been buried in the Old Minster were exhumed, identified, and reburied in the new cathedral.[63] St Swithun was not only received into the new church with great honour, but also the cathedral's dedication was expanded to 'St Swithun and SS Peter and Paul'.[64] The Anglo-Saxon calendar was continued, as were the majority of customs in the *Regularis Concordia* as witnessed by the Holy Sepulchre chapel in the north transept arm that continued the Anglo-Saxon *Visitatio Sepulchri* drama.[65]

Much has been made of the non-Norman architectural features at Winchester,

---

[60] See Klukas, 'Winchester, Ely, Canterbury . . .' For a description of the enlarged east end begun during Anselm's archiepiscopacy see the description of Gervase as recorded in Willis, *English Cathedrals*, i, 41-4.

[61] See T. Symons, ed., *The Monastic Agreement*; for a comparison of the *Decreta* with the *Regularis Concordia* see Appendix I.

[62] There is much controversy over the custom of crown-wearings. H. G. Richardson and G. O. Sayles consider the custom to be an ancient Anglo-Saxon inheritance. Herbert E. J. Cowdrey disagrees and considers the crown-wearing custom to be no earlier than Edward the Confessor and of Norman derivation. See Cowdrey, 'The Anglo-Norman *Laudes Regiae*', *Viator* 12, 1981, 37-78. Coronation customs that include a ceremonial reception of the crown are certainly Anglo-Saxon and derive from Carolingian Germany, see D. H. Turner, *The Claudius Pontificals*, London 1971, xxx-xxxv. See also M. Biddle, ed., *Winchester Studies* i, Oxford 1976, 311n.

[63] *Annales Monasterii de Wintonia*, ed. R. H. Luard, RS 36, London 1865, ii, s.a. 1093.

[64] *Annales Monasterii de Wintonia*, s.a. 1093.

[65] The extant chapel of the Holy Sepulchre is decorated with twelfth-century frescoes but its position between the northern crossing piers seems original. For a discussion of the play see G. B. Bryan, *The Monastic Community at Winchester and the Origin of English Liturgical Drama*, Bloomington, Indiana 1971.

especially the western transepts, aisled eastern transepts, and rectangular ambulatory. These features may well be explained by the conscious desire of the king and bishop to maintain liturgical continuity with the past. These unusual features were creative formal solutions to the traditional liturgical functions. For example, Martin Biddle's recent excavation of the cathedral's west front brought to light the massive foundations of a Norman westwork.[66] Biddle reconstructs this as a twin-towered façade, but I would concur with A. W. Clapham that its elevation more probably resembled that of Ely, its liturgical sister, with an axial tower and flanking transept arms.[67] The ground floor would have provided for a central narthex flanked by chapels, dedicated to SS Mary and Swithun as in the Old Minster. Above the narthex would have been the royal loggia, with perhaps a balcony facing onto the square as well as into the nave. It would have been here that William and his heirs wore their crowns each succeeding Easter until 1108.[68] From this loggia William would have had an uninterrupted view down the nave to the altar of the Holy Cross, or people's altar, before the stone pulpitum of the monastic enclosure. Thus the function of the Saxon westwork would have been continued in the stylistically new Norman westwork.

In the new Norman cathedral the aisled south transept and the entire choir were cut off from the nave and crypt by gates and were therefore strictly a part of the monastic enclosure. Pilgrims reached the crypt entrance via the north transept. The eastern aisles and eastern tribunes of the transepts were planned as chapels, while the western aisle of the south transept was fitted out as the sacristy. The transept bridges not only connected the nave tribunes to the eastern ones, but also functioned as singers' galleries as required in the *Regularis Concordia*.[69] These bridges allowed for the complete perambulation of the cathedral at the tribune level. We know of a documented procession in the tribunes in 1122 when the monks processed backwards counter to the sun with their processional crosses turned upside down. This was to protest the actions of Bishop Gifford, who immediately conceded to the monks.[70] This humorous incident points again to the acute architectural problem of providing for episcopal and monastic functions within one building as we saw at Canterbury. The Norman architect provided a solution to this problem at Winchester by raising the monks' east end on a large hall crypt and ambulatory. This enormous crypt, which amply housed the cathedral's relics, provided for the large number of pilgrims who wished to see the Anglo-Saxon saints enshrined there.[71]

Above the crypt the monastic life of Winchester could continue without interruption. The monastic choir stalls were placed under the lantern. To the east was the high altar at the chord of the apse. Behind the high altar was the venerable shrine

[66] Biddle, *Winchester Studies* i, 310-11.

[67] A. W. Clapham, *After*, 30: 'The axial western tower found at Ely, Bury, and Winchester is a Saxon inheritance.'

[68] See Biddle, *Winchester Studies* i, 311. The court spent Easter at Winchester annually until 1108, and the king wore his crown in the cathedral. After 1108 the court was seen less often at Winchester.

[69] Symons, *Monastic Agreement*, 36. For an explanation of its significance see Klukas, 'Architecture and Liturgy: Deerhurst Priory as an expression of the *Regularis Concordia*', *Viator* 15, 1984, forthcoming.

[70] For the documentation of the event see *Annales de Wintonia*, 48-9; the event is discussed by Diana Greenaway, 'Bishop William Giffard . . .' *Winchester Cathedral Record*, 1977, 10-12.

[71] The *Chartulary of Winchester Cathedral*, ed. Arthur Goodman, Winchester 1927, 3 records that Bishop Henry of Blois removed the relics of the saints from the crypt and placed them around the high altar. The crypt thus had served as the main repository for relics.

of St Swithun (which contained the monks' portion of his remains).[72] The presbytery aisles allowed the monks to process behind the high altar to venerate Swithun's shrine and provided access to the axial chapel where the matutinal mass could be celebrated and the Anglo-Saxon custom of a second office in honour of All Saints and the Dead could be properly maintained.[73] Surrounding this axial arrangement of the conventual altars there were at least seventeen subsidiary altars solely within the monastic enclosure. Thus the new Norman church not only perpetuated, but enlarged and dignified, the liturgical prescriptions laid out in the Old Minster.

We thus see remarkable liturgical divergences expressed in strikingly different formal arrangements. At Canterbury the monks remained in their stalls for both the morrow and high masses and almost all of the offices,[74] while at Winchester the community moved from their stalls where they had sung the office to the chapel of All Saints where the morrow mass was celebrated and then returned to their stalls for the high mass. The additional offices of All Saints and the Dead were said in the chapel of All Saints as well. This created two distinct liturgical foci within the monastic enclosure at Winchester and necessitated the processional space provided by the ambulatory. The royal functions of the Winchester western tribune did not immediately concern the monks except for the singing of the *Laudes* at crown-wearing ceremonies.[75]

Thus both Canterbury and Winchester had the dual responsibility of providing for episcopal and monastic functions. Both buildings utilised crypts as a means of providing public access to their collections of relics and both provided altars dedicated to the Holy Cross in their naves. But here the parallels end. Canterbury did not provide either a western gallery or an axial chapel outside the choir. Canterbury's tribunes did not provide for continuous circulation around the interior. Canterbury's apse-echelon plan allowed only simple processions from the choir aisles across the presbytery, or from the west door to the pulpitum; Winchester provided processional space around the east end on two levels as well as processions to stations at the nave font and the transept arms. Canterbury's plan thus provided an austere and simplified arrangement for Lanfranc's austere and simplified liturgical customs.

But what architectural influence did Lanfranc have on other monastic houses in Britain? We have already mentioned that fifteen houses had some direct connection with Lanfranc and his *Decreta*. For our purposes some of these houses must be eliminated because their extant architectural evidence dates either before the *Decreta* were instituted (e.g. St Augustine's, Canterbury; Battle; Westminster), or date decades after Lanfranc's death (e.g. Dover). Other monuments are too decayed or rebuilt to provide sufficient evidence for a reconstruction of their Romanesque plan and elevation (e.g. Eynsham and Great Malvern). We will therefore concentrate our discussion on the remaining nine monuments.

---

[72] St Swithun's relics are mentioned in the context of both the crypt and presbytery. His remains were translated from the Old Minster in 1093 (*Annales de Wintonia*, 295) ostensibly to the area behind the high altar, but more relics of St Swithun and of other saints were discovered during the demolition of the Old Minster in 1094 (*Annales de Wintonia*, 37) and placed in the crypt of the new cathedral.

[73] Symons, *Monastic Agreement*, 15: 'Post quas eundum est ad Matutinales Laudes De Omnibus Sanctis, decantando antiphonam ad venerationem sancti cui porticus ad quam itur dedicata est . . .' See also my forthcoming article in *Viator*.

[74] *Decreta*, 4-5, outlines the ordinary day with the morrow mass first, then the chapter meeting and rest in the cloister before returning to the choir for high mass.

[75] See note 62.

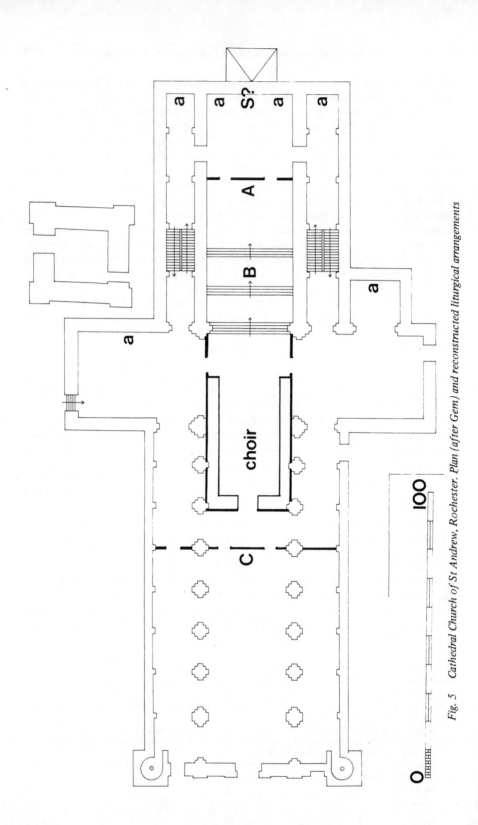

Fig. 5   Cathedral Church of St Andrew, Rochester. Plan (after Gem) and reconstructed liturgical arrangements

Lanfranc assured the obedience of his archdiocese to his concept of reform when he appointed Gundulf as Bishop of Rochester in 1077. Gundulf had been a monk at Bec under Lanfranc's priorship, went with him to Caen in 1063 and joined him at Canterbury in 1070.[76] Rochester was the seat of the suffragan bishop of the archdiocese, and Lanfranc and Gundulf introduced a cell of monks from Christ Church to maintain complete uniformity between the two cathedrals of the archdiocese. The liturgical arrangements must have been correspondingly parallel, for as F. W. Fairweather suggests, the church which Gundulf built was nearly identical to Lanfranc's cathedral in its layout (Fig. 5).[77] Recent excavations have proven Fairweather's assumptions to be correct, even if his reconstruction has been supplanted by more recent work.

Rochester was poorly endowed and was therefore dependent upon Canterbury for financial support. This poor endowment is certainly the reason for Rochester's reduced scale and extensive use of rubble construction. Lanfranc paid for much of the construction from his own revenues and worked diligently to regain estates that had once belonged to Rochester.[78] As at Canterbury, Rochester's nave of eight bays had a three-storey elevation but unlike Canterbury the tribune is false. No vaulting could ever have been intended for the aisles or nave because a wall passage cuts through the tribune piers. Nor were western towers or a lantern intended. The presbytery, as at Canterbury, was raised over a crypt and consisted of three bays. Unlike Canterbury, however, the east end did not terminate in apses but rather the eastern chapels were finished as rectangles.

Rochester must have followed Christ Church closely in its liturgical layout. The monks' stalls extended from the crossing west to the second bay of the nave. Screens separated the monastic enclosure from the rest of the church at the third pair of piers west of the crossing.[79] The matutinal altar stood at the first bay of the presbytery with the high altar in the third bay of the presbytery. Access to the presbytery altars was by means of stairs flanking the crypt entrance or through doors cut through the solid walls of the presbytery at the fourth bay. As a smaller community Rochester did not have the number of altars that Canterbury required. The total number of side altars within the monastic enclosure could not have been more than four. In spite of this disparity in the number of side altars, the two communities worshipped within nearly identical liturgical plans.

At Evesham[80] the parallels continue as its presbytery was raised over a crypt, as

---

[76] For the life of Gundulf see R. Thomson, ed., *The Life of Gundulf, Bishop of Rochester*, Toronto 1977. Gundulf was Bishop of Rochester from 1077 to 1108. See also R. A. L. Smith, 'The Place of Gundulf in the Anglo-Norman Church', *EHR* 58, 1943, 257-72.

[77] For the architectural history of Rochester see W. H. St-John Hope, 'The Architectural History of the Cathedral Church and Monastery of St Andrew at Rochester', *Arch. Cantiana* xxiii, 1898, 194-328. F. H. Fairweather disagrees with St-John Hope's reconstructed plan and proposed his own which is in agreement with recent excavation findings, see 'Gundulf's Cathedral and Priory Church, Rochester: some critical remarks on the hitherto accepted plan', *Arch. Journ.* 86, 1929, 187ff. Clapham, *After*, 24, agrees with him. For recent evidence and a new plan see R. Gem, 'The significance . . .', 12 who shows how very parallel Rochester is to Canterbury in its plan.

[78] Gibson, *Lanfranc*, 155-6.

[79] The remains of this arrangement are still to be seen in the nave, see Vallence, *Screens*, 46-7. By c.1240 the monks' stalls were moved eastwards and the rood screen was placed at the west side of the crossing.

[80] The best history of the abbey is to found in A. A. Locke, 'Abbey of Evesham', VCH *Worcestershire*, London 1906, 112-26. The best archaeological discussion is F. B. Andrews, 'The Benedictine Abbey of Evesham', *Birmingham Archeological Society Transactions* 35, 1909, 34-56.

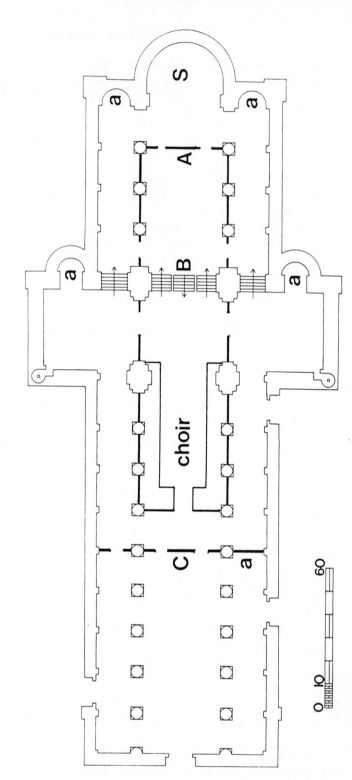

Fig. 6   Abbey Church, Evesham. Reconstructed liturgical plan

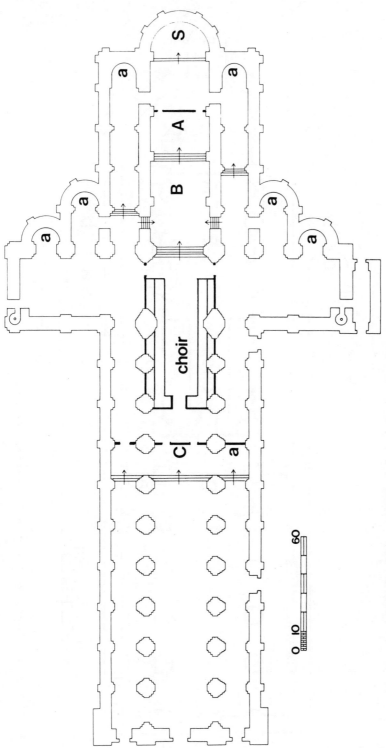

Fig. 7   Abbey Church of St Alban, St Albans. Reconstructed liturgical plan

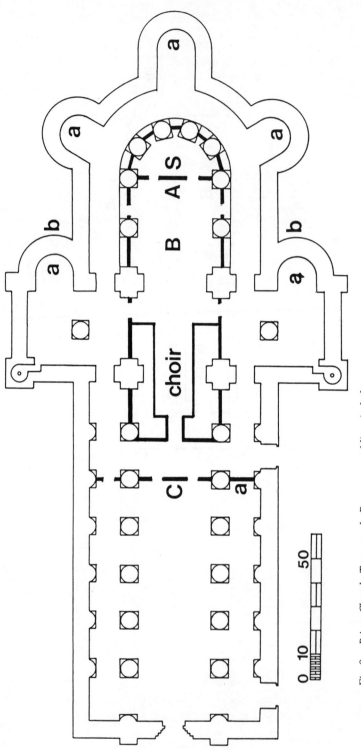

Fig. 8   Priory Church, Tynemouth. Reconstructed liturgical plan

at Canterbury and Rochester (Fig. 6). Although Evesham was not a cathedral as the other two buildings were, its extraordinary collection of relics including the shrine of St Egwin, and consequent number of pilgrims may have necessitated the crypt as a means of public access, as was true at Canterbury and Winchester. This crypt was a part of the large church begun by Walter of Cerisy (1070-1104) and completed by his successor, Robert of Jumièges (1104-30). The plan of the east end is now uncertain because of a later rebuilding which included a rectangular ambulatory.[81] It is more probable that the east end was originally an apse-echelon plan similar to that of Canterbury Cathedral. No evidence exists for its elevation.

At St Albans Lanfranc's *Decreta* was perfectly fulfilled in the new church his nephew Paul began in 1077 (Fig. 7).[82] St Albans was built on a vast scale, its total length of approximately 360ft was double that of Rochester. Remarkably, St Albans retains the screen and pulpitum placements of the eleventh-century plan.[83] At the fourth piers west of the lantern stands the lay altar, dedicated to the Holy Cross, above which originally stood a great Rood, with the rood screen acting as the pulpitum west face. The monks' stalls extended from the pulpitum east face into the lantern area. A screen closed off the monks' precinct from the nave in the north aisle. A Lady altar almost certainly stood at the end of the south aisle two bays west of the cloister door. Unlike Canterbury, St Albans had no functional tribunes or transept bridges and therefore placed all of its side altars on the main floor-level within the monastic enclosure. The shrine of St Alban and the high altar of the church, as with the pulpitum, remain today in their original positions. The shrine stood at the chord of the great apse and the high altar stood one bay west of the shrine. Doors were cut through the solid walls of the presbytery in the first and fourth bays to give access to the shrine in a circulation pattern that included the transept north arm, north choir aisle, the processional space between the high altar and shrine, and return through either the presbytery south aisle or back the way the pilgrim began. The doors in the presbytery first bay were on an alignment of doors across all seven apses and gave the sacristan, whose sacristy was adjacent to the cloister, direct access to all the chapels within the east end of the church. The matutinal altar must have stood within the second presbytery bay east of the crossing. It is the only item missing at St Albans from the arrangement required in the *Decreta*. Thus at St Albans the seven apse-echelon plan and elongated presbytery provide exactly the same number of altars as provided at Canterbury within a liturgical layout identical to Lanfranc's own cathedral priory.

A recent extensive bibliography has been compiled by D. C. Cox, 'A Bibliography of Evesham Abbey', *Research Papers* 3, 1971, 11-25 and *Research Papers* 4, 1972, 19-51.

81 The rebuilding of the east end is recorded in *Chronicon Abbatiae de Evesham ad Annum 1418*, ed. W. D. Macray, London 1863, 86ff. The only plan of Evesham is that of the Gothic rebuilding of the east end as excavated by E. Rudge in 1811. It is recorded in 'Memoir on the Antiquities discovered in excavating the ruins of the Abbey Church of Evesham ...', *Vetusta Monumenta* 5, 1835, 1-11.

82 St Albans was begun in 1077 and Lanfranc contributed 1000 marks towards its construction. The dedication was in 1115 but the church was certainly in use when Abbot Paul died in 1093. For the history of St Albans see Matthew Paris, *Chronicon Maiora*, ed. H. Luard, RS 57, London 1880; *Gesta Abbatum Sancti Albani*, ed. H. T. Riley, RS 28, London 1867-69. For the architectural history of the church see Clapham, *After*, 22-3; D. T. van Zanten, 'The Romanesque Church of St Albans', *Gesta* 4, 1965, 23-7; and R. Wittkower, 'St Albans Abbey: A Bibliography', *Arch. Journ.* 102, 1945, 167ff. Because of the disastrous nineteenth-century 'restoration' of the Abbey it is important to see presentations of its earlier condition, which are collected by J. W. C. Carr, *The Abbey Church of St Albans*, London 1877.

83 See A. Vallance, *Screens*, 89.

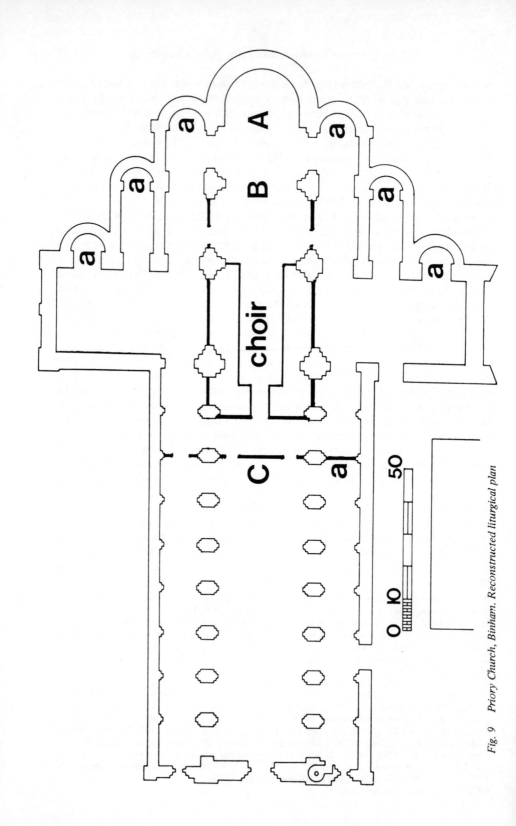

Fig. 9   Priory Church, Binham. Reconstructed liturgical plan

St Albans had several priories of which three survive in some recognisable Romanesque form — Wymondham, Binham and Tynemouth. All three priories remained in close communication with their founding house throughout the medieval era and would thus have remained in liturgical uniformity as well. We shall closely examine the remaining archaeological evidence to see whether this uniformity was also architecturally true. Tynemouth was colonised with monks from St Albans in 1090 and their church was begun soon after their arrival.[84] The church was not large, consisting of a seven-bay nave and a two-bay presbytery (Fig. 8). There was a crossing tower but no western towers. The transept arms each had one apsidal chapel and probably bridge-chapels at the transept terminations.[85] The elevation was of three storeys but the middle level was a triforium rather than a tribune, as at St Albans. The choir is a break in plan from St Albans, however, for W. H. Knowles reported that in his 1910 excavation he found the foundations for an ambulatory with three radiating chapels. This plan had been swept away in the later Gothic rebuilding of a rectangular presbytery. Why Tynemouth should have an ambulatory, in contrast to all the other examples we have mentioned, can only be a matter of conjecture. Perhaps since Tynemouth had been a centre of pilgrimage since the martyrdom of St Oswin in 651, the new church built after 1090 had to provide access to his shrine for monk and pilgrim alike. The site did not allow for a crypt because it is on top of a sheer stone cliff. The only common alternative to a crypt was an outer-crypt, or ambulatory.[86] Pilgrims would have access to the shrine, placed within the great apse, via the north transept and north aisle of the presbytery. The central space of the presbytery and crossing was reserved for the monastic community who had access to the shrine behind the high altar. This altar stood at the chord of the apse with the matutinal altar one bay to the west. The monks' stalls occupied the crossing and the first bay of the nave.[87] The rood screen would have been one bay west of the pulpitum, with a Lady altar adjacent to it in the nave south aisle. If we accept the probability of bridge chapels in its transepts, Tynemouth would have provided seven subsidiary chapels within its enclosure as did its motherhouse.

The plan and elevation of Binham (Fig. 9) are even closer to the plan and elevation of St Albans than is Tynemouth.[88] From the extant nave we can conclude that Binham had a three-storey elevation with a triforium with evidence of a similar elevation in the choir from the extant south-east crossing pier. The seven chapels of its apse-echelon plan are identical to those of its motherhouse, the only difference at Binham is that its two-bay presbytery was only half that of St Albans. This may be the result of Binham's lack of major relics and the much smaller community of

---

[84] For Tynemouth see W. H. Knowles, *Arch. Journ.* 67, 1910, 1ff; Clapham, *After*, 36; and R. N. Hadcock, *Tynemouth Priory and Castle*, London 1952.

[85] Stated by R. Gem at the Durham Conference of the British Archaeological Association on 29 March 1977.

[86] For a discussion of the development of the ambulatory from the crypt see Jean Hubert, '"Cryptae inferiores" et "cryptae superiores" dans l'architecture religieuse de l'époque carolingienne', *Mélanges d'histoire du moyen âge dédié à la mémoire de Louis Halphen*, Paris 1951, 351-7 and Warren Sanderson, 'Monastic Reform in Lorraine and the Architecture of the Outer Crypt, 950-1100', *Transactions of the American Philosophical Society*, 61, 1971, 1-37.

[87] The remains of a rood screen on the western side of the crossing are of a later date. A. Vallence, *Screens*, 121 considers it to be c.1095. The position of all the ritual area was radically modified with the construction of the new Gothic east end.

[88] For the history of Binham see *Gesta Abbatum Sancti Albani*, 51; *Monasticon* iii, 345. See also F. H. Fairweather, *Ingleby's Supplement to Blomefield's Norfolk*, n.d., 324; and Clapham, *After*, 27.

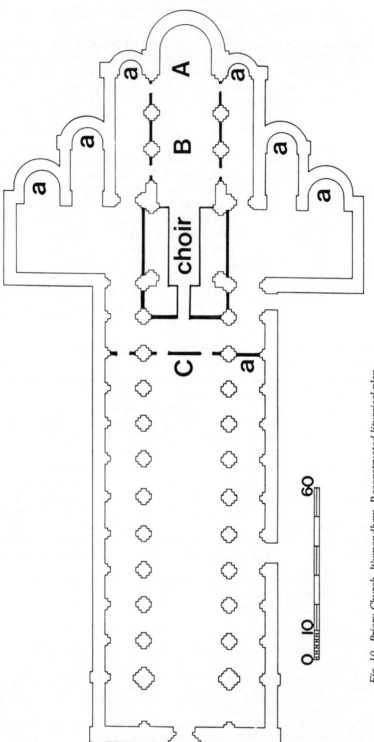

Fig. 10 Priory Church, Wymondham. Reconstructed liturgical plan

monks which officiated there. As at St Albans the monks' stalls stood under the lantern and extended into the first bay of the nave. The rood screen, in the same position as now extant, extended across the nave at the second pier west of the crossing. As no towers were intended, Binham is a reduced-size version of its proto-type at St Albans.

Wymondham, also in the same county as Binham, was founded from St Albans in 1107.[89] As with Binham, its east end is now known only by excavation (Fig. 10). Again, as with Binham, the rood screen of the monastic priory became the east wall of the post-dissolution parish church, but because of a controversy between the monks and townsfolk in the fifteenth century, a tall lantern was built by the monks on top of the rood screen. The nave elevation of Wymondham also parallels Binham and St Albans in that it is a three-storey elevation; as with Binham the original aisles are now lost, and because of this the disposition of the tribune/triforium can no longer be determined. The plan of the east end also leaves some unanswered questions. The three bay presbytery is flanked by aisles with apsidal endings, and apsidal chapels open to the extremities of the transept arms. Traces of a foundation slightly to the south-east of the transept north arm chapel suggests that a chapel of two bays stood between the transept terminal chapel and the aisle of the presbytery.[90] If this is the case Wymondham would have had a seven chapel apse-echelon plan in accord with Binham and St Albans.

The internal arrangements at Wymondham can be reconstructed in the same man-ner as at Binham. The rood screen divided the nave from the monks' enclosure at the second pair of piers west of the crossing, exactly as at Binham and St Albans. The screen may also have been the west face of the pulpitum, for the narrow width of the aisle bays left little space for stalls west of the crossing. The monks' stalls extended into the crossing and the matutinal altar was within the first bay east of the crossing. The high altar probably stood within the easternmost bay of the pres-bytery with a processional path in front of it. Wymondham had no major relic and did not need a processional space for the laity outside the monks' area. Thus two out of three priories of St Albans follow their motherhouse in their apse-echelon plan and all three share common elevational schemes and internal arrangements.

Durham Cathedral was refounded as a Benedictine priory by Bishop William of St-Carilef in 1083.[91] It is certain that he looked to Lanfranc for direction in ordering his monastic community, for not only does Durham still possess an early copy of Lanfranc's *Decreta*, but also the majority of the books given to Durham during William's episcopacy were Christ Church products.[92] The plan of Durham, however,

89 For the history of Wymondham see *Monasticon* iii, 323 ff; J. C. Cox, 'Abbey of Wymondham', VCH *Norfolk* ii, London 1906, 336-42. For the excavations at the site see H. Harrod, 'Some Peculiars relating to the History of the Abbey Church of Wymondham in Norfolk', *Archaeologia* 43, 1871, 264-72; Clapham, *After*, 43.

90 A recent plan, published without author, is to be found in J. G. T. Thomas and C. F. Jarvis, *The Abbey Church of . . . Wymondham*, Bury St Edmunds 1975, 13.

91 For the history of Durham Cathedral see H. Wharton, *Anglia Sacra* i, 689-789; J. E. Bygate, *The Cathedral Church of Durham*, London 1922. For the architectural history of the church see R. W. Billings, *Architectural Illustrations and Description of . . . Durham*, London 1843; J. Bilson, 'On the Recent Discoveries at the East End of the Cathedral Church at Durham', *Arch. Journ.* 63, 1869, 1-18; Clapham, *After*, 25-6. See also M. G. Snape, 'Documentary Evi-dence for the Building of Durham Cathedral . . .', *Medieval Art and Architecture at Durham Cathedral*, London 1980, 20-37.

92 See A. Lawrence, 'The Influence of Canterbury on the collection and production of manu-scripts at Durham', *The Vanishing Past: Studies of Medieval Art, Liturgy and Metrology presented*

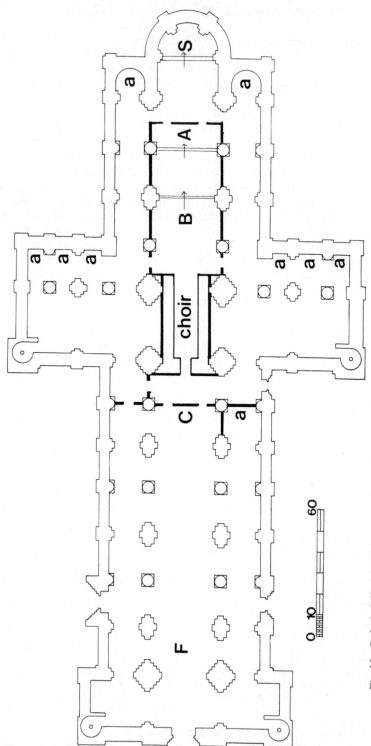

Fig. 11 Cathedral Church, Durham. Reconstructed liturgical plan

is not modelled on that of Christ Church (Fig. 11). It is much closer to the plan of St Albans, with an apse-echelon plan at the extremity of an elongated presbytery of four bays. The transepts break with Norman tradition by replacing apsidal chapels with an eastern aisle of four bays.[93] This provided two more side chapels than at St Albans. If Durham's plan is a break with Norman tradition, its elevational scheme is a return to the proportional system of Jumièges: above a tall arcade is a low tribune, paved and lighted by small windows. These tribunes cannot be ritually useful, for the windows are only a few inches from the floor and could not have had altars in front of them. Any other use is unknown.

As at Tynemouth, Durham housed the shrine of a beloved Northumbrian saint, Cuthbert, and therefore had to provide access for pilgrims to the shrine, as well as an enclosed environment for the monks. St Cuthbert's shrine was placed within the great apse, as at St Albans; however, the placement of the presbytery altars and the monks' stalls is far from certain. The later rebuilding of the eastern end of the Cathedral completely altered the positions of the Romanesque internal fittings. St-John Hope has reconstructed the thirteenth-century arrangements of the choir and presbytery with the pulpitum at the eastern side of the crossing, the monks' stalls in the next two bays, and the high altar within the fourth bay east of the crossing.[94] This arrangement assumes that the matutinal altar within the presbytery had been replaced by a Lady altar *outside* the presbytery, a custom which did not gain acceptance until the thirteenth century.[95] Our concern is with the original Romanesque arrangement which required two altars within the presbytery. Since the nave Lady altar was located in the south aisle next to the monks' cloister door (as at Christ Church and many other houses), and since the cloister door usually gave access to the passage between the rood screen and pulpitum, the logical placement of the pulpitum would be between the western piers of the crossing and the rood screen one bay farther west. The matutinal altar probably stood on a platform at the second bay east of the crossing. The high altar would have stood two bays farther east with a passage between it and the shrine. As at St Albans the shrine was entirely within the monastic enclosure. Access for pilgrims was provided through a gate in the nave north aisle.

Durham's priory at Lindesfarne[96] follows its mother church in style and function (Fig. 12). Built as a miniature Durham it included the characteristic drum piers and the massive ribs of its prototype. Lindesfarne also included a three-storey elevation in its nave, but its middle level was a triforium rather than a tribune. The short transepts opened to apsidal chapels and the aisleless presbytery of two bays terminated in an apse. The original presbytery was extended two bays eastward only a few years

to Christopher Hohler, edited by A. Borg and A. Martindale, Oxford 1981, 95-104.

93 Winchester was the earliest building in post-Conquest England to have aisled transepts. Continental churches such as St-Rémi de Reims and Orléans Cathedral seem to have had them by the beginning of the eleventh century. Single aisles on the east are rare in Romanesque churches, Peterborough and Bury St Edmunds being the only other examples known to me.

94 See A. Vallence, *Screens*, 37-9 and St-John Hope, *Archaeologia* 68, 73 for plans and a discussion of the evidence.

95 The earliest documented Lady Chapel at Durham was within the Galilee by 1189, see *Muniments of the Dean and Chapter of Durham*, 2.1. Ebor. 16. The custom of singing a mass in honour of the Virgin became standard practice in English Benedictine houses by the Council of Oxford in 1216, Knowles, *Monastic*, 542-3 discusses its origins.

96 For the history of Lindesfarne see H. Warton, *Anglia Sacra* i, 689-789. An architectural description is provided by A. H. Thompson, *Lindesfarne Priory*, London 1975. See also Clapham, *After*, 53.

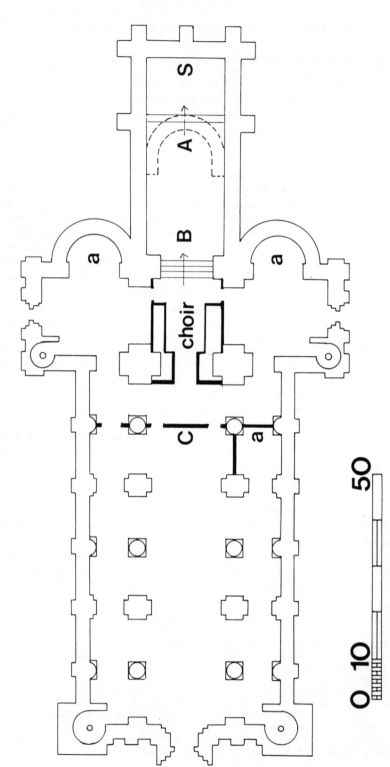

Fig. 12 Priory Church, Lindesfarne. Reconstructed liturgical plan

after its construction.[97] This was undoubtedly due to the cramped placement of the two presbytery altars within one bay of the earlier apse. The new east end allowed the easternmost bay to become a *sacrarium* or place to house relics, with the high altar directly in front of it and the matutinal altar in the middle of the original square. The monks' stalls were placed, as at Durham, under the lantern with the pulpitum set between the western piers of the crossing and the rood screen one bay west of the pulpitum. Thus the monks of Lindesfarne continued the monastic routine of their motherhouse in a ritual arrangement identical to that at Durham.

From the small priory at Lindesfarne to the immensity of St Albans Abbey, all the churches related to Lanfranc's *Decreta* show a striking uniformity of ritual plans. In each building which housed shrines the high altar was placed to the west of the shrine with a processional space between them. Iron grills, or some other form of screen, closed the presbytery from the processional space and presbytery aisles. In every building the matutinal altar was placed at least one bay west of the high altar — all within the space determined by the presbytery bays. In each case the choir stalls were placed under the crossing and were enclosed at their western ends by a pulpitum. One bay west of the pulpitum a rood screen supported a large crucifix and cut off the monastic precinct from the laity who worshipped in the nave. In several cases the rood screen also functioned as the western face of the pulpitum, as at St Albans. In every case but one (Rochester) the altar beneath the crucifix was dedicated to the Holy Cross. In the majority of cases we have primary evidence for a chapel dedicated to the Virgin terminating the nave aisle nearest the monks' cloister door.

In architectural terms there was also a remarkable uniformity. Of the monuments whose floorplans are certain, all but one (Tynemouth) were variations on the apse echelon plan. All but the two smallest (Rochester, Lindesfarne) provided six chapels to flank the central apse. None provided chapels or other ritual spaces at their west ends, indeed only two had even towers at their west ends (Canterbury, Durham).

The ritual arrangements for the entire group were strictly within the monastic enclosure at the east end and were on one level. Crypts were provided only where the number of relics and the press of pilgrims required space separate from the monks' presbytery (Canterbury, Rochester, Evesham). Only two buildings in this group had functional tribunes (Canterbury, Durham) and two had transept bridges (Canterbury, Tynemouth), but in all cases, the tribunes were not used for ritual purposes; instead the transept bridges provided additional space for side altars, as had also been the case at St-Étienne de Caen.

The cohesiveness of the Lanfranc-related houses is even more striking if we compare them to other families of post-Conquest churches in Britain. The formal complixity of experimental monuments like Winchester with its westwork, Ely with its western transept, or Worcester with its range of tribune chapels seem far removed from the simplicity and regularity of the Lanfranc-related monuments. This simplicity and regularity in architectural terms is the end result of a simplicity and regularity in the liturgical life which was carried on in these monuments. The way in which these buildings related to the *Decreta Lanfranci* shows us how directly liturgical practices can influence architectural form.

---

[97] The original screen positions have been identified by A. H. Thompson, *Lindesfarne*, 15 and the extension of the east end is dated by Thompson, *Lindesfarne*, 10 to a decade after the original construction.

Key used for Liturgical Furnishings

A	High altar
B	Matutinal altar
C	Rood altar
F	Font
S	Sacrarium, or relic repository
a	Side altar at ground level
b	Side altar at gallery level
c	Cathedra, or bishop's throne
sac	Sacristy
0-50	Measurement in feet
▬▬▬	Screen
	Stairs with direction up

APPENDIX I

A Comparison of the Decreta Lanfranci *with the* Regularis Concordia

We have already mentioned that the *Decreta Lanfranci* show a strong influence from Cluniac sources, especially that of the Customary which Bernard completed in 1067.[1] The *Regularis Concordia* also indicates some influences from the Cluny-related customs of Fleury,[2] but its primary influence came from another source, that of the Gorze-Brogne monastic reform movement.[3] Indeed, Dom Kassius Hallinger came to the conclusion that the text of the *Regularis Concordia* is the purest Gorze-Brogne family of customaries to survive.[4]

Hallinger noted eight characteristics which distinguish Gorze-Brogne customaries from Cluny-related customaries. I have used these characteristics as a means of contrasting the *Regularis Concordia* with the *Decreta Lanfranci*. The most evident distinguishing feature between the Gorze-related and Cluny-related customaries is that of the liturgical play at Easter known as the *Visitatio Sepulchri*.[5] This play is unknown in any Cluniac-related customary but it is consistently found in all Gorze-related customaries.[6] The most complete early description of it is found in the *Regularis Concordia*. Less significant distinguishing characteristics include three incensations at Cluny-related Easter vigils, while Gorze-related customaries mention it once. On Palm Sunday the Gorze-related rites require an asperges procession during the matutinal mass rather than after High Mass, as in Cluny customs. During Holy Week the custom in Gorze-related houses was to have the office of Tenebrae three times using twenty-four or twenty-five candles. Cluny-related customaries mention this custom for Thursday night only and specify fifteen candles. An unusual dramatic prop is mentioned in Gorze-related customs; this is the use of a candlestick in the shape of a serpent or dragon which was carried in procession. No Cluniac customary (other than Fleury) mentions it. Further contrasts during Holy Week included the new fire kindled three times in Gorze rites while only once on Holy Saturday in Cluniac rites. The procession of the new fire at Cluny prescribed the singing of Psalm 50, while Gorze rites usually specify silence. The final contrast is that Cluniac houses recited the entire Psalter on Good Friday in the cloister while Gorze rites mention the recitation of the Psalter in the choir. As the table on p.170 shows, the *Decreta Lanfranci* differs from the *Regularis Concordia* in every instance.

---

[1] *Consuetudines cenobi Cluniacensis* (Paris, Bibl. Nat. MS Latin 13). Graham discusses this and other early Cluny customaries in 'The relation of Cluny . . .', 179 ff.

[2] The *Regularis Concordia*, 3, mentions that advisors were sent to Winchester from Fleury to give advice in its composition. See my discussion of the sources of the *Regularis* in *Altaria Superioria*, 469-78.

[3] Dom Kassius Hallinger, *Gorze-Kluny*, Rome 1950-51, 909 ff.

[4] Hallinger, *Gorze-Kluny*, 928.

[5] See Karl Young, *The Drama of the Medieval Church*, London 1933, which lists all known references to the *Visitatio Sepulchri* play.

[6] Hallinger, *Gorze-Kluny*, 909 ff.

A Comparative Table of English and Norman Liturgical Observance

Key to the Table

Palmarum: Palm Sunday
Sacrum Triduum: Maundy Thursday, Good Friday, Holy Saturday

Palmarum

Asperges: Common to Gorze customs is the blessing of the convent with Holy Water on Palm Sunday by one priest with acolyte before (Pre) the morning mass. Cluny rites specify after the morning mass (Post).

Silence: Gorze rites specify that the Palm Sunday procession to the stational church be done in silence (S) while the Cluny rites specify the recitation of Psalm 50 (Ps).

Host: From Lanfranc's day in Normandy it became the Norman custom to carry the consecrated Host in the Palm Sunday procession to symbolise Christ's entry into Jerusalem. Use of this observance is indicated by a cross (x).

No. Stations: Number of stations on Palm Sunday processional route; the Bec customs specify four.

Sacrum Triduum

Psalter Said: Cluny observances require the monks to recite the entire Psalter on Good Friday in the cloister (Cl), while Gorze-related rites specify the same custom for all the *Sacrum Triduum* in the choir (Ch).

Office M/S: During Holy Week the Gorze rites usually maintain the ancient Roman secular office (S) while the Cluny rites have a monastic office (M).

New Fire: Cluny customs require the New Fire to be lit on Saturday (1), Gorze customs often require this to be repeated Thursday to Saturday (3).

No. Candles: At *Tenebrae* on Maundy Thursday the Cluny rite mentions fifteen candles while the Gorze rite mentions twenty-four. The number of candles specified in each house is recorded.

Serpent: After the lighting of the New Fire in Gorze rites the fire is carried in procession in a candlestick made in the shape of a serpent. Use of this practice is indicated by a cross (x).

Responses: A custom unique to the *Regularis Concordia* is that the Maundy Thursday responses be sung across the choir from flanking *porticus*. Use of this observance is indicated by a cross (x).

Cross Burial: On Good Friday the Anglo-Saxon rites follow the Veneration of the Cross with a symbolic burial of it in a tomb. Use of this custom is indicated by a cross (x).

Easter

Lit. Play: Common to Gorze rites is the performance of liturgical plays for each season, especially the *Visitatio Sepulchri* at Easter.

Office M/S: Same as above under *Sacrum Triduum*.

Other

Vesper Pro.: Daily processions to a chapel outside the choir for a second Vespers in honour of All Saints is a common Anglo-Saxon custom. Use of this observance is indicated by a cross (x).

All Saints: The singing or recitation of a second office of Matins or Vespers in honour of All Saints, the Dead, or a particular saint on his or her day of commemoration is a common Anglo-Saxon custom. Use of this custom is indicated by a cross (x).

Font Pro.: Processions to the font (F) are common in Anglo-Saxon rites while Cluny-Lanfranc rites specify the Rood (R) instead.

A Comparative Table of English and Norman Liturgical Observance

Monument	Palmarum				Sacrum Triduum							Easter		Other		
	Asperges	Silence	Host	No. Stations	Psalter Said	Office M/S	New Fire	No. Candles	Serpent	Responses	Cross Burial	Lit. Play	Office M/S	Vesper Pro.	All Saints	Font Pro.
England																
Regularis Concordia	Pre	x	–	–	Ch	S	3	24	x	x	x	x	S	x	x	x
Barking	–	Ps	x	–	Ch	S	1	24	–	–	x	x	S	x	x	x
Worcester	–	–	–	–	–	S	–	23	–	x	x	x	S	x	x	R
York, St Mary	–	–	–	–	–	–	–	–	–	–	–	–	–	–	–	–
Mixed English																
Norwich	Pre	Ps	x	4	–	S	3	25	x	–	x	x	–	x	–	F
Sarum	–	Ps	x	4	–	–	–	–	–	–	–	x	–	–	–	–
Normandy																
Liber Officiis	–	–	–	–	Ch	S	3	24	x	x	x	x	S	x	x	F
Rouen	–	–	x	–	Ch	S	3	24	x	x	x	x	S	x	x	F
Bayeux	–	–	x	–	–	–	–	–	–	x	–	–	–	–	–	–
Decreta Lanfranci	Post	Ps	x	4	Cl	M	1	15	–	–	–	–	M	–	–	R
Bec	Post	Ps	x	4	Cl	M	1	15	–	–	–	–	M	–	–	R
Caen	Post	Ps	x	4	Cl	M	1	15	–	–	–	–	M	–	–	R

WILLIAM THE CONQUEROR AND THE CHURCH OF ROME
(FROM THE EPISTOLAE)

Pier Andrea Maccarini

The relations between *sacerdotium* and *imperium* in the Middle Ages went through alternate phases, and the two centres of power were sometimes enemies and at other times of reciprocal aid and support.

Gregory VII's work was itself in part prepared for by events of the thirty years before his accession.

So, when in the eleventh century the Church of Rome passed through one of its darkest periods, the Emperor Henry III delivered the papacy from the hands of the local Roman families, as *Defensor Ecclesiae*, deposing straight away three popes (Synod of Sutri, 1046), Benedictus IX, Silvester III and Gregory VI, and instituted a succession of German popes (starting with the bishop Suigerius of Bamberg who took the name of Clement II), who between 1046 and 1057 began to exercise more firmly the authority of the Church.

Leo IX (1048-54), in particular, took a strong lead in seeking to extirpate the moral abuses which contemporary reformers so vociferously condemned.

From 1059 Hildebrand, the future Gregory VII, stood near to the centre of affairs as archdeacon of the Roman Church; and it was with him that there took shape that reform of the Church already begun in Cluniac circles. When he became pope he sought with an altogether new resolution and zeal to bring to fruition the work which his predecessors had initiated. Simony and clerical marriage quickly became and always remained the objects of his energetic action. But he also sought wider ends which had been foreshadowed but not clearly articulated before, that is, to secure the reform of the Church, to achieve what he and his supporters called its 'liberty'.

This cardinal concept of the Gregorian reform meant the freeing of the Church from every kind of subordination, and the exclusive lordship of St Peter as prince of the apostles and as recipient of Christ's commission to feed his sheep.

This led to the 'Investiture Contest' with the Emperor Henry IV, and the conflict brought the excommunication of the Emperor and led to the famous meeting in Canossa (28 January 1077).

The Emperor then occupied Rome in 1083, enthroning an antipope, Guibertus of Ravenna (Clement III), who crowned him in Campidoglio (31 March 1084); the Roman Curia with almost all the Cardinals took sides with the winner of that moment, and Gregory VII was forced to flee.

At this time Matilda of Canossa, being Gregory's faithful ally in Italy, acted as a *Defensor Ecclesiae*. She was careful to notify the German princes faithful to Gregory that the seal of the pope had been stolen in Rome, thus preventing them from giving credence to anything not emanating from her or her legates.[1]

---

[1] MGH, SS, t.viii, Hannover 1848, 463 (*Hugonis Chronicon*, lib.ii).

It seems to me of particular interest to study the relations between *sacerdotium* and *imperium* in England in their early stages, since the Church of Rome and the Kingdom of England are the only institutions so far existing in the world with a continuous history in the last millennium (the eleventh to twentieth century). In this light the figure of William the Conqueror seems of greater importance, as we can see from the collected correspondence. It is relevant here to remember how William of Malmesbury[2] described the king as a religious man. Moreover, this king arrived in England as the supporter and the leader of that ideal of the reform of the Church which from Leo IX onwards was going to be realised in Europe, and which also condemned some members of the Old English Church, including bishops not exempt from simony and nicholaism.[3]

Besides, for a long time Lanfranc of Bec had been the esteemed counsellor of William the Conqueror; and Lanfranc in 1059 had obtained from pope Nicholas II[4] the dispensation for the marriage of William and his cousin Matilda of Flanders.

Ever since the death of Edward the Confessor in 1066 William had claimed his right to the succession to the English throne usurped by Harold. Alexander II, who had good reasons to avoid supporting Harold, acknowledged the justice of William's claims and also sent him a banner, to win God's protection for his army. This policy was quite probably due to Hildebrand who, later on, in a letter to William (IX) reminded the king how much he owed to his intervention.[5] Because of this the Norman expedition to England looked like a sort of 'holy war'.[6]

In this way the Church was provided with an ally in the reform of the English clergy. So, with William as king, Stigand, archbishop of Canterbury, was removed because of simony and schism, and Lanfranc succeeded him (1070). William had immediately expressed his will to purge the English bishops, getting his coronation from the archbishop of York (25 December 1066).

The relations between England and the continent became closer under William the Conqueror, and especially closer with Italy: we must remember that a relic of St Edmund had been brought to the church of St Martin of Lucca by abbot Baldwin of St Edmund, from Rome, in 1071; and that Englishmen were most devout to that saint, patron of their kings.[7] The links with the world of reform are also shown by the relations between William the Conqueror and Anselm's town, Lucca, which lasted even after his death. Some evidence of these links is given by the veneration of the 'Volto Santo', the famous crucifix, dating back to the eighth century and placed in Lucca cathedral: its veneration spread all over Europe from the eleventh century,

---

[2] *De gestis regum*, ii, 326. 'Inprimis, Dei famulis humilis, subjectis facilis, in rebelles inexorabilis erat. Religionem Christianam, quantum secularis poterat, ita frequentabat, ut cotidie missae assisteret, cotidie vespertinos et matutinos hymnos audiret.'

[3] R. Manselli, *L'Europa medievale*, UTET, Torino 1979, viii, 482, 653.

[4] Nicholas was enthroned pope in Rome (Lateran) on 24 January 1059 with the help of Matilda of Canossa and in his short reign (1059-61) reformed the laws governing papal elections, being throughout his pontificate advised by Hildebrand, later Gregory VII.

[5] 'Notum esse tibi credo, excellentissime fili, priusquam ad pontificale culmen ascenderem, quanto semper te sincere dilectionis affectu amavi, qualem etiam me tuis negotiis et quam efficem exhibui, insuper, ut ad regalem fastigium cresceres, quanto studio laboravi' (Letter IX, 24 April 1080).

[6] Migne, *Patrologia Latina* (henceforth *PL*), 146, 1277. *Gesta Guillelmi*, 154; *De gestis regum*, ii, 302.

[7] R. Manselli, *Lucca e Lucchesi nei loro rapporti con la prima crociata*, Bollettino storico lucchese, 1940, 158.

not least in England, so that William's son, king William Rufus, used to swear *per Vultum de Luca*.[8] Later, the Lucchesi sailed on the First Crusade together with the English, on English ships, even though they were quite near Pisa and not far from Genoa. The Lucchesi also followed English events, narrating them in a famous letter.[9]

In England, under king William, new cathedrals and monasteries were built, and the life and culture of the clergy were improved by regulations applied with severity. Synods were held in order to strengthen the principles of reform, and a separate system of ecclesiastical courts was instituted (1076) for the application of canon law. Lanfranc brought the English Church into line with continental practice, in government, in law and in the liturgy.

A clear idea of the king's personality emerges from Eadmer's description of the relations between William and Anselm of Canterbury: 'There was no earl or countess in England, or any other important person, who did not consider that he had lost a chance of gaining merit with God, if he happened not to have shown any kindness to Abbot Anselm of Bec at that time. Even King William who had seized England by force of arms and was reigning at that time – although he seemed stiff and terrifying to almost everyone because of his great power – nevertheless unbent and was amiable with Anselm, so that to everyone's surprise he seemed an altogether different man when Anselm was present.'[10]

The *epistolae* which I have collected relating to William the Conqueror show a lesser-known aspect of a king who volunteered his services faithfully to the Church of Rome. Unfortunately, of the many letters written also by king William either to Alexander II or to Gregory VII, and of which we know the existence by reference in answers to them, we have so far only one, though this is of great importance as we shall see. Instead we have many letters of Gregory VII, of which nine are addressed to king William, two to queen Matilda and one to their son Robert. To all of these I have added one of the two we know addressed to the king by Alexander II, and the only letter we have addressed to the king by Anselm, bishop of Lucca, after his uncle Anselm, former bishop of Lucca, became pope Alexander II. In the past the letters of the eleventh century have been closely analysed. Many of the letters of Gregory VII appear to have been personally dictated by Gregory himself, and criteria have been suggested[11] by which such letters may be recognised: they include peculiarities of vocabulary, the use of favourite biblical and other quotations, the use of first person singular, warm expressions of personal emotion, and appeal to the theological springs of papal action as Gregory understood them. Other letters

---

8 *De gestis regum*, ii, 373. There is evidence of the veneration of the Holy Face (*Volto Santo*) in England from the pre-Conquest period. Leofstan, abbot of Bury St Edmunds (d.1065) is said to have brought back a copy of the Lucca Crucifixion on his return from a pilgrimage to Rome, and the Volto Santo has been held to be the prototype of the larger of the two roods at Langford, Oxfordshire. In addition, the church of St Thomas in London had a Chapel of the Holy Face (source, P. Lazzarini, *Il Volto Santo di Lucca*, M. Pacini Fazzi publisher, Lucca 1982, 199-201).

9 P. Riant, *Inventaire critique des lettres historiques des Croisades*, Paris 1880, 224 (Epistola cleri Lucensis de victoria mirabile contra Turcas. Scripta anno 1187, quo obiit Urbanus papa III) and in H. Hagenmeyer, *Epistulae at chartae ad historiam primi belli sacri spectantes*, Innsbruck 1901, 166.

10 *The Life of St Anselm . . . by Eadmer*, ed. R. W. Southern, Oxford, Clarendon Press 1972, 56.

11 O. Blaul, *Studien zum Register Gregors VII*, *Archiv für Urkundenforschung*, iv, 1912, 113-228; E. Caspar, *Studien zum Register Gregors VII*, N.A., xxxviii, 1913, 144-226.

may probably have been drafted on Gregory's behalf by the clerks of his *curia* and seen by him before fair copies were made, sealed with a lead *bulla* and dispatched; Gregory himself was concerned that *bullae* taken from his letters might be affixed to forged documents,[12] or, as said above, that a stolen seal could have been used. We may certainly trust items which were preserved by chroniclers and letter collectors who were in a position to know where their material came from: in this light the letters relating to William the Conqueror deserve the greatest confidence, both those of Gregory VII, and those of Alexander II and Anselm of Lucca: the same three personalities emerged in previous studies on Matilda of Canossa[13] as her most strict counsellors.

Alexander II, who had already sent (as noted above) 'ad Guillelmum comitem Nortmanniae ... vexillum ut Haroldum tyrannum ... expelleret'[14] in 1066 – thus almost sanctioning the Norman expedition to England – sent thereafter other letters to the king, two of which have survived.[15] The most interesting of these is the first, of 1071, in which he praises the king's faith and entrusts to him the defence of ecclesiastical persons and the rights of Lanfranc (I).

More numerous are the letters of Gregory VII concerning king William. In the first (II), of 20 November 1073, the pope writes to Lanfranc of Canterbury on the matter of the unworthy bishop Arfast, and reminds him that he also informed king William of this problem – 'Guilielmum regem, carissimum et unicum filium sanctae Romanae ecclesiae'. The second (III), of 4 April 1074, is interesting for the warm expressions of personal emotion, but especially because it reveals that the king had written to him letters expressing feelings of filial apprehension for the Church, and Gregory remarks that among the kings he has only him – 'inter reges te solum habemus, quem aliis diligere supra scripta credimus' – with this corroborating all that he had already written to Lanfranc six months before. At the same date, and therefore by the same messenger, the pope wrote to queen Matilda (IV), referring to the letters he had received and adding an interesting note on the king, whereby he recalled from the Scriptures that if a man unfaithful is saved by a faithful wife, a faithful husband becomes even better with a faithful wife.

A letter of 1076 concerning bishop Juhel of Dol (V) was probably drafted on Gregory's behalf by the clerks of his *curia*. In it Gregory requests the king's help in the expulsion of the bishop, because of his scandalous life, and because he, Gregory, had already consecrated a successor for his see. This subject occurs again in the next letter (VI), of 31 March 1077, written from the castle of Bianello, where the pope was the guest of Matilda of Canossa, after the famous events of two months before with the emperor Henry IV at Canossa, three miles from Bianello. Clearly the situation of the bishop of Dol was still unsatisfactory and necessitating a more direct

---

[12] H. E. J. Cowdrey, *The 'epistolae vagantes' of pope Gregory VII*, Oxford University Press 1964, 110.

[13] P. A. Maccarini *et al.*, 'Il patto tra Matilde di Canossa e il doge veneziano Vitale I Michiel', in *Studi matildici*, Deputazione di Storia Patria, Modena 1971 (Atti del II Convegno matildico); Maccarini, 'Matilde di Canossa: una vita per il potere o al servizio di un'idea?' *Bollettino storico reggiano* xi, 1978, 38; 'Aspetti della religiosità di Matilde di Canossa', *Reggiolo medievale*, Reggio Emilia 1979; 'Diplomazia autonoma di Matilde di Canossa, *In memoria di Leone Tondelli*, Reggio Emilia 1980; 'Anselme de Canterbury et Mathilde de Canossa' (Colloque international d'Etudes anselmiennes, Le Bec Hellouin 1982), Institute de Recherche et d'Histoire des Textes, Paris, CNRS, 1982 (forthcoming).

[14] *PL*, 146, 1277.

[15] *PL*, 146, 1365 and 1413.

intervention of the pope. In this letter we find again a reference to letters of the king which have not survived, together with final expressions of blessing for queen Matilda and their sons. Dated 4 April 1078, we have a letter of the pope to the king (VII) concerning the archbishop of Rouen, and we find, in spite of the official style, the expression *Fili Karissime*. In addition, here the legate Hubert is named for the first time: he served several times as intermediary between Gregory VII and William the Conqueror.

In our chronological order we insert next the unique letter of king William to Gregory VII, which for many reasons we date to 1079 (VIII). It is of great interest because it shows the king unwilling to swear fealty to the pope, although ready to send Peter's Pence, as his predecessors had done. It finishes with reference to the faithful archbishop Lanfranc, and requests prayers because the king wishes to love sincerely and to listen obediently to the pope above all people. The pope knew that he was able to trust king William to ensure the triumph of reform, but the king was jealous of his own independence, and was anxious to have an absolute power over all his subjects, laymen or ecclesiastics: this letter of the king relates to the highest point of the conflict which broke out in 1079. Undoubtedly it had also been a misunderstanding, and the conflict resolved itself thanks to the reciprocal will on both sides. The cooling between the king and the pope was without consequence, and from 1080 the correspondence of the pope with the king of England assumed once more a friendly atmosphere.[16]

Thus we have the letter of 24 April 1080 (IX), one of the more important, both because it has a particularly affectionate tone and because it reveals the affection of the pope for the king, dating from before Hildebrand's elevation to the papacy when, as counsellor of Alexander II, he had supported William in the war against Harold. It is a letter with a pastoral and exhortative tone, and reminds the king how from humble origins ('ex servo peccati misero et pauperculo') God made him *potentissimum regem*.

Similar but shorter is the following letter of 8 May 1080 (X), which reveals more the spiritual counsellor than the pope, and urges the king to the love of God, who will enlarge the kingdom with his powerful arm. After this letter, and of the same date, we have the second surviving letter of Gregory VII to queen Matilda (XI), from which we know that she had been in correspondence with the pope; and we learn also how warm were the relations between the queen and Gregory, still warmer than six years before (*filia karissima*), the pope pointing out her merits greater than any other treasure, and helpful to her husband. On the same date again Gregory VII writes another letter (XII), this time to the king's son, Robert. This letter appears important as it shows how the pope had resumed a very good relationship with the king, so much so as to want to help him in the war with his son. He warns the son Robert to respect the father and to adapt to his will, not listening to the advice of evil people. Evidently Gregory VII was referring to Robert's rebellion against his father, dating from 1074 and caused by the king's refusal to give Robert real authority in his Norman dominion. This rebellion ended in 1079 with the siege of Gerberoi by the Conqueror and his younger son William Rufus. These letters written on the same day to the members of the royal family of England may remind us of the similar treatment by Gregory VII of another eminent family and the many letters

---

[16] A. Fliche, *Storia della Chiesa dalle origini fino ai nostri giorni*, Italian edition by P. Frutaz, Saie Publishers, Turin 1959, viii, 168.

to Beatrix of Lorena and her daughter Matilda of Canossa, each of them *filiae karis-simae*.

The last remaining letter of Gregory VII to William the Conqueror (XIII) dates from late 1083, and lacks an end, but it is important for its beginning wherein the pope declares his long friendship with the king through their common love of and sincere devotion to the apostle St Peter, and then scolds him gently for his treatment of his brother (Odo of Bayeux), without full consideration of the honour due to priests even if unworthy.

Finally there remains, from 1085, a unique letter of Anselm of Lucca (XIV), the great counsellor of Matilda of Canossa,[17] a letter probably written after the death of Gregory VII (25 May 1085), very long and interesting chiefly in its demonstration that the relations of king William with the Church were not only formal as between him and pope; for we may also see how deep was the consideration of Anselm, a great personality of that time, towards the king. Anselm praises the king, summarising all his glory so that 'non solum occidentis partes . . . verum etiam aliae mundi regiones remotissimae, iam ex longo tempore plena attestatione cognoscunt'. Then the letter continues in pastoral tone with admonitions and suggestions for a Christian behaviour towards both the persons and churches under his jurisdiction. Next Anselm expresses the wish that the king will not lessen his faith in Peter, a faith which will last for ever in the Roman Church, to which he ought to come *quasi ad matrem tuam*, as if to his mother. Finally Anselm, recalling the letters which the king sent to him, specifies that this letter has been written by him *propria manu* and sent only to the king.

We may say that the letter of Anselm who, as bishop of Lucca had close links with the English, not least through devotion to the *Volto Santo*, attests and re-affirms, with the same tone, all the letters of Gregory VII, of whom he had been, with Matilda of Canossa, the most faithful interpreter, and attests also to a long correspondence with the Conqueror which has unfortunately not survived.

And at this point I think it is very suitable to report the last words of William the Conqueror, as they have been transmitted to us, which recall those suggested by Anselm in his letter — 'Ecclesiam Dei, matrem scilicet nostram, numquam violavi; sed ubique, ut ratio exegit, desideranter honoravi. Ecclesiasticas dignitates numquam venundedi.'[18]

We may conclude that William the Conqueror had a rôle with regard to the Church of Rome similar to those of Henry III of Germany and of Matilda of Canossa, who for her merits was buried in St Peter in Rome: William also has full right to be considered a *Defensor Ecclesiae*.

---

[17] Rangerius, *S. Anselmi lucensis episcopi vita*. De La Fuente, Madrid 1870.
[18] Orderic, iv, 90.

Acknowledgements
I would like to express my special appreciation to Father Angelo Galletti O.S.B. (Abbey S. Giovanni Evangelista, Parma) for his help in preparing this paper, and to Professor Reginald Allen Brown (University of London, King's College) for his help with its presentation.

APPENDIX

1. List of letters cited

Abbreviations

Briefs.   *Briefsammlungen der Zeit Heinrichs IV*, ed. C. Erdmann and
       N. Fickermann, MGH, Weimar 1950
Ep. vag.   *The epistolae vagantes of Pope Gregory VII*, ed. H. E. J. Cowdrey,
       Oxford 1964
PL   *Patrologia Latina*, ed. J. P. Migne
Reg. Greg.   *Register Gregors VII*, ed. E. Caspar, MGH, Berlin 1920

I   'Omnipotenti Deo' (*PL*, 146, 1365) Alexander II to king William,
       Rome, 1071
II   'Non minima' (*Reg. Greg.* 51) Gregory VII to Lanfranc of Canterbury,
       S. Germano, 20 November 1073
III   'Merore mentis' (*Reg. Greg.* 101) Gregory VII to king William,
       Rome, 4 April 1074
IV   'Auditis nobilitatis' (*Reg. Greg.* 102) Gregory VII to queen Matilda,
       Rome, 4 April 1074
V   'Compertum esse' (*Ep. vag.* 44) Gregory VII to king William,
       s.l., post 27 September 1076
VI   'Causam unde' (*Reg. Greg.* 322) Gregory VII to king William,
       Bianello, 31 March 1077
VII   'Officii nostri' (*Reg. Greg.* 382) Gregory VII to king William,
       Rome, 4 April 1078
VIII   'Hubertus legatus' (*PL*, 148, 748) King William to Gregory VII,
       s.l., probably 1079
IX   'Notum esse' (*Reg. Greg.* 499) Gregory VII to king William,
       Rome, 24 April 1080
X   'Credimus prudentiam' (*Reg. Greg.* 505) Gregory VII to king William,
       Rome, 8 May 1080
XI   'Ingenuitati vestrae' (*Reg. Greg.* 507) Gregory VII to queen Matilda,
       Rome, 8 May 1080
XII   'Certi rumores' (*Reg. Greg.* 508) Gregory VII to Robert son of king William,
       Rome, 8 May 1080
XIII   'Communis amor' (*Reg. Greg.* 630) Gregory VII to king William,
       s.l., end of 1083
XIV   'Quanta virtutis' (*Briefs.* 15) Anselm of Lucca to king William,
       s.l., about 1085

2. Texts of letters cited

I

Alexander episcopus, servus servorum Dei, charissimo filio Willelmo glorioso regi Anglorum, salutem et apostolicam benedictionem.

Omnipotenti Deo laudes gratiasque referimus quod, in hoc tempore, licet mundus in maligno positus plus solito pravis incumbat studiis, tamen inter mundi principes et rectores egregiam vestræ religionis famam intelligimus et, quantum honoris sanctæ Ecclesiæ tum Simoniacæ hæresis vires opprimendo, tum catholicæ libertatis usus et officia confirmando vestra virtus impendat, non dubia relatione cognoscimus. Sed quia non iis qui bona demonstrant, justitia sed in fine probatis præmium et corona promittitur, excellentiam vestram plena dilectione monemus ut in studio Christianissimæ devotionis vestræ persistatis, et primo quidem ecclesias Christi quæ in regno vestro sunt, religioso cultu et iustis dispositionibus exornetis, commissa vobis regni gubernacula ita justitia tenendo tractetis ut, ex operum rectitudine, quod scriptum est: *Cor regis in manu Dei* (*Prov.* xxi, 1), vobis manifeste congruat.

Rogamus etiam dilectionem vestram ut ecclesiasticas personas ab injuria defendatis, viduas, et orphanos, et oppressos misericorditer relevando protegatis. Quoniam licet ille Rex regum et supernus arbiter totius regni quod vobis tradidit rationem a vobis exigat pro his tamen districtius appellabit quibus non fuerunt vires et arma nisi vestra potentia. Ad hæc igitur perficienda et aliarum virtutum incrementa percipienda, fratris nostri Lanfranci Cantuariensis archiepiscopi monitis et consiliis gloriam vestram hortamur acquiescere, quem charissimum membrum et unum ex primis Romanæ Ecclesiæ filiis lateri nostro assidue non adjunctum esse dolemus sed ex fructu quem Ecclesiæ in regno vestro tribuit consolationem ejus absentiæ sumimus.

Præterea eminentiæ vestræ notum esse volumus quod causa Alricii, qui olim Cicestrensis Ecclesiæ præsul dictus, a suppositis legatorum nostrorum depositus est, non ad plenum nobis tractata videtur, ideoque, sicut in canonibus cautum est, in pristinum locum debere restitui judicavimus. Deinde causam ejus, juxta censuram canonicæ traditionis, diligenter retractandam et definiendam prædicto fratri nostro archiepiscopo Lanfranco commisimus. Item sibi negotium de discernenda lite quæ inter archiepiscopum Eboracensem et episcopum Dorcacestrensem de pertinentia diœcesis eorum est firmiter injungendo commendavimus, ut hanc causam diligentissima perquisitione pertractet, et justo fine determinet. In causis autem pertractandis, et definiendis ita sibi nostræ et apostolicae auctoritatis vicem dedimus, ut quidquid in eis, justitia dictante, determinaverit, quasi in nostra præsentia definitum, deinceps firmum et indissolubile teneatur. Multa vobis præter hæc significata dedissemus, nisi quod ea in hujus dilectissimi fratris nostri Lanfranci et ejusdem fidelissimi vobis ore posuimus, ut ejus viva voce et nostræ dilectionis affectum plenius cognoscatis et reliqua nostræ legationis verba attentius audiatis. Deus autem omnipotens det vobis quæcunque sibi sunt placita velle et posse, ut et hic auctor sit vestri gubernaculi et retributor in gloria sempiterni gaudii.

II

Gregorius episcopus servus servorum Dei Lanfranco Cantuariorum in Anglia archiepiscopo salutem et apostolicam benedictionem.

Non minima ammiratione dignum ducimus, qua fronte, qua mente Arfastum dictum episcopum sancte Romane ecclesie illudere et beate memorie Alexandrum predecessorem nostrum eiusque decreta contempnere patiamini. Prudentiam quippe vestram ad plenum cognoscere nos non latet sanctam Romanam ecclesiam iure a Deo dato sibi defendere ecclesiarum sacerdotum episcoporum consecrationes et a nullo sumpta licentia debere et posse celebrare, suis et prebuisse et Deo annuente prebituram firmissimam etiam in hoc defensionem, quia Romam venerint et sedis apostolice consilium et auxilium petierint. Quibus Arfastus dictus episcopus, qua nova audacia resistat, nisi fortasse ista: 'Ponam sedem meam ad aquilonem et ero similis Altissimo', ignoramus. Ad quid etiam dilectio vestra super his sileat, non nimium miramur. Verum quia de vobis non aliter quam de nobis dubitamus, fraternitatem vestram confidenter deprecamur, ut vice nostra Arfasti nugas penitus compescatis et sancti Eadmundi abbatiam contra decretum decessoris nostri inquietari nullo modo sinatis. Qui etiam, cum eundem abbatem in presbyterum ordinari Rome fecisset, ipsum et monasterium, cui preest, in tutelam apostolice sedis accepit. Unde iniurias illius in nos redundare dissimulare non possumus, presertim cum ad despectum auctoritatis nostre eas sibi irrogari perpendimus. Unde etiam Guilielmum regem, carissimum et unicum filium sancte Romane ecclesie, precibus nostris et vice nostra super his admonere dilectionem vestram precamur et, ne Arfasti vanis persuasionibus adquiescat, in quo sua singularis prudentia supra modum diminuta et contracta ab omnibus cognoscitur. Si vero Arfastus contra hec recalcitrare abhinc temptaverit, apostolica auctoritate sibi et Balduino abbati precipite, ut sedem apostolicam ad hec determinanda petant. Data ad Sanctum Germanum XII. Kalendas Decembris, Indictione XII.

III

Gregorius episcopus servus servorum Dei Guilielmo regi Anglorum salutem et apostolicam benedictionem.

Merore mentis tue, fili dilecte, ex decessu antecessoris nostri beate memorie Alexandri, tui etiam hylaritate ex nostre promotionis certo rumore absque dubio credimus te ex corde matri tue sancte Romane ecclesie adherere eamque totis viribus, ut debes, diligere. Nam, quia eius quasi viduitate audita graviter angebaris, consolatione etiam sua de nostri promotione vero gaudio letaris statumque nostrum te velle scire per litteras tuas obnixe et humiliter precaris, affectum boni filii, affectum filii matrem ex corde diligentis ostendis. Exsequere ergo operibus, fili dilecte, quod ore confiteris, imple efficaciter quod dicis, ut consentias ipsi Veritati clamanti: 'Qui diligit me, sermones meos servabit'; et alibi: 'Probatio dilectionis exhibitio est operis'. Sermones matris tue hi sunt et huiusmodi: Iustitie per omnia, cum oportunum est, inmodo insudare ne desinas, ecclesiis tibi ad defendendum commissis sic consulere, ut fomenta salutis anime tue conficias, peccatorum maculas deleas, virtutum odores sic tibi introducas, ut cum apostolo dicas: 'Christi bonus odor sumus'. Honorem Dei et omnia que Dei sunt tuo et mundanis omnibus preponere consulimus admonemus et precamur, cum hoc ex certo sit unum, quo neglecto sepius tue dignitatis potestates solet perdere et ad inferos trudere. Hec ideo, karissime, tibi inculcavimus, quia inter reges te solum habemus, quem pre aliis diligere supra scripta credimus.

Statum vero nostrum, quem te scire suppliciter oras, sic accipe: Navem inviti ascendimus, que per undosum pelagus violentia ventorum et impetu turbinum et fluctibus ad aera usque insurgentibus in incerta deicitur; saxis occultatis et aliis a longe in altum apparentibus, licet cum periculo, obviat tamen et ex animo. Sancta quippe Romana ecclesia, cui licet indigni et nolentes presidemus, diversis temptationibus quam plurimis persecutionibus ypocritarum et hereticorum insidiis et dolosis obiectionibus continue et cotidie quatitur, mundanis vero potestatibus occulte et evidenter per diversa distrahitur. Quibus omnibus obviare et his et quam plurimis aliis summopere cavere post Deum et inter homines nostri est officii et cure, specialiter horum cura die noctuque coquimur, his et similibus continue divellimur; licet pro tempore ab huius mundi filiis hec nobis videantur arridere, que tamen, grates Deo referimus, mundana coguntur nobis displicere. Sic vivimus et Deo annuente vivemus.

Privilegium vero sancti Stephani, de quo mandasti, anime tue salus est. Et pro eodem tibi consulimus sic ratum te habere, prout legati nostri Petrus et Iohannes Minutus canonice observandum iudicarunt. Si tamen superhabundans aliquid privilegio tibi videtur adscriptum, quanto plura pro Deo et sancto Petro beato Stephano concesseris, tanto maiora in retributione ab his procul dubio habebis.

Rebus vero sancti Petri, que in Anglia colliguntur, sic te ut tuis invigilare admonemus, sic liberalitati tue ut tua committimus, ut pium et propitium debitorem Petrum repperias et eum tibi ex debito subvenire admoneas, quem sibi multa te tribuisse non latebit. Data Rome II. Nonas Aprilis, Indictione XII.

IV

Gregorius episcopus servus servorum Dei Mathildi regine Anglorum salutem et apostolicam benedictionem.

Auditis nobilitatis tue litteris liberalitatem tuam, filia dilecta, dilectioni et humilitati invigilare intellegimus, ex quibus tue salutis indicium et spem certam hilariter accepimus. Non quippe dubitandum de eius salute fore credimus, que humilitati et dilectioni, in qua lex ex toto continetur, ex corde inservire dinoscitur. Munera hec et similia a te expectamus, immo toto mentis desiderio accipere cupimus, ut, que nobilis es sanguine, nobilior vivas sanctorum more honestate. Insta viro tuo, anime utilia suggerere ne desinas. Certum enim est, si vir infidelis per mulierem fidelem, ut ait apostolus, salvatur, vir etiam fidelis per mulierem fidelem in melius augmentatur. Data Rome II. Nonas Aprilis, Indictione XII.

V

Gregorius episcopus seruus seruorum Dei excellentissimo filio W. glorioso regi Anglorum salutem et apostolicam benedictionem.

Compertum esse celsitudini tuae non dubitamus quod dictus episcopus Dolensis ecclesiae, quae Britannicae provinciae principalis est sedes, suae salutis immemor et sanctorum canonum decreta conculcans, eamdem ecclesiam per simoniacam haeresim impudenter inuaserit et prolixo iam tempore oppresserit uiolenter. Datis namque comiti Alano copiosis muneribus, quae usque hodie ad probamentum prius nequitiae in propatulo extant, non per ostium in ouile Christi sed ut fur et latro aliunde irrepsit. Qui etiam nec hoc scelere contentus iniquitatem super iniquitatem apposuit et, quasi simoniacum esse parum et pro nihilo deputaret, nicolaita quoque fieri festinauit. Nam in ipso tam perniciose adepto episcopatu nuptiis publice celebratis scortum potius quam sponsam ducere non erubuit, ex qua et filios procreauit; ut qui iam spiritum suum animarum corruptori per simoniaca commercia prostituerat, per foedae libidinis incestum corpus suum ita in contumeliam diabolo consecraret; et sic in eo nullus locus superesset Conditori quem intus exteriusque obligatum totum sibi aduersarius non uendicasset. Nec tamen huc usque conatus malitiae substitit, sed etiam atrocissimum facinus turpissimumque flagitium horrendo etiam sacrilegio cumulauit. Nam adultas ex illicito matrimonio filias, praediis ecclesiae et redditibus nomine dotis collatis atque alienatis, scelere immanissimo maritauit. His iniquitatibus coopertus, eamdem tamen ecclesiam dilaceratam dissipatamque, si liceat, incubare molitur. Quibus de causis celsitudo tua nouerit illum iam beati Petri apostoli spiculo perfossum et nisi sceleris resipuerit anathemate mortifero esse damnatum. Quapropter paterna caritate te ammonere et causam breuiter exponere studuimus, ne fortasse per ignorantiam tam scelesto homini tandiu in tenebris suis iacenti ulterius auxilium praebeas neue sceleris eius te participem facias; sed sedi apostolicae nostrisque monitis modeste parendo illum a te repellas, uel etiam ut tandem aliquando sibi consulat atque ad remedium paenitentiae confugiat blande suadendo, si poteris, inducas. Nam tales in malo perseuerantes fouere et adiuuare nihil est aliud quam iram Domini contra se prouocare. Nos uero supradictae ecclesiae afflictionem diutius non ferentes, Deo inspirante, uirum uita probabilem et compertae religionis inibi ordinauimus et consecrauimus, uidelicet S. Melanii abbatem; qui cum ob alias causas quas explicare prolixum est ad nos uenisset, pontificatus onus ex insperato subire compulsus est. De quo confidimus in Domino quia si, ut desideramus litterisque nostris multipliciter implorare curauimus, principum terrae bonorum uirorum gratiam et studia habere meruerit, Domino cooperante, sub beati Petri patrocinio ecclesiam in melius restaurabit.

VI

Gregorius episcopus servus servorum Dei Wilielmo regi Anglorum salutem et apostolicam benedictionem.

Causam, unde nos in litteris vestris rogastis, ita iam ad extremum deductam esse putavimus, ut nichil in ea quod ulterius retractandum esset, restare videretur. Nam cum in Dolensi ecclesia episcopum ordinavimus, ita hunc, pro quo excellentia vestra intervenit, ad deiectionem suam ex propriis facinoribus et ad ultimum ex inoboedientia ac precipitasse non solum per clericos et religiosas personas illius ecclesie, sed etiam per legatum nostrum Teuzonem monachum intellexeramus, ut magis sibi de malis in ecclesiam commissis et corruptissima vita sua timendum et plangendum, quam pro recuperatione episcopatus proclamandum aut quicquam sperandum fore iudicaremus. Attamen, deprecationem vestram sine ea qua oportet cura et benignitate suscepisse videamur et, si aliquis per subreptionem, quod non credimus, nos fefellit, ad inquirendum et corrigendum minus solliciti inveniamur, legatos nostros, videlicet confratrem nostrum Hugonem venerabilem Diensem episcopum et dilectum filium nostrum Hubertum sancte Romane ecclesie subdiaconum et ipsum etiam Teuzonem monachum, si ereptum ab infirmitate poterimus, illuc mittere decrevimus, qui causam diligenti inquisitione discutiant et, si quid in ea dictante iustitia mutandum vel emendandum fuerit, consequenti ratione et auctoritate exequi studeant. Nusquam enim hoc negotium rectius aut diligentius quam in eadem ecclesia pertractari posse videtur, ubi et hic et illi presentes esse valeant et vestri etiam interesse fideles, qui rationem et iustitiam plene percognitam certis assertionibus vobis indicare queant. Nec dubitamus equidem, quin vestra celsitudo diffinitioni iustitie concorditer adquiescat, quoniam, licet in vobis per misericordiam Dei multe et egregie sint virtutes, hec tamen est preclara et famosissima et que gloriam vestram Deo precipue commendat et hominibus, quod iustitiam, quam vos facere prompti estis, aliis etiam facientibus diligitis atque probatis. De cetero scitote eminentiam vestram et sepe cognitam devotionem eius nobis gratissimam fore, qui et vos ipsos et, quicquid ad gloriam sublimitatis vestre Deo auctore proficere potest, semper in corde et visceribus nostris cum magno desiderio et affectu intime caritatis amplectimur et ad voluntatem vestram in omnibus, que apud nos impetrare quesiveritis quoad possumus et secundum beneplacitum Dei nos audere cognoscimus, flecti et annuere parati sumus. Quia vero prefatum filium nostrum Hubertum ad vos usque dirigere destinavimus, plura vobis scribere non necessarium duximus, quoniam in omnibus, que ex nostra parte vobis referet, ipsum quasi certissimam epistolam nostram et verba nostra fideliter continentem fore nec nos dubitamus nec vestram excellentiam dubitare volumus.

Deus autem omnipotens meritis et intercessionibus apostolorum Petri et Pauli et omnium sanctorum suorum tibi et serenissime regine Mathildi uxori tue et clarissimis filiis vestris omnium peccatorum vestrorum indulgentiam et remissionem et absolutionem tribuat et, cum vos de rebus mundanis exhimi iusserit, ad eternum regnum suum et veram gloriam transire faciat. Data Bibianello XII, Kalendas Aprilis, Indictione XV.

VII

Gregorius episcopus servus servorum Dei Guilielmo regi Anglorum salutem et apostolicam benedictionem.

Officii nostri cura exigit, ut ecclesiis pastoribus viduatis sollicite subvenire properemus. Quia vero inter reges tum more, honestate, qua nites, tum liberali prudentia, qua muniris, te speciali dilectione amplectimur, dignum est, ut ecclesiis, que sunt in regno divina dispositione tibi commisso, specialiter cavere studeamus. Unde Rotomagensi ecclesie, quam dudum pastore destitutam egritudine impediente audivimus, succurrere hoc modo disposuimus. Hubertum sancte R. ecclesie subdiaconem, quem experimento nobis et tibi fidelem didicimus, liberali glorie tue, fili karissime, mittimus; qui cum viris religiosis, episcopis et abbatibus, eiusdem etiam ecclesie fratribus, predictum archiepiscopum adeat, diligenti et pia consideratione examinet, an pastorali moderamini preesse, ut oportet, valeat. Si vero valitudine corporali sic iudicent destitutum, ut amodo episcopali non sit aptus regimini, piis ammonitionibus sibi persuadere non desistant, si oportuerit etiam auctoritate apostolica, ut suo consensu ordinetur ecclesia. At si valitudo sic eum oppresserit, ut insensatum et officii sui obliviosum reddiderit, non diiudicans, quanti sibi et universe patrie egritudo sit detrimenti, precipimus auctoritate apostolica virum tanto ponderi competentem, bene moratum et sapientem universorum consensu canonice eligi et in archiepiscopum promoveri. Data Rome II. Nonas Aprilis, Indictione I.

VIII

Excellentissimo sanctæ Ecclesiæ pastori Gregorio gloriosus gratia Dei Anglorum rex et dux Northmannorum Willelmus salutem cum amicitia.

Hubertus legatus tuus, religiose Pater, ad me veniens ex tua parte, me admonuit quatenus tibi et successoribus tuis fidelitatem facerem et de pecunia, quam antecessores mei ad Romanam Ecclesiam mittere solebant, melius cogitarem; unum admisi, alterum non admisi. Fidelitatem facere nolui, nec volo, quia nec ego promisi, nec antecessores meos antecessoribus tuis id fecisse comperio. Pecunia tribus fere annis, in Galliis me agente, negligenter collecta est; nunc vero divina misericordia me in regnum meum reverso, quod collectum est per præfatum legatum mittitur; et quod reliquum est, per legatos Lanfranci archiepiscopi fidelis nostri, cum opportunum fuerit, transmittetur. Orate pro nobis et pro statu regni nostri, quia antecessores vestros dileximus et vos præ omnibus sincere diligere et obedienter audire desideramus.

IX

Gregorius episcopus servus servorum Dei Guillelmo regi Anglorum salutem et apostolicam benedictionem.

Notum esse tibi credo, excellentissime fili, priusquam ad pontificale culmen ascenderem, quanto semper te sincere dilectionis affectu amavi, qualem etiam me tuis negotiis et quam efficacem exhibui, insuper, ut ad regale fastigium cresceres, quanto studio laboravi. Qua pro re a quibusdam fratribus magnam pene infamiam pertuli summurmurantibus, quod ad tanta homicidia perpetranda tanto favore meam operam impendissem. Deus vero in mea conscientia testis erat, quam recto id animo feceram sperans per gratiam Dei et non inaniter confidens de virtutibus bonis, que in te erant, quia, quanto ad sullimiora proficeres, tanto te apud Deum et sanctam ecclesiam, sicut et nunc Deo gratias res est, ex bono meliorem exhiberes. Itaque nunc tanquam dilectissimo filio et fideli sancti Petri et nostro, sicut in familiari colloquio facerem, consilium nostrum et, quid te postmodum facere deceat, paucis aperio. Quando enim complacuit ei, qui exaltat humiles, ut sancta mater nostra ecclesia ad regimen apostolice sedis invitum satis ac renitentem Deo teste me raperet, continuo nefanda mala, que a pessimis filiis suis patitur, officii mei, quo mihi clamare et nunquam cessare iniunctum est, necessitate compulsus amore quoque ac timore devinctus dissimulare non potui; amore quidem, quia sanctus Petrus a puero in domo sua dulciter nutrierat et quia caritas domini Dei nostri me quasi aliquid estimans tanti pastoris vicarium ad regendam sanctam matrem nostram elegerat; timore autem, quia terribiliter divina lex intonat dicens: 'Maledictus homo, qui parcit gladio suo a sanguine', id est qui doctrinam subtrahit ab occisione carnalis vite. Nunc igitur, karissime et in Christo semper amplectende fili, cum et matrem tuam nimium tribulari conspicias et inevitabilis nos succurrendi necessitas urgeat, talem te volo et multum pro honore tuo et salute in vera et non ficta caritate moneo ad omnem oboedientiam prebeas, ut, sicut cooperante Deo gemma principum esse meruisti, ita regula iustitie et oboedientie forma cunctis terre principibus esse merearis tot procul dubio in futura gloria principum princeps futurus quot usque in finem seculi exemplo tue oboedientie principes salvabuntur; et si quidam illorum salvari noluerint, tibi tamen retributio nullatenus minuetur; non solum autem sed et in hoc mundo tibi et heredibus tuis victoria honor potentia sullimitas amplius celitus tribuetur. Exemplum tibi te ipsum propone. Sicut enim velles ab eo, quem ex misero et pauperrimo servo potentissimum regem fecisses, non immerito honorari, sic et tu, quem ex servo peccati misero et pauperculo – ita quippe omnes nascimur – potentissimum regem Deus gratis fecit, honoratorem tuum protectorem atque adiutorem tuum omnipotentem Iesum honorare semper studiose festina. Nec ab hec impediat te pessimorum principum turba; nequitia enim multorum est, virtus autem paucorum; gloriosius est probato militi multis fugientibus in prelio stare; pretiosior illa est gemma, que rarius invenitur. Immo quanto magis potentes huius seculi superbia sua et impiis actibus excecati corruunt in profundum, tanto magis te, qui pre illis multum Deo carus inventus es, pie humiliando decet erigi et oboediendo sullimari, ut sit, sicut scriptum est: 'Impius impie agat adhuc et qui in sordibus est sordescat adhuc et iustus iustificetur adhuc.' Plura tibi adhuc exhortando scriberem, sed quia tales misisti, qui me satis de tua prudentia honestate iustitia simul cum filio nostro Huberto letificaverunt, sapienti viro satis esse dictum iudicavi sperans, quia omnipotens Deus supra quam dicimus in te et per te ad honorem suum dignabitur operari. Que vero in litteris minus sunt, legatis tuis viva tibi voce dicenda commisimus. Ipse autem omnipotens Deus et pater noster hoc tuo cordi, karissime fili, ita inspirare atque plantare misericorditer dignetur, quatinus et in hoc seculo merito virtutum tuarum regnum tuum et potentiam augeat et in futuro cum sanctis regibus ad regna supercelestia inexcogitabiliter meliora feliciter introducat. Amen.

Cenomannensi episcopo tuis precibus iustitia dictante faventes officium episcopale reddidimus. Abbatem quoque monasterii sancti Petri, quod est Cinomanni, absolvimus. Data Rome VIII. Kalendas Maii, Indictione III.

X

Gregorius episcopus servus servorum Dei Guilielmo regi Anglorum salutem et apostolicam benedictionem.

Credimus prudentiam vestram non latere omnibus aliis excellentiores apostolicam et regiam dignitates huic mundo ad eius regimina omnipotentem Deum distribuisse. Sicut enim ad mundi pulchritudinem oculis carneis diversis temporibus representandam solem et lunam omnibus aliis eminentiora disposuit luminaria, sic, ne creatura, quam sui benignitas ad imaginem suam in hoc mundo creaverat, in erronea et mortifera traheretur pericula, providit, ut apostolica et regia dignitate per diversa regeretur officia. Qua tamen maioritatis et minoritatis distantia religio sic se movet christiana, ut cura et dispositione apostolica dignitas post Deum gubernetur regia. Quod licet, fili karissime, tua non ignoret vigilantia, tamen, ut pro salute tua indissolubiliter menti tue sit alligatum, divina testatur scriptura apostolicam et pontificalem dignitatem reges christianos ceterosque omnes ante divinum tribunal representaturam et pro eorum delictis rationem Deo redditturam. Si ergo iusto iudici et qui mentiri nescit creaturarum omnium creatori tremendo iudicio te sum representaturus, iudicet diligens sapientia tua, an debeam vel possim saluti tue non diligentissime cavere et tu mihi ad salutem tuam, ut viventium possideas terram, debeas vel possis sine mora non oboedire. Provideas ergo, ut pro te incessanter insistas, ut te diligis Deum, honorem Dei tibi tuoque proponere honori, Deum munda mente totis viribus integro corde diligere. Crede mihi, si Deum pura mente, ut audis et ut scriptura precipit, dilexeris, si Dei honorem, ut debes, in omnibus tuo proposueris, qui ficte nescit diligere, qui potens est etiam te proponere, hic et in futuro te amplexabitur et regnum tuum omnipotenti suo brachio dilatabitur. Data Rome VIII. Idus Maii, [I]ndictione III.

XI

Gregorius episcopus servus servorum Dei Mathildi regine Anglorum salutem et apostolicam benedictionem.

Ingenuitatis vestre lectis litteris, quam fideli mente Deo oboedias, quanta dilectione fidelibus suis adhereas, intelleximus. Nos quoque quomodo mentis tue memoria presentes contineat, ex amplitudinis tue promissionibus non minus percipimus, quibus designastis, ut, quicquid de vestris vellemus, si notum vobis fieret, sine mora susciperemus. Quod, filia karissima, qua suscepimus dilectione et que munera a te obtamus, sic intellegas. Quod enim aurum, que gemme, que mundi huius pretiosa mihi a te magis sunt expectanda, quam vita casta, rerum tuarum in pauperes distributio, Dei et proximi dilectio? Hec et his similia a te munera obtamus, ut integra et simplicia diligas, nobilitatem tuam precamur, dilecta obtineas, habita nunquam derelinquas. His armis et similibus virum tuum armare, cum Deus tibi oportunitatem dederit, ne desistas. Cetera, que dimisimus, per Hubertum filium nostrum et fidelem communem mandamus. Data Rome VIII. Idus Maii, [I]ndictione III.

XII

Gregorius episcopus servus servorum Dei Roberto filio regis Anglorum salutem et apostolicam benedictionem.

Certi rumores tuorum morum et tue prudentie et liberalitatis, qui usque ad nos pervenere, partim dilectione parentum partim tua nos letificaverunt. Qui vero econtra quorundam pravorum consilio aures nostras molestaverunt, ut priores hilarem, sic sinistri nos reddidere tristem. Nunc vero, quia per Hubertum filium nostrum audivimus te paternis consiliis adquiescere, pravorum vero omnino dimittere, letamur. Insuper monemus et paterne precamur, ut menti tue semper sit infixum, quia, quam forti manu quam divulgata gloria quicquid pater tuus possideat, ab ore inimicorum extraxerit, sciens tamen se non imperpetuum vivere, sed ad hoc tam viriliter insistere, ut eredi alicui suo dimitteret. Caveas ergo, fili dilecte, admonemus, ne abhinc pravorum consiliis adquiescas, quibus patrem offendas et matrem contristeris. Sint tibi indissolubiliter infixa precepta et monita divina: 'Honora patrem et matrem, ut sis longevus super terram'; et illud: 'Qui maledixerit patri vel metri, morte moriatur'. Si vero ex honore patris et matris longior tibi tribuitur vita, econtra si dehonestas, quid tribuatur, liceat videas. Si autem ex maledictis mortem filio divina scriptura intonat, multo certius ex malefactis certiorem mortem insinuat. Quid ergo restat, si membrum Christi vis vivere et in mundo isto honeste conversari? Pravorum consilia ex officio nostro precipimus penitus dimittas, patris voluntati in omnibus adquiescas. Data Rome VIII. Idus Maii, [I]ndictione III.

XIII

Gregorius episcopus servus servorum Dei Gilielmo regi Anglorum salutem.

Communis amor et sincera devotio, quam erga beatum P. apostolum gerimus, ex longo iam tempore inter nos amicitiam iunxit atque adeo invicem inde magis convaluit, quia et ego te pre ceteris tui ordinis apostolice sedi devotum animadverti et tua me claritudo inter aliquos predecessores meos circa honorem apostolice sedis credidit amplius desudasse. Denique cum in malis moribus idem velle et nolle pernitiosam sepe factionem conficiat, consequens videtur, ut in bonis rebus idem studium animique desiderium diverso quamlibet spatio terrarum disiunctos in unum dilectionis glutino copulet. Verum licet quidam regie potestatis non modicum doleant et in nos sepissime murmurent se quodamodo contemni, conquerantur se non sic ab apostolica sede diligi nec ita factis aut sermonibus per nos honorari, minime tamen nos penitet nec deinceps Deo favente penitebit. Speramus etenim celsitudinis tue industriam in eadem sancte ecclesie devotione iustitieque studio semper mansuram ac in melius etiam opitulante Domino de cetero dilatandam. Unde merito nos oportet in eiusdem dilectionis tenore perseverare, immo per diuturnitatem temporum crescentibus meritis magis ac magis excrescere.

Unum tamen interea nos tangit et tangendo angustat atque inter regalium tuarum virtutum insignia monimenta leticiam in amico corde violenter obnubilat, videlicet quod in capiendo germanum tuum episcopum non sicut decuit proprie honestati prospitiens sed secularem cautelam et rationem divine legi preponens sacerdotalem reverentiam minus vigilanter attendisti. Et quidem non latere tuam prudentiam credimus scriptum esse, quod de sacerdotibus maxime oportet intelligi: 'Qui vos tangit, tangit pupillam oculi mei', et alibi: 'Nolite tangere christos meos'; et quod Dominus ipse sacerdotibus, licet pravis et valde indignis, honorem deferre non sit dedignatus. Quam rem pie memorie Constantinus precipuus videlicet imperator intelligens, in Nicena sinodo nullam in episcopos ab ipsis etiam episcopis accusationem voluit suscipere nullumque contra eos iuditium presumpsit inferre dicens: Vos dii estis, a vero Deo constituti; ideo non oportet, ut nos homines deos presumamus iudicare. Quanta etiam sit sacerdotii dignitas quantaque sublimitas episcopalis, beatus Ambrosius, doctor scilicet eximius, vestram doceat magnitudinem vestramque instruat prudentiam, in pastorali suo sic ponens: 'Honor igitur, fratres, et sublimitas episcopalis nullis poterit comparationibus adequari. Si regum fulgori compares et principum diatemati, longe erit inferius, quam si plumbi metallum ad auri fulgorem compares' . . .

XIV

Divine dispensationis providentia G. duci Normannorum et regi Anglorum A. sancte Lucensis ecclesie indignus episcopus eterne felicitatis beatitudinem.

Quanta virtutis potentia et felicitatis gloria invictissima Dei dextera te sublimaverit et quanto laudis preconio per diversas usquequaque gentes extulerit, non solum occidentis partes, in quo hec gesta sunt, testes existunt, verum etiam alie mundi regiones remotissime iam ex longo tempore plena attestatione cognoscunt. Fortia etenim facta et magnarum rerum gesta excellentia, non ex te, sed divinitus tibi collata, per multarum terrarum intervalla diffusa, ora hominum quieta esse non patiuntur.

Et ideo tota vice et obnixis viribus recurrendum est tibi ad creatorem tuum, qui tibi dedit et in hostilibus preliis multotiens triumphare et regni gubernacula in pacis iam tranquillitate possidere. Quamvis enim per te, non tamen ex te gesta sunt ista, sed illius imperio, cuius est terra et plenitudo eius, qui mutat gentes et regna et rerum naturas, in quas voluerit transferre conditiones. Tu namque malleus, quo contrite sunt gentes, tu securis, qua cesi sunt populi, divina manu teneris et regeris et, quocumque Dei sapientia et fortitudo voluerit, versaris et percutis. Sed quibus astringeris manibus, istiusmodi moderationis deputata est alternatio. Testificatur hoc per prophete labia spiritus Dei dicens: *Numquid elevabitur securis contra tenentem se aut gloriabitur serra contra eum, a quo trahitur?* Sic Cyro regi Persarum, antequam natus esset, per eximium prophetarum Deus promiserat, quod *subiceret ante eum gentes et dorsa regum verteret, portas ereas contereret et vectes ferreos confringeret, et daret ei thesauros absconditos et archana secretorum* revelaret, ostendens quod omnia, que rex ipse facturus esset, ipse per regem perficeret, quoniam ea prius et per prophetam predixisset et postea pleniter peregisset. Nabuchodonosor etiam Chaldeorum regem ad destructionem Hierusalem properantem Dominus servum suum profitetur in hac eadem causa sibi servientem, quod et terram in solitudinem redigat et populum Iudeorum per LXX annorum spatia iugo durissime opprimat servitutis. Cognoscat ergo cordis tui preclara prudentia, quod omnia illa magnifica et excelsa, que per te acta sunt, divina virtus effecit, cui semper gratie sunt agende, cui laudes incessanter habende, cui iugiter corde et ore dicendum: *Omnia opera nostra, Domine, operatus es in nobis.*

Hoc ergo moneo, hoc suadeo, rex illustrissime, ne in aliquo operum tuorum de te umquam presumere velis nec cor tuum elevetur fiduciam habens in propriis viribus, sed omnem spem et gloriam tuam ad eum transferas, qui tibi et victoriam de celo ministravit et gentium multitudine decoravit et divitiarum opulentia sublimavit. Ecclesias, quas in tua ditione concessit divina potestas, variis exorna muneribus, sacerdotes earum et clerum decenter honorifica, viduarum et pauperum memor esto, iustitie rigorem cum misericordie tranquillitate subditis exhibe. Humilitatis mansuetudinem, misericordie decora retine, omnibus modis, quibus vales, Deo adhere, quatinus de hac transitoria et inani gloria ad illam pervenias, que est sine fine continua.

Ego autem memor beneficiorum, que in me tua benivolentia contulit, omni conamine secundum Deum servitium meum tue dignitati impendere, si preceperis, non gravabor.

Omnipotens Deus, qui te in hoc seculo, supra quam sperari potuit, exaltavit, ad eterne claritatis gloriam te provehere et secum semper guadere sempiterna felicitate concedat.

Non sine causa gladium portas, Dei enim minister es ad vindictam malorum, ad laudem vero bonorum. Dispensationem itaque tibi a Deo creditam in exhibendo cognosce et ad gloriam et laudem eius ministerium tuum imple. Ipse siquidem in plene felicitatis gloria auxilio tuo non indiget, sed quoniam in terra ista miserie in membris suis multa opprobria et irrisiones sustinet, in adiutorium sponse eius, que constuprata est usque ad verticem, vir potentissime, accingere. Fides autem Petri, quia pro ea Christus rogavit, numquam deficiet, que in Romana ecclesia inconvulsa permanet usque in finem. Ad quam quasi ad caput et matrem tuam te oportet venire, ut illam, quantum in te est, de manu alienorum festines eruere. In te enim singulariter confidit, quia pre ceteris principibus maiorem iam fiduciam ex multis tuis impendiis et probitate morum in te haurit. Sed sapienti pauca: tibi itaque nunc ista sufficiunt, et propter periculosa tempora, que nunc imminent, in exequendis, que ad partes nostras litteris mandasti et que rescripta sunt tibi, viriliter age, caute prudenterque sollicitudinem tuam impende. Hec ego propria manu scripsi et committo tibi soli. Potentiam tuam incolumem Dominus ad exaltationem ecclesie sue conservet.

THE NORMAN CATHEDRAL AT LINCOLN

Dorothy Owen

Peter of Blois, in expounding a difficult law-suit to the Pope, remarked on the confusion of customs in English cathedral churches: some have a dean, he says, some not, some a treasurer, some not, in some the cantor is a minor canon, in others the treasurer is one of the greater canons. In fact, one cannot generalise about what one will find there.[1] My theme today is an attempt to discover what happened when one such a cathedral church was founded, and how the circumstances of the foundation affected the particular organisation which evolved there.

A good deal of time and thought has gone in the last thirty years to the consideration of the rôle assumed by the cathedrals in the Anglo-Norman church and of the purposes served by such institutions within the dioceses, and in the two national churches. Professor Douglas, and more recently, Dr Bates, have demonstrated the importance of the new or re-founded cathedral chapters in the ecclesiastical revival (reformation is not, perhaps, too strong a word) in Normandy.[2] Professor Barlow has looked rather sceptically at the place of the new or revived chapters in the post-Conquest church in England,[3] and Miss Edwards surveyed thirty years ago, in a magisterial work, the origins of the English secular cathedrals.[4] Such general surveys have been based on, or followed by, important archaeological and architectural studies of individual minsters and cathedral churches, which allow us to see that in late Anglo-Saxon England cathedrals were scarcely to be distinguished, except as the place where the Bishop kept his chair and consecrated the holy oils, from a range of imposing hundredal minsters served in some cases by groups of priests, and exercising some degree of primacy over the churches and inhabitants of a wide area.[5] A good example of the latter type was Aylesbury in Buckinghamshire, where, according to Domesday, the freemen of eight hundreds in its circuit paid each a load of corn to it for every hide of land they held.[6]

Some of these minsters were already the property of the diocesan by 1066: one thinks of Beverley, Ripon, and Southwell in the diocese of York in this context. It seems certain, nevertheless, that after the Conquest churchmen regarded the bishops' own churches, where their chairs were placed, and perhaps even the bishops themselves, with greater respect than had been usual in Anglo-Saxon England. Christopher Brooke has looked at some aspects of this changed scene in an early study of the

[1] *Patrologia Latina*, ed. J. P. Migne, xxvii, 497.
[2] D. C. Douglas, 'The Norman Episcopate before the Conquest', *Cambridge Historical Journal* xiii, 1957, 101-15; D. Bates, *Normandy before 1066*, London 1982, especially 189-235; L. Musset, 'Recherche sur les communautés de clercs séculiers en Normandie au xie siècle', *Bulletin de la société des Antiquaires de Normandie* lv, 1959-60, 5-38.
[3] F. Barlow, *The English Church 1066-1154*, London 1979, 234-61.
[4] K. Edwards, *The English Secular Cathedrals in the Middle Ages*, Manchester 1949.
[5] F. Barlow, *Durham Jurisdictional Peculiars*, Oxford 1950, ix, xv.
[6] DB f.143v.

chapter of St Paul's, and in several shorter papers,[7] and Kathleen Edwards examined the origins of the new foundation at Old Sarum, in a memorable contribution to the *Victoria History of Wiltshire*.[8] More recently, in his essay in the recently published *History of York Minster*, Professor Brooke discussed afresh the origins of the new Anglo-Norman secular chapters and has suggested that a common purpose animated St Osmond of Salisbury, Remigius of Lincoln and Thomas of York in the arrangements they made for the service of their new cathedrals.[9]

I want here to look at the Lincoln evidence and, if I can, carry discussion further. Were the post-Conquest Norman bishops in England introducing a 'new model' of the purposes to be served by a cathedral and, if so, what was it? The first evidence for the establishment of a cathedral at Lincoln is in the royal charter of about 1072 in which the King commanded Bishop Remigius, after consultation with the Pope and his legates, presumably, as the editors of *Councils and Synods I* have suggested, at the legatine council of 1070, to remove his chair from Dorchester to Lincoln.[10] The King gave Remigius an area of toll-free land in the city, and here by 1086 the bishop was established: *sancta Maria de Lincolnia in qua nunc est episcopatus*.[11]

Henry of Huntingdon, writing in the first half of the twelfth century, described his own schooling in Lincoln, late in the previous century, when a new church dedicated to the Blessed Virgin had already appeared at the top of the hill, next to the castle, *in mercatis ipsis praediis*, which seems to imply an area of trading, though not, perhaps, a localised and identifiable market.[12] There is every reason to suppose that when the castle was first established, a market grew up at its eastern gate, and that here, subsequently, the cathedral was built, but the phrase is tantalisingly vague.

Orderic, writing not much later than Henry, says little about the foundation of the cathedral, and the Anglo-Saxon chronicle is equally silent, although Orderic reports the castle building of 1067 and 1068 at Lincoln, Huntingdon and Cambridge.[13] Thirty years after the event William of Malmesbury plausibly suggested that Remigius himself chose to go to Lincoln because of its prosperity and its large trading population.[14] None of these writers has anything to say about the actual events of the cathedral foundation, although Henry describes the early chapter. It is clear, however, that someone wrote an account of it, for the chapter library included a copy of a *liber fundationis* in 1160.[15] There, it seems, Giraldus Cambrensis used it, or something very like it, together with the chapter's archives, to compile a *Vita sancti Remigii*, which seems to be the first stage of a canonisation process which was later abandoned.[16] He makes the interesting comment that Remigius built his cathedral

---

7 C. N. L. Brooke, 'The Composition of the Chapter of St Paul's', *Cambridge Hist. Journ.* x, 1951, 111-13; 'Gregorian Reform in Action', *Medieval Church and Society*, London 1971; 'Continental Influences on English Cathedral Chapters in the Eleventh and Twelfth Centuries', *xie congrès des Sciences Historiques, Stockholm, 1960, Résumé des Communications*, 120-1.

8 K. Edwards, 'The cathedral of Salisbury', VCH *Wiltshire* iii, 1956, 156-209.

9 G. E. Aylmer and R. Cant, *History of York Minster*, Oxford 1977, 25 and note 73.

10 C. W. Foster and K. Major, *Registrum Antiquissimum of the Cathedral Church of Lincoln*, Lincoln Record Society, vols i-x, 1931-73, i, no. 2 (pp. 2-3); D. Whitelock, M. Brett and C. N. L. Brooke, *Councils and Synods I*, Oxford 1981, 566 and note.

11 C. W. Foster and T. E. Longley, *The Lincolnshire Domesday*, Lincoln Record Society, xix, 1924, 4 (DB f. 336b).

12 Huntingdon, 212.

13 Orderic, ii, 219.

14 *De Gestis Pontificum*, 312.

15 The library list is printed by J. F. Dimock, *Giraldi Cambrensis Opera* vii, RS 1877, 165-71.

16 Dimock, vii, pp. xxii, xxvi.

in a place highly suitable for a great church, and moreover, on the north bank of the River Witham, so as to defy the claims of the Archbishops of York that Lindsey belonged to their diocese and province.

Drawing on Giraldus' work, a copy of which he had given to the chapter library, and also on the known traditions of the place, Bishop Sutton's registrar, John of Schalby, who had spent his whole life in the service of the cathedral and diocese, set down, over two hundred years after the event, an account of the foundation which for the first time describes the site on which the cathedral was built.[17] It was founded, he says, where the church of St Mary Magdalen in the Bail of Lincoln had previously stood. The parishioners of that church were served at an altar of the same dedication, in the cathedral nave, by a priest provided by the cathedral, until Bishop Sutton gave them a separate church at the west gates of the minster enclosure (the 'Exchequer Gate'), and assigned a parish to it.

I shall return to Schalby's story later, but in the meantime it becomes necessary to consider the background for the cathedral move. The large diocese of Dorchester/ Leicester/Lindsey, to which Remigius was called almost immediately after William I's coronation, had existed in that form only since 1004, and its disparate make-up was clearly reflected in the words of the revised profession which Remigius made to Lanfranc after the removal of Stigand, to whom he had originally professed obedience:

> Ego Remigius Dorcacensis et Legovacensis et Lincoline provincie et ceterarum
> provinciarum quibus antecessores mei prefuerunt.[18]

The original diocese of Lindsey seems to have been co-terminous with the kingdom and the former administrative county of the same name: north of Witham, east of Trent. The site of its cathedral is still uncertain,[19] but there is no doubt of the existence within the area of several other important religious establishments. In 1066 there were large churches associated with such royal estates as Louth, Caistor, Horncastle and Kirton Lindsey, each apparently a hundredal minster. At Stow Earl Leofric in 1061 re-endowed a large and important church which had plainly existed before as the minster of a large and important estate in which the Bishop had a considerable financial interest.[20]

In Lincoln itself the Bishop's holdings at Domesday included two churches, presumably those of St Martin and St Laurence which William I had given him, and a little manor 'near the city' which seems to be that of Willingthorpe to the north-west of the castle. In addition, as part of the endowment of St Mary (that is, of the cathedral) he had thirty messuages which in 1066 had been held by Tochi son of Uti, and a carucate of land in the fields.[21]

---

[17] Dimock, vii, 193-216 (appendix E). A translation by J. H. Srawley appeared as Lincoln Minster pamphlet 2, in 1949.

[18] *Councils and Synods*, 573.

[19] For a recent suggestion that the cathedral of the bishops of Lindsey was at Louth, see A. E. B. Owen, 'Herefrith of Louth', *Lincolnshire History and Archaeology*, 15, 1980. It should be pointed out that the church of St Martin, with which is associated the issue in the early tenth century of St Martin's pennies, may have been, for a time at least, an episcopal church of some importance, if not the cathedral of the bishops of Lindsey. Recent work by Mr David Stocker, who has discussed the matter with me, and to whom I am very obliged, suggests that the parishes of the western side of the lower town seem to have been formed from the large area originally attached to St Martin; this church would seem in the light of this to have been the first church in that area, and possibly an episcopal foundation.

[20] H. E. Salter, *Cartulary of Eynsham*, Oxford Historical Society, xlix and li, 1906-7, 1908, i, 28-30.

[21] Foster and Longley, 3 (DB f.336a).

In South Lincolnshire, which had been outside the kingdom and diocese of Lindsey, there were several large and important churches. By 1086 the hundredal church of St Wulfran of Grantham already belonged to Salisbury, and Sleaford had been granted to Remigius, who also held parish churches on the manors of Dunsby and Bitchfield.[22] It is difficult to believe that the great church of Hough on the Hill, close by the hundred meeting place of Loveden Hill had not also been a hundredal minster and there may have been others. In Holland, by contrast, the leading ecclesiastical establishment was undoubtedly St Guthlac of Crowland.

The shire town of Leicester must once have had a cathedral and an episcopal palace and these were presumably represented at Domesday by the two churches and various houses said to have been held by Wulfwig in 1066.[23] So far as the diocese of Dorchester itself is concerned there were in it in 1066 many churches of size and importance which suggest an episcopal framework of some size, even though none is an obvious candidate for a head minster or episcopal church.[24] In Buckinghamshire, for example, there was the two-hundredal church of Aylesbury, which has already been mentioned, and the town chapel of the shire town of Buckingham, both of which had belonged to Bishop Wulfwig.[25] In Northamptonshire Dr Franklin has identified several hundredal churches, but the proximity of Peterborough abbey may explain why none is clearly an episcopal church.[26] Dorchester, apparently served by secular canons, was the cathedral of the diocese and there was a sizeable monastic foundation at Eynsham, while in the shire town of Bedford the Bishop owned the church of St Mary. There were, in addition, a minster, served by secular canons, which was soon to be diverted to a monastic foundation at Newnham, and a hundredal church on the royal manor of Leighton Buzzard which the Bishop already held.[27] By contrast, in Huntingdon, Ely, Cambridgeshire and North Hertfordshire there were no obvious episcopal churches and the scene was dominated by the great monastic houses of Ramsey, Ely, Thorney and St Albans.

This is a hasty survey, in a field which deserves fuller investigation, and its purpose is no more than to suggest the difficulties which faced Remigius at the outset: the extent of the diocese, the competing jurisdictions within it, his own relatively limited endowments. How could a diocesan administration with a cathedral in its south-western corner, two hundred miles from its northern boundaries, have functioned at all? It seems clear that Wulfwig had delegated to the few churches he owned, or to the great monastic establishments, the arrangements for distributing chrism, and collecting the dues for it. Elsewhere he plainly relied on the monastic presence for a variety of functions. The monastic sacrist of Ely, for example, had always performed a number of episcopal duties within the Isle of Ely, as he continued to do when the diocese of Ely was formed,[28] and it seems probable that Eynsham, Peterborough, Crowland, Thorney, and even more St Albans, did the same within their own spheres. Wulfwig had in fact, from sheer necessity, devised a rudimentary archidiaconal system operated through the monastic houses: it was left to his successor

---

[22] Foster and Longley, 46-7 (DB ff. 343d, 344c).
[23] DB f. 230v.
[24] DB f. 155.
[25] DB f. 143a.
[26] M. J. Franklin, 'Ministers and Parishes: Northamptonshire Studies', unpublished Ph.D. dissertation, Cambridge, 1982.
[27] DB f. 209a.
[28] C. L. Feltoe and E. H. M. Minns, *Vetus Liber Archidiaconi Eliensis*, Cambridge Antiquarian Society, 1917, xxii-xxiii.

to arrange the archidiaconal framework which provided a more efficient solution to the problem.

Remigius and the King must have appreciated the difficulties presented by the inchoate diocese from the first and William seems to have acted very quickly to build up the episcopal forces. Along with his pastoral staff Remigius received the important royal manor of Wooburn in Buckinghamshire and quite soon after the King gave him the house and properties of Eynsham, the rich church of Sutton in Northamptonshire and a house on the castle site at Huntingdon.[29] In Huntingdonshire his position was further strengthened by Earl Waltheof's gift of the manor and church of Leighton Bromswold.[30] It was however in the county of Lincoln, presumably after the change of cathedral site was decided on, that the most substantial additions were made to the episcopal estate. The large manor of Welton by Lincoln seems to have been the principal secular gift but this was accompanied by important churches which were intended no doubt to facilitate episcopal control in the city and the county. In this way the royal churches of Caistor and Sleaford and the city churches of St Martin and St Laurence were added to the episcopal holdings by the King, and would, in due course, be given to the cathedral.[31]

The first four or five years after 1066 presented a series of threats to the stability of the new Norman régime and it seems certain that William rightly anticipated as the most dangerous of these a Viking attack on the eastern half of the country, a repetition as it were, of the attempt foiled by Harold at Stamford Bridge. This seems to explain the construction in 1067-68 of large and important castles on the strategic route from London to the north, at Huntingdon, Cambridge and Lincoln. The establishment of the castles in these places was followed so soon by a fresh Viking threat to Yorkshire, and by the Atheling's determined attempt to land in North Lincolnshire, that the safety of the new castles themselves, and even more of their lines of communication, was at risk, and it was necessary to have at hand a powerful and resolute supporter of the Norman régime. This, it seems, was the role for which Remigius was cast by the King; the need for such a presence goes a long way to account for the move of the cathedral from Dorchester to Lincoln.

Most authorities on the period seem to be agreed that Remigius was an enthusiastic and forceful character on whose assistance the King must have felt that he could rely. No other assumption could explain the large share of castle guard at Lincoln with which he was entrusted for the bishopric, and the assignment to him of 'a dwelling near the castle' and in its Bail.[32] The strategic significance of Lincoln in the defence of the kingdom against the Vikings, and its relative ease of communications for this purpose, and for the control of the important area included in the diocese, must have been jointly responsible for the decision at which the King and the Bishop arrived, to transfer the cathedral to it.

The town was sited at the junction of the Fossway, which led to Leicester and beyond into the borders of Oxfordshire, with Ermine Street running north from London to the Humber through the eastern half of the midland shires, and providing easy access to Northampton, Huntingdon, Cambridge, Bedford and the northern half of Hertfordshire. It housed a wealthy and important trading community worthy

[29] DB ff.144, 203; *Registrum Antiquissimum* i, no. 2.
[30] *Registrum Antiquissimum* i, no. 2.
[31] *Registrum Antiquissimum* i, no. 2.
[32] J. W. F. Hill, 'Lincoln Castle, Constables and Castle Guard', *Assoc. Arch. and Arch. Soc.* lx, 1932-3; the bishop owed 45 knights at Lincoln.

of a cathedral city; it had easy water communication via the Witham with the east coast and the continent and, all things considered, Remigius could have chosen no more suitable site for his new foundation.

There was probably another reason for the choice, more closely related to ecclesiastical politics and the integrity of the diocese. Since the early eleventh century and the addition of Lindsey to the Leicester/Dorchester bishopric the archbishops of York had been claiming that the area really belonged, as did Nottinghamshire, to the diocese and province of York. It was inevitable that the bishops of Dorchester should have resisted this claim, and as recently as 1061 Pope Nicholas II had pronounced in Dorchester's favour for its right to:

> the *parochia* of Lindsey and its appendages in Newark and Stow, which Ailric the archbishop of York had improperly invaded.

Archbishop Thomas revived the claim after 1070 and although it was rebutted in 1072, as Hugh the Chanter reported, it was not finally withdrawn until Remigius' successor, Robert Bloet, succeeded in persuading (*bribing* according to York sources) William II to pronounce decisively in his favour.[33] There were other threats to the diocesan authority in the south and east, where the abbots of Ely and the monks of St Albans were claiming a large measure of independence, and it was no doubt to counter such claims, and the York attack, that Remigius decided to establish himself firmly at Lincoln to ensure possession of the northern part of his diocese. Giraldus was perhaps echoing common knowledge when he reported that Remigius deliberately built his cathedral in Lindsey, north of the Witham.

We already know a good deal from the writings of Sir Francis Hill and the work of the archaeologists who have been busy there in recent years, about the town of Lincoln.[34] It is situated on a crossing of the river Witham where the limestone ridge (cliff, or edge), along which Ermine Street runs due north through the county, was breached by the river and its flood plain which to the west of the town spread out into a wide area of pool and marsh. The Roman roads were carried over this flood plain on a causeway street along which the Romans and their successors had built an extensive and populous suburb, housing many merchants, which in 1066 was known as Wigford.

The upper town, on the hill to the north of the Witham crossing, was enclosed by its Roman walls, the north, south and east gates of which were still visible, and in use. A further area of the town, enclosed by later but still Roman walls, lay on the slope of the hill and terminated just above the flood plain where the Stone Bow still crosses the High Street.

It was in the south-west corner of the upper town, overlooking the flood plains not only of the Witham but also of the Trent which ran only a few miles to the west, and commanding the main route via Fossway from the south-west, that William I established his castle, to build which he seems to have demolished a large number of houses. The bailey of the castle covered the whole walled area of the upper town and it was within this bailey (The Bail of Lincoln), on a flat site in the south-east corner of the upper city and butting against the eastern walls, that the new cathedral was established on the land given, or assigned, by William I. The intention to found

---

[33] *Registrum Antiquissimum* i, nos. 4, 247; Hugh the Chanter, trans. C. Johnson, *History of the Church of York, 1066-1127*, Nelson Med. Texts, 1961, 8.
[34] M. Jones, B. Gilmour and K. Camidge, 'Lincoln', *Current Archaeology* 83, August 1982, 366-71.

a cathedral at the gates of the castle, and in close conjunction with it, seems to have been quite clear. The site, as we have seen, lay within the bailey not more than two hundred yards from the castle gate and facing it across a small open square. The resemblance with the cathedral site at Old Sarum is very marked, and parallels could be found all over western Europe.

The ecclesiastical map of the upper town of Lincoln before the cathedral appeared there is by no means easy to draw, and not all the problems it presents can be resolved in the current state of knowledge.[35] There is no doubt of the existence, in the north-west half of the enclosure, of the parish of St Paul on a site close to the forum of the Roman city which had evidently been occupied by a sequence of ecclesiastical buildings from the fifth century. By the time its parochial area can be ascertained it seems to have been bounded by the central street of the town. North and east of St Paul, and close to the north gate, lay St Clement, but nothing remains to indicate which church served the inhabitants of the houses destroyed to make the castle, unless it is that of All Saints, which lay north of the street now called Eastgate and which has not existed since the early fourteenth century. Two churches lay outside the eastern wall of the city but close enough to it to serve some of its inhabitants, St Margaret, and Holy Trinity in Pottergate, and there were others just below the southern ditch.

Sir Francis Hill suggested that the site of the cathedral itself had been occupied by an old minster dedicated to St Mary,[36] and others have assumed on this basis that this must have been the episcopal church of the bishops of Lindsey. The case for there having been a church of importance on the site was strengthened by the reported finding there of 'pre-conquest stones' and by a papal privilege of 1163 enforcing the ancient right of St Mary of Lincoln to a levy of 'thraves': *quod in Lincolnsira parochiani eiusdem scire ab antiquo concesserunt* – and which was known as 'Marycorn'. Such a levy, Sir Frank Stenton pointed out, was the usual mark of an old minster. The 'pre-conquest stones' were two tomb slabs reported and illustrated in 1926 by Canon D. S. Davies. These have been recently examined by Mr David Stocker in the course of a survey of Anglo-Saxon sculptured stones in the area. He reports that the time and place of their finding is uncertain, although they are now in the cloister, that he is unable to date them more precisely than to the mid eleventh century, and that they do not in themselves constitute evidence of any large earlier church on the cathedral site, even if they were found on it.[37] The Marycorn evidence is more difficult to evaluate. If it were levied before the Conquest from Lindsey alone it might indeed constitute proof that we have in St Mary an ancient episcopal church, a 'head minster' for the independent diocese of Lindsey. The claim of 1163 is, however, for the payment of the due from the whole of Lincolnshire, from Kesteven and Holland as well as Lindsey, and there is no clear evidence that these areas can have been regarded as belonging to the original diocese of Lindsey.[38]

---

[35] I have discussed this paragraph with Miss Kathleen Major, with Michael Jones and David Stocker of the Lincoln Archaeological Research Committee, and with my husband, to all of whom, and to those who commented on the paper at Battle, I am very grateful. They are in no way responsible for the conclusions I have reached.
[36] J. W. F. Hill, *Medieval Lincoln*, Cambridge 1948, 64-81. I myself accepted this theory in *Church and Society in Medieval Lincolnshire*, 1971, 37.
[37] D. S. Davies, 'Pre-conquest carved stones in Lincolnshire', *Arch. Journ.* lxxxiii, 1926, 1-20. I am very grateful to Mr Stocker for discussing this matter and allowing me to quote his views.
[38] *Registrum Antiquissimum* i, no. 255.

Negative evidence is rarely satisfactory, and the absence of pre-Conquest documentation for the county makes it particularly unconvincing, yet a post-Conquest mention of the payment of Marycorn might have been expected to turn up in some source, if it existed, and so far nothing has been noted. The 1163 privilege is not easy to explain in the absence of other evidence. Can it have been an attempt by a Dean who was familiar with the payment of thraves elsewhere, in Yorkshire for example, to find a similar source of income for Lincoln? Alternatively, can it be based on the survival of a folk memory of a levy exacted in the years just before 1066 by a church dedicated to St Mary?[39]

It seems inherently improbable that such a church could have been an episcopal possession. Nothing in the Domesday survey suggests that the second component in the diocese of Dorchester, that is Leicester, had retained a 'Head minster' with episcopal privileges. Why, therefore, should Lindsey have kept one? Moreover, if there were a surviving episcopal church in Lincoln, it might have been expected to figure in the papal privilege of 1061 by which the claims of Dorchester to the diocese of Lindsey, with its appurtenances in Newark and Stow, were confirmed.[40] Besides, if there had been an episcopal minster in the upper town at Lincoln one might have expected traces of its pre-Conquest endowments to be found in Domesday. There is only one entry which may be crucial, in the account of the twelve carucates which lay in the fields of Lincoln: 'residuum dimidiam carucatam terre habuit et habet sancta Maria de Lincolnia in qua nunc est episcopatus'. The words *habuit et habet* certainly suggest that St Mary existed in 1066, but there is no trace of other endowments held by the church at this point. The half carucate indeed compares rather poorly with the whole carucate and twelve tofts of All Saints in the Bail. Outside the town there is no other Domesday evidence of lands held by St Mary in 1066. The manor of Welton, which in 1086 was in the Bishop's possession and held by six canons, was not apparently Bishop Wulfwig's in 1066, when it was in the holding of Sven who was seemingly a layman; there is no mention of St Mary in connection with it.[41] Can it be, in fact, that there was, somewhere on the cathedral site, a parish church of St Mary, no larger, and less well-endowed, than others in the upper town?

There are no other clues as to what stood on the cathedral site in addition to this church, if it existed. It is true that seventy-four houses outside the castle walls were reported as wasted since the Conquest in addition to those on the castle site and some at least of these may have been in the south-east corner of the upper city. As to Schalby's story of St Mary Magdalen, a church of this dedication might well have been destroyed, along with the houses of its parish, at the building of the castle. This would account for the revival of the dedication in a nave altar in the cathedral, especially as the parish assigned to the church, when it was given a separate existence, included the castle, while the existence of a church dedicated to St Mary the Virgin, to be completely obliterated by the cathedral, explains Schalby's confusion of it with St Mary Magdalen.

It is not clear why Remigius was slow in completing the building of his cathedral, which was ready for consecration only just as he died in 1091, and I do not propose to discuss here the form or extent of the building, which will be thoroughly examined by Dr Peter Kidson in the History of Lincoln Minster which will be published fairly

---

[39] The incidence of thraves in Beverley is discussed by A. F. Leach, *Memorials of Beverley Minster* i, Surtees Soc. 98, 1898, xcviii-cv.
[40] *Registrum Antiquissimum* i, no. 247.
[41] Foster and Longley, 48 (DB f. 344a).

soon, and of which the present essay is a by-product. The chapter itself was clearly in existence by 1086 and presumably occupying old or temporary buildings on the site. There is nothing to suggest, as Christopher Brooke has hinted, that until the very eve of the consecration Remigius was toying with the idea of a monastic chapter.[42] On the contrary, six canons drew their living from Welton by 1086 and it seems certain that a full chapter was already sketched. The members of this new establishment were evidently seen from the start as an episcopal staff, who were to be the Bishop's assistants in the administration of an unwieldy diocese. The urgent need for such a staff (eight archdeacons) and the undoubted example of the Norman Church, where new or re-founded cathedral chapters were used as centres of diocesan administration, evidently inspired Remigius. Dr Diana Greenway's investigation of the first two centuries of the chapter's existence has demonstrated that before Remigius' death seven archdeacons, and perhaps also the eighth, had begun work in the diocese together with a dean, precentor, treasurer and possibly a *magister scolarum* and/or chancellor.[43] I do not propose at this point to discuss further where in Normandy this plan originated. Henry of Huntingdon said explicitly that before Remigius' death twenty-one canons had been named and had received prebends, although their identification, and even more that of their prebendal estates, is virtually impossible. It is clear from Domesday, as we have seen, that the manor of Welton was already held by six canons, but whether they had divided it, or held in common, is not certain. The Domesday entries, and the foundation charters, also indicate that the Bishop held the churches of Sleaford, Louth, Kirton Lindsey, Caistor and Wellingore, St Martin and St Laurence in Lincoln, Bedford St Mary, Leighton Buzzard, Buckingham and Aylesbury, and the manors of Leighton Bromswold and Wooburn, which were soon to form the endowment of St Mary of Lincoln. The assignment of these to separate prebends, along with the acquisition of other properties and the building up of an entirely separate endowment for the Deanery mostly from royal estates in the midlands, went on until the mid twelfth century, and is clearly traceable in *Registrum Antiquissimum*.

Meanwhile it seems possible that as late as 1160 a form of common life was practised by the chapter. About that year Dean Adelm confirmed to the chapter land he had bought on the south side of the church *ad faciendas domos ad opus commune*. The heading of this entry in *Registrum Antiquissimum* is *de bederna canonicorum* and this seems significant, for *bederna* is the term used at Beverley Minster and elsewhere to describe the common establishment in which the canons ate and lived. It seems likely that this charter hints at a similar institution in Lincoln, especially when it is remembered that about the same time Bishop Robert Chesney gave to the canons an annual pension of one hundred shillings, to be spent on bread and ale.[44] It seems probable that a common hall or building of some sort survived, for as late as 1180 x 1184 Samson canon of Lincoln gave to the dean and chapter in case they wished to make a cloister, a plot which lay between his own *curia* and the gate of the Bedern.[45] It is not clear where the building of Samson's time lay, nor

---

[42] In *York Minster History*, 25 and note 93.
[43] D. E. Greenway, *J. Le Neve, Fasti Ecclesie Anglicane 1066-1300, Lincoln*, 1977, ix and appendix ii, 51-64.
[44] *Registrum Antiquissimum* ii, no. 366; D. M. Smith, *English Episcopal Acta: Lincoln 1067-1185*, British Academy, 1980, no. 158.
[45] *Registrum Antiquissimum* ix, no. 2603; Leach, *Beverley*, p.cv.

whether the cloister as we know it was made on this site, but common living there was in the mid twelfth century.

Miss Major has demonstrated that in the early stages of the cathedral's existence no residence houses were owned by the church; individual dignitaries, like the earlier bishops, made what arrangements they could and until Bishop Alexander acquired the Eastgate of the Bail from the Crown (probably after the disastrous fire of 1125) no precise location is known for an episcopal dwelling.[46] One would like to know where the house of Bishop Bloet was in which, as a member of the household, Henry of Huntingdon was taught by Albinus of Angers. Is it possible that the first dignitaries lived there, with the Bishop, while they were in Lincoln and only gradually, as house sites became available, moved 'out of court'?

Such a suggestion seems to be borne out by what the records imply: that the earliest dignitaries were associates, or even relatives of the bishops.[47] Simon Bloet, son of the Bishop, was for example the second dean. The known names of the earliest members of the chapter indicate that they were Normans, and it is possible to understand how easily dynasties could be created within the chapter, as for example in the two archdeaconries of Huntingdon and Stow. Even after such arrangements had ended it is certain that bishops and dignitaries continued to nominate relatives and friends to vacant places. It is equally clear, as Dr Brett has remarked, that royal influence was also exerted quite frequently in cathedral appointments; the prebend of Corringham was endowed by Henry I for Brand the priest who held the church, and for his son Brand who was to succeed him.[48] It may well be that the same King's augmentation of Aylesbury with his own royal manor of Sutton in Northamptonshire formed part of a similar move to control an important prebend which was soon to provide an endowment for the archdeaconry of Buckingham.

The rôle of the cathedral chapter in the diocese, and its association with the eight *provincie* or archdeaconries is not easy to distinguish before the late twelfth century, when a deliberate attempt to involve the archdeaconries in the rebuilding began, probably at the instigation of St Hugh himself. Before this date some at least of the archdeacons, and notably David, fifth archdeacon of Buckingham and brother of Bishop Alexander (1142 x 1176), played a considerable part in the endowment of monasteries in south Lincolnshire, and as witnesses in the episcopal court.[49] Other archdeacons show little sign that they were called on as episcopal representatives in their *provincie* and such devotion to the bishop and the cathedral as can be detected outside Lincolnshire, where the archidiaconal synods were held in the cathedral,[50] is represented by the supply of chrism from Lincoln and even more by the institution of Pentecostal processions, which brought parochial offerings from the diocese to the cathedral. The processions can never have been easy to enforce and it is clear that as early as Bishop Alexander's time the processions and offerings of Hertfordshire, south Bedfordshire and Oxfordshire had been diverted to St Albans and Eynsham.[51] For the rest, by the time we have record, pentecostals (one penny from each hearth alight in the manner of the church scot payable at Martinmas,

---

[46] K. Major, *Minster Yard*, Lincoln Minster Pamphlets, 2nd ser. no. 7, 1974.
[47] Greenway; D. E. Spear, 'The Norman Empire and the Secular Clergy', *Journal of British Studies* xxi, 1981-2, 1-10.
[48] M. Brett, *The English Church under Henry I*, Oxford 1975, 188-9.
[49] D. M. Smith.
[50] BL MS Cotton Vesp. E. xviii, f.82v; Cotton Vesp. E xx, f.197v.
[51] *Registrum Antiquissimum* i, no. 307, ii, nos. 321-2; Eynsham, i app. ii.

according to Edgar's code, to the old minsters) were collected outside Lincolnshire by the archdeacons; Pentecostal processions, a fruitful source of dispute and violence, continued to come to the cathedral only from its immediate neighbourhood.[52]

I have already disclaimed any intention of discussing whether Remigius, in the cathedral establishment which he devised for Lincoln, was deliberately following the practice of Rouen, as Giraldus and John of Schalby had said he did, or whether, as Bradshaw and Wordsworth suggested, the chapter more closely resembles that of Bayeux.[53] Kathleen Edwards, following Lewis Loyd, has considered the question thoroughly and no more need be said here. It is otherwise, however, with the liturgical and other customs of the church, which is what I suspect Giraldus and John meant. Passing references by Edmund Bishop in an important paper on Holy Week observances at Hereford were taken up by Christopher Brooke. Both have declared that Lincoln, like Hereford, drew its special Holy Week observances from the treatise of John of Avranches, *De officiis ecclesiasticis*, which was adapted for the use of Rouen by Archbishop Maurilius in the mid eleventh century.[54]

It is possible to test these hypotheses in some measure against our knowledge of the liturgical arrangement of the first cathedral, some information about which can be inferred from the unwritten customs recorded by John of Schalby in the Black Book.[55] We can see for example that there were several altars, the offerings from which had been granted by Remigius to the canons, and that they included the high altar, dedicated presumably to the Blessed Virgin, before which Bishop Bloet was buried, and a rood altar at the entrance to the sanctuary, where Remigius himself was buried. The place of the Bishop's chair is not named, but it seems certain that he had both a stall and a chair in the sanctuary, for holy water was to be carried to him *sive in stallo, sive in sede sua*. Conceivably the chair stood, as it still does at Norwich, behind the high altar.[56] Above and behind the high altar was a beam on which candles were placed on certain feasts; a bronze candelabrum for seven candles was used in the sanctuary on Christmas Eve and for the five succeeding days. The pulpitum was used for the reading of the epistle and gospel. The chief evidence however comes from the officers' customary which Schalby also included in the Black Book, some of the information in which can be tested not only against John of Avranches, but also against a fragmentary Rouen ordinal of a late date which Dom Martène has printed.[57] As Bishop suggested for Hereford, the Palm Sunday procession carrying the *corpus domini* out of the church seems to derive from Rouen, where the Host was carried in solemn procession to the church of St Gildard and on its return:

> cum autem processio ad portam civitatis ornatam venerit sex pueri turrim ascendant ac hos versus festive cantent Gloria laus et honor.

At Lincoln the evidence for the custom appears among the duties of the cathedral carpenters[58] who

52 Owen, *Church and Society*, 42, 107.
53 H. Bradshaw and C. Wordsworth, *Lincoln Cathedral Statutes*, two parts in three volumes, Cambridge 1892, i, 35.
54 E. Bishop, *Liturgica Historica*, Oxford 1918, 276-300; R. Delamare, *Le De Officiis Ecclesiasticis de Jean d'Avranches*, Paris 1923.
55 Bradshaw and Wordsworth, i, 365-79.
56 Cf. pp.136 ff above.
57 E. Martène, *De Antiquis Ecclesie Ritibus*, Rouen 1700-1702, iii, 76.
58 Bradshaw and Wordsworth, i, 291-3.

ought on Palm Sunday to prepare the canons' seats everywhere where the procession is made, and hang a cloth at the gate of the Bail or elsewhere when the boys sing *Gloria Laus*.

Still in the manner of Rouen, on Holy Thursday the carpenters are to find water and basins to wash the altars and the feet, and to heat the water. On Ascension Day they hang a cloth at the front of the church where *Non vos relinquam* is sung. They have their duties too in the three festivals succeeding Christmas — St Stephen for the deacons, St John the Evangelist for the priests, and Holy Innocents for the boys of the choir — all of which usages can be paralleled in John of Avranches' treatise and, it seems, at Canterbury where the same rites are said to stem from Lanfranc and Bec. There are no verbal parallels, the Lincoln hints are very slight and there is no surviving ordinal. It is interesting, however, that Gilbert of Sempringham, when in the mid twelfth century he came to devise a rite for the use of his new order, used the same Holy Week observances and other practices which he had experienced in Lincoln, and thus it seems very likely that the rites recorded by Schalby are those known to the early twelfth century cathedral.[59] The whole adds a further stroke in the picture of the new cathedral of the diocese and its popular appeal to the parishioners of the city of Lincoln. By the time of St Hugh's death the city had absorbed the cathedral, which was no longer an alien element in its life but a source of pride, but that is another story.

[59] R. M. Woolley, *The Gilbertine Rite*, Henry Bradshaw Soc., vols 51-2, i, 26-8.

Mural Paintings Westmeston Church.
Western Face of the East Wall of Nave.

Plate 1 Westmeston: nave east wall. Christological scenes and Agnus Dei. Destroyed. From copy by Mrs Heathcote Campion

THE 'LEWES GROUP' OF WALL PAINTINGS IN SUSSEX

David Park

The 'Lewes Group' comprises five related schemes of wall painting, executed within the period c.1080-1120, in the Sussex parish churches of Clayton, Coombes, Hardham, Plumpton and Westmeston.[1] It is possible that either Clayton or Hardham, or both, were owned by the Cluniac Priory at Lewes when the paintings were executed. The name of the group has arisen from the belief that there was a connection between the paintings and Lewes Priory, and it is retained here for convenience, though it will be argued below that even if the connection did exist its significance should not be over-emphasised.[2] Three of the five churches — Clayton, Plumpton, and

I am indebted to Dr J. J. G. Alexander and Dr G. D. S. Henderson, who supervised my research on the Lewes Group at Manchester and Cambridge respectively. I am also grateful to Dr Richard Gem, for providing the Appendix to this paper, and to Mrs Eve Baker, Dr Timothy Hudson, Dr Christopher Norton and Dr E. Clive Rouse for their helpful advice. The present paper is based partly on my M.A. thesis (see n.12), and on my unpublished lecture to the International Symposium on Wall Painting Conservation (Farnham and Oxford 1979). At the request of the editor, illustrations have been kept to a minimum, and therefore confined to the Lewes Group paintings themselves; the location of comparative illustrations is indicated in the footnotes.

[1] Certain other wall paintings have on occasion been considered either definitely or possibly products of the same school: Binsted, Botolphs, Keymer, Maresfield, and Slaugham, in Sussex; Great Bookham and Witley, in Surrey; and Finchampstead, in Berkshire. For all these, see E. W. Tristram, *English Medieval Wall Painting: the Twelfth Century*, Oxford 1944, and references therein. The paintings at Binsted, Witley and Finchampstead are certainly not by Lewes Group artists; thus the window painting at Binsted differs from those of the Lewes Group in being not merely decorative, whilst its (sadly deteriorated) figure of St Margaret is similar in style to the figures on the lead font at Lower Halstow (Kent), for which see G. Zarnecki, *English Romanesque Lead Sculpture*, London 1957, figs 40, 43-4 (I owe this comparison to Mr Neil Stratford). The Witley paintings, dating probably from the first third of the twelfth century, show important stylistic and iconographical differences to the Lewes Group; see D. Park, 'The Romanesque Wall Paintings of All Saints' Church, Witley', *Surrey Archaeological Collections* lxxiv, 1982, 157-67. It is most unlikely that the painting at Great Bookham is by Lewes Group artists; whilst none of the confused remains on the nave east wall at Botolphs appears to be in a Lewes Group style. The destroyed painting at Slaugham included diaper ornament, like some of the Lewes Group work, but it seems very improbable that it belonged to the Group; and, in the case of the destroyed paintings at Maresfield, there is insufficient evidence to determine whether any might have been by Lewes Group artists. Some of the painting discovered and destroyed in the nineteenth century at Keymer, near Clayton, may have been by artists of the Group, but no firm decision can be reached on the basis of the short and confused account published at the time: C. H. Campion, 'Mural Paintings, Keymer Church', *Sussex Archaeological Collections* (hereafter *SAC*) xvii, 1865, 249-50. At Angmering (West Sussex), small fragments of painted plaster have been excavated, the colours similar to those of the Lewes Group paintings; see O. Bedwin, 'The Excavation of the Church of St Nicholas, Angmering, 1974', *SAC* cxiii, 1976, 31. For fragments of painted decoration at Lewes Priory, see below, n.128.

[2] The connection with Lewes Priory is first proposed in the writings of P. M. Johnston, who uses the term 'Lewes Group' in his 'Mural Paintings in Sussex Churches', *Memorials of Old Sussex*, ed. P. D. Mundy, London 1909, 246. For a discussion of the possible link with the Priory, see below, pp.229-33.

Westmeston – lie at the foot of the South Downs, near Lewes. Coombes is in the Adur Valley, near Bramber, while Hardham is some distance away from the other churches, on Stane Street, a mile to the south of Pulborough. The churches themselves are all fairly primitive and small, consisting of a rectangular nave and chancel, though Clayton may also originally have had low transepts and Coombes a west tower.[3] The walls are of flint or other rubble, pierced by very small single-splayed windows; these have since been replaced or complemented by larger openings, at some damage to the wall paintings. Although the siting of all the churches now seems rather remote – especially Coombes, which is only reached by crossing a field – at the time the paintings were carried out the Sussex Downs and coastal plain were a prosperous and heavily populated area, with considerable arable farming, a thriving salt industry, and an important port at Shoreham.[4] The present high importance of the Lewes Group paintings derives from their exceptionally early date, the comparatively large amount of painting which still survives; and the fact that they *are* a group, rather than just isolated survivals like virtually all other Romanesque wall paintings in England.

Unfortunately, although five Lewes Group schemes are known, one of them has been destroyed completely. The paintings discovered beneath post-Reformation layers at Westmeston in 1862 were almost immediately destroyed, and are now known largely from the poor account and copies published by the Revd Heathcote Campion.[5] On the nave east wall (pl. 1) were the *Agnus Dei* and angels, and four Christological subjects; the Adoration of the Magi and *Traditio Legis*, on the lower part of the wall, having been partly destroyed by the insertion of altar recesses later in the Middle Ages. The subject-matter on the north wall included the Betrayal, and the remains of a subject probably showing St George, which may well have formed part of a cycle of scenes devoted to this saint.[6] At Plumpton, much painting was uncovered in 1867 and subsequently destroyed, and likewise unsatisfactorily published by Campion.[7] On the nave east wall was Last Judgment subject-matter, on the west wall of the chancel the Flight into Egypt, and on the chancel arch itself the *Agnus Dei*. Further painting was uncovered by E. Clive Rouse in 1955-8, on the nave north wall: a representation of Heaven, and the Procession of the Blessed towards it, as part of the nave Last Judgment programme; scrollwork decoration on

---

[3] The chancel has been rebuilt at Coombes, Plumpton and Westmeston, but was probably originally rectangular in each case; a south aisle has also been added to Westmeston, and a west tower to Plumpton. For the architecture of the churches, see below, pp. 227, 229, 236-7.

[4] See H. C. Darby and E. M. J. Campbell (eds), *The Domesday Geography of South-east England*, Cambridge 1962, 444, 456, 474-7, etc. For Shoreham, see F. Aldsworth and D. Freke, *Historic Towns in Sussex, an archaeological survey*, London 1976, 60-1.

[5] C. H. Campion, 'Mural Paintings in Westmeston Church', *SAC* xvi, 1864, 1-19, pls 1-7; E. W. Tristram, *English Medieval Wall Painting: The Twelfth Century*, Oxford 1944, 30, 149-52.

[6] Campion, 'Westmeston', 10-14, pl.6; see below, p.221. On the soffit of the chancel arch were Signs of the Zodiac and, below them, 'in the panel on the south side . . . a demon, with open mouth and large claws, threatening a figure in a shroud' (Campion, 'Westmeston', 3). The description of the 'demon' corresponds closely to the Coombes atlas figure (pl.3); and, since Campion mistook the Betrayal at Westmeston as being a representation of the Adoration of the Magi, it is possible that he also misinterpreted this chancel arch painting. The Coombes figure has white 'clouds' to the left, and it is conceivable that Campion mistook this sort of decoration for 'a figure in a shroud'.

[7] C. H. Campion, 'Mural Paintings in Plumpton Church', *SAC* xx, 1868, 198-202; Tristram, *Twelfth Century*, 31, 142-3.

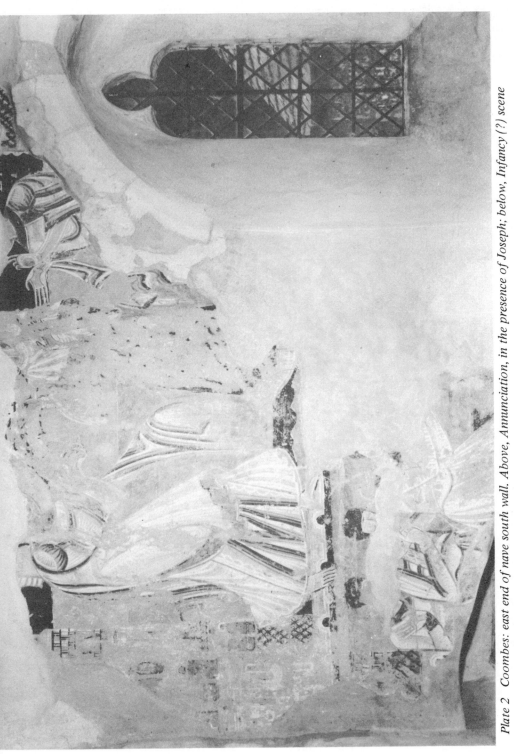

Plate 2 Coombes: east end of nave south wall. Above, Annunciation, in the presence of Joseph; below, Infancy(?) scene

Plate 3 Coombes: *nave east wall (detail).* Traditio Legis, *with Evangelist symbols above, and geometric ornament in dado. Fragments of post-Reformation texts survive over part of the wall*

a window; and the remains of unidentified subject-matter below.[8] At Coombes, all the Lewes Group wall painting now extant, as well as some later painting partly overlying it, was uncovered by Rouse in 1949-52. On the side walls of the nave are the remains of a cycle of scenes of the Infancy of Christ (pl. 2), and, on the north wall, also possibly of a St George cycle. On the east wall, the painting includes a Majesty flanked by the Evangelist Symbols and seraphim, and a *Traditio Legis* to the north of the chancel arch (pl. 3). On the arch itself is a very striking atlas figure (pl. 4), doubtless originally one of a pair, with pelta pattern decorating the soffit above. In the chancel, two key-pattern borders of the same date partly survive above and around the chancel arch.[9] The paintings at Clayton, first uncovered in the 1890s, comprise the remains of a very impressive Last Judgment programme on the east, north and south walls of the nave (pls 5-7). Subsequent treatment of the paintings has included a major programme of cleaning and conservation work in the 1960s under the direction of Mrs Eve Baker.[10] A small fragment of painting of the same scheme was also exposed at this time on the chancel north wall, and it is possible that there is more painting to be revealed here.[11] At Hardham, the painting largely survives in both the nave and chancel, providing the most complete scheme of English Romanesque wall painting now existing. The paintings were first revealed in 1866, and further uncovering and conservation work has included that by P. M. Johnston in 1900, and by Mrs Baker in the 1960s. The scheme comprised originally over forty subjects, most of which survive. There is a very long Christological cycle in the nave and chancel; a St George cycle on the north wall of the nave; Last Judgment and Apocalyptic subject-matter, including Hell scenes covering the entire nave west wall; and Labours of the Months beside the chancel arch (pls 8-11).[12]

There can be no doubt that the five schemes are all the product of the same group of artists, and not merely similar works surviving from the same period. There are numerous stylistic, iconographical and other links between the various schemes. For instance, at both Westmeston and Hardham the *Agnus Dei* supported or flanked by angels is represented on the east wall of the nave, above the chancel arch (pls 1, 8); both schemes share similar Christological as well as other subject-matter (if, as seems likely, St George scenes were represented on the nave north wall at Westmeston); and both show the same characteristic use of ornamental diaper pattern (pls 1, 8-11). The Westmeston paintings were so close to

---

8 E. C. Rouse, 'Wall Paintings in St Michael's Church, Plumpton', *Sussex Notes and Queries* xlv, 1956, 187-9. Rouse comments (p.189) that there is possibly more painting to be uncovered in the nave.

9 E. C. Rouse and A. Baker, 'The Early Wall Paintings in Coombes Church, Sussex, and their Iconography', *Arch. Journ.* cxxxvi, 1979, 218-28. For the extensive remains of painting of c.1300 in the chancel, see E. W. Tristram, *English Wall Painting of the Fourteenth Century*, London 1955, 158.

10 For the Clayton paintings, see especially A. M. Baker, 'Lewes Priory and the Early Group of Wall Paintings in Sussex', *Walpole Society* xxxi, 1942-3, 1-44; A. M. Baker, 'The Wall Paintings in the Church of St John the Baptist, Clayton', *SAC* cviii, 1970, 58-81; and E. Baker, 'The Wall Paintings of Clayton Church, Sussex', in G. R. Grove, *Clayton: A Guide to the Church of St John the Baptist*, 1966, 11-15.

11 See Baker, 'Clayton', 65. Since this painting is at the east end of the wall, the chancel cannot have been lengthened in the thirteenth century, as stated by VCH *Sussex* vi, 1940, 142.

12 For Hardham, see especially P. M. Johnston, 'Hardham Church, and its Early Paintings', *SAC* xliv, 1901, 73-115; Tristram, *Twelfth Century*, 27-8, 128-33; D. Park, *The Romanesque Wall Paintings of Hardham Church, Sussex, with reference to those in the other churches of the 'Lewes Group'*, unpublished M.A. thesis, University of Manchester, 1974.

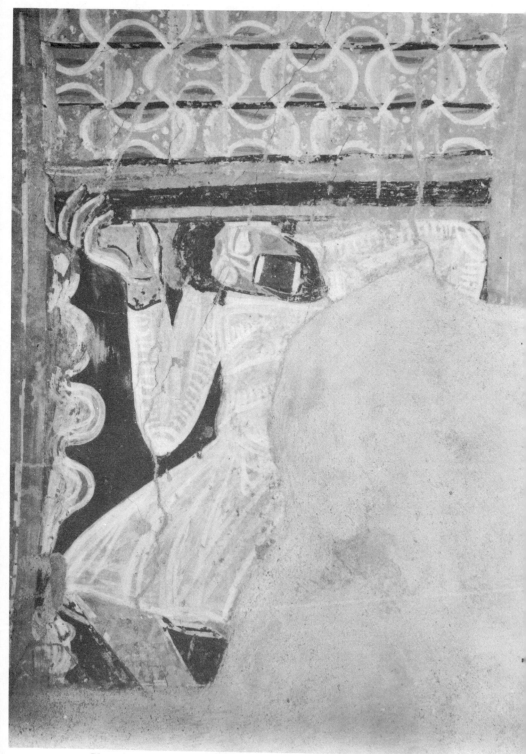

Plate 4 Coombes: chancel arch. Atlas figure, and pelta pattern above

those at Hardham, in fact, that crude though the nineteenth-century copies are, they help in deciphering some of the now fragmentary painting at Hardham. Thus, as in the Flagellation scene at Westmeston (pl. 1), in the same subject on the chancel east wall at Hardham, Christ can similarly be seen looking out from behind the white column with its coloured capital to which he was bound, and the remains of the grotesque profile head of a scourger can be seen to the left. There must be a distinct possibility that the very same painter was at work here and at Westmeston. Likewise, although the Westmeston paintings were closest to Hardham, they also included on the east wall of the nave the rather rare *Traditio Legis* subject (pl. 1), which, though not found at Hardham, is similarly represented on the nave east wall at Clayton (pl. 5) and Coombes (pl. 3). The bold drapery folds over Christ's shoulder in the Clayton and Coombes representations were paralleled in that at Westmeston, though there the groups of three dots scattered over the draperies are similar to those seen in the Annunciation and elsewhere at Hardham (pl. 8). The paintings at Clayton and Coombes are so close stylistically and technically that the possibility must again arise that the same painter worked on both; the very close similarities are obvious, for example, from a comparison of the *Traditio Legis* scenes. Technically, all the surviving Lewes Group paintings are in fresco; that is, painted on successive patches of plaster while they were still wet.[13] This technique has the advantage that the pigments and plaster are bound together by a chemical reaction which helps the painting to survive in good condition. A varying amount of final detail in the paintings was then added when the plaster had dried. Fresco is now known to have been the technique generally used in Romanesque wall painting in England,[14] as opposed to the secco technique (painting on dry plaster) normally used in the Gothic period. Some of the other Romanesque fresco paintings, as in Winchester and Canterbury cathedrals, have much richer colour schemes, and even a small amount of gold is sometimes used. The Lewes Group, however, as befits paintings in humble parish churches, are characterised by the use of cheap and locally obtainable pigments: red and yellow ochres, lime white and carbon black. Various different shades were produced by mixing these pigments. Blue, which was used extensively in such paintings as those of Canterbury and Winchester, was an expensive mineral pigment. It was imitated at Hardham and Coombes, as in the simulated draperies and lozenge decoration (pl. 3) of their respective dados, by a blue-grey colour produced by a combination of white and black. Probably the most expensive pigment used in the Lewes Group was green, which is found in a few details at Hardham, most notably in several of the haloes on the nave east wall – a particularly prominent part of the scheme.[15]

The subject-matter in the Lewes Group paintings is arranged in two tiers on each wall. These tiers may show different types of subject-matter (e.g. pl. 9), or both the same (e.g. pl. 11). However, no individual scene is ever shown forming part of both

---

[13] For the technique, see Rouse and Baker, 222, 225; Baker, 'Clayton', 58-9.

[14] See e.g. D. Park, 'The Wall Paintings of the Holy Sepulchre Chapel', *British Archaeological Association Conference Transactions . . . 1980. VI. Medieval Art and Architecture at Winchester Cathedral*, London 1983, 40, n.11; and E. Baker, 'St Gabriel's Chapel, Canterbury Cathedral', *Canterbury Cathedral Chronicle* no. 63, 1968, 5 (which states, however, that most of the St Gabriel's painting was finished in secco).

[15] Baker, 'Clayton', 59, also notes the use of a small amount of green in the Clayton paintings. The green pigment at Hardham was found, on analysis, to be a green copper carbonate, probably natural malachite; Tristram, *Twelfth Century*, 132.

tiers, which are normally firmly separated by a horizontal border.[16] Within each tier, the narrative unfolds along a single line, the only exception to this rule being provided by the two scenes on the nave north wall at Hardham of the Dream of Joseph and the Dream of the Magi (pl. 9). This exceptional arrangement must have been influenced by a particular model, perhaps in a manuscript. A miniature of the somewhat later Winchester Psalter, of c.1150, similarly shows the two Dream scenes one above the other, with the reclining figures beneath semi-circular arches as at Hardham.[17] In the Bayeux Tapestry, which will be shown to provide many comparisons to the Lewes Group, a manuscript model has been suggested for the one interruption of the single-line narrative, in the two death-bed scenes of Edward the Confessor.[18] Stylised towers are often used in the Lewes Group paintings, particularly at Hardham and Coombes, to separate consecutive subjects (pl. 8), or to close the end of a tier (pl. 2). Towers are used in a similar way to close scenes in the Bayeux Tapestry, and both here and in the Lewes Group this device derives ultimately from classical painting.[19] Considerable use is made of inscriptions in some of the wall painting: for example, the explanatory inscriptions, in the form of leonine hexameters, occupying the borders above the scenes on the nave east wall at Westmeston (pl. 1), and the similar inscription surviving above the Annunciation and Visitation at Hardham (pl. 8). There is evidence of a few other inscriptions in the borders at Hardham,[20] and it seems likely that all or most of the scenes were originally identified in this way. Although enclosed in borders, and in white Lombardic lettering, the explanatory inscriptions are reminiscent of the long inscriptions running above the scenes in the Bayeux Tapestry. And, just as in the Tapestry certain figures are individually identified by their name inscribed beside their head, the same device occurs at Coombes (pl. 3), and in the destroyed paintings at Plumpton and Westmeston. It is a matter for speculation as to who would have been able to read the inscriptions in the wall paintings: presumably few, if any, of the congregation, and perhaps not even the parish priest.[21]

The location of the different types of subject-matter on the various walls of the churches is a curious mixture of the traditional and the *ad hoc*. Thus, the *Traditio Legis* is always represented on the nave east wall, and this is perhaps a distant reflection of the original location of this subject, in Early Christian churches, in the apse

---

[16] Against this, it has been suggested that in the painting at the east end of the nave south wall at Coombes (pl. 2), the figures in the lower tier are Jews spying on a scene of Joseph's Doubts above (Rouse and Baker, 226-7). However, the lower figures are not looking up at the scene above, which should in any case be interpreted as the Annunciation; see below, p. 211. The lower tier may have been a continuation of the cycle of Infancy scenes, and the three figures at the east end are reminiscent of the kings in certain Ottonian representations of the Adoration of the Magi where they are similarly shown bare-headed; for examples, see J. J. G. Alexander, *Norman Illumination at Mont St Michel 966-1100*, Oxford 1970, 137, n. 4. On the other hand, this position on the south wall would be an odd one at which to show the Adoration, since the Nativity and Flight into Egypt, between which the subject might logically be expected to occur, are both represented on the opposite wall.
[17] BL, MS Cotton Nero C. IV, f.13; F. Wormald, *The Winchester Psalter*, London 1973, 19, ill. 16.
[18] F. Wormald in *BT*, 26, pl. 33.
[19] See *BT*, 26, pls 17, 19, 31.
[20] For the inscriptions at Hardham and Westmeston, see Johnston, 'Hardham', 89, and Tristram, *Twelfth Century*, 129, 150-1.
[21] The level of education of parish priests at this period is briefly discussed by M. Brett, *The English Church under Henry I*, Oxford 1975, 220-1.

at the east end.[22] At Coombes and Westmeston the *Traditio Legis* is represented as one subject, as is usual: Christ is shown enthroned, with SS. Peter and Paul on either side (pls 1, 3). At Clayton, however, there was insufficient room on either side of the splendid chancel arch to represent the whole subject, so it was split into two (pl. 5). Christ was therefore represented twice, which left one of his hands unoccupied in each case. This problem was solved by showing this hand holding a small orb in the St Peter scene, and raised in blessing in the other. At Hardham (pl. 9), and almost certainly in the destroyed paintings at Westmeston, St George subject-matter appears in the lower tier of the nave north wall; this is possibly also the case at Coombes.[23] In the Hardham scheme, however, the St George cycle is allowed to carry over on to the adjacent east wall, where the last subject – probably the Burial of St George – is represented to the north of the chancel arch (pl. 8). The corresponding subject on the south side of the chancel arch is the Baptism of Christ, which is represented below a semi-circular arch, which of course makes no sense iconographically; however, it does balance that above the Burial of St George, and this is presumably why it was included.[24] Between the Baptism and the chancel arch are two small Labours of the Months, and it is possible that more Labours were originally painted on the soffit of the arch, which was stripped of its plaster in the nineteenth century. In Romanesque schemes the chancel arch is the location usually adopted for showing the Labours of the Months or Signs of the Zodiac (which appeared on the arch at Westmeston), the curve of the arch conveniently simulating the rise and fall of the year. However, at Hardham there would barely have been room on and around the arch to show all twelve Labours, nor do the surviving Labours appear to represent November and December, which would have been appropriate to their position had there been a complete cycle. In fact, one further Labour is represented at Hardham, but it is so damaged, and in such a curious position, that it has not previously been recognised. In the left-hand spandrel of the arch over the Baptism is represented a small figure apparently digging – which must be the most strangely located subject in the entire Lewes Group.[25]

Much of the iconography of the Lewes Group paintings is of the greatest rarity. For example, in the Adam and Eve cycle at Hardham (pl. 11), Eve is shown milking a cow as her Labour. This is probably unique; normally she is shown spinning in this subject.[26] Also represented in a very unusual way is the subject directly below the milking scene, uncovered in the 1960s, and showing Adam and Eve hiding their

---

[22] See C. Davis-Weyer, 'Das Traditio-Legis Bild und Seine Nachfolge', *Müncher Jahrbuch* xii, 1961, 7-45.

[23] See below, p. 221-2.

[24] An earlier example of a Baptism within an architectural frame is provided by a ninth-century Carolingian ivory; see G. Schiller, *Iconography of Christian Art*, i, London 1971, fig. 366. It is most unlikely that such a work had any influence on the Hardham scene.

[25] Johnston, 'Hardham', pl. 2, confused by the curving double hem-line of the figure's knee-length tunic shows a roundel in this position; Tristram, *Twelfth Century*, 130, pl. 33b, believed that there was a figure here belonging to the Baptism, and identified it as an angel bearing Christ's garments.

[26] Above left of the milking scene, the partly destroyed figure of Adam holding branches (?) is reminiscent of the scene in the Anglo-Saxon Hexateuch of Adam and Eve hiding their nakedness with leafy branches; BL MS Cotton Claudius B. IV, f.7v. (second quarter eleventh century). However, at Hardham it seems more likely that Adam's Labour is represented here, especially as Adam and Eve are shown covering their nakedness in the scene below, and also with the lower part of their bodies covered in the scene beneath the Temptation on the other side of the chancel arch.

nakedness. The two figures are shown seated back-to-back, covering their nakedness with their arms, and each peering back over their shoulder. The only parallel for this back-to-back representation of the figures appears to be on a sculptured portal, of the first half of the twelfth century, at Andlau (Alsace), where however there is a tree between the figures.[27] The Christological iconography of the Lewes Group also shows many rare features. Thus, in the Visitation scene at Coombes, instead of the two women alone being represented, as is usual, a male figure — probably Zacharias — is shown pointing at them.[28] To the east of this is a very rare representation of the Annunciation in the presence of Joseph (pl. 2), for which a parallel can be found in paintings of c.1200 from Puigreig in Spain.[29] To consider just one of the many unusual features in the Hardham Christological cycle, in the Baptism (pl. 8) St John is shown holding an open book beside Christ's head, and pointing at it with his other hand. This motif can be traced back to the Early Christian period; on a sarcophagus of c.280 in Rome, the Baptist is shown holding an unfolded scroll above Christ's head.[30] On either side, in this latter representation, is the tree with leaves and the withered tree referred to in the Baptist's sermon on repentance, and it may be that the book in the Hardham scene should be interpreted as representing this sermon. The only close parallel for the motif in English Romanesque art is on the carved font of c.1120 at West Haddon (Northants.).[31]

As might be expected, various types of influence, at different removes, can be discerned in the iconography of the Lewes Group. It is argued below that part of the Last Judgment programme at Clayton may be Byzantine-derived.[32] In the nave at Hardham there is a cycle of scenes of the martyrdom of St George, and such a cycle also probably existed at Westmeston, and may still do so in fragmentary form at Coombes.[33] The earliest known cycles of the martyrdom of this eastern military saint, popularised in the West at the time of the First Crusade, are in tenth- and eleventh-century Byzantine wall painting, and it is therefore possible that this element of the Lewes Group iconography may owe something to Byzantine prototypes.[34] Ottonian influences are very evident in the Lewes Group, as may be seen from an examination of some of the Christological iconography at Hardham. In the Annunciation (pl. 8) the standing Virgin, with hands upraised, is of Ottonian type.[35] In the Last Supper the representation of St John leaning on Christ's breast (now very faint) is a feature which first appears in Ottonian art, as also seems to be the case with the long straight table at which the figures sit, and the isolation of Judas in front of this.[36] On the chancel south wall the Washing of the Feet, with its row of the twelve apostles seated facing the (now destroyed) figure of Christ is particularly closely paralleled in Ottonian art.[37] The Dives and Lazarus cycle on the nave south wall

---

[27] See H. Haug and R. Will, *Alsace romane*, La Pierre-qui-Vire 1965, 261-2, pl.121.

[28] Rouse and Baker, 225-6, pl.lvii.

[29] O. Demus, *Romanesque Mural Painting*, London 1970, fig. 30; see also above, n.16.

[30] Sarcophagus from the Via Lungara, Rome; now Rome, Museo Nazionale, see Schiller, 132-3, fig. 349.

[31] See G. Zarnecki, *English Romanesque Sculpture 1066-1140*, London 1951, 33, fig. 44.

[32] See below, p.000.

[33] See below, p.000.

[34] For Byzantine St George iconography, see T. Mark-Weiner, *Narrative Cycles of the Life of St George in Byzantine Art*, Ph.D. thesis, New York University 1977 (University Microfilms International, Ann Arbor 1980).

[35] See Alexander, *Mont St Michel*, 142.

[36] Alexander, *Mont St Michel*, 143-5.

[37] This scene was partly uncovered in the 1960s; its identification as the Washing of the Feet

is now very damaged, but even so it is clear that it showed the same subjects, in the same sequence, and in much the same way, as representations of this parable in Ottonian art. For instance, the Death of Dives at the end of the cycle (pl. 10) may be compared with the same subject in the Echternach Golden Gospels (c.1040):[38] in both, Dives is shown lying in bed, with his wife and a male figure lamenting at its head, and large devil carrying off his soul above the foot of the bed. In the Ottonian miniature, Hell is represented immediately to the right of the Death of Dives; at Hardham, the painter has so contrived it that the Death scene is next to the representation of Hell covering the adjacent west wall.

At least some of the Last Judgment iconography of the Lewes Group seems likely to be of Anglo-Saxon derivation. Wormald and others have examined the interest in Last Judgment subject-matter at Winchester and elsewhere in the Anglo-Saxon period,[39] and the likely influence of pre-Conquest traditions on Romanesque illustrations such as those of the Pembroke Gospels (c.1130) and Winchester Psalter (c.1150),[40] which share such features with the Lewes Group as Christ displaying the Wounds (at Clayton, pl. 5), and angels supporting the cross (Clayton, and formerly Plumpton).[41] Early evidence for the veneration of Christ's Wounds and the Instruments of the Passion is found in two miniatures of the Athelstan Psalter (before 939).[42] A particularly interesting parallel for the iconography of the wall paintings is provided by an Anglo-Saxon walrus ivory plaque of c.1000, which shows Christ displaying the wounds in his bared breast and upraised hands as at Clayton; and two angels supporting the cross, flanked by eight figures that are now very damaged but appear to be standing, and may well be apostles.[43] The apostles on

was first suggested by A. Baker in *Survey of Mural Paintings in Sussex Churches: Draft Report – Part I*, unpublished report, c.1964, 22. The long row of apostles is paralleled in the Gospels of Henry III, Escorial Cod. Vetr. 17, f.152v: see H. Giess, *Die Darstellung der Fusswaschung Christi in den Kunstwerken des 4.-12. Jahrhundert*, Rome 1962, pl. 42. The remonstrating gesture of St Peter at the head of the row in the Hardham scene is particularly closely paralleled in the Book of Pericopes of Henry III of the second third of the eleventh century, Berlin, Kupferstichkabinett MS 78 A 2, f.35; Giess, pl. 36.

[38] Nuremberg, Germanisches Museum MS 156142, f.117v; P. Metz, *The Golden Gospels of Echternach*, London 1957, pl.123.

[39] See, e.g., F. Wormald, 'Anniversary Address', *Antiqs. Journ.* xlvii, 1967, 162-5; Wormald, *Winchester Psalter*, 73.

[40] Pembroke Gospels: Cambridge, Pembroke College MS 120, f.6v.; E. Parker, 'A Twelfth-century Cycle of New Testament Drawings from Bury St Edmunds Abbey', *Proceedings of the Suffolk Institute of Archaeology* xxxi, 1969, 272, pl.xliii. Winchester Psalter: London, BL MS Cotton Nero C. IV, ff.31-9; Wormald, *Winchester Psalter*, 27-8, 72-3, ills 34-42, 57.

[41] See Baker, 'Clayton', 65-6. For the Plumpton angels, see Campion, 'Plumpton', 201-2, pl. opposite p.201. According to Campion, both angels supporting the cross in this painting were shown holding spears, as were three others on the same wall. This unusual feature is paralleled in one of the Judgment miniatures of the Winchester Psalter (f.33), showing angels holding Instruments of the Passion (though not the cross), where five of them are represented with spears; Wormald, *Winchester Psalter*, 27, ill. 36.

[42] London, BL MS Cotton Galba A. XVIII, ff.2v. 21; see E. Temple, *Anglo-Saxon Manuscripts 900-1066*, London 1976, 36-7, ills 32-3. As well as in Anglo-Saxon and later English art, Christ is shown displaying the Wounds, and angels supporting the cross, in, e.g., the wall painting at Burgfelden (Württemberg), of c.1075-1100 (see Baker, 'Lewes Priory and the Early Group of Wall Paintings', 5, pl. ivb); and in the twelfth-century sculptured tympana of Beaulieu (c.1130-40), and Conques (second quarter twelfth century), see B. Rupprecht, *Romanische Skulptur in Frankreich*, Munich 1975, pls 50-1, 114-17.

[43] Cambridge, Museum of Archaeology and Ethnology. J. Beckwith, *Ivory Carvings in Early Medieval England*, London 1972, nos. 18, 38, 121, ill. 41. Beckwith describes the lower figures as standing, and interprets them as apostles, or saints or representations of the Blessed.

either side of the Majesty at Clayton are similarly shown standing (pl. 5), rather than seated as is usual in Last Judgment compositions. In the ivory plaque, the angels are shown supporting the cross directly below the Majesty, and this was probably also the case in the original model for Clayton, where, however, because of lack of space on the east wall, this part of the subject-matter had to be fitted in rather awkwardly at the east end of the south wall. On the north wall at Clayton and Plumpton, the polygonal representation of Heaven, and long procession of the Blessed approaching it, are particularly closely paralleled by the Last Judgment illustration in the *Liber Vitae* of the New Minster, Winchester (probably 1031).[44] The three frontal figures inside the Clayton Heaven, with their hands raised in adoration, have been variously interpreted: for example, as the Trinity, or as perhaps Moses, Christ and Elias.[45] However, it is more likely that they are simply representative figures of the Blessed, as those in the *Liber Vitae* Heaven also appear to be, and which are shown with their hands raised in adoration to a Majesty depicted within the Heaven.[46] A Majesty is likewise represented within the very damaged Heaven at Plumpton, and was presumably similarly shown being adored by figures of the Blessed. Although much of the Lewes Group Judgment iconography is thus paralleled in Anglo-Saxon art, it is very difficult to decide — in this case, as with the iconography and style of the wall paintings generally — to what extent it might actually have been derived from sources in pre-Conquest wall painting. This is, of course, because so little Anglo-Saxon wall painting survives, or is known from documentary references. However, both the most significant surviving fragments of wall painting of certain or probable Anglo-Saxon date may have formed part of Last Judgment compositions. The tenth-century fragment excavated at Winchester may have belonged to a composition of Christ in Majesty surrounded by saints, like the miniatures of the Athelstan Psalter already referred to, one of which shows a central Christ of the Last Judgment displaying the wound in his breast.[47] The paintings on the nave east wall at Nether Wallop (Hants.), for which a pre-Conquest date has been persuasively argued, show flying angels supporting what was originally probably a mandorla enclosing a Majesty. If so, this painting would have anticipated the Clayton iconography in this position (pl. 5) and it may have formed part of an overall Last Judgment composition.[48]

A major part of the Clayton Last Judgment has been seriously misinterpreted in some of the more important literature on the Lewes Group. Immediately to the west of the angels supporting the cross at the east end of the upper tier on the south wall, stands an angel holding a lance with a white banner, and confronting a long procession of figures (pl. 6), corresponding in their position to the procession of

[44] BL MS Stowe 944, ff.6v-7; Temple, no.78, 95-6, ills 247-8. This parallel is pointed out by Baker, 'Lewes Priory and the Early Group of Wall Paintings', 7-8; and Baker, 'Clayton', 68.

[45] See Baker, 'Lewes Priory and the Early Group of Wall Paintings', 9; and Baker, 'Clayton', 68.

[46] On the Last Judgment tympanum of Autun (c.1130-45), several small figures of the Blessed are shown within the Heaven, two of them with their hands raised in the same, ultimately Early Christian, *orans* position as at Clayton; see Rupprecht, pl.172.

[47] For the Winchester fragment, see F. Wormald, 'Anniversary Address', *Antiqs. Journ.*, xlvii, 1967, 162-5, pl.xxiii; and Wormald, *Winchester Psalter*, 73. As Wormald demonstrates, the painting is stylistically related to the Athelstan Psalter, and other works of the first half of the tenth century. I am grateful to Dr Gem for the view that, on other grounds, its dating hitherto to before c.903 is unconvincing.

[48] For a discussion of the Nether Wallop painting, see R. Gem and P. Tudor-Craig, 'A "Winchester School" wall-painting at Nether Wallop, Hampshire', *Anglo-Saxon England* ix, 1981, 115-36; the parallel to the Clayton Majesty and angels is pointed out on p.131.

Plate 6   Clayton: nave south wall, upper tier (detail). Angel repelling the Damned

the Blessed on the north wall. The lance-holding angel is in a vigorous and contorted pose, with one hand raised and pointing at the figures before it, and the other stretched back across its body to hold the lance. It has been thought that this angel is beckoning, or blessing the figures before it, and that these are therefore the Blessed, or penitent figures seeking salvation 'at the foot of the cross'.[49] Many of the figures are shown with raised hands, and this has been interpreted as a gesture of adoration.[50] However, there can be no doubt that the entire procession is in fact of the Damned, on the left hand of God, and that the angel is rejecting them.[51] One or more angels are commonly shown repelling the Damned in Last Judgment compositions, and are often similarly armed with a lance. There is such an angel, for example, in the late eleventh-century wall paintings at Burgfelden (Württemberg), wielding its lance to unmistakable effect.[52] The Damned at Burgfelden are shown in a row, facing the angel (and, therefore, also facing the Majesty, and angels supporting the cross behind), and in this are similar to the Clayton figures. At the rear of the Burgfelden procession, a devil is shown pulling the Damned towards Hell by a rope or chain round their necks, which parallels to some extent the figure of a mounted devil at the end of the Clayton procession, shown pulling the rearmost figure back by the hair (pl. 7). The Clayton Damned have faces that are obviously very mournful, with slanting eyes and downturned mouths, and their hands are raised, not in adoration, but in despair. Both the facial expressions and the gestures are paralleled in, for example, the miniature of the Damned in the Winchester Psalter,[53] which also provides an interesting comparison to another feature of the Clayton Damned. In the wall painting, the row of heads looking backwards, behind the main figures, recalls the rows of disembodied heads facing in opposite directions at the top of the Psalter miniature. At Clayton, this feature must be interpreted as showing figures of the Damned, already rejected, on their way to Hell; while those in front, facing the angel, are either about to be, or are in the process of being rejected. There are many parallels, besides that provided by the Burgfelden wall painting, for the devil assisting the passage of the Damned to Hell. For example, in the Anglo-Saxon *Liber Vitae* illustration, three devils are shown taking or attempting to take souls down to Hell, two of them wearing jagged skirts like the Clayton devil, and one of them similarly holding his victims by the hair. What is possibly unparalleled in other western representations of the Last Judgment is that the Clayton devil is shown mounted (the hooves of this horse-like beast are shown trampling another figure of the Damned). A standard element of Byzantine Last Judgments, immediately to the right of the Damned being repelled by angels, is a representation of Satan holding a small figure of Antichrist in his lap, and seated on a monster or monsters, this beast-throne typically shown swallowing one or more of the Damned.[54] Admittedly, none of the

---

49 The first interpretation is put forward by Tristram, *Twelfth Century*, 114; the second by Baker, 'Lewes Priory and the Early Group of Wall Paintings', 12-14, and Baker, 'Clayton', 68-9.
50 Tristram, *Twelfth Century*, 114.
51 The figures were correctly interpreted as the Damned by P. M. Johnston, 'Mural Paintings', 257; and T. Borenius and E. W. Tristram, *English Medieval Painting*, Florence and Paris, 1927, 15.
52 Demus, pl. 241, fig. 43. In the Last Judgment tympanum of Conques (second quarter twelfth century), one of the two angels confronting the Damned is shown, as at Clayton, holding a lance with a large three-tailed banner; see Rupprecht, pl.119.
53 f. 37; Wormald, *Winchester Psalter*, ill. 40.
54 See, e.g., the illustration in an eleventh-century Gospel Book, Paris, Bibliothèque Nationale MS Grec. 74, f. 51v.; S. Jónsdóttir, *An Eleventh-century Byzantine Last Judgment in Iceland*, Reykjavik 1959, pl. 3. For other examples, see Jónsdóttir, pls 2, 4-6.

Plate 7. Chrétien's name, as it appears above the medallion. The Bodmer manuscript

early representations of the mounted Satan are very close to the Clayton figure. However, there are later examples, such as that in the fourteenth-century wall paintings of Dečani (Yugoslavia), which show Satan or another devil mounted, and without the figure of Antichrist, which do bear a distinct resemblance to the Clayton figure.[55] Further evidence that this part of the Last Judgment may show Byzantine influence is perhaps provided by the red background behind the mounted devil, which has been unconvincingly interpreted as a curtain.[56] In Byzantine representations of the Last Judgment, a stream of fire is shown emanating from Heaven to Hell, against which the mounted Satan is often set. It is possible that this is what is represented at Clayton, whether or not the painter understood the motif.[57] As to where Hell itself was represented in the Clayton scheme, the group of figures between the mounted devil and the angel blowing the Last Trump to the west (pl. 7) are clearly not already there; although undoubtedly Damned, they are not yet shown undergoing any physical torments. Very little painting survives in the lower tier on this wall, and what there is does not seem to belong to a Hell;[58] such a position would in any case be a very odd one for hell scenes. A curious feature of the Clayton scheme is that it ends, with the trumpet-blowing angels, two-thirds of the way down the side walls of the nave. This abrupt ending, with the west end of the church left unpainted, is paralleled at Coombes, and in certain other early schemes.[59] It is possible that at Clayton, at least, there was an internal partition, possibly of wood, or lath and plaster, separating off the west end of the church. If so, this may have been covered with Hell scenes, like the nave west wall at Hardham.[60]

The St George iconography of the Lewes Group is of particular interest with regard to the dating of the paintings. At Hardham, the scene at the west end of the St George cycle is of the saint in battle against the Infidel (pl. 9). He is shown mounted on a white horse, and with a white four-tailed banner suspended from his lance, charging one or more figures to the right. The remains of painting in this right-hand area are obscure, and not yet fully uncovered, but the kite-shaped shield of one of the saint's opponents can be clearly seen in the upper part. Beneath the saint's horse, part of a naked figure was uncovered in the 1960s conservation work, its legs stretched out horizontally and with bleeding wounds. The appearance of St George in this scene corresponds closely to that as described in various accounts of the Battle of Antioch, on 28 June 1098, during the First Crusade. Thus, the

---

55 D. Milošević, *The Last Judgment*, Vaduz 1964, ills on pp. 26, 68.

56 Baker, 'Clayton', 64.

57 On the other hand, this colour may well be just decorative background, with no special significance. Baker, 'Clayton', 64, refers to 'Drapery lines' over the painting here, but this effect seems to be produced simply by damage to the painting, as also over the adjacent figures, and mount of the devil. What Baker refers to as the similar background behind the lance-holding angel repelling the Damned is merely this angel's upraised wings. The 'red peebles (sic) or perhaps embers' mentioned by Baker beneath the rear hooves of the devil's mount are in fact the feet of the Damned, and the semi-circular notches in the ground-line below the figures. For a recent argument that Byzantine influences are to be seen in the twelfth-century Last Judgment tympanum of Autun, see D. Denny, 'The Last Judgment Tympanum at Autun: Its Sources and Meaning', *Speculum* lvii, 1982, 532-47.

58 The chief surviving fragments are the remains of three figures towards the east end of the tier; Baker, 'Clayton', 64, pl. xvib.

59 At East Shefford (Berks.), where the paintings end only about a third of the way down the side-walls; and in the painting above the north arcade at Ickleton (Cambs.). For both these, see below, n. 90.

60 For the Hardham Hell, see Tristram, *Twelfth Century*, 131.

Plate 8 Hardham: nave east wall. In upper tier, Infancy scenes and Agnus Dei. Below, Burial of St George, Labours of the Months, and Baptism

almost contemporary *Gesta Francorum* records: 'There also appeared from the mountains a countless host of men on white horses, whose banners were all white. When our men saw this, they did not understand what was happening . . . until they realised that this was the succour sent by Christ, and that the leaders were St George, St Mercurius and St Demetrius.'[61] Because of this close resemblance, the Hardham scene was interpreted by Johnston as almost certainly representing St George at the Battle of Antioch, thus providing for the paintings as a whole a *terminus post quem* of 1098.[62] Although the other saints are not represented at Hardham, this does not necessarily militate against the Antioch interpretation, since the cycle as a whole within which the scene occurs is devoted to St George, and Hardham church itself was very probably dedicated to St George at the time the paintings were executed. It is now dedicated to an Anglo-Saxon saint, St Botolph, but in a twelfth-century charter the dedication is recorded as being to St George.[63] The present dedication is probably a reversion to the original, which, as was often the case with Saxon dedications to obscure saints, would have been changed after the Norman Conquest.[64] It may well be, at Hardham, that an earlier church on the site was replaced, and the new building dedicated to St George, and painted with St George scenes amongst others, all at the same time in the early twelfth century. The closest parallel to the Hardham battle scene is provided by the doorhead of Fordington church (Dorset), carved with a scene which has also been identified as St George at the Battle of Antioch, and dated in a recent study to 1098-c.1110.[65] This similarly shows St George mounted, and with a large, tailed banner attached to his lance, riding down a group of infidels at right; the banner in this case has a cross on it, and a row of small crosses is also shown suspended from the horse's harness.[66] The doorhead differs from the Hardham scene in that two Christian knights are shown kneeling at left, their hands raised in wonder or adoration at the apparition of the saint. Fordington church is known to have been dedicated to St George in the late eleventh century, as it still is today.[67] There does, therefore, seem to be a strong case for identifying the Hardham scene as St George at the Battle of Antioch. Even if there were doubt as to whether it represented this specific battle, it might be considered very unlikely that a scene showing the saint in battle with the infidel would pre-date the beginning of the First Crusade, in 1095. St George, according to legend, was martyred in Palestine in the Early Christian period, for refusing to worship heathen idols; and

---

61 *Gesta Francorum*, ed. and trans. R. Hill, London 1962, 69. Similar accounts are given e.g. by William of Malmesbury, and Orderic Vitalis; for the latter, see Orderic, v, 113-15.

62 Johnston, 'Hardham', 98, 112. Subsequently, the scene was mistakenly interpreted by Tristram, *Twelfth Century*, 131, pl. 33a, as St George and the Dragon, his drawing showing the kite-shaped shield as one of its wings.

63 See *The Chartulary of the Priory of St Pancras of Lewes*, pt ii (Sussex Record Society, xl), ed. L. F. Salzman, 1934, 80. The charter, of c.1175, records a grant to the church.

64 The old dedication would have continued to be used locally, and in time its replacement would have fallen into disuse. For the phenomenon of post-Conquest rededications to more orthodox saints, see e.g. VCH *Sussex*, vi, i, 1980, 119, where the dedication of Botolphs Church, near Coombes, is discussed. This church (for the paintings of which, see above, n.1) seems originally to have been dedicated to St Botolph, but to have been rededicated to St Peter after the Conquest.

65 S. Alford, *Romanesque Sculpture in Dorset: A Selective Catalogue*, unpublished M.A. Report, University of London 1981, 6-14, 50, pls 1-2. The comparison with the Hardham scene was first made by Johnston, 'Hardham', 100, ill. on p.99.

66 The Fordington St George thrusts the *butt-end* of his lance into the mouth of one of the infidels, and he similarly appears to be using this end of his lance at Hardham.

67 Alford, *Romanesque Sculpture in Dorset*, 10.

scenes of his martyrdom, of course, constitute the remainder of the Hardham cycle.[68] Although he had been venerated in Byzantium as a military saint for long before the period of the Crusades, there do not appear to be any earlier representations of him in battle against the Infidel, either in Byzantine or western art.[69] The saint was comparatively little venerated in the West before the late eleventh century, but from the period of the First Crusade his cult increased enormously.[70] Nevertheless, it might be wise to introduce a note of caution, and not place absolute reliance on the Hardham battle scene providing a 1095 or 1098 *terminus post* for the paintings. St George is also recorded as having intervened on behalf of the Christians against the Moslems, at the battle of Alcoraz in Spain in 1096 – that is, a little before the Battle of Antioch; and Geoffrey Malaterra, writing shortly after 1098, records the saint's intervention on behalf of the Normans at Cerami in Sicily in 1063.[71] Neither subject is likely to be that represented at Hardham, but they serve to illustrate the general veneration of St George as a military saint at this period, outside the context of the First Crusade itself. Orderic Vitalis, who describes the intervention at Antioch in much the same words as the *Gesta Francorum*, records in another passage in his chronicle the activity of Gerold, clerk of Hugh of Avranches, Earl of Chester (1071-1101), in collecting edifying tales of 'the combats of holy knights', including St George, without specific reference to any events of the First Crusade.[72] A pre-1095 date for the Hardham scene is, perhaps, therefore conceivable. However, if the slight doubts raised here, that the St George battle scene at Hardham may not provide a firm *terminus post quem* are unfounded, it may well be that the other St George iconography in the Lewes Group also provides a post-1095 dating, and is present as a result of the saint's increased veneration as a consequence of the First Crusade. In the Westmeston paintings, which were so close in many ways to those at Hardham, a damaged scene on the nave north wall showed an enthroned figure, identified by an inscription as Datianus, and with an attendant figure standing behind. Datian was the Roman provost at whose order St George was martyred. It therefore seems probable that at least one St George subject was represented at Westmeston, and indeed the whole of the lower tier of the north wall may have been occupied by a St George cycle as at Hardham.[73] At Coombes, again in the lower tier of the nave north wall, the chief surviving fragment of painting shows an enthroned figure with an attendant standing behind, and is very reminiscent of the

68 Tristram, *Twelfth Century*, 131, pl.31.
69 Nor are any episodes of the saint in battle recorded in H. Delehaye, *Les Légendes grecques des saints militaires*, Paris 1909. The motif of the saint trampling a figure is sometimes seen in eastern representations of St George, particularly in Georgia, where he tramples his persecutor, the emperor Diocletian; see, e.g., K. Weitzmann, *The Icon*, London 1978, 57, pl.9. However, this cannot be the subject represented at Hardham, which is clearly a battle scene. The motif of a horseman trampling a naked figure can be traced back ultimately to classical representations of riders triumphing over barbarians.
70 See, e.g., C. M. Kauffmann, 'The Altar-Piece of St George from Valencia', *Victoria and Albert Museum Yearbook* ii, London 1970, 85.
71 P. Deschamps, 'La Légende de Saint Georges et les Combats des Croisés dans les Peintures Murales du Moyen Age', *Fondation Piot, Monuments et Mémoires* xliv, 1950, 113. This article discusses a number of representations of St George as a military saint in Romanesque and later wall paintings in France. Deschamps (115, fig. 2) interprets a damaged scene in the twelfth-century wall paintings of Poncé-sur-Loir (Sarthe) as having represented SS. George, Mercurius and Demetrius in battle with the Infidel.
72 Orderic, iii, 217.
73 See Campion, 'Westmeston', 10, pl. 6; Tristram, *Twelfth Century*, 151.

presumed St George subject at Westmeston. It is possible, therefore, that a St George cycle occupied this tier at Coombes; though, on the other hand, the enthroned figure could equally well represent Herod ordering the Massacre of the Innocents, and the subject thus have formed part of the nave cycle of scenes of the Infancy of Christ.[74]

Whether or not the St George iconography provides a *terminus post quem* in the 1090s for some of the Lewes Group paintings, the style of the paintings points clearly to a dating in the late eleventh or early twelfth century. This style is early Romanesque and characterised by the striped draperies and other features so typical of Anglo-Norman painting of the last decades of the eleventh century and the period around 1100. In the stylistic development of English painting, therefore, the paintings are in a later phase than that of the pre-Conquest period, but at an earlier stage than the Byzantine-influenced painting typical of much of the twelfth century. The various characteristics of the Lewes Group style may be summarised here. The figures, mostly drawn with a firm, bold outline, tend to be elongated, and with relatively small heads. Many are in vigorous or mannered poses, with expressive gesturing hands; for example, the figures of Adam and Eve in the Hardham Temptation (pl. 11). Other figures, however, such as those of Christ on the east wall at Clayton (pl. 5), are very stiff and hieratic, and their effect is monumental and imposing. A similar stiffness is seen in the angels supporting Christ's mandorla here, which are certainly intended to be flying, but appear virtually motionless, and almost as if they are kneeling. On the other hand, the right-hand angel is equally typical of the Lewes Group style in the very contorted nature of its pose, with one arm twisted back behind its head to support the mandorla frame. There is little attempt to achieve a naturalistic effect either in the figures, or their draperies, in the various paintings of the Group. Characteristic of the figure-style, for example, are stylised red cheek-patches (pls 3-4); and hair piled up in compact beret- or helmet-like masses (e.g., pls 2, 7). Nor are the settings of the figures in any sense naturalistic. No effort is made to show them in space: the backgrounds are in the main merely decorative, consisting either of broad horizontal bands of different colours (e.g., pls 3, 5, 8), or of diaper pattern (pls 8, 11). Likewise, the figures are not shown standing on a naturalistic ground; in some of the paintings they stand on a ground-line consisting of a narrow horizontal band with semi-circular notches in the lower edge (e.g., pls 2, 5). Only a few colours are used in the paintings, and these tend to be bright and harsh. Again, these colours are used less for any purposes of naturalism than to achieve a decorative effect; thus, white draperies are shown with red folds (e.g., pls 2, 6), and in some cases robes are even represented with different-coloured sleeves (pls 3, 6). In general, the style is very formal, with a considerable emphasis laid on symmetry and balance. This is demonstrated very clearly by the painting on the east wall at Clayton (pl. 5); and also by that on the same wall at Hardham, with the scenes in the lower tier painted with matching architectural canopies (pl. 8).[75]

Although certain features of the Lewes Group style are, in fact, derived ultimately from Anglo-Saxon painting, the overall effect of the wall paintings is purely Romanesque, and very different from that of pre-Conquest work. Their formal, monumental style contrasts strongly with the sketchy, impressionistic and somewhat undisciplined nature of late Saxon painting, which derived to a considerable extent from Carolingian

---

[74] Rouse and Baker, 227-8.
[75] See above, p. 210.

painting of the Reims school.[76] The firm, strong outline of figures in the Lewes Group paintings is in marked contrast to the thin, nervous line found in such earlier works as the Nether Wallop wall painting, and the illustrations of the *Liber Vitae*.[77] Similarly, the rather fussy, fluttering draperies of these Anglo-Saxon works contrast with the bold, striped draperies of the Lewes Group. The difference between the wall paintings and these earlier works is exemplified by a comparison of the flickering, windswept lower hems in the *Liber Vitae*, and the severe, almost straight lower hems typical of the wall paintings (e.g., pls 2, 5). On the other hand, the *Liber Vitae*, and other manuscripts of similar date, such as the Grimbald Gospels (c.1020),[78] do show in an earlier form many of the stylistic characteristics which in the Lewes Group are certainly derived from Anglo-Saxon painting: the elongation of figures, and their mannered poses and expressive gestures; their large, hunched shoulders, and small, rather square heads pushed forward on long necks; and the long swinging drapery folds hanging down from the wrist or shoulder. Such features are also found in the Tiberius Psalter,[79] and other manuscripts of a few decades later than the *Liber Vitae*, which are still in the same basic style as the earlier illumination, though in a somewhat harder and less delicate version. Even so, the style represented by the Tiberius Psalter is still much less stiff and disciplined than that of the Lewes Group. With regard to the dating evidence it provides, it is of some importance that the Tiberius Psalter, although it has traditionally been assigned to c.1050, is now thought very likely to date from as late as the 1070s.[80] In some other illumination, which has again normally been dated to the immediate pre-Conquest period, the drapery folds are so thick and firmly drawn that they do give a certain impression of striping. This is particularly the case in the illumination of the Pembroke Gospels[81] and Hereford Troper,[82] though even here a close parallel is not yet provided for the disciplined, straight and often parallel folds of the Lewes Group. It is, again, noteworthy that the Troper at least may be of post-Conquest date.[83] In these manuscripts, as in earlier Anglo-Saxon illumination, the figures are still represented standing on semi-naturalistic grounds, which as already noted do not occur in the Lewes Group (though a distant reflection of this device is perhaps seen in the wavy edge of the lower background band in the *Traditio Legis* at Coombes (pl. 3), and Flagellation at Westmeston (pl. 1)). Likewise, the sketchy illusionistic backgrounds of much late Anglo-Saxon painting, derived ultimately from classical painting, and seen for example in the Sacramentary of Robert of Jumièges (c.1020),[84] find almost no echo in the wall paintings. All that remains of this device, in the Lewes Group, are a few small areas of 'wavy cloud' in the background to some of the painting (pls 4, 11), performing little or no illusionistic function, but present once again mainly for decorative effect. By the first decades of the twelfth century, this device had become almost extinct in English painting.[85]

[76] See Temple, 22.

[77] BL, MS Stowe 944, ff.6-7; Temple, ills 244, 247-8.

[78] BL, MS Add. 34890; Temple, no. 68, 86-7, ills 215, 218.

[79] BL, MS Cotton Tiberius C. VI. See F. Wormald, 'An English eleventh-century Psalter with pictures', *Walpole Society* xxxviii, 1962, 1-13, pls 1-30; Temple, no. 98, 115-17, 302-11.

[80] I am grateful to Mr Christopher Hohler for the view that this manuscript is probably of post-Conquest date.

[81] Cambridge, Pembroke College, MS 302; Temple, no. 96, 112-13, ills 290-2.

[82] BL, MS Cotton Caligula A. XIV; Temple, no. 97, 113-15, ills 293-5.

[83] I am grateful to Mr Sandy Heslop for this information.

[84] Rouen, Bibliothèque Municipale, MS 274 (Y, 6); Temple, no. 72, 89-91, ills 237-40.

[85] It is still seen, however, e.g. in the wall painting at Witley, for which see above, n.1.

If the fully Romanesque style of the wall paintings shows that they are later in date than Anglo-Saxon paintings, despite the debts which they owe to the latter, it is equally true that their style shows no signs of the Byzantine influences which, in various ways, affected so much English painting of the twelfth century. Byzantine stylistic influences are seen as early as c.1100 in manuscript illumination at Canterbury; and at a later date in surviving wall paintings at Canterbury and elsewhere.[86] Such Byzantinising characteristics as careful facial shading in green and other tints, and damp fold draperies (i.e., draperies which often appear to cling to the body as if damp, and are characterised by oval or other-shaped panels separated by curving folds) nowhere appear in any of the paintings of the Lewes Group, whatever the possibility of some Byzantine influence on their iconography.[87]

The closest stylistic parallels to the Lewes Group paintings are provided by works of the Anglo-Norman period. Following the Conquest, interchange between patrons, artists, and illuminated manuscripts, in England and Normandy, helped to produce a very similar painting style on both sides of the Channel. This Anglo-Norman style, though very heavily influenced by Anglo-Saxon painting, shows all the tendencies of a hardening of outline, greater solidity of painting, and formalisation referred to above in the general characterisation of the Lewes Group style. As has justly been said, 'it would be more realistic to speak of an Anglo-Norman art of the period from 1070 to 1100 than to try to separate the paintings of England and Normandy'.[88] Whether the Lewes Group paintings are all, or partly, as early as this; or whether, as is conceivable, since they are provincial paintings, they could date from as late as the first decades of the twelfth century, they are certainly by far the most significant surviving wall paintings in this Anglo-Norman style. As already mentioned, the other English wall paintings which have been suggested to belong to the Group, are destroyed, or in small fragments, or are later in date. The painting at Witley (Surrey), though it shows some similarities to the Lewes Group, as in its overall colouring and the banded backgrounds to the scenes, has a rather different figure-style characterised by less movement, and in some cases rather larger heads in proportion to the rest of the body, which may suggest a slightly later date.[89] The wall paintings uncovered in the early 1970s at East Shefford (Berks.) may be late eleventh-century in date, but are very damaged, and do not seem particularly close in style to the Lewes Group, though like many Romanesque wall paintings they include some 'pelta' pattern, a variety of which is also seen on the chancel arch at Coombes (pl. 4).[90]

[86] For the Canterbury manuscripts, e.g. Cambridge University Library MS li.3.12, see A. Lawrence, 'The Influence of Canterbury on the Collection and Production of Manuscripts at Durham in the Anglo-Norman Period', *The Vanishing Past: Studies of Medieval Art, Liturgy and Metrology presented to Christopher Hohler*, ed. A. Borg and A. Martindale, B.A.R. International Series III, Oxford 1981, 95-103. See also Kauffmann, 62, 79, where these manuscripts are however dated to c.1130. The wall paintings in St Gabriel's Chapel, Canterbury Cathedral, show some stylistic resemblance to these manuscripts, and have sometimes been dated to about the 1130s; see e.g. Demus, 509. However, it has recently been argued that they are as late as c.1160; D. Kahn, 'The Structural Evidence for the Dating of the St Gabriel's Chapel Wall Paintings', *Burlington Magazine*, April 1984.

[87] See above, pp. 215-17.

[88] C. R. Dodwell, *Painting in Europe 800-1200*, Harmondsworth 1971, 86-9; see also Kauffmann, 19-20.

[89] See Park, 'Witley', 164-5. For this and the other wall paintings, see above, n.1.

[90] See E. Baker, 'East Shefford Church, Berkshire', *Trans. of the Ancient Monuments Society* xix, 1972, 40-5; 1. Bulmer-Thomas, *East Shefford Church* (guide), London 1978, 2-5, 22-3, 26. For the pelta motif, see Bulmer-Thomas, 3, and references in his n.7. It occurs in classical

In Normandy itself, relatively little Romanesque wall painting survives but, further to the south, the paintings at Château-Gontier (Mayenne), of c.1100,[91] provide some particularly interesting comparisons to the Lewes Group. For instance, they similarly show the use of diaper pattern in the background of a scene, and of a long inscription in white letters in the border above, and also extremely similar stylised scroll-work to that of the borders dividing the tiers at Clayton (pls 5-7), and decorating a window in the south wall at Coombes.[92]

Because of the relative lack of surviving wall paintings of the Anglo-Norman era, most of the best stylistic parallels to the Lewes Group paintings are provided by illuminated manuscripts, though some also by Anglo-Norman sculpture, and by one other work already referred to on several occasions: the Bayeux Tapestry. The Tapestry is, of course, a prime example of the close connections in the art of England and Normandy at this period, since it appears to have been made in England, but for a Norman patron (Bishop Odo of Bayeux), some time before 1082.[93] Although it is probably slightly earlier than any of the Lewes Group paintings, it has already been shown that it displays certain general similarities to the wall paintings, as in its use of inscriptions and dividing towers. The figure-style also shows many similarities, such as the prominent humped shoulders, small heads pushed forward on long necks, and hair represented in a compact beret-like form. And, in much the same way that in the Tapestry horses are sometimes represented with legs of different colours, so in the Lewes Group paintings some of the figures are shown with different-coloured sleeves (pls 3, 6).

As far as the surviving manuscript illumination of the period is concerned, none of it is exactly similar in style to the Lewes Group, but enough is sufficiently close to show that these are works of the same stylistic phase.[94] The Carilef Bible, one of

---

art, and is seen in the fragment of tenth-century wall painting excavated at Winchester (see above, p.213; as well as in the Romanesque wall paintings at Kempley (Glos.), Copford (Essex), Ickleton (Cambs.), and elsewhere. For the Kempley paintings, see Tristram, *Twelfth Century*, 42-4, 134-6, pls 56-66, 89. They show striped draperies, but of a different kind from the Lewes Group; they are more similar to those of the Shaftesbury Psalter (BL, MS Lansdowne 383; Kauffmann, no. 48, 82-4, ills 131-4). The Kempley paintings probably date from c.1140. The Ickleton paintings, mostly uncovered following a fire in 1979, also seem later; their figure-style indicates a mid twelfth-century date. See P. Clark, unpublished B. A. dissertation, University of East Anglia 1982; and also T. Sladen, in *Ickleton, Cambridgeshire* (guide), no date.

[91] See Demus, 423, pl.143; and M. Thibout, 'Découverte de peintures murales dans l'église de Château-Gontier', *Bulletin Monumental* ci, 1942-3, 5-40.

[92] For the Château-Gontier scrollwork, see Thibout, 29. Other wall paintings, further south than Château-Gontier, and dating from c.1100 and later, show general stylistic similarities to the Lewes Group. See, e.g. M. Rickert, *Painting in Britain: The Middle Ages*, 2nd edn, Harmondsworth 1965, 76; Baker, 'Clayton', 73, 75; Park, 'Hardham', 254-60. See also n.103 below, for the white highlights in the wall paintings at Saint-Savin.

[93] Wormald, in *BT*, 33.

[94] Some of these manuscripts have already been compared to the Lewes Group by Baker, *et al.*; see e.g. ns. 97, 102 below. The comparisons which Baker has also made with eleventh-century Flemish manuscripts such as Saint Omer, Bibliothèque Municipale MS 698 are generally less convincing; see Baker, 'Lewes Priory and the Early Group of Wall Paintings', 27-32, and Baker, 'Clayton', 76. However, the draperies in a Liège manuscript of the second quarter of the eleventh century (Paris, Bibliothèque Nationale MS Lat. 819, f.8v.; Baker, 'Lewes Priory . . .', pl.viiid) do show some similarities to those at Clayton and Coombes. It may also be noted that the background of one of the Evangelist portraits in the Leofric Gospels, of c.1040 (Oxford, Bodleian Library, MS Auct. D. II.16, f.72v.) has bold geometric ornament reminiscent of some of the

a group of manuscripts apparently made for the bishop of Durham, William de St Calais (Carilef), while he was in exile in Normandy in 1088-91, shows a number of similarities to the Lewes Group style.[95] Once again, we see the same rather square faces, the high piled-up hair, and rather similar draperies with, for example, the characteristic feature also seen at Clayton, of the lower draperies swinging to one side.[96] This last feature is also found throughout a Gospel Book from Jumièges, which though rather fussy and inferior in quality, is extremely close in style to the Clayton and Coombes paintings.[97] The figure-style of the manuscript shows the same tall, slender figures, in excited poses and with large gesticulating hands, and small heads poked forward on long necks. The jewelled borders of the draperies of many of the figures in the wall paintings, their long swinging folds of drapery falling from the arm, and the hard striped effect of the folds in the lower draperies and elsewhere, are also very closely paralleled in the Jumièges manuscript, although in this rather inferior work the 'jewelled' convention is somewhat less realistic and used for many other features besides. In addition, the distinctively shaped crowns worn by certain figures of the Blessed and Damned in the Clayton Last Judgment are also found in this manuscript. Other close parallels are afforded by manuscripts produced at Rouen in this period; for example in a Bible of c.1070-1100, with illustrations showing very bold striped draperies, we again see the same squarish faces and dense piled-up hair.[98] In addition to some general similarities of figure-style and draperies, a Bible illuminated at Jumièges in the last quarter of the eleventh century also provides an even closer parallel than those in the Bayeux Tapestry to some of the towers in the Lewes Group, with their partial differentiation into two vertical sections, and their arcading, domes and triangular gables.[99] An extensive use of bold comb-like white highlights, as in some of the Lewes Group paintings

Lewes Group painting; see J. J. G. Alexander, 'A little-known Gospel Book of the later eleventh century from Exeter', *Burlington Magazine* cviii, 1966, fig. 10. Comparisons which have been made between the style of the Clayton paintings and that of the whalebone plaque of the Adoration of the Magi in the Victoria and Albert Museum are unconvincing. Not only is the style of the plaque rather dissimilar, but it was probably carved not in England or Flanders, but in Spain. For its comparison with the Clayton paintings, see J. Beckwith, *The Adoration of the Magi in Whalebone*, Victoria and Albert Museum 1966, 25; and Baker, 'Clayton', 77. For its probable Spanish provenance, see J. Hunt, 'The Adoration of the Magi', *Connoisseur* cxxxiii, 1954, 154-61; and P. Williamson, *An Introduction to Medieval Ivory Carvings*, London 1982, 16. The reliefs from the choir screen of Chichester Cathedral, which have also been compared to the wall paintings (see, e.g., Baker, 'Clayton', 77), show significant differences as well as similarities in style; for example, in the treatment of the draperies.

[95] For these manuscripts, see H. Swarzenski, 'Der Stil der Bibel Carilefs von Durham', *Form und Inhalt: Kunstgeschichte Studien für Otto Schmitt zum 60. Geburtstag*, Stuttgart 1950, 89-95; Kauffmann, 20; Lawrence, 95-103.

[96] Durham, Cathedral Library, MS A. II. 4, f.87v; R. A. B. Mynors, *Durham Cathedral Manuscripts to the End of the Twelfth Century*, Oxford 1939, pl. 17.

[97] BL, MS Add.17739; see C. R. Dodwell, 'Un Manuscrit enluminé de Jumièges au British Museum', *Jumièges, Congrès Scientifique du XIIIe Centenaire* ii, Rouen 1955, 737-41. The style is compared to Clayton by Dodwell, 741, and by Baker, 'Clayton', 78.

[98] Rouen, Bibliothèque Municipale MS 467 (A.85); Dodwell, *Painting in Europe*, 87-8, pl.106. Although not in a Norman manuscript, a figure of Christ in Majesty within an initial of a Beauvais manuscript of c.1100 provides quite close parallels both for the jewelled draperies at Clayton and Coombes, and especially for the bold parallel folds over Christ's shoulder in the *Traditio Legis* scenes; see F. Avril, 'Un Manuscrit de Beauvais et le Maître des Evangiles de Corbie (Manuscrit Amiens 24)', *Cahiers Archéologiques* xxi, 1971, fig.1.

[99] Rouen, Bibliothèque Municipale, MS 8 (A.6); *Trésors des Abbayes Normandes*, Rouen and Caen 1979, 120.

(e.g., pls 2-4), is also found in a Gospels illuminated at Exeter in c.1080,[100] and in the Mont-Saint-Michel Sacramentary, perhaps of c.1070-1100.[101] Particularly close parallels for the Lewes Group highlights and other aspects of the style are found in a Gospels from Les Préaux, of the end of the eleventh century.[102] The highlights in the St Luke portrait of this manuscript include rows of 'cusped' white highlights along the edges of the draperies, similar to those occurring particularly in the figure of the angel in the Annunciation scene at Coombes (pl. 2).[103] Other comparisons can be made with the striped and jewelled draperies of the Les Préaux manuscript, where the device of sprinkling draperies with groups of three white dots is also found, as at Hardham and Westmeston; the square faces of the figures, with their stylised red cheek-patches, and high dense masses of hair. The extensive use of diaper-pattern in the background of some of the wall paintings is not so characteristic of contemporary manuscripts, though it occurs for example in one of the full-page illustrations of the Canterbury *St Augustine, De Civitate Dei* manuscript now in Florence.[104] A love of geometric pattern is very characteristic of English and Norman sculpture of this period.[105]

The architectural evidence for dating the Lewes Group churches is considered by Dr Gem in the Appendix to this paper, but some of the arguments may be briefly summarised here. The most notable of the five buildings is Clayton, with its powerfully moulded chancel arch (pl. 5). This arch, far from being an interesting survival of pre-Conquest architecture, as has been thought,[106] is much more likely to be a crude copy of the kind of arch found in the major Romanesque buildings being constructed in the region in the late eleventh century. A more probable dating therefore would be in the 1080s or 1090s, though it could certainly be as late as the early twelfth century. The fact that the churches at Clayton, Coombes and Plumpton are mentioned in Domesday Book is not evidence that the fabric of the existing buildings dates from before 1086. Coombes and Hardham are both good examples of a small, primitive type of church common in south-east England generally, and especially in Sussex. These churches are characterised typically by a simple two-cell plan, rubble walling, small single-splayed windows, and chancel arch constructed in the *arc-fourré* technique (i.e. with rubble infilling between the voussoirs

---

100 Paris, Bibliothèque Nationale, MS Lat. 14782; Kauffmann, no. 2, 54, ills 3-6.

101 New York, Pierpont Morgan Library, MS 641; Alexander, *Mont St Michel*, pls 42a, 43, etc. The Sacramentary is dated to c.1050-65 by Alexander, but, perhaps more convincingly, towards the end of the eleventh century, by Dodwell, *Painting in Europe*, 87, pl. 105.

102 BL, MS Add. 11850. See Dodwell, *Painting in Europe*, 88, pl. 108 (where it is attributed to Saint Ouen, Rouen); and *Trésors des Abbayes Normandes*, no. 128. The facial style and draperies are compared to the Clayton paintings by Baker, 'Lewes Priory . . .', 31, pl. viiia-b; and Baker, 'Clayton', 76-7, pl. xviia.

103 f.91v.; J. Backhouse, *The Illuminated Manuscript*, Oxford 1979, pl. 9. Rather similar highlighting is found in some English twelfth-century illumination − e.g., that of the Apocrypha Master in the Winchester Bible (Winchester, Cathedral Library) − and in French wall painting at Saint-Savin-sur-Gartempe. These have been discussed together by Ayres, in proposing an 'Angevin Style' in English and French painting of the twelfth century; L. M. Ayres, 'The Role of an Angevin Style in English Painting', *Zeitschrift für Kunstgeschichte* xxxvii, 1974, 193-223.

104 Florence, Biblioteca Mediceo-Laurenziana, MS Plut. XII.17, f.2v., Kauffmann, no.19, ill. 50. For this manuscript, see also Lawrence, 100.

105 See e.g. G. Zarnecki, 'Romanesque Sculpture in Normandy and England in the Eleventh Century', *ante* i, 1978, 180-1.

106 E.g., by H. M. and J. Taylor, *Anglo-Saxon Architecture*, Cambridge 1965, 159; E. A. Fisher, *The Saxon Churches of Sussex*, Newton Abbot 1970, 82, 85.

of either face).[107] Dating of such churches is impossible with precision, though a late eleventh- or early twelfth-century date seems most likely. Plumpton and Westmeston churches were also of this type, though both have since been much altered.[108] It is reasonable to assume that the churches, with their rubble walling, would have been plastered as soon as they were built; and, since the Lewes Group paintings are in the fresco technique, the plaster surface on which they are executed is certainly contemporary with them. As far as such technical evidence for dating the wall paintings is concerned, it has in fact been noted that the plaster at Clayton is laid directly on to the stone (mainly flint) walling, which would indeed suggest that it is coeval with the building, or at least not significantly later.[109] It is highly unlikely that any earlier layer of plaster would have been scraped off before the existing layer was applied. However, until there has been much more detailed study of the techniques of English medieval wall painting, such evidence must be treated with caution.

The documentary evidence concerning the connection, or lack of it, of the various churches of the Group with Lewes Priory, is of interest regarding the possible patronage of the paintings, and consequently also of their dating. However, in both respects the evidence is unfortunately inconclusive. Coombes church seems to have had no connection with Lewes Priory; it is very likely that at this period the advowson was owned by the lord of the manor.[110] Neither Plumpton nor Westmeston church belonged to the Priory, but part of the tithes of each are recorded as having been granted to it, in the general confirmation charter of the tithes owned by the Priory, issued by Ralph, Bishop of Chichester (1091-1125).[111] In an earlier study of the documents it has been claimed that a confirmation charter of grants to Lewes Priory, issued by Henry I, shows that Clayton church was given to the Priory by William de Warenne, first earl of Surrey. He had founded the Priory, with his wife Gundrada, in 1077, and he died in 1088/9. Reference is made, in the same earlier study, to two supposed general confirmation charters of the second earl, referring to Clayton church and other possessions of the Priory.[112] However, the second earl was likewise named William, and Henry I's charter, which dates from 1107-18, simply refers to the grants of 'William de Warenne, Earl of Surrey'.[113] Of the supposed general confirmation charters of the second earl, the first, of which there are four copies in the Chartulary of Lewes Priory, and which on the evidence of witnesses

---

[107] At Coombes, the chancel side walls were rebuilt in c.1300 on the same alignment as those of the nave, but the width of the original narrower chancel is indicated by the horizontal key pattern border surviving on the west wall; see Rouse and Baker, 218-19, fig. 2. The church may originally have had a west tower; see D. Park, 'The West End of Coombes Church', *SAC* cxviii, 1980, 382-3. For the architecture of Hardham Church, see Taylors, 283-4; F. G. Aldsworth and J. Hadfield, 'Investigations at Hardham Church 1978 and 1981', *SAC* cxx, 1982, 222-8.

[108] For these churches, see VCH *Sussex* vii, 1940, 111-12; 116, 118.

[109] Baker, 'Clayton', 58.

[110] The earliest record of the advowson is apparently of 1261, when it seems to have been held with the manor, as it was thenceforward until the present century, see VCH *Sussex*, vi, i (1980), 218. In 1086 the manor was held of William de Braose, lord of Bramber rape, by William son of Norman; and it continued to be held of Bramber rape thereafter (VCH *Sussex*, vi, i, 216).

[111] The charter confirms 'two parts of the tithe of Frechesend of Plumptune', and also the tithes of Robert de Petraponte of Plumpton and Westmeston. See M. S. Holgate, 'Lewes Priory Tithes', *Sussex Notes and Queries* i, 1926-7, 50.

[112] Baker, 'Lewes Priory . . .', 42-3; see also Baker, 'Clayton', 80.

[113] *Ancient Charters Royal and Private prior to AD1200*, ed. J. H. Round, Pipe Roll Society, x, 1888, no. 4.

would if authentic be datable to 1091-7, is a later fabrication of before c.1306.[114] The second, although at one time thought to be a charter of the second earl, is in fact of the *third* earl, also named William, and dates from 1147.[115] Indeed, the very charter by which William de Warenne II gave Clayton and five other churches to Lewes Priory still survives, and can be dated to 1106-18.[116] It is therefore not clear whether Clayton church was in the possession of Lewes Priory at the time the paintings were executed. As has been shown above, the closest stylistic parallels for the paintings are of the late eleventh century and c.1100; whilst, on architectural grounds alone, the building itself might seem most likely to date from the end of the eleventh century. However, it is perfectly possible that the donation of the church to Lewes Priory in 1106 x 18 may have occasioned its rebuilding and decoration. Hardham church is an even more complicated case than Clayton. A charter, which again survives, records the gift of the church to Lewes Priory by Alan son of Eudes; this charter has been dated to c.1120.[117] The Priory's ownership of the church is recorded in the general confirmation charter of the Priory's possessions issued by Archbishop Ralph of Canterbury (1121), which however does not mention who gave it.[118] Contrary to the evidence of the c.1120 charter, the general confirmation charter of King Stephen (1135-54) records the gift of Hardham church to Lewes Priory by Robert of Arundel.[119] Round identified this Robert with Robert Fitz Tetbald, a major landholder in the area, who is recorded in Domesday Book as holding the manor of Hardham, and who died in 1087.[120] What reliance can be placed on the Stephen charter is unclear. Its authenticity is suspect, and although it is nevertheless considered reliable as to its record of the possessions of the Priory, it may not always be correct in its attribution of the gifts.[121] On the other hand, it could record an informal gift by Fitz Tetbald, the formal charter not being given until c.1120.[122] As in the case of Clayton, the question arises as to whether the gift of the church to Lewes Priory might have occasioned its rebuilding and decoration. If the gift was made in c.1120, it is by no means inconceivable that the church and paintings date from as late as this. It has been seen that the inclusion in the paintings of a scene of St George in Battle makes a dating of the scheme before the end of the eleventh century improbable. On the other hand, the links between the Hardham paintings and the others of the Lewes Group make a dating of c.1120 rather later than might otherwise have been expected. Certainly a dating any later than c.1120 would seem

---

[114] *Early Yorkshire Charters, viii, The Honour of Warenne* (Yorkshire Record Society, Extra Series, vi), ed. C. T. Clay, 1949, 62-6. For a translation of the first copy of the charter, see *The Chartulary of the Priory of St Pancras of Lewes*, pt i (Sussex Record Society, xxxviii), ed. L. F. Salzman, 1932, 9-20.

[115] Clay, no. 33. It is dated by Salzman, i, 20, to c.1095; but this dating is amended to 1147 by Salzman, ii, p. xxiii.

[116] PRO Anc. Deed A.15412; Clay, no.15, pl. vi. The other churches in the grant include Keymer, for the wall paintings of which see above, n.1.

[117] PRO Anc. Deed A.14163; Salzman, ii, 78.

[118] *Ancient Charters*, no. 8. The authenticity of this charter is suspect; see C. R. Cheney, *English Bishops' Chanceries, 1100-1250*, Manchester 1950, 28.

[119] *Regesta* iii, no. 444; *Cal. Docs. France*, no. 1391.

[120] See J. H. Round, 'Some Early Grants to Lewes Priory', *Sussex Arch. Colls.* xl, 1896, 64-6. Round does not refer here to the c.1120 charter. See also VCH *Sussex* i, 1905, 378, 431. Baker, 'Lewes Priory . . .', appears to identify the Robert mentioned in King Stephen's charter as Robert de Bellême, earl of Shrewsbury and lord of Arundel rape, 1098-1102.

[121] On its reliability, see *Regesta* iii, 168; and J. H. Blair, 'The Surrey Endowments of Lewes Priory before 1200', *Surrey Archaeological Collections* lxxii, 1980, 99.

[122] I am grateful to Dr Richard Gem for this suggestion.

most unlikely. In any case, it should be noted from the evidence as analysed above that *none* of the Lewes Group churches can definitely be said to have been in the possession of Lewes Priory at the time the paintings were executed.

Even if Lewes Priory did own two of the churches at the relevant period, it is not clear what significance this may have had as far as their painted decoration is concerned. Little if any evidence survives from this early period, certainly in England, as to whether a monastery had any formal responsibility for the wall paintings in the parish churches in its possession. If a monastery did have any such responsibility, it is unclear whether this would have been confined to the decoration of the chancel, or whether it would have extended throughout the church. It is noticeable that in the almost complete surviving paintings at Hardham, the scheme continues uninterrupted from the nave into the chancel; and there is also evidence of Lewes Group painting in both nave and chancel in three of the other four churches. Most of what is known about the responsibilities of monasteries for the churches in their possession dates from the period after 1200.[123] It seems very unlikely that its possession of the tithe, or part of the tithe, would have resulted in any sort of artistic patronage on the part of a monastery.

It is worth examining the paintings themselves to see whether they display any specifically Cluniac elements. Their style is certainly in no sense Cluniac; as has been seen, it is purely Anglo-Norman, similar to that of other works in England and Normandy in the late eleventh and early twelfth centuries. There is, in fact, no such thing as a specifically Cluniac style, since the paintings and sculptures of different Cluniac monasteries tend to be in the general style of their respective regions. Thus, even if the Lewes Group paintings were, to some extent, the result of Cluniac patronage, they are in a radically different style from that of the approximately contemporary paintings of the Cluniac chapel of Berzé-la-Ville in Burgundy, which is already strongly Byzantinising, with elaborate damp fold draperies and heavy facial modelling.[124] A study of English Cluniac sculpture of the Romanesque period has shown that there is no consistent style in these works.[125] A surviving figured capital from Lewes Priory itself is in a very different style from that of the Lewes Group.[126] Nor does there appear to be anything specifically Cluniac in the iconography of the Lewes Group paintings, except conceivably the inclusion in three of the schemes of the rather rare subject of the *Traditio Legis* (pls 1, 3, 5). The Cluniacs had a special veneration for St Peter, to whom Cluny itself was dedicated, and a version of the *Traditio Legis* occurs in the apse frescoes of the Cluniac chapel of Berzé-la-Ville (early twelfth-century).[127] The Cluniac pope, Urban II, preached the First Crusade in 1095, and it is perhaps possible that Cluniac involvement with the crusading ideal was partly responsible for the inclusion of the St George subject-matter in the Lewes

---

123 I am indebted to Dr M. Franklin for discussing this question with me at the conference.
124 For the Berzé paintings, see Demus 416-17, pls 110-21, pp.53, 63; and for Cluniac art generally of this period, J. Evans, *Cluniac Art of the Romanesque Period*, Cambridge 1951.
125 R. B. Lockett, 'A Catalogue of Romanesque Sculpture from the Cluniac Houses in England', *Journ. BAA*, 3rd ser., xxxiv, 1971, 43-61.
126 Lockett, 53; G. Zarnecki, *English Romanesque Sculpture 1066-1140*, London 1951, 37-8, fig. 71.
127 Demus, 416, pls 110-15; see also Baker, 'Clayton', 67, for a comparison with the Berzé painting; and for the general view that there is little if anything specifically Cluniac in the style or iconography of the Lewes Group paintings. The 'Cluniac' nature of the wall paintings had earlier been emphasised by Johnston, 'Mural Paintings', 245-6, and Tristram, *Twelfth Century*, 27, 34-5.

Plate 11   Hardham: chancel west wall. Adam and Eve scenes

Group. It may be asked whether the Lewes Group schemes would not have derived from the painted scheme of a great church, just as the architecture of Clayton seems to have been partly modelled on that of a major building in the area. If so, could this great church have been that of Lewes Priory? It is certainly possible that a major scheme of painting then existing in the region may have had an important influence on those of the Lewes Group. Nevertheless despite the many similarities of the various Lewes Group schemes to one another, there are so many differences of layout, and — as will be emphasised shortly — instances of the use of different models, for representation of the same subject in different churches, that it is clear that these schemes are by no means wholly dependent on a single prototype. In the case of Lewes Priory there is very little certain information about the architecture of the first church, dedicated perhaps in 1091 x 1098, and the few minor fragments of wall painting which have come to light in the Priory are of uncertain date.[128] However, the high quality of some of the Lewes Group painting, particularly that at Clayton and Coombes, does suggest that an important source of patronage may ultimately have lain behind this workshop. It is now impossible to be certain whether this would have been a monastery, or perhaps even a major land-holding family in the region, such as the de Warennes who founded Lewes Priory. Direct patronage of wall paintings is recorded on behalf of Roger de Montgomery (d.1093), lord of Arundel rape, who gave a series in the refectory of Cluny itself.[129]

It is possible to form only a very general idea of who the painters themselves were. Although the documentary evidence in the Romanesque period is severely limited, it seems likely that at this time and later in the Middle Ages most wall paintings were executed by professional lay painters, often travelling individually or in teams from one commission to another.[130] The Lewes Group is of particular value in that it affords a rare opportunity to study how a workshop operated. From variations of style and quality within the Group as a whole, some estimate can be made of the number of different artists. The surviving paintings at Clayton may all be the work of one hand, and this may also be the case at Coombes. As has already been noted, these two schemes are so close stylistically that it is also just possible that the same painter worked on both. Both are somewhat different in style from the surviving painting at Plumpton, which is again different from the Hardham and Westmeston paintings. As has again been pointed out already, the painter of part of the scheme at Hardham may also have been responsible for the Westmeston paintings. Within the Hardham scheme itself, it seems possible to distinguish at least two, and possibly three, different hands. Thus the crude and rather wooden painting in parts of the nave, as in the Infancy subjects of the upper tier on the north wall (pl. 9), is clearly inferior to some of the expressive painting in the chancel, such as the Adam and Eve scenes (pl. 11). Of course, this kind of 'connoisseurship' can become rather subjective, but it appears the Lewes Group paintings which survive are the work of between about four and seven different artists. With regard to the models which the artists were using, it seems most likely that they were working partly from memory, and partly from model-books. Some subjects are represented in such a similar way in the different schemes, that it seems a common model must have lain

---

128 For the architecture, see J. T. Smith, 'A Note on the Architectural History of Lewes Priory', *SAC* cii, 1964, 33-8, and references therein. The remains of painting are briefly described in J. L. André *et al.*, 'Mural Paintings in Sussex Churches', *SAC* xliii, 1900, 238.

129 Evans, 20.

130 See Park, 'Winchester', 49, and ns. 93-5.

behind them; this applies, for example, to the *Traditio Legis* scenes (pls 1, 3, 5). On the other hand, the same subject is sometimes represented in a very dissimilar way in the different paintings of the Group; for example, the scenes of the Flight into Egypt at Hardham (pl. 9) and Coombes, are very dissimilar from that formerly at Plumpton.[131] It is clear, therefore, that the Lewes Group painters had a very extensive stock of models on which they could draw. One scene at Hardham – the Temptation – is painted to simulate a textile hanging (pl. 11). In the background of the scene drapery folds are represented, and at the top a row of loops and a horizontal white rail with hooks. Although simulated draperies are often represented in Romanesque wall paintings at dado-level – and indeed there is an example of this on the nave north wall at Hardham itself (pl. 9) – such a *trompe-d'oeil* hanging on the upper part of the wall is most unusual, if not unique. It is noticeable how much more care was taken in the Temptation scene to imitate a hanging accurately, than in the very stylised example in the dado. It is conceivable, therefore, that the Hardham scene may imitate an actual hanging, since examples with figure-subjects are known to have been used in churches in the twelfth century and earlier.[132]

In conclusion, it is worth emphasising two general points. The first concerns the general tendency which there has been to regard the period from the Norman Conquest to c.1120 as one of 'iconophobia'. Surviving sculpture of the period is characteristically confined to minor architectural members such as capitals, and much of the contemporary manuscript illumination is in the form of small-scale decorative initials.[133] In wall painting of the period, too, there is evidence that even in major churches simple decoration was sometimes preferred to pictorial cycles; thus the surviving late eleventh-century painting in York Minster, and Blyth church (Notts.) consists merely of masonry patterns, and also in the latter case scrollwork decoration on a capital.[134] According to an influential study of the 1960s:

> The ban on pictorial narrative in religious art – for this is what is amounted to – lasted until about 1120 when simultaneously, in the north and south of England, fully fledged picture cycles suddenly made their appearance . . . this unparalleled outburst of pictorial narrative is one of the most astonishing phenomena in the history of medieval art, second in importance only to the sudden rise of monumental sculpture.[135]

However, this view can no longer be sustained. It has been seen that the Lewes Group paintings are at least in part likely to date from within this period. If such paintings, with their extensive narrative cycles, existed in relatively humble parish churches, it might be expected that other, greater schemes once existed at that time in more major buildings. There is indeed documentary evidence of paintings in great churches at this period: thus, in Canterbury Cathedral, paintings were provided by Lanfranc, and by priors Ernulf (1093-1107) and Conrad (1107-26); and a painting was executed above the main altar of St Albans Abbey, between 1077 and 1093.[136]

131 Campion, 'Plumpton', ill. opposite p.198.
132 See Wingfield Digby, in *BT*, 46-8; and C. R. Dodwell, *Anglo-Saxon Art*, Manchester 1982, 129-36.
133 See G. Zarnecki, *English Romanesque Sculpture 1066-1140*, London 1951; and Kauffmann, 19-20, 55-6, 59-62.
134 For Blyth, see Tristram, *Twelfth Century*, 99-100.
135 O. Pächt, *The Rise of Pictorial Narrative in Twelfth-Century England*, Oxford 1962, 13.
136 See Dodwell, *Anglo-Saxon Art*, 226-7. Although these documentary references all appear to be to major paintings they are very brief, and none refer specifically to figure-subjects.

Significantly, Gilbert the Sheriff, who founded Merton Priory in 1114, is described as having 'handsomely decorated it with paintings and other images, as was customary'.[137] Recently, it has been shown that of the three manuscripts with the 'fully fledged picture cycles' referred to above, one is earlier than c.1120; the *Bede. Life of St Cuthbert*, illuminated at Durham, is datable rather to c.1100-1104.[138] It has been seen above that the Tiberius Psalter, with its cycle of full-page Christological scenes, may date from the 1070s. Likewise, in the field of monumental sculpture, the famous reliefs from the choir screen of Chichester Cathedral may well date from as early as the dedication of the church in 1108, rather than from c.1120 or even later as has been thought.[139] The small-scale Christological scenes on the crossing capitals of Southwell Minster are also datable to c.1109-14.[140] The Bayeux Tapestry, though not a work of religious art, shows a positive genius for narrative invention. For all these reasons, it is now clear that the early Romanesque period in England was very far from being one of iconophobia. This leads on to the second general point: that the importance which can be attached to certain later manuscripts, such as the St Albans Psalter,[141] would thereby seem to be diminished. This and other manuscripts of about the second quarter of the twelfth century have been regarded as very innovatory and influential, in such respects as their extensive borrowings from Ottonian art. But it has been seen that there are significant Ottonian influences in the wall paintings of even such a modest church as Hardham, which paintings would seem to date from c.1120 at the very latest. Further work is still required on the dating and sources of such twelfth-century manuscripts as the Shaftesbury Psalter,[142] the Bury Gospels,[143] and the detached psalter leaves now divided between London and New York,[144] as well as of the St Albans Psalter itself. The immediate sources of the iconography of these manuscripts, and the precise nature of their relationship to one another,[145] are at present unclear. However, a study of the Lewes Group suggests that wall paintings may have been at least as important as manuscript illumination in the post-Conquest period, and that therefore no study of the latter can afford to ignore them.

[137] A. Heales, *Records of Merton Priory*, London 1868, 2; see also L. F. Salzman, *Building in England down to 1540*, Oxford 1967, 160-1.

[138] M. Baker, 'Bede's "Life of St Cuthbert"', *Journal of the Warburg and Courtauld Institutes* xli, 1978, 20-1.

[139] I am grateful to Mr Sandy Heslop for discussing the dating of these reliefs with me. They are dated in the second quarter of the twelfth century by G. Zarnecki, 'The Chichester Reliefs', *Arch. Journ.* cx, 1953, 106-19.

[140] L. Stone, *Sculpture in Britain: The Middle Ages*, Harmondsworth 1955, 51, pl. 30b.

[141] Hildesheim, St Godehard. The Psalter is dated to c.1120-30 by R. M. Thomson, *Manuscripts from St Albans Abbey 1066-1235* i, University of Tasmania 1982, 25; but assigned to as late as the 1140s by C. J. Holdsworth, 'Christina of Markyate' in *Medieval Women*, ed. D. Baker, Oxford 1978, 193-5.

[142] BL, MS Landsowne 383; Kauffmann, no. 48.

[143] Cambridge, Pembroke College, MS 120; Kauffmann, no. 35.

[144] Kauffmann, no. 66.

[145] For a discussion of their iconographical similarities, and Ottonian and other sources, see Kauffmann, 31-2.

THE 'LEWES GROUP' OF WALL PAINTINGS
ARCHITECTURAL CONSIDERATIONS

Richard Gem

The paintings here under discussion occur in buildings of different architectural character none of which, however, is closely dateable. The earliest of the group architecturally may be Clayton, which has been generally claimed as Anglo-Saxon, but the pre-Conquest date of which is far from assured. The most important feature of Clayton is the Early Romanesque chancel arch, the jambs of which are decorated on their reveal with a half column against a dosseret, while a further half-column on each face bridges the difference in thickness between the dosseret and the wall: the same elements are repeated in the arch itself. The arrangement has some resemblance to such mid-eleventh-century Anglo-Saxon Romanesque or proto-Romanesque buildings as Stow (Lincolnshire) in that it uses half-columns that may be read as on the face of the wall. However, a more accurate interpretation might be to see the whole composition as derived from an orthodox Anglo-Norman Romanesque arch of two orders: the inner order with a half-column on a dosseret, the outer order with recessed angle-colonnettes. The presence of the half column against a dosseret makes the latter interpretation more likely. It has been argued in these *Proceedings* (v, 1982,126-8) that the influence of Norman Romanesque ideas at parochial level is less likely to represent an infusion direct from Normandy than the copying of major Romanesque buildings on this side of the Channel. The date of Clayton is therefore likely to depend on that of the major post-Conquest Anglo-Norman Romanesque buildings in the surrounding region, such as for example the geographically close Lewes Priory (founded c.1078 or 1078 x 1082 and with the first church dedicated 1091 x 1098?). A date earlier than c.1080 seems, therefore, unlikely; but how much later it might be is difficult to judge with certainty. That the church is a rebuilding — of the one extant at the time of the Domesday Survey — following the donation to Lewes Priory in 1106 x 1118 cannot be ruled out for sure. The possibility that the later medieval plan, with low chapels flanking the east end of the nave, may go back in origin to the same date as the chancel arch need not conflict with a post-Conquest date. This type of plan is indeed of Anglo-Saxon occurrence, but is found in the late eleventh and early twelfth centuries also — as, for example, at Stoughton (Sussex).

Hardham has also been claimed by various writers as of possibly Late Anglo-Saxon date: but it is difficult to see on what this claim is based. The building is indeed extremely simple in detail, but it contains no single feature that relates specifically to a recognised Anglo-Saxon tradition of construction. Hardham and Coombes belong in fact to an extensive group of Sussex churches, of comparative simplicity in plan and detail, which can be attributed with some confidence to the post-Conquest period, but which can be dated little more precisely than late eleventh- or early twelfth-century. In the case of Hardham it is not possible to state with certainty whether the architecture precedes or succeeds 1120 (the donation to Lewes): but it is entirely possible that the present fabric was already existing by that year. This is a case where the wall paintings themselves must allow a greater degree of precision in dating than does the architecture.

It should perhaps be added that the existence or not of a church in the Domesday Book does not constitute evidence for the dating of the fabric of particular buildings, despite H. Poole's worthwhile attempts ('Domesday Book Churches of Sussex', *SAC* lxxxvii, 1948). It is now recognised as likely that the greater part of the medieval parochial system was in existence already by the time of the Conquest and that the appearance or not of churches in the Survey is conditioned most often by factors other than whether there was a building in existence. A substantial proportion of surviving Romanesque parish churches is thus likely to be replacements of earlier buildings and it cannot be argued from the coincidence of a Domesday reference and the existence of arguably eleventh-century fabric that an existing building is likely to be earlier rather than later than 1086.

AN EARLY CHURCH OF THE KNIGHTS TEMPLARS
AT SHIPLEY, SUSSEX

Richard Gem

The twelfth-century church of St Mary the Virgin at Shipley, Sussex, has received only scant attention in print. This paper seeks to redress the situation and argues that the church is of considerable interest and importance as one of the earliest buildings of the Knights Templars to survive in England.

History

The most substantial historical account of the Templar connexion with Shipley was for long that of Blaauw published in 1857,[1] but this was highly inaccurate and claimed a date for the foundation of Shipley earlier than the date usually accepted for the introduction of the Templars to England. Lees' classic work of 1935[2] set the historical record straight: yet still the erroneous date was repeated by Knowles and Hadcock.[3] The very implausibility of this date has hitherto distracted architectural historians from looking at the church with more than perhaps a sceptical curiosity, and has prevented them from analysing its real significance.

The church of Shipley is first mentioned in 1073 when William de Braose included the tithe and church among his donations to his newly founded collegiate church of St Nicholas at Bramber.[4] Thereafter Shipley seems to have been associated with the complicated fortunes of this new foundation. Circa 1079-80 William gave the church of Bramber to St-Florent-de-Saumur to form the endowment for a daughter house at Briouze: the donation apparently included 'the church of Shipley, the land of one plough et cetera'.[5] However, the new abbey of Briouze was never founded, and St-Florent itself came to establish a priory at Sele near Bramber.

In a charter of 1126[6] Philip de Braose confirmed his father's gift to St-Florent, mentioning the priory of Sele. With reference to Shipley, however, it is stated that

---

[1] W. H. Blaauw, 'Sadelscombe and Shipley, the preceptories of the Knights Templars in Sussex', *Sussex Archaeol. Coll.* ix, 1857, 227-74. This account was followed by L. F. Salzman, VCH *Sussex* ii, 1907, 92f.

[2] B. A. Lees, *Records of the Templars in England in the Twelfth Century (British Acad., Rec. Social and Econ. Hist.* ix, 1935).

[3] D. Knowles and R. N. Hadcock, *Medieval Religious Houses, England and Wales*, London 1971, 295.

[4] J. H. Round, *Calendar of Documents Preserved in France*, London 1899, no. 1130 (p.405). In Domesday Book it is mentioned in passing that William de Braose was the holder of the manor of Shipley in 1086, but no details of the manor are given under that name: VCH *Sussex* i, 1905, 439-40. Shipley lay immediately adjacent to the de Braose castle of Knepp.

[5] Round, no. 112 (pp.396-7, also xlii). L. F. Salzman, *The Chartulary of the Priory of St Peter at Sele*, Cambridge 1923, no. 1 (pp.1-3).

[6] Date assigned by C. Brook, cit. Knowles and Hadcock, 91. The charter is Round, no. 119 (p.401); Salzman, no. 2 (p.3).

'the monks of St-Florent exchanged the church of Shipley for the church of Washington'; yet they still had an income of 4s a year and all the tithe of the demesne from Shipley.[7] The interpretation of this is not without difficulties, but for the present purpose it is probably reasonable to conclude that Shipley church, after being held for a time by St Nicholas of Bramber and then by St-Florent-de-Saumur under William I de Braose (died c.1093 x 1096),[8] by c.1126 was back in the hands of Philip de Braose, except for a part of the revenues. The next historical point of reference is the charter of donation to the Templars.[9] By this charter Philip de Harcourt, Dean of Lincoln, granted to the Knights of the Temple 'the estate of Shipley with all things pertaining to it and the church of the same vill . . . that they may have it as my brother Richard gave it all to me and likewise the church . . . All this my brother Richard had and held from Philip de Braose, his and my relative (*patruus*)'. Probably on the same occasion as this charter a confirmation was granted by William de Braose, son of the Philip mentioned.[10]

Lees discussed the degree of relationship indicated by the word *patruus*, but concluded that there could be no certainty other than that the Braose and Harcourt families were akin and friendly.[11] What is evident, however, is that Philip de Braose before his death (c.1134 x 1155)[12] had given the manor and church of Shipley to his relative Richard de Harcourt, who had in turn given them to his brother Philip: the latter was thus in possession prior to the donation to the Templars.

What is of especial interest is the actual date of the charter of donation. A *terminus post quem* is provided by Philip's appointment as Dean of Lincoln. Le Neve[13] gives Philip's first certain recorded occurrence in this office as c.1133(?); but there are two possibly earlier occurrences in 1129 x 1138 and 1131 x 1141. A *terminus post quem* based on Philip's appointment in the early 1130s would coincide with that derived from the confirmatory charter which must have been issued after William II de Braose succeeded his father in 1134 x 1155. A *terminus ante quem* must be provided at least by the end of Philip's term of office as Dean of Lincoln, which seems to have occurred in 1141 or 42 when he left England and was subsequently elected Bishop of Bayeux.[14] Lees, however, thought it likely that the granting of the charter preceded Philip's appointment as Chancellor to King Stephen, in June 1139 (and his election in March 1140 to the bishopric of Salisbury – a position in which, however, he was not confirmed).[15] The most probable date for the foundation that emerges from the charter, therefore, is c.1134 x 1139.

A date in the 1130s Lees sought to place in its historical context.[16] The English province of the Templars had probably been instituted in 1128 and the house at Holborn may have been founded as its headquarters at this time. However, it was not until the accession of King Stephen in 1135 that any rapid development may be traced. About sixty charters, royal and private, in favour of the Templars are known from Stephen's reign, though the only one that is actually dated is that concerning Cressing in 1137. The foundation of Shipley, therefore, in the early years of Stephen's reign places it among the first houses of the Order in England.

---

7 *Monasticon* iv, 669.

8 VCH *Sussex* vi. i, 1980, 4.

9 Lees, 227-8.

10 Lees, 228.

11 Lees, cxlviii.

12 VCH *Sussex* vi. i, 1980, 4.

13 J. le Neve, *Fasti Ecclesiae Anglicanae 1066-1300* iii, *Lincoln*, compiled D. E. Greenaway (Inst. Hist. Research 1977), 8.

14 Le Neve, as above.

15 Le Neve and Lees, 227.

16 Lees, xxxviii-xli.

For the subsequent twelfth-century history of the Templars at Shipley there is unfortunately little documentary evidence, not least because the Sussex roll is absent from the 1185 Inquest. However, one surviving document indicates that the Templars came into conflict with the monks of Sele regarding the tithes of Shipley and that this was settled, in 1181, by a compromise which recognised the established rights of Sele (to the ancient demesne tithes and certain others, and to 4 s per annum) but granted the remaining tithes to the Templars.[17]

Knowles and Hadcock included Shipley in their gazetteer as 'a lesser house, or . . . lacking contemporary information' for its exact status — though they did record the suggestion that another Sussex house was a *camera* of Shipley.[18] Lees, however, stated her view (without further discussion) that Shipley was a preceptory, and suggested that the preceptor c.1185 was perhaps the William de Matunville who is then recorded as General Procurator of the Templars in Sussex.[19]

If, as seems perhaps likely, Shipley was indeed the Templar's preceptory for Sussex, an interesting question arises as to the exact relationship of this house and the parish church. Before the bull of Innocent II granted on 29 March 1139, permitting the Templars to build their own *oratoria* and to bury in their own graveyards, it might be expected that their houses had a close relationship with existing churches. The likelihood, then, that the Shipley house was founded before June 1139 might make it probable that it was established in direct relationship with the parish church. Even after 1139, however, there are clearly evidenced cases of Templar establishments making use of parish churches which had been granted to them, in place of (or in addition to) chapels in their own houses. A case in point is the Sussex house of Sompting where the church, granted to the Templars in 1154 by Philip and William de Harcourt and William de Braose, was appropriated to the Templars *in usus proprios* by the beginning of the thirteenth century.[20]

Architecture of the Church

The church is set on ground which, a short distance southwards, falls down to the River Adur, while to east and north the churchyard is bounded by a moat. Within the churchyard, to the south of the church, there are reports of the discovery of 'the angle of a wall, a quantity of building rubble, some oyster shells and medieval pottery',[21] but whether these belonged to the domestic offices of the supposed preceptory is unknown.

The church itself is constructed throughout with walls of thin, carefully laid, slabs of sandstone. The external quoins and dressings to the openings use larger sandstone ashlars; but most of the internal and some of the external ashlar is different and appears to be Caen stone.

In general plan and elevation (Figs 1, 2) the twelfth-century church comprised a long unaisled nave (some 15 by 65 feet), a central tower without flanking transepts, and a rectangular chancel.[22] The dramatic axial design was somewhat spoiled, however, by the addition of a north aisle in 1893, to the design of J. L. Pearson.

Of its original details the nave retains a south doorway, of two plain rectangular

[17] Lees, 230.   [18] Knowles and Hadcock, 295.
[19] Lees, cl and n.   [20] Lees, cxlix-cl.
[21] M. M. Hickman, *The History of Shipley, a Wealden Village*, 1947, 10.
[22] W. H. Godfrey, 'Sussex church plans: St Mary, Shipley', *Sussex Notes and Queries* viii, 1940, 50-1.

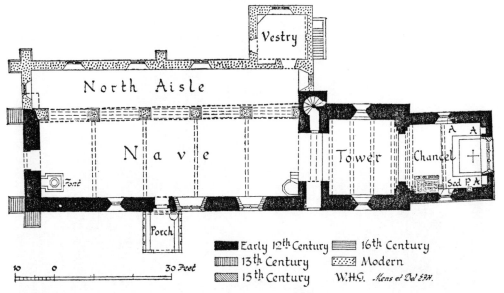

Fig. 1   Shipley church, Sussex. Plan after Godfrey (1940)

orders, and one of the windows (Fig. 3B). The window is most remarkable in that, despite its considerable size, it is of double-splayed form. The west doorway is of a later twelfth-century style than the rest of the church and must be an insertion.

The nave is divided from the tower by an extraordinarily thick wall, opened with an arch of two orders. The outer order is plain, but on its west face has a hood decorated with a small 'jelly-mould' motif. The inner order of the arch (Fig. 4B) is enriched with an angle roll, penetrated by horizontal chevrons alternating with a clasping rectangular 'bracket' motif. This arch is carried on scallop capitals and short lengths of half-column which stop on magnificent corbels carved with grotesque heads. The half-columns are thus stopped to allow for openings below them, set in the reveals of the jambs. The north opening is a doorway leading to a stair turret attached to the north-west corner of the tower. The south opening is a broader, barrel-vaulted passageway, leading to an external doorway. This passageway is evidently designed to give access to the eastern part of the church from the outside without going through the nave and, at the same time, without piercing the walls of the tower or chancel: this suggests that the walls needed to be left available for other purposes.

The eastern tower-arch, towards the chancel, is cut through a thinner wall than that on the west, but it is of three orders (Fig. 4A). The orders are plain on their east faces and decorated only on their west. The outer order is quite plain and has only a quirked and chamfered hood. The intermediate order has an angle roll penetrated by miniscule horizontal chevrons (looking almost like blanks for carving beak-heads). The inner order is decorated, in the arch only, with a recessed quadrant roll to the angle. One feature of particular interest is that the moulding of the intermediate order stops a few feet from the floor, as though it were adjoined at this point by some piece of furniture. This feature, taken in conjunction with the position of the entrance passage already referred to, suggests a most likely arrangement as

Fig. 2   Shipley church, Sussex. Exterior from south-east

being that choir stalls were set the length of the north and south walls of the tower. Such a choir area would have been lit by the large windows, again of double-splayed form, set higher up in the north and south walls.

The chancel retains of its clearly original features only the windows in its north and south walls. These are double-splayed, and have part of an outlining design of geometric motifs painted in red ochre: this decoration could be twelfth-century, though rather restored. Of the several aumbries set in the chancel walls, some may be original, but of this it is difficult to be certain.

The central tower rises two levels above the ground story. The intermediate level had a plain lintelled doorway opening westward towards the roof space of the nave; there is also, in the north wall, a window with monolithic round head. More impressive is the top level of the tower, which presumably from the first served as a bell chamber. In each wall at this level is a single plain, arched, opening, which runs back almost as a barrel-vaulted passageway through the full thickness of the wall (Fig. 3A). The three levels of the tower are connected by the stair turret at the north-west angle.

Discussion of Design and Date

The church stands out from the average twelfth-century parish church on a number of counts. In the first place it is constructed, despite its simplicity of plan, on a fairly monumental scale. Secondly, it has been shown that there was a particular care taken to provide independent access to the eastern part of the building, while leaving space

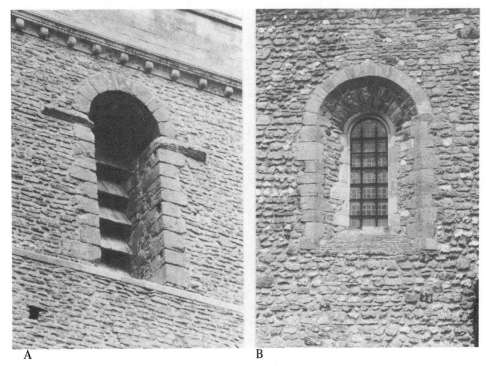

A   B

Fig. 3 Shipley church, Sussex. A Opening in top stage of tower. B Double-splayed window in nave

probably for choir stalls under the central tower. This might lead to the supposition that the church was built by and for the Templars: but what of the internal evidence for its date?

The only decorative details to go on are those of the two tower arches. These are idiosyncratic and, for that reason, perhaps not closely dateable; but a context in the second quarter of the twelfth century seems probable (and certainly not earlier if the beak-head like character of the ornament is accepted).[23] Where, however, does this leave the double-splayed windows — which are sometimes claimed as evidence of the survival of Anglo-Saxon influence? The fact is that double-splayed windows are a feature of fairly common occurrence in domestic buildings (both monastic and secular) through a large part of the twelfth century in England — in contexts where there is no reason to think of any 'Anglo-Saxon influence'. As local examples may be cited late eleventh-century windows at Lewes Priory, and late twelfth-century ones at Arundel Castle. What is unusual about the Shipley windows is only their context and scale (the latter perhaps explained by the former): such windows by the twelfth century were essentially a domestic type, but here were used in a church. One quite close parallel to the scale and prominent position of the windows is

[23] Jeffrey West, to whom I am most grateful for discussing with me the decoration of Shipley, suggests that the stylistic date should be c.1140 and anyway not earlier than 1130.

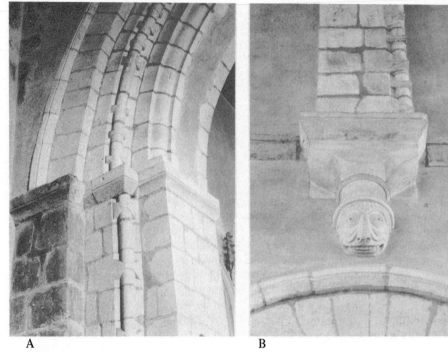

A   B

*Fig. 4 Shipley church, Sussex. A East arch of tower, detail of north jamb.
B West arch of tower, detail of south jamb*

provided, although not in a church, by the domestic offices of the abbey of St-André-en-Gouffern, near Falaise, built c.1130-43.[24]

There are other features which may also, perhaps, be seen as bearing some resemblance to domestic or military architecture. One of these is the entrance passage contrived in the thickness of the wall: it speaks as much or more of the thinking that went into the design of the circulation system in a twelfth-century *donjon*, as it does of the wall-passage system in a major church. Then there are the openings in the bell-chamber of the tower: without any ornamental articulation, their stark form speaks of military functionalism. It is perhaps no more than an impression, and one that would be difficult to demonstrate conclusively, but the church is one that could well have been designed by a mason or engineer more accustomed to military or domestic work than to ecclesiastical — and it may be added that the crude execution of the tower-arch ornament is hardly commensurate with a church of such a scale, where an accomplished mason might be expected to have been employed.

The general type of the building is not one that would be particularly remarkable in a twelfth-century context. There was an already established tradition in England at the time of the Conquest of churches with an unaisled nave and a central tower and chancel: but in these the tower was flanked by transeptal *porticus*. A pre-Conquest date has also been claimed for a number of churches with an unaisled

---

[24] A. de Caumont, *Statistique Monumentale de Calvados* ii, Paris and Caen 1850, 428. The abbey was founded from Savigny in 1130 by William Talvas, son of Robert de Bellême; the church was dedicated in 1143.

nave and central tower but with no flanking transepts or *porticus*:[25] however, some, if not all, of this group are likely to be post-Conquest (e.g. Dunham Magna, Norfolk; Langford, Oxfordshire). Whatever the precise date of the earliest example of this type in England, it certainly continued right through the twelfth century to enjoy a place in the pattern book of parish church designs: for example, it is represented elsewhere in Sussex at Newhaven and Iford. Shipley should not be seen, therefore, as a particularly archaic building in twelfth-century terms. Although it does indeed exhibit certain peculiarities, these are not throw-backs to the eleventh century. The church is in fact one that would fit comfortably a date towards the middle of the twelfth century. If this is the case, then the most likely theory is that it was built (or, rather, rebuilt) very shortly after the donation to the Templars in 1134 x 1139: a date in the late 30s or c.1140 is therefore put forward here.

Shipley and Early Templar Architecture

Shipley has perhaps not figured prominently in discussions of early Templar architecture in England, not only on account of uncertainties about its date, but also because it did not fit into the prevailing preconception that the architectural form specific to the Order was essentially the rotunda. It is several years since Lambert sought to counter this misconception,[26] yet the early Templar material in England has not been comprehensively re-evaluated. This is not the place to undertake this task, though it can be stated categorically that the rotunda form was certainly in use at an early date − that is, before the move of the English headquarters to the New Temple in 1161. To take but one example, the church of the preceptory at Bristol, founded before 1147, has been shown by excavation to have been a rotunda.

However, even in anticipation of a comprehensive survey, the church of Shipley allows certain deductions to be made about Templar architecture in England prior to 1161. The New Temple was one of the most lavish and fashion-conscious buildings of its day in England, and this raises the question of whether or not it represented a departure from an earlier and simpler tradition. The Templars had, after all, been founded under the influence of St Bernard, who must surely have expected to see in the Knights something of the devotion to stark simplicity that he was striving to impress upon the Cistercians? The answer to this question, to judge by Shipley, is that early Templar architecture was totally different in character from the New Temple.

At Shipley there was no attempt to create a grand evocation of the Dome of the Rock or of the Holy Sepulchre. Instead, the simplest type of contemporary Anglo-Norman church design was adopted (the simplest, that is, consistent with its use both by the parish and by the Knights): a plain unaisled nave, a choir and a sanctuary. In this a comparison might be made with the earliest churches of the Cistercians and other reformed religious orders. The principal difference in form is that the monastic churches had no crossing towers but did have transepts (with additional chapels − i.e. a functional requirement): Shipley had no transepts but did have a tower.

It is not only the choice of plan and basic elevation that exemplifies the simplicity of Shipley, however, but also the style of the building: the similarity in certain points

[25] H. M. Taylor, *Anglo-Saxon Architecture* iii, Cambridge 1973, 1009-10.
[26] E. Lambert, 'L'architecture des Templiers', *Bul. Mon.* cxii, 1954, 7-60, 129-65.

to military and domestic architecture; the starkness of the detailing; the general absence of other than a rather rudimentary and crude ornamentation. In all but the grotesque-animal corbels of the west tower arch, Shipley is surely a building of which St Bernard would have approved: it is in any case one that speaks eloquently of the early character and ideals of the Knights of the Temple before power and wealth subverted them.